I0085768

TRANSFORMING
BORNEO

The **ISEAS – Yusof Ishak Institute** (formerly Institute of Southeast Asian Studies) is an autonomous organization established in 1968. It is a regional centre dedicated to the study of socio-political, security, and economic trends and developments in Southeast Asia and its wider geostrategic and economic environment. The Institute's research programmes are grouped under Regional Economic Studies (RES), Regional Strategic and Political Studies (RSPS), and Regional Social and Cultural Studies (RSCS). The Institute is also home to the ASEAN Studies Centre (ASC), the Singapore APEC Study Centre and the Temasek History Research Centre (THRC).

ISEAS Publishing, an established academic press, has issued more than 2,000 books and journals. It is the largest scholarly publisher of research about Southeast Asia from within the region. ISEAS Publishing works with many other academic and trade publishers and distributors to disseminate important research and analyses from and about Southeast Asia to the rest of the world.

TRANSFORMING BORNEO

From Land Exploitation
to Sustainable Development

CHUN SHENG **GOH** · LESLEY **POTTER**

ISEAS YUSOF ISHAK INSTITUTE

First published in Singapore in 2023 by
ISEAS Publishing
30 Heng Mui Keng Terrace
Singapore 119614
E-mail: publish@iseas.edu.sg
Website: <http://bookshop.iseas.edu.sg>

All rights reserved. No part of this publication may be reproduced, stored in a retrieval system, or transmitted in any form or by any means, electronic, mechanical, photocopying, recording or otherwise, without the prior permission of the ISEAS – Yusof Ishak Institute.

© 2023 ISEAS – Yusof Ishak Institute, Singapore

The responsibility for facts and opinions in this publication rests exclusively with the authors and their interpretations do not necessarily reflect the views or the policy of the publisher or its supporters.

ISEAS Library Cataloguing-in-Publication Data

Name(s): Goh, Chun Sheng, author. | Potter, Lesley M., author.
Title: Transforming Borneo : from land exploitation to sustainable development / Goh Chun Sheng and Lesley Potter.
Description: Singapore : ISEAS-Yusof Ishak Institute, 2023. | Includes bibliographical references and index.
Identifiers: ISBN 9789815011647 (paperback) | ISBN 9789815011654 (ebook PDF)
Subjects: LCSH: Land use—Borneo. | Economic development—Borneo. | Sustainable development—Borneo. | Agriculture—Economic aspects—Borneo.
Classification: LCC HD880.8 G61

Cover design by Lee Meng Hui
Index compiled by Raffaie Nahar
Typeset by Superskill Graphics Pte Ltd
Printed in Singapore by Markono Print Media Pte Ltd

Contents

PART IV: CONCLUSION

List of Figures, Tables and Boxes

Tables

Boxes

Preface I

I was twelve when, first in my lifetime, I was told to put on a white dust mask before stepping out of the house. A thick haze blanket shimmered across my hometown, Penang, blocking the sun's rays from reaching the surface. It was 1997, and the particle-laden air persisted for months. As I was told, the source of this greyish matter came from the land fires in Indonesia. The reason for the fires was reduced to a set of clichés in the understanding of the general public in Malaysia: the fire was set by the "irresponsible" farmers in Indonesia who used fire to clear forest land for farming. Interestingly, the region was experiencing drastic changes at the same time—in both financial and political landscapes. The most significant change would be the fall of Suharto's dictatorship following the financial crisis in 1998.

I was twenty-eight when I made my first trip to Central Kalimantan as a junior researcher at Utrecht University, working on a research project called "Large-scale Investment in Food, Fibre, and Energy: Options for the Poor". Central Kalimantan is one of the most affected areas that generate massive haze during prolonged, severe droughts. With a local friend, Pak Agustinus, we rode across the province on a motorbike and went deep into the mountains, forests, plantations, and gold mining sites on large rivers and small streams. In these few months, I met a wide range of people, including indigenous people, migrants from other islands, urban settlers, local officials, entrepreneurs, activists, and plantation workers. I was, however, struggling to put all the pictures together—there are no simple ways of framing the fire events with complex on-ground socio-economic dynamics. While many uncontrolled fires were made unintentionally (such as a carelessly discarded cigarette butt), there were also reports about massive fires set purposely for land clearing. Ironically, many oil palm companies operating in these fire-prone areas are owned by Malaysians and have close patronage relationships with the government, if not actually government-linked.

Coincidentally, in later years I was involved in several projects related to agriculture and forestry in both Malaysian and Indonesian Borneo in different capacities, including policy design, industrial development, and research. These experiences have contributed to a greater understanding of the land-use dynamics in Borneo from various perspectives. I learnt that people from different backgrounds, sectors, disciplines, positions, ethnicity, and nationality tend to have very different views on land-based development and conservation. On the one hand, advocates for "modernization" argue that Borneo should not be left behind in economic development. On the other hand, conservationists urge prioritizing environmental protection and restoration in Borneo. These have sparked plenty of debates and generated more heat than light on many occasions. However, the interconnected nature of economic productivity and conservation in Borneo implies that people have to work together and find the right combination of strategies to address the various issues related to land use and sustainability. Especially, the variation by places and timing of implementations must be carefully considered.

How to improve livelihoods without causing further environmental impacts but also repairing the damage done in the past? This big question has motivated Lesley and me to write a book about Borneo, specifically on land use and sustainable development. This monograph considers not only the seven subnational territories on the island but also Borneo as a regional entity that shares many similarities in both agroecological and socio-cultural aspects. This approach makes this book an interesting compilation of information and analyses that offers both ground-level views and high-level perspectives of land-based development on one island but two countries. We tried to identify the similarities and differences in regional experience and domestic priorities against national and global development. We drew interesting comparisons and lessons from what happened in 2000–20, describing the history, status, and future perspectives of transforming Borneo from land exploitation to sustainable development, as well as questioning how economies and societies were (re)structured within and beyond artificial boundaries.

In total, it took us about three years to complete the writing. It seems impossible to acknowledge everyone who has contributed to a book with a broad coverage like this one: some too many people have fed us the knowledge and information needed. We apologise for not being able to list all of those names.

Chun Sheng Goh
April 2022

Preface II

My experience with this book began rather later than that of Chun Sheng. During his post-doc at Harvard in 2020, he had compiled a draft, but lacking access to either the university library or interested staff because of COVID-19, he was unsure of some of the data and his conclusions. He asked me to check the manuscript, which I agreed to do, but then I began to discover gaps and to proceed to fill them. The result has been a substantial rewrite by both of us over the succeeding three years and our agreement to produce a joint volume.

Following completion of my PhD in Guyana (South America), for McGill University (Montreal), I moved to the University of Adelaide and began field studies in Borneo (mainly Kalimantan) in 1983. My initial introduction to Banjarmasin was to a city living on private generators, as the level of the hydropower dam was too low to be operational and there was a serious El-Niño drought. This soon developed in the logging regions of East Kalimantan into a large-scale forest fire, brought about by the "changed condition of the forest", according to a leading commentator. After several field seasons resident in Banjarese and other villages in the Upper Riam Kiwa, I shifted my focus, from a concentration on the forests and the active deforestation and grassland formation still taking place, to attempted reforestation and replanting, eventually of oil palm, the new "golden child". This brought a move to field sites in West Kalimantan, then a leading oil palm centre, especially to Dayak smallholder villages in Sanggau district. Consultancies also followed with the Centre for International Forestry Research (CIFOR). Later work also involved first-hand knowledge of various transmigration sites in Central Kalimantan, including the notorious "Million Hectare Rice Scheme". I had meanwhile been involved in research in the environmental history of Borneo through archives in the Netherlands and collaboration in work of the KITLV anthropological group in Leiden. I managed to acquire some knowledge of Sabah, Sarawak and Brunei through overland travel and conference attendance, while residence on logging company sites, oil palm estates and in national parks like Kayan Mentarang (North Kalimantan) helped to fill in my "Borneo" experience and enabled me to understand the rapid changes taking place. I have been grateful to always find a welcome from local villagers and fellow researchers, who have been keen to assist me to understand the complexities of life on this large island. My special thanks goes to Jennifer Sheehan of the Cartographic & GIS Services of the Australian National University (ANU) for drawing the maps for Figures 1.1, 2.1a and b, 2.2 and 5.4.

Lesley Potter
May 2022

Glossary

ADB	Asian Development Bank
AI	Artificial Intelligence
AMAN	Aliansi Masyarakat Adat Nusantara (Alliance of Indigenous People of the Archipelago)
APL	Areal Pengunaan Lain (Other use zone: non-forest)
APP	Asia Pulp and Paper
APRIL	Asia Pacific Resources International Holdings Limited
BAPPENAS	Badan Perencanaan Pembangunan Nasional (National Development Planning Agency)
BFCP	Berau Forest Carbon Partnership (East Kalimantan)
BIG	Badan Informasi Geospatial (National Geospatial Information Agency)
BIMP-EAGA	Brunei-Indonesia-Malaysia-Philippines-East-ASEAN-Growth-Area
BMF	Bruno Manser Fund (Sarawak)
BOLEH	Biodiversity Observation for Land and Ecosystem Health (Sabah and East Kalimantan)
BPDPKS	Badan Pengelola Dana Perkebunan Kelapa Sawit (Oil Palm Fund Management agency)
BRG	Badan Restorasi Gambut (Peatland Restoration Agency)
BPS	Badan Pusat Statistik (Indonesian Central Statistics Agency)
BSR	Basal Stem Rot (disease of oil palm)
CBD	Convention on Biological Diversity
CBM	Community Biodiversity Management (Sar)
CDM	Clean Development Mechanism
CIFOR	Center for International Forestry Research
CPO	Crude Palm Oil
CU	Credit Union

Dayak Misik	Dayak Indigenous peoples, generally in more remote areas (Central Kalimantan)
DOSM	Department of Statistics, Malaysia
DTE	*Down to Earth* (journal)
EFB	Empty Fruit Bunches (oil palm)
EIA	Environmental Impact Assessment
ES	Ecosystem Services
EU-ETS	European Union Emissions Trading Scheme
FAOSTAT	Food and Agricultural Organization Statistical Databases
FCPF	Forest Carbon Partnership Facility (East Kalimantan)
FELCRA	Federal Land Consolidation and Development Authority (Malaysia)
FELDA	Federal Land Development Authority (Malaysia)
FFB	Fresh Fruit Bunches (oil palm)
FGV	Felda Global Ventures (oil palm plantation corporation)
FLEGT	Forest Law, Enforcement, Governance and Trade Action Plan
FORMADAT	Forum Masyarakat Adat Dataran Tinggi Sarawak *(*Forum of Indigenous People of the Uplands of Sarawak, NGO).
FORCLIME	Forests and Climate Change Programme (Aid Agency funded, for eastern Indonesia).
FPIC	Free, prior and informed consent
FREL	Forest Reference Emission Levels (Indonesian government)
FS	Forever Sabah (NGO)
FSC	Forest Stewardship Council
GAR	Golden Agri Resources (oil palm company)
GEM	Global Energy Monitor
GFED	Global Fire Emissions Database
GHG	Greenhouse Gas
GIZ	German Aid Agency
GIZFORCLIME	Project on sustainable rubber in Kapuas Hulu (West Kalimantan)
HCS	High Carbon Stock
HCV	High Conservation Value

HoB	Heart of Borneo (see Figure 2.1b)
HTI	Hutan Tanaman Industri (Industrial Plantation Forest)
hutan adat	customary forest
hutan desa	village forest
ILUC	Indirect Land Use Change (EU)
IKN	Ibu Kota Negara (Capital City) (New capital in East Kalimantan)
INOBU	Earth Innovation Research Institute (Central Kalimantan)
IoT	Internet of Things
IPBES	Intergovernmental Science Policy Platform on Biodiversity and Ecosystem Services
IPOP	Indonesian Palm Oil Pledge
IR 4.0	Industrial Revolution 4.0
IPCC	Intergovernmental Panel on Climate Change
ISPO	Indonesian Sustainable Palm Oil
IUCN	International Union for Conservation of Nature
JA	Jurisdictional Approach
JATAM	Jaringan Advokasi Tambang (Mining Advocacy Network)
JCSPO	Sabah Jurisdictional Certified Sustainable Palm Oil
JICA	Japanese International Cooperation Agency
Jokowi	(President) Joko Widodo
Kabupaten	district, regency
Kaharingan	Animistic Dayak religion in Central Kalimantan
Kalbar	Kalimantan Barat (West Kalimantan)
Kalsel	Kalimantan Selatan (South Kalimantan)
Kaltara	Kalimantan Utara (North Kalimantan)
Kalteng	Kalimantan Tengah (Central Kalimantan)
Kaltim	Kalimantan Timur (East Kalimantan)
Kecamatan	subdistrict
Kemitraan	partnership
KFCP	Kalimantan Forests and Climate Partnership (Australia)
KKPA	Kredit Koperasi Primer untuk Anggota (Primary Credit Co-operative for Members) (oil palm smallholder scheme)

Konsep Baru	"Land Reform" Sarawak
Kota	Municipality, city
Kota Terpadu Mandiri	New town on former transmigration site.
Kotim	Kotawaringin Timur subdistrict (C. Kal.)
Kutim	Kutai Timur subdistrict (E. Kal)
Lahan Kritis, Lahan Sub-optimal	Degraded land, unproductive land
M2M	Machine to machine
MARDI	Malaysian Agricultural Research and Development Institute
MCO	Movement Control Order (during COVID-19) Malaysia
MoA	Ministry of Agriculture, Indonesia
MODIS	Satellite Imagery
MoEF	Department of Environment and Forestry, Indonesia
MPOB	Malaysian Palm Oil Board
MRP	Million Hectare Rice Project (also PLG: Pengembangan Lahan Gambut) (Central Kalimantan)
MSPO	Malaysian Sustainable Palm Oil
MSW	Municipal Solid Waste
MTCS	Malaysian Timber Certification Scheme
NBS	National Biomass Strategy (Malaysia)
NCR	Native Customary Rights (Sarawak)
NGO	non-government organization
NDPE	No Deforestation, Peat, Exploitation (pledge by some oil palm companies)
NKEA	New Key Economic Areas (Malaysia)
OMP	One Map Policy (Indonesia)
padi paya(k)	Wet swidden (West Kalimantan)
padi pulut	Sticky rice (West Kalimantan)
PEFC	Programme for Endorsement of Forest Certification
PES	Payment for Ecosystem Services
PHPL	Pengelolahan Hutan Produksi Lestari (Sustainable Production Forest Management)
PIR	Perkebunan Inti Rakyat (Nucleus Estate and Smallholder Scheme, Indonesia)

PIR-Trans	Perkebunan inti Rakyat Transmigrasi (as above, for transmigrants)
PKO	Palm Kernel Oil
PKS	Palm Kernel Shell
PLN	Indonesian State Electricity Company
POIC	Palm Oil Industrial Cluster (Sabah)
POME	Palm Oil Mill Effluents
RECODA	Regional Corridor Development Authority (Sarawak)
RED	Renewable Energy Directive (EU)
REDD (+)	Reducing Emissions from Deforestation and Forest Degradation. (REDD + includes conservation, sustainable management of forests and enhancement of forest carbon stocks).
RFID	Radio Frequency Identification Tags
RHAP	Regional Haze Action Plan
RIL	Reduced Impact Logging
ROW	Rest of the World
RSPO	Roundtable on Sustainable Palm Oil
SAIP	Sabah Agro-industrial Precinct
SALCRA	Sarawak Land Consolidation and Rehabilitation Agency
SBABB	Quality Oil Palm Seedlings Assistance Scheme (Malaysian Palm Oil Board)
SBC	Sarawak Biodiversity Centre
SCORE	Sarawak Corridor of Renewable Energy
SDC	Sabah Development Corridor
SDGs	Sustainable Development Goals
SFM	Sustainable Forest Management
SLDB	Sabah Land Development Board
SPOC	Sustainable Palm Oil Clusters (Malaysia)
SPU	State Planning Unit, Sarawak
STLVS	Sarawak Timber Legality Verification System
SVLK	Sistem Verifikasi Legalitas Kayu (Indonesian Legal Timber Verification System)
TLAS	Timber Legality Insurance System (Sabah)
Toba	Kecamatan in Sanggau district (West Kalimantan)
TORA	Tanah Obyek Reforma Agraria (Agrarian Reform) (Indonesia)

ULC	Underutilized Low Carbon Land
UN-COMTRADE	Database of detailed global annual and monthly trade statistics
UNCTAD	United Nations Conference on Trade and Development
UNFCCC	United Nations Framework Convention on Climate Change
WALHI	Wahana Lingkungan Hidup Indonesia (Indonesian Forum for the Environment; Friends of the Earth, Indonesia, NGO)
WTO	World Trade Organization
WWF	World Wide Fund for Nature
Yayasan Sabah	Sabah Foundation (an organization providing educational and economic opportunities for Sabahans).

PART I

INTRODUCTION

Replanting oil palm in Gunung Meliau (West Kalimantan) (taken by Potter in 2013).

Photos on previous page

1. Coal barge in Mahakam River, Samarinda (East Kalimantan) (taken by Potter in 2010).

2. Remnant forest along Buntok Road (Central Kalimantan) (taken by Potter in 2010).

3. Main Drain in the MRP site (Central Kalimantan) (taken by Potter in 2010, before much oil palm development).

4. Selling watermelons along the Main Drain (Central Kalimantan) — one successful crop! (taken by Potter in 2010).

5. Dedicated coal road near Banjarmasin (South Kalimantan) (taken by Potter in 2010).

1

Introduction

The past five decades of land-use change in Borneo mark an unprecedented, vivid example of land exploitation to induce economic development. Borneo, the world's third-largest island located in Southeast Asia (Figure 1.1), was endowed with one of the oldest rainforests in the world. However, since the 1970s the island has experienced rampant timber extraction on a massive scale; a huge amount of valuable tropical wood was logged and exported, either as raw logs or plywood, resulting in millions of hectares of deforestation and forest degradation. In total, about 20 million ha of old-growth forests were destroyed from 1973 to 2018, largely due to human activities (CIFOR 2020).

In the 1980s, the cultivation of oil palm, a lucrative cash crop grown mainly for export, was introduced throughout the island. By 2018, about 22 million tonnes of the world's vegetable oils (12 per cent) came from the island, compared to 5 million tonnes in 2000 (FAOSTAT 2021). The widespread logging and replacement of forests with oil palm and other crops has resulted in serious degradation of peatland (mainly in Central Kalimantan, Sarawak and West Kalimantan) and greatly escalated the risk of fires, especially during periodic long droughts (Santika, Budiharta, et al. 2020). Repeated peat and forest fires have led not only to enormous carbon stock loss but also transboundary haze that has exerted detrimental health impacts over the entire region (Zhang and Savage 2019).

While land-based developments over the past five decades have substantially reduced poverty, these achievements have been secured at the expense of the environment. Such exploitative activities have generated quick revenues for Malaysia and Indonesia, but peoples' livelihoods have also been threatened, from immediate local health risks to long-term global climate change (Santika, Wilson, Budiharta, Kusworo, et al. 2019; Santika, Wilson, Budiharta, Law, et al. 2019). There is also evidence that the newly generated wealth has been mostly concentrated in the hands of a small group of elites, creating huge wealth gaps among the people. Communities

FIGURE 1.1
Location of Borneo

continuing to seek traditional livelihoods (planting dry rice in swiddens, creating rubber, rattan, or mixed fruit gardens, engaging in small-scale mining, hunting, fishing, or collecting forest products), as well as those working as day labourers on plantations, have found themselves victimized or "left behind" in the wave of development.

Today, many parts of the island are plagued by social conflicts, poor governance, corruption, and ineffective law enforcement. The over-reliance on the exports of primary products for fiscal revenues has also exposed Borneo to periodic economic crises due to fluctuations in commodity prices, making incomes unstable and unpredictable. All these drawbacks imply that such a development pathway is unsuitable for continuation into the future. To avoid further environmental degradation and ensure long-term sustainable development, proper strategies with the right incentives must be put in place to transform conventional land-based economies (Ogg 2020).

Globally, the broad concept of "bio-economy" has caught people's imagination in producing more food and bio-based materials while dealing with the environmental issues of conventional land-based development (Bugge, Hansen, and Klitkou 2016). This concept is mainly championed by "productivists", i.e., advocates of productivity. It asks for increasing economic output while reducing resource consumption through improving system efficiency. The underlying motivation is that the economy has to keep growing, and it is believed that this can be done within safe and sustainable operating boundaries. Especially in developed countries, "climate neutrality" is emphasized as a central piece of the bio-economy (Fritsche et al. 2020). The concept illustrates the transition from a fossil-fuel-based to a bio-based economy by using cutting-edge biological knowledge and technological innovation to optimize the potential of land and biological resources. The spectrum of bio-economy strategies is wide, covering the different components from upstream (e.g., intensifying primary production) to downstream (e.g., creating new products and markets) (Jordan et al. 2007; Shen, Worrell, and Patel 2010). Along these lines, rural development is also emphasized in terms of job creation, income generation, and infrastructure construction (Johnson and Altman 2014). Pressing the importance of increasing overall economic productivity, it seeks to offer a strategic means to reconcile socio-economic progress with environmental sustainability.

Meanwhile, alternative conservation-oriented economic strategies proposed by some conservationists have also received an enthusiastic resonance across the world (Kitchen and Marsden 2009). While the term "bio-economy" has been widely discussed for its definition and scope, there is no common term with that level of attention for alternative strategies in the context of land-based economic activities. Only for a broad indication, they may be loosely placed under the broad concept of "eco-economy". Generally, such a concept stresses the multifunctionality of land-based activities, advocating the need to observe the biological capacity of the Earth system when optimizing the human use of nature (Marsden and Farioli 2015). Unlike the bio-economic concept, the urgency of economic growth over fixing past damages is questioned. While it seeks alternative economic opportunities to restore previously damaged landscapes, maintaining a harmonious relationship with nature is prioritized over economic productivity (Karsenty, Vogel, and Castell 2014). In general, the concept portrays a self-sufficient landscape with small-scale farming systems and alternative income-generation programmes, such as ecosystem restoration, banking on international carbon market mechanisms, and other "green" businesses like eco-tourism (Gómez-Baggethun et al. 2010; Sills et al. 2014; Das and Chatterjee 2015).

Along with these two broad directions of "bio-economy" and "eco-economy", a variety of strategies have been formulated, to drive economic transformation in different parts of Borneo, albeit with a different order of priority over the environment, economy, and society. The choices of strategies, however, depend highly on local complexities shaped by endogenous political, agroecological, social, economic, and cultural factors (Goh et al. 2018). The transformation process becomes more complicated with non-local factors like international trade, foreign investment, migrations, climate change, and other transboundary impacts (Delphin et al. 2016; Goh, Wicke, Faaij, et al. 2016; Nobre et al. 2016; Radel et al. 2019).

While there is no strict dichotomization between the two concepts as the development processes are mostly hybridized, general differences do exist. In the northern part of Borneo, the two Malaysian states, with greater autonomy from the federal government, have tended to prioritize economic development with multiple "bio-economy" policies implemented, although Sabah has also seen more involvement of international organizations in pushing for alternative development strategies and conservation plans. Meanwhile, the less developed Indonesian provinces in the south have been receiving relatively more influence from international conservation efforts with more "eco-economy" initiatives launched. That said, the more urbanized and industrialized eastern coastal areas, particularly East Kalimantan, have also actively engaged in productivity-based strategies, especially utilizing their bountiful coal resource. Generally, the Kalimantan provinces have less freedom to differ from some Central Government policies than their Malaysian counterparts, though decentralization in 2000 resulted in challenges to some central policies, notably on land and forests. These variations make Borneo a very interesting case as it may generate new perspectives in comparing the different tracks chosen by individual territories, despite their geographical, climatic, and socio-cultural continuities.

PREVIOUS WORKS

To fully understand the dynamics of such economic transformation, careful attention must be paid to territorial-specific characteristics and on-ground realities, including historical land-use patterns. General country studies focusing on land-based economies especially agriculture, forestry, and to a lesser extent mining are available. Examples are the books edited by Vincent and Ali (1997) and Jomo, Chang, and Khoo (2004) which lucidly illustrate the strategies deployed by the Malaysian government in the 1980s to jump-start the economy using the country's natural resources, with timber and oil palm among the major contributors. Similarly for Indonesia, edited books by Pierce Colfer and Resosudarmo (2002) and McCarthy and Robinson (2016) provide detailed accounts of the respective development pathways in Indonesia, with attention given to oil palm expansion, forest conservation, and land reform and a "way forward" in the modern era. Specifically, on oil palm expansion, the equally relevant volume edited by Cramb and McCarthy (2016) discusses and analyses issues arising in both Malaysia and Indonesia.

Several books covering aspects of Borneo Island appeared at the end of the 1980s and during the 1990s. This was an era of transition from "traditional" to "modern" livelihoods, leading to a considerable flowering of scholarship concerning local traditions and the inevitability and direction of change. They included *People of the Weeping Forest: Tradition and Change in Borneo*, by Avé and King (1986). It was followed by *Borneo: Change and Development*, by Cleary and Eaton (1992); *The Peoples of Borneo*, by King (1993); *In Place of the Forest*, by Brookfield, Potter, and Byron (1995), and *Borneo in Transition: People, Forests, Conservation, and Development*, by Padoch and Peluso (1996) (with an updated edition in 2003).

These books all dealt with the forests, the transformation of the Borneo environment, and strategies for development, but the approaches differed somewhat. Borneo, in that particular period, was seen alternately as a "resource frontier" (Brookfield, Potter, and Byron 1995), an "underdeveloped periphery" (Cleary and Eaton 1992), "a neglected island" (King 1993), or most importantly, as a region with "complex, diverse and dynamic" social and ecological reality (Padoch and Peluso 1996). The five books also discussed shifting cultivation (a contentious issue) and other farming systems, ethnicity, land settlement, transmigration, and resource rights, such as those of the Penan (Cleary and Eaton 1992). King (1993) was more concerned with the socio-political organization and material culture of the Dayak and Islamic groups, while Brookfield, Potter, and Byron (1995) raised issues of environmental history such as drought, forest fire, and the origin of the *Imperata cylindrica* (*alang-alang*) grasslands. Oil palm was only mentioned briefly for that period, except in Avé and King (1986) and King (1993) where the early developments, especially in Sabah, were analysed. The book by Kaur (1998) on the economic history of Sabah and Sarawak since 1850 also made a sound contribution at that time.

Two more recent books have continued to represent the whole island. The first, *Reflections on the Heart of Borneo*, edited by Persoon and Osseweijer (2008), raises many questions about the Heart of Borneo, that "large transborder area of high conservation value shared by the three countries", about which the contributions ranged widely, canvassing conservation issues throughout the island. A second edited volume, *Borneo Transformed: Agricultural Expansion on the Southeast Asian Frontier*, by De Koninck, Bernard, and Bissonnette (2011), skilfully combined and compared the developments in both the Malaysian and Indonesian territories in Borneo at a subnational level. One new work, edited by Ishikawa and Soda (2019), *Anthropogenic Tropical Forests*, has further extended the scope of transdisciplinary research in Borneo, albeit with a special focus on Sarawak compared to the other parts of Borneo. It represents a comprehensive collection of knowledge from both natural and social scientists on topics related to commodity chains, material cycles, and food webs in the dimensions of environmental and societal changes.

While the more recent books mentioned above provided useful background up to the 2010s, they did not further examine the potential pathways beyond primary production, e.g., downstream bio-based industries, and eco-tourism that open new opportunities for economic transformation, and how different strategies can work together or against each other. Recent years have not seen efforts to consolidate knowledge across both sides of "bio-economy" (productivity-centric) and "eco-economy" (conservation-centric) for the case of Borneo as a whole. Such a comprehensive study will have to take many years and a large number of specialists to complete.

While this present book aims to fill in some of the gaps, it is not envisaged that it would be as ambitious. However, a comprehensive review with updated information in a territorial context and comparative analyses across sectors and disciplines can be a timely work, neatly filling in the knowledge gap given the rapid changes in social, economic, and political aspects across the island from 2000 to 2021. This allows the authors to verify the robustness of different strategies and narrow the set of possible alternatives that can be employed in different contexts, by examining questions like "does what makes sense for big players also work for smallholders?", "does what fails in Central Kalimantan also fail in Sabah?". By putting these pieces of the puzzle together, this book provides a more complete picture of how Borneo has been transformed in the past two decades, with different strategies or interventions producing good, bad, or mixed results in different territories. The experience in Borneo can also be relevant for other tropical communities, which have seen more calls for the transformation of exploitative land-based economies, especially in South America and Africa.

Scope and Structure

This book attempts to systematize the strategies proposed or implemented to transform the land-based economies in Borneo and explores the underlying dynamics in addressing the big question: how to improve livelihoods, not only without causing further environmental impacts but also repairing the damage done in the past. It is further guided by three sub-questions: (i) what strategies are implemented or proposed to transform the land-based economies? (ii) what are the current status, opportunities, and challenges of these strategies from different perspectives? and (iii) how do they complement or contradict each other in a territorial context?

The framework of the book was established based on the authors' years of experience in varied parts of Borneo and discussions with various actors (local communities, governments, researchers, industries, international organizations, non-governmental and civil society organizations) while working in different capacities, following which the content gradually evolved through a careful analysis of the now voluminous literature.

This book is organized into 14 chapters grouped into four parts. Part I consists of this introduction and Chapter 2, in which both quantitative and qualitative background information about the island is provided, including a summary of the post-independence land-based developments in chronological order.

The chapters in Part II describe five productivity-oriented strategies for transforming land-based economies in Borneo. Chapter 3 gives an overview of the first strategy, i.e., boosting upstream productivity of oil palm and timber, the two major commodities in Borneo's export-oriented economies. It provides a detailed account of the biological and physical limitations, as well as the problems associated with small farmers and labour availability. The next strategy, activating underutilized low-carbon land resources for future production, is analysed in Chapter 4. Both the biophysical and non-biophysical characteristics of such land resources are examined, and the factors that affect the mobilization of these land resources are identified.

The next three chapters primarily deal with strategies related to downstream activities and markets. The efforts in upgrading and diversifying downstream activities, particularly the oleochemical industries and biorefineries are elaborated upon in Chapter 5. This is followed by a discussion about the importance and the current status of infrastructure and investment. Chapter 6 provides a broader perspective of value creation through strategic branding of the two aforementioned commodities, i.e., timber and palm oil. The market status, schemes, impacts, and challenges are analysed. Lastly, the strategy of establishing domestic demand for bio-resources to boost local growth and supply security is reviewed in Chapter 7. The motivation and effectiveness of implementing this strategy in the food, energy, and manufacturing sectors are assessed.

Part III consists of Chapters 8 to 12 which cover conservation-oriented development strategies. These five chapters are arranged in a way analogous to the five chapters in Part II. Corresponding to the productivity-boosting strategy described in Chapter 3, enhancing agroecological resilience is portrayed as an alternative strategy for ensuring long-term growth in Chapter 8. Adoption of a landscape approach in (re)designing the land-use system, with a special focus on peatland restoration, is deemed the key to enhancing the resilience of the land-use systems in Borneo. In addition, commodifying ecosystem services is perceived as a revolutionary approach to addressing the perennial issue of environmental degradation as described in Chapter 9. It is fundamentally different from most of the other strategies as it does not measure the outputs in terms of biological products or human-based services. Instead, it attempts to arbitrarily create value for ecosystem services and markets to trade them. The issues of measurement, monetization, scheme design, and implementation are elaborated.

As the counterpart of Chapter 5, Chapter 10 portrays the potential of establishing eco-based tertiary sectors, such as eco-tourism, as an alternative to conventional industrialization. Meanwhile, Chapter 11 focuses on marketing products from smallholdings to create new value propositions. This strategy is complementary to the one described in Chapter 6, but with different focuses and approaches. Chapter 12 represents more of an ideological approach than an economic strategy. It describes the idea of a self-sufficient farming-hunting-gathering system in rural areas largely linked to traditional lifestyles. This is discussed in the context of urban-rural transition, ethnicity, and land-use practices.

The last part of this book, Part IV, has two chapters. Chapter 13 explores the potential impacts of the ongoing digital revolution on Borneo, particularly the application of new technologies for realizing transformative strategies. Chapter 14 discusses future perspectives, especially in light of current climate change predictions.

2

Recapping the Five Decades of Land-Based Development

This chapter lays a foundation for the other chapters, especially for readers not familiar with Borneo Island. First, the geographical background is provided before the chapter moves into a brief history of land-based development in Borneo. The summary is divided into five parts: the period of massive timber extraction in 1970–2000; the rise and fall of mega land-based projects from the 1990s; the concurrent growth of coal mining; the era of oil palm expansion in the first two decades of the twenty-first century and the ongoing, gradual shift to sustainable development beginning about 2010. For readers interested in understanding the detailed history of land-based development in Borneo, the books and publications described in Chapter 1, in the paragraphs before the section "Scope and Structure", are recommended for further reading.

Special thanks to Jennifer Sheehan at the Australian National University (ANU) for drawing the maps in this chapter.

GEOGRAPHICAL BACKGROUND

Borneo is the world's third-largest island located in Southeast Asia. The name "Borneo" relates to the phrase "Brunei Darussalam", which possibly has a Sanskrit root of *Váruṇa*, i.e., the Hindu god of rain. The island is also called "Kalimantan" by the Indonesians, likely a derivation from *Kālamanthāna*, a Sanskrit word that carries the meaning of burning and hot air. The island has an area of 73 million ha, almost thrice the size of the United Kingdom, or eighteen times the size of the Netherlands. There are long swampy coastlines, a mountainous interior, and extensive river networks. As swampy and mountainous environments are generally less suitable for agriculture and not easily accessed, most settlements are concentrated in drier flat areas, traditionally along riverbanks.

Borneo is politically divided between Malaysia (26 per cent) and Indonesia (73 per cent), with the remainder forming Brunei Darussalam. The current political division in Borneo is a result of colonial history. The northern territories were under British control, while the south was colonized by the Dutch. Physically, the north and the south of the island are divided by a central spine of rugged mountains that vaguely form the political boundary between Malaysian and Indonesian Borneo (Figure 2.1). After a short "unification" under the Japanese during World War II, the Dutch-controlled territories were merged into the Republic of Indonesia in 1945. Kalimantan's internal boundaries have undergone several changes, the most recent being in 2012 when the northern part of East Kalimantan was recognized as a new province, North Kalimantan. Meanwhile, the regions of Sarawak and Sabah formed the Federation of Malaysia in 1963 together with Peninsular Malaysia and Singapore. Brunei Darussalam, however, chose to remain an independent sultanate.

Despite the political division, border control is relatively loose between Malaysian and Indonesian Borneo. Naturally, there are more trade, people, and cultural flows between Sabah and North Kalimantan, both via the sea route and across the land border. On the other side, although sharing borders with three Kalimantan provinces, Sarawak has more communication with West Kalimantan (including periods of intense smuggling via the many small "rat" paths [jalan tikus] which access the porous border) but limited exchange with the other two provinces due to the largely mountainous border terrains.

The highest points in Kalimantan, Sabah, and Sarawak are noted in Figure 2.1a. A comparison between the elevation and the population density (Figure 2.2) will emphasize the general limitations posed by the uplands on human settlement in Borneo. However, a high proportion of this upland area is included in the "Heart of Borneo" (Figure 2.1b), much of it already protected, containing a large part of the remaining forest and amazingly biodiverse natural environments on the island.

The tropical island is now inhabited by about 23 million people. Figure 2.3 illustrates the population growth in Borneo. The population of Kalimantan was 5.1 million by 1970 and reached 16.6 million by 2020 (BPS 2020). A large increase occurred between the 1980s and 2000s, predominantly due to transmigration from other parts of Indonesia. Kalimantan was one of the main targets of the transmigration programme that involved transporting poor families, largely from overpopulated Java to government-organized settlements in the "outer islands", including Kalimantan. Meanwhile, the populations of Sabah and Sarawak also grew,

FIGURE 2.1

Borneo: Physical Structure: (a) Elevation; (b) River Systems and Major Protected Areas

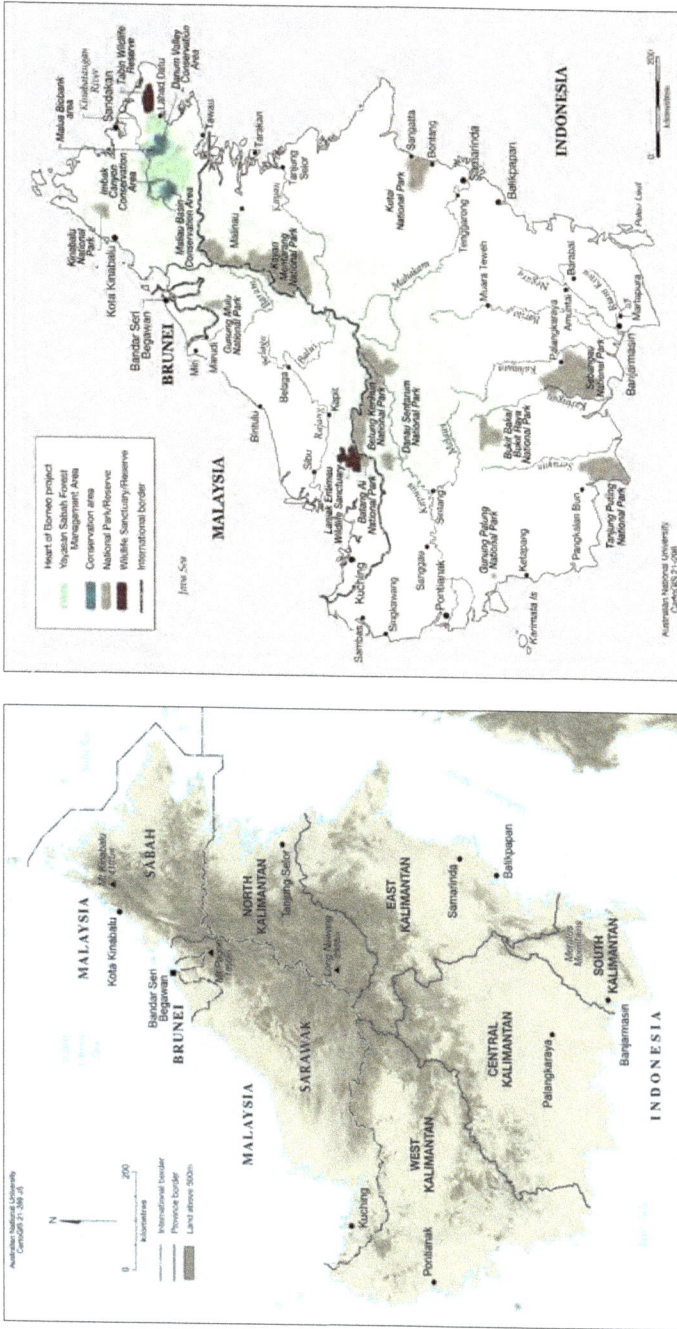

FIGURE 2.2
Borneo: Population Density per District, 2020

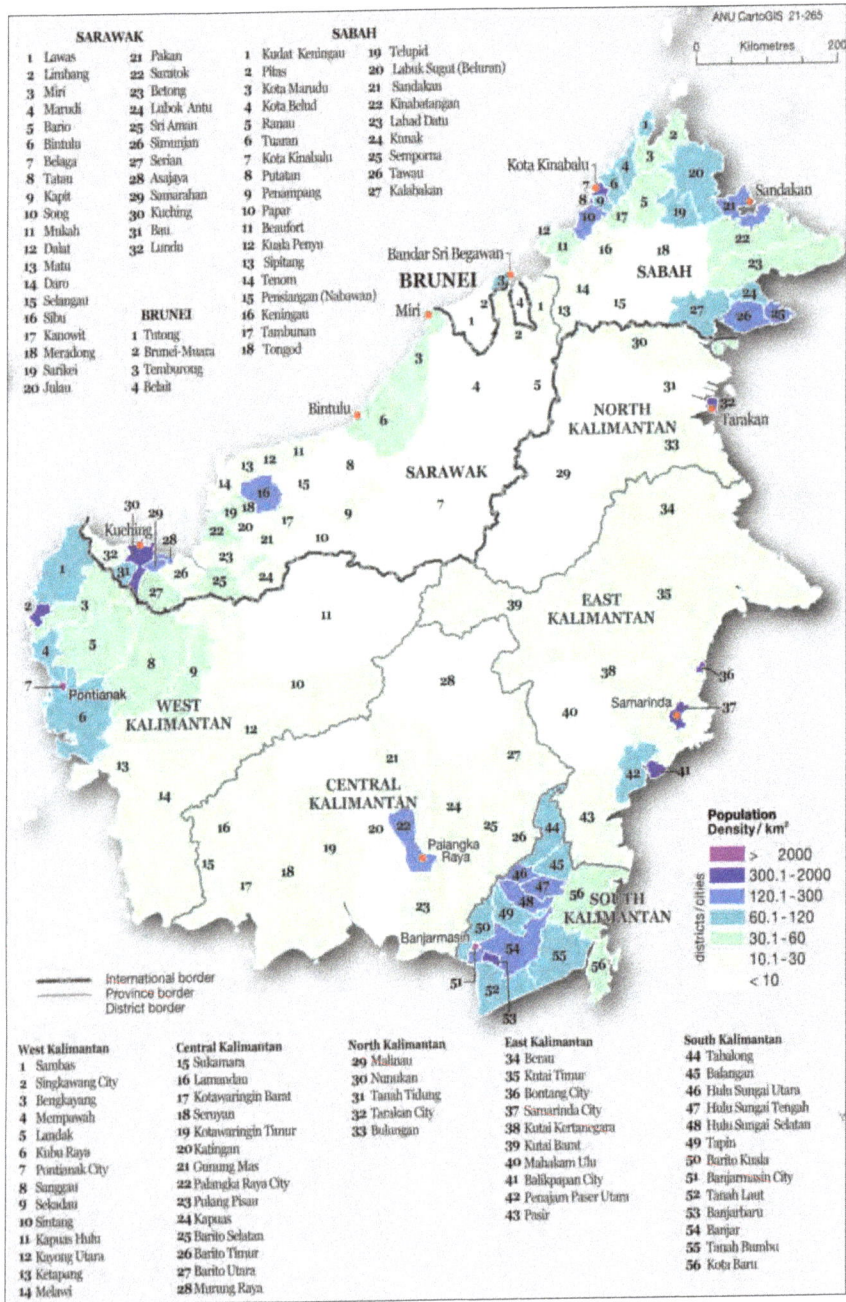

ANU CartoGIS 21-265

SARAWAK

1 Lawas	21 Pakan
2 Limbang	22 Saratok
3 Miri	23 Betong
4 Marudi	24 Lubok Antu
5 Bario	25 Sri Aman
6 Bintulu	26 Simunjan
7 Belaga	27 Serian
8 Tatau	28 Asajaya
9 Kapit	29 Samarahan
10 Song	30 Kuching
11 Mukah	31 Bau
12 Dalat	32 Lundu
13 Matu	
14 Daro	
15 Selangau	
16 Sibu	**BRUNEI**
17 Kanowit	1 Tutong
18 Meradong	2 Brunei-Muara
19 Sarikei	3 Temburong
20 Julau	4 Belait

SABAH

1 Kudat Keningau	19 Telupid
2 Pilas	20 Labuk Sugut (Beluran)
3 Kota Marudu	21 Sandakan
4 Kota Belud	22 Kinabatangan
5 Ranau	23 Lahad Datu
6 Tuaran	24 Kunak
7 Kota Kinabalu	25 Semporna
8 Putatan	26 Tawau
9 Penampang	27 Kalabakan
10 Papar	
11 Beaufort	
12 Kuala Penyu	
13 Sipitang	
14 Tenom	
15 Pensiangan (Nabawan)	
16 Keningau	
17 Tambunan	
18 Tongod	

0 ——— Kilometres ——— 200

Population Density / km²

- > 2000
- 300.1 - 2000
- 120.1 - 300
- 60.1 - 120
- 30.1 - 60
- 10.1 - 30
- < 10

(districts / cities)

International border
Province border
District border

West Kalimantan
1 Sambas
2 Singkawang City
3 Bengkayang
4 Mempawah
5 Landak
6 Kubu Raya
7 Pontianak City
8 Sanggau
9 Sekadau
10 Sintang
11 Kapuas Hulu
12 Kayong Utara
13 Ketapang
14 Melawi

Central Kalimantan
15 Sukamara
16 Lamandau
17 Kotawaringin Barat
18 Seruyan
19 Kotawaringin Timur
20 Katingan
21 Gunung Mas
22 Palangka Raya City
23 Pulang Pisau
24 Kapuas
25 Barito Selatan
26 Barito Timur
27 Barito Utara
28 Murung Raya

North Kalimantan
29 Malinau
30 Nunukan
31 Tanah Tidung
32 Tarakan City
33 Bulungan

East Kalimantan
34 Berau
35 Kutai Timur
36 Bontang City
37 Samarinda City
38 Kutai Kertanegara
39 Kutai Barat
40 Mahakam Ulu
41 Balikpapan City
42 Penajam Paser Utara
43 Pasir

South Kalimantan
44 Tabalong
45 Balangan
46 Hulu Sungai Utara
47 Hulu Sungai Tengah
48 Hulu Sungai Selatan
49 Tapin
50 Barito Kuala
51 Banjarmasin City
52 Tanah Laut
53 Banjarbaru
54 Banjar
55 Tanah Bumbu
56 Kota Baru

FIGURE 2.3
Population Growth in Borneo, 1970–2020

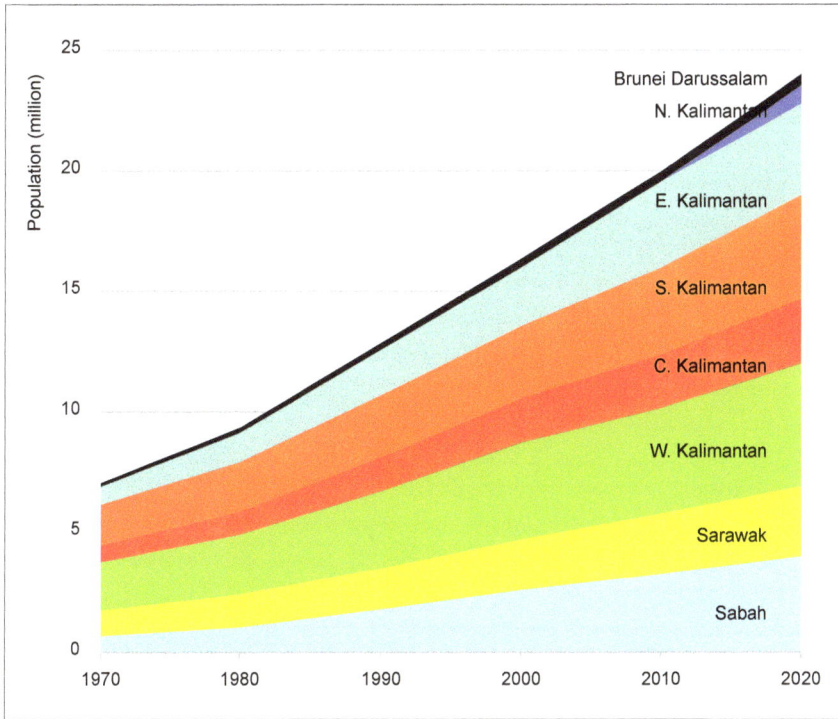

Source: BPS (2020); DEPS (2020); DOSM (2020).

from 0.7 million and 1.0 million, respectively, (Kaur 1998) to 3.9 million and 2.9 million (DOSM 2020). Brunei Darussalam remains less populated with about 0.5 million (DEPS 2020). Interestingly, West Kalimantan (5.4 million) and South Kalimantan (4.1 million) are both more populated than either Sarawak or Sabah. As its area is small, South Kalimantan is the most densely populated "state" in Borneo although its political freedom from the Central Government does not approach that of its Malaysian counterparts.

The population spread across the island is ethnically diverse and broadly organized into several loose ethnoreligious blocks. The umbrella term "Dayaks" refers to the non-Muslim indigenous group, with many variants, for example, Iban, Bidayuh, Kenyah, Kayan, Ngaju, Ot Danum, Ma'anyan, and Punan/Penan. Meanwhile, Malay, Melanau, Banjarese and Bajau are broadly recognized as Muslims. There are also Chinese descendants, especially in Sarawak and West Kalimantan, as well as other indigenous people (mainly in

Sabah), who neither recognize themselves as Dayaks nor Muslims (Kadazan, Dusun, Murut, Sungai, etc., including Sino-Native with mixed-parentage). Some recent migrants (many undocumented) from other islands, especially Java, Sulawesi, Flores, and the southern Philippines, may not be included in the previously mentioned ethnoreligious blocks. However, one should note that there are significant differences in terms of culture and origins even among the people within the same "block".

The main cities in Borneo are located along the coastline, several being also important trading seaports. One prominent exception is Palangka Raya (Central Kalimantan) situated inland on the Kahayan River, though not far from the coast. There are some arguments as to which city is the largest. Samarinda (East Kalimantan) is listed by the 2020 Indonesian census as having a population of 827,994. According to the State Planning Unit (SPU) of Sarawak, Kuching had 812,900 in 2018 (including Kuching City, Bau, and Lundu) (SPU 2019). Another contender is the conurbation of Banjarmasin-Banjarbaru in South Kalimantan, which had 911,105 people in 2020. Today, the majority of the Chinese population resides in the major cities of Sarawak, Sabah, and West Kalimantan. The Muslims are mainly spread along the coasts and several rivers. The largest group of Muslims, the Banjarese, occupy South Kalimantan, with sizeable Banjarese minorities in Central and East Kalimantan. The other ethnic groups are widely dispersed across the landscape, with many, such as the Sarawak Iban and Kelabit, now also living in cities.

The changes in GDP per capita in Borneo by territories are illustrated in Figure 2.4a. Brunei Darussalam has enjoyed the highest GDP per capita owing to its rich petroleum resources and relatively small population. Sarawak and East Kalimantan also stand out from the other regions due to their oil and gas resources. Both have surpassed the national average since the rise of oil prices in the 2010s. Interestingly, Central Kalimantan also outpaced Indonesia's national average in 2018 in terms of GDP per capita. In contrast, Sabah has been falling behind the national average with a widening gap since the 2000s. This gap in GDP per capita corresponded to the rapid growth in population over the same period. However, as displayed in Figure 2.4b, the Kalimantan provinces still maintained a commodity-based economic structure for many decades post-independence with relatively small manufacturing sectors compared to Peninsular Malaysia and Java. Primary industries, i.e., agriculture, forestry, and fisheries, as well as extractive industries such as mining contributed up to 50 per cent of the GDP in many of these territories. The following sections briefly outline the land-based development in the Bornean territories since 1970.

FIGURE 2.4
(a) Trends of GDP per capita at Current Price in Borneo in 1970–2020;
(b) Distribution of GDP by Sector in 2010 and 2018

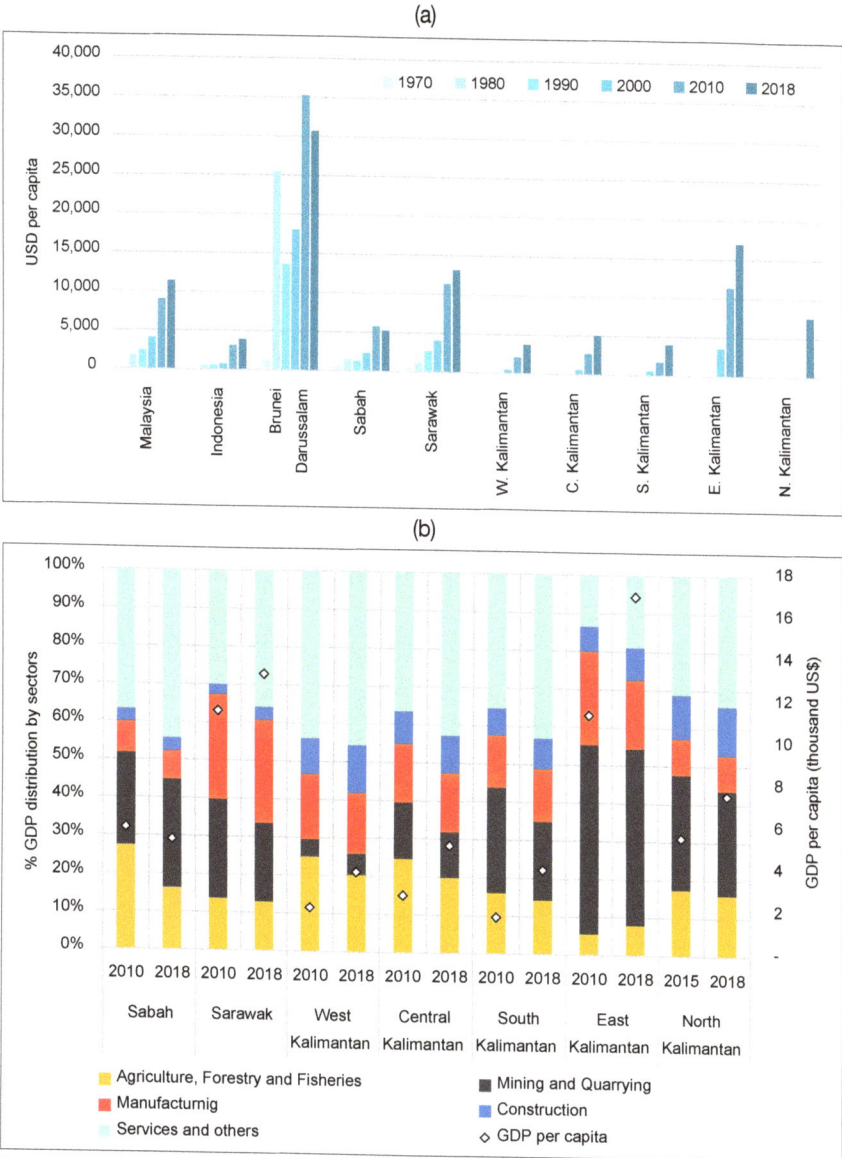

(a)

(b)

Sources:
1. Sabah: (DOSM 2020) for 2010-2019; (Hashim 1998) for 1970–2000.
2. Sarawak: (DOSM 2020) for 2010–19; (DOSM 1991) for 1980-2000; (Drabble 2000) for 1970 (estimation).
3. Provinces of Kalimantan: (BPS Kalbar 2020); (BPS Kalteng 2020); (BPS Kalsel 2020); (BPS Kaltim 2020); (BPS Kaltara 2020) for 2000–19. No data before 2000. As North Kalimantan only existed after 2012, the earliest data available is for 2015.
4. Brunei Darussalam, Malaysia, and Indonesia: (World Bank 2020b),
5. Currency exchange based on (World Bank 2020b).

Massive Timber Extraction, 1970–2000

As it was bestowed with vast forests, large-scale exploitation of timber resources was deemed a rapid way of developing the Borneo economies. Until the early 1970s, the island still possessed huge stretches of biodiverse rainforests. Since then, most territories in Borneo have undergone massive forest destruction on an unprecedented scale, except Brunei Darussalam which has been relying on its petroleum revenues (Bryan et al. 2013). Rapid timber extraction has resulted in severe deforestation and environmental degradation (see Figure 2.5). From 1990 to 2000, the forest loss in Borneo surged rapidly. corresponding to the increase in the export of timber shown

FIGURE 2.5
Changes in Forested Areas in Borneo Excluding Brunei Darussalam

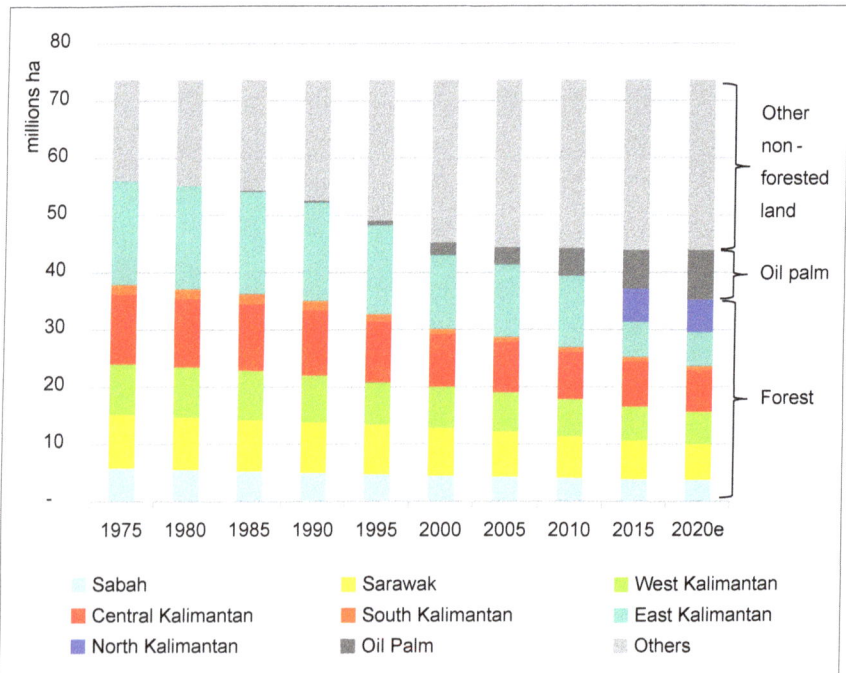

Sources:
1. Forested land: CIFOR (2020) for 1973 and 2001–18; Aden et al. (2001) for Kalimantan in 1985 and 1997; Kaur (1998) for Sarawak in 1977.
2. Oil palm: MPOB (2021) for Sabah and Sarawak; (DG Estate Crop Indonesia 1996) (DG Estate Crop Indonesia 1996, 2012, 2016, 2018) for Kalimantan in 2011–18; BPS (2007) in 2001–7; missing years were interpolated.
3. Extrapolation for 2020.

in Figure 2.6. Many of the remaining forests have been highly degraded, as demonstrated by the dense network of logging roads penetrating those in Sarawak and Sabah (Bryan et al. 2013).

Demand from the emerging economies in the region was the main driver of timber extraction in Borneo. Timber and plywood from Borneo were a major source of building and industrial materials, especially in Japan and to a lesser extent Korea and Taiwan (Barbier et al. 1995). Since the 1960s, Japan had adopted an import-oriented policy for its wood-based industry. Japan alone has been contributing about US$2 billion per year to the timber export business in Indonesia and Malaysia since 1990 as shown in Figure 2.6a. Japanese companies like Mitsui, Mitsubishi, and Sumitomo played active roles in the early years of logging in Borneo, especially in Kalimantan (Nectoux and Kuroda 1989). It can be roughly assumed that timber shipped to Japan came from Borneo, especially in the case of Malaysia as log exports were banned in the Peninsula (Brookfield and Byron 1990; Samejima 2020). Sabah's exports remained quite high throughout the period. Kalimantan's were similar until 1986 when the Indonesian government banned exports of raw logs so the country could make its own plywood. The volume of exports from Sarawak started small but grew rapidly in the 1980s to be a similar size to Sabah's, replacing Kalimantan in the Japanese market for logs, though Kalimantan's plywood later became dominant.

It was timber revenues that largely financed the Malaysian states until the 1990s (Kaur 1998). Sarawak had to surrender its petroleum resources to the federal government in 1975, being compensated with 5 per cent of royalties. In such a situation, land-based economic activities, which were out of federal control, became the major revenue source. The then state administration, under Chief Minister Taib Mahmud (1981–2014) held a very clear policy direction: pushing large-scale "modern" land development to "liberalize" the economic values of the vast "idle" land resources in the state. Timber extraction was the most important activity in the first stage of such a development pathway. In the stiff contests for rents between the elites, including the "big six" timber tycoons with political patronage, huge areas of forest were ruinously degraded and destroyed. Sarawak experienced one of the most rapid log clearances in Southeast Asia—about 76 per cent of the land was forested in the late 1970s, and by 1990 almost the entire forested area had been licensed for logging (Faeh 2011). Until the 2010s, as concluded by Faeh (2011), "the sparse remaining loggable forest is being keenly fought over by a few large-scale timber conglomerates, the land rights of indigenous groups are usually still being denied and the problems of illegal timber logging and smuggling remain to this day".

FIGURE 2.6
(a) Imports of Hardwood Logs to Japan by Source, 1970–87; (b) Export Values of Wood and Articles of Wood from Malaysia and Indonesia to Japan and the Rest of the World (RoW)

(a)

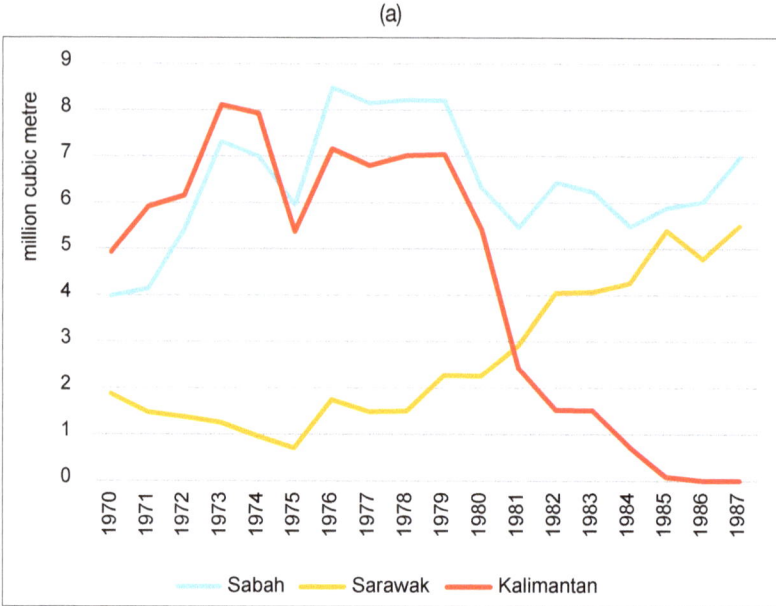

(b)

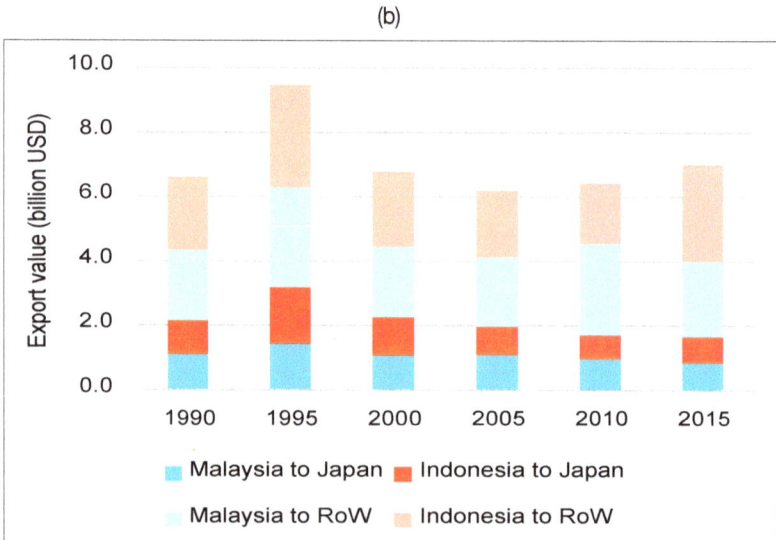

Source: a. Nectoux and Kuroda (1989); b. UN COMTRADE (2021).

Until recently the situation was no better in Sabah. Apart from some small private concessions, the territory was directly involved in the timber business through a statutory body, the Sabah Foundation (Yayasan Sabah). Almost 1 million ha of forests were allocated for industrial harvesting under this body, which was supposed to manage the forests sustainably for the benefit of the people (Reynolds et al. 2011). Unfortunately, the foundation was widely known as "a cash register for politicians" with many politicians, including a recent Chief Minister, Musa Aman, publicly accused and charged for siphoning off funds during his time in office from 2003 to 2018 (Butler 2012). However, Reynolds et al. (2011) also reported that the management of the forestry department had been improving in the 2000s, expanding strict conservation areas and instituting several forest restoration efforts, including internationally funded projects.

Between 1970 and 2000, large-scale logging was also conducted throughout Kalimantan. In contrast to Sarawak and Sabah, the central government in Jakarta had direct control over the forests in Kalimantan through the Basic Forestry Law of 1967 (and continued despite some minor changes in the revised Forestry Law of 1999) (see Chapter 4). In the 1980s, the government demarcated the boundaries of the "Agreed Forest Land Use Zones" (TGHK) without consulting the local forest dwellers. Nearly one-half of the land in Kalimantan or about 25.6 million ha was placed under the category of "production forest" (Potter 2005). Sustainable logging was not practised as initially expected, as many companies were just there to "cut and run", taking out the big trees without nurturing the medium and small ones.

Meanwhile, the "conversion forest", usually in more accessible locations, was made available for agriculture and settlement and could be clear-felled. The boundary between the production and conversion forests was always contentious, as officials sought suitable degraded forests that could then be reclassified and clear-felled. Under the control of Bob Hasan, a businessman who was closely linked to President Suharto, the logging and plywood industries in Kalimantan grew rapidly. In the 1980s and 1990s, Indonesia became the world's leading exporter of tropical plywood. The exports tripled between 1984 and 1991, with much of the plywood being exported to Japan. Due to the depletion of natural timbers in the early 1990s, it was suggested that the golden age of plywood was over.

Other uses were being planned for the forests by the large conglomerates controlling the industry, as interest shifted to pulp and paper plants. In 1989 the official selective logging system was renamed the "selective felling and planting system" as all holders of forest concessions were expected to replant worked-out sections of their holdings in "industrial" timbers (Hutan Tanaman Industri, HTI), the most popular of which was *Acacia mangium*. The acacia is a fast-growing tree, ideal for pulp, but subject to disease and pest attacks. A "reforestation fund" was established to aid the transition, but concession holders were slow to respond.

Some abandoned their holdings, which were then taken over by a government group, Inhutani, the aim being to speed reforestation. Even a transmigration scheme was devised (HTI-Trans), with mainly Javanese migrants being used as a source of labour for planting acacia. That scheme was not very popular, as no land was provided for the migrants. It was described by one NGO as "akin to slavery in a modern guise" (Potter 1996). Now, most of Indonesia's pulp and paper plants are located in Sumatra, with the original plans for Kalimantan (up to ten plants) not viable. Only one pulp plant, PT Kertas Nusantara, is still in operation in Berau, East Kalimantan but it has experienced many problems, mainly with the supply of fibre for its large mill. Much acacia grown in Kalimantan is used, however, to support the needs of the Sumatran plants, the two largest of which (Indah Kiat and RAPP, both in Riau province) are some of the biggest in the world.

Also important to note is the existence of illegal logging throughout Borneo. There is limited accurate information about the actual timber produced from Borneo in recent decades due to rampant illegal logging throughout the island (Smith et al. 2003; Lawson and MacFaul 2010). In Kalimantan, the level and type of "illegal" logging initially took the form of small-scale timber removal from the large, often foreign concessions by local people, frustrated at being deprived of a traditional "common property" resource (Potter 1988). In 1995, the magnitude of timber theft from fifty concessions in Kalimantan was reported to be equal to the officially recorded production (Resosudarmo 2002).

Following the end of the Suharto regime in 1998 and the decentralization policy in 2000, illegal logging became more widespread, including in both national parks and logging concessions. The timbers were moved across the international borders, as traders from Sabah and Sarawak set up sawmills in Indonesian border locations (Tagliacozzo 2001; Casson and Obidzinski 2002; Smith et al. 2003; Wadley and Eilenberg 2005). Many people in the border regions came to rely on these forestry activities as their major income source, although what they obtained was only a fraction of the true value of the timber. One observer remarked that "Malaysia receives a cow, but the Indons only get a chicken" as reported in *Kompas* (9 August

2000) (Potter 2009b). However, Malaysia eventually banned the import of timber from Indonesia in 2004.

MEGA LAND-BASED PROJECTS FROM THE 1990S

Due to the predatory nature of logging activities in Borneo as described earlier, the forestry sector began to face the depletion of high-value timber in the 1990s. In the post-logging era, economic transformations were needed for new wealth sources. Against this backdrop, two prominent land-based mega projects were launched in Sarawak and Central Kalimantan. Meanwhile, coal mining rapidly increased in East and South Kalimantan.

Construction of Dams for Hydropower in Sarawak

In Sarawak, plans for constructing large-scale hydroelectricity dams in the interior were made to take advantage of the state's abundant land and water resources. Hydropower was perceived as the growth engine of the Sarawak Corridor of Renewable Energy (SCORE) to accommodate energy-intensive businesses, such as aluminium smelting (Howe and Kamaruddin 2016). The construction of dams, however, came at great expense to both the natural environment and the displaced populations. The first dam, Batang Ai, was built in Lubuk Antu between 1982 and 1986. Although comparatively small in size, it still provoked criticism about the resettlement process involving 3,000 Iban, supposed to change from their traditional swidden cultivation to cash cropping of oil palm or cocoa (Taswell 1986). However, it was dwarfed by the Bakun Dam on the Balui River, a tributary of the Rajang River, the biggest dam in the region with a 2,400 MW capacity, involving the destruction of nearly 70,000 ha of tropical forests. Although it was begun in 1996, it was only completed in 2011 due to the Asian Economic Crisis. The original plan to transfer 90 per cent of the power by undersea cable to Peninsular Malaysia was shelved, and this highly centralized, industrial-focused power supply scheme has failed to realize its original development goals for the rural areas (Sovacool and Bulan 2012).

Construction of the dam was also strongly criticized for the inadequate arrangements in the relocation of indigenous communities and the subsequent deterioration of their livelihoods (Sovacool and Bulan 2011; Aeria 2016), not to mention the political and financial scandals surrounding the project. The same issue was reported for a third dam which was completed on the Murum River (944 MW) in Belaga in 2015. It drew strong protests from the displaced people, largely Penan, about the inadequacy of housing built to accommodate them, poor food security, little hope of economic opportunities in the settlement area, and no safe transport for children to the "makeshift" schools (Sarawak Report 2013, 2014).

The "mega dams" plan was even scheduled to take place in the more remote regions of the state, both to provide power for local energy and to sell electricity to neighbours such as West Kalimantan, Brunei, and Sabah. One dam in Baram, if built, would have been likely to displace 20,000 people and submerge 400 km² of the rainforest. In 2015, the Adenan Satem government decided against proceeding with that construction, noting that it was not needed with the other dams already constructed (Gaworecki 2015a, 2015b). Lobbying against the dams by environmental NGOs such as "Save Sarawak Rivers" had also been intense. However, the present government of Abang Johari now seems set to revive the former policy, with the announcement in 2017 of the construction of the 1,295 MW Baleh Dam in Kapit (to be completed by 2025) to be followed by the Trusan Dam, aiming to supply both water and power to Brunei and Sabah (Sulok 2017; Alamgir et al. 2020).

Large-Scale Coal Mining in East and South Kalimantan

Coal mining has also been developed rapidly in Borneo, especially in East and South Kalimantan. PT Kaltim Prima Coal, the world's largest single producer of thermal coal, started mining at Sangatta in East Kalimantan in 1990; PT Adaro, the second-largest producer, began operations in Tanjung, South Kalimantan in 1991 (Lucarelli 2010). However, the dramatic rise in Kalimantan's coal production and export occurred from 2000 to 2019. East Kalimantan is Borneo's leader in coal production, with South Kalimantan not far behind (Figure 2.7). Indonesia is currently the world's biggest coal exporting country (replacing Australia), having doubled its exports over the past decade, largely to China, India, Japan, and South Korea (Chatham House 2021). Coal is the major power source for the country, accounting for nearly 60 per cent of the country's energy generation (Coca 2021).

Like the construction of hydropower dams in Sarawak, this type of land-based activity in Kalimantan has been accompanied by serious environmental and social impacts. The extensive open-cut mines pollute and contaminate water sources and occupy formerly productive farmlands, while worked-out properties are often simply abandoned with no attempts at landscape restoration, leaving deep and dangerous acidic ponds in which many village children have drowned.

In East Kalimantan, the city of Samarinda and the adjoining district of Kutai Kartanegara have many small to medium companies lining the banks of the Mahakam River (formerly occupied by sawmills) and encroaching on the outer suburbs of the city. Long lines of barges convey the coal along the

FIGURE 2.7
Location of Coal Mines in Borneo

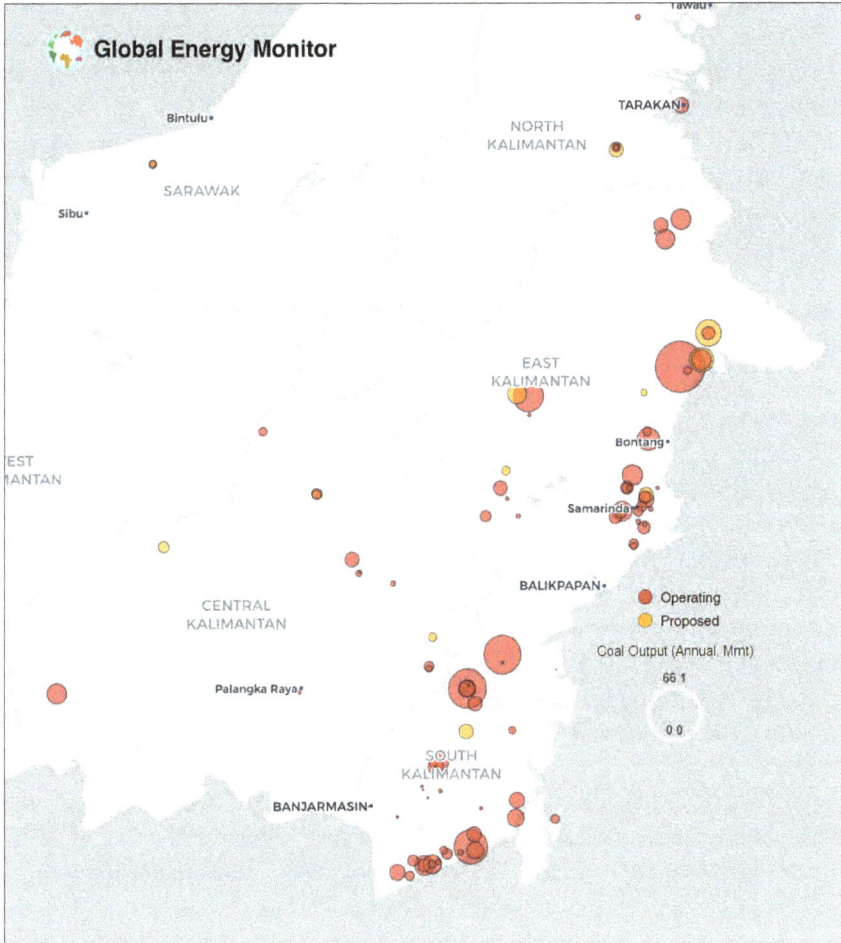

Source: GEM (2022).

river to the port of Samarinda. There are 394 unrestored abandoned coal pits within Samarinda's city limits, and the river water is heavily polluted (Siti Maimunah and Agustiorini 2020). Upriver, the rapidly growing city of Tenggarong was described as "a boom town built on coal" (DTE 2010). In 2016, it was claimed that 748 mining concessions had been granted around the Mahakam (Siti Maimunah and Agustiorini 2020), with 40 per cent of provincial land earmarked for coal concessions (Yovanda 2019).

In South Kalimantan, the giant Adaro and Arutmin mines, with the latter designated as a "National Vital Object" by the Indonesian government, have a total annual production of 100 million tons (Idris 2021) out of a provincial total in 2018 of 150 million tons (Susanto 2019). JATAM (Mining Advocacy Network) estimated that 33 per cent of the land area of the province was allocated for coal mining permits (Mulyana 2021). Research by the Auriga group reported that as much as 41 per cent of the Meratus Mountains, from which flowed several streams, were burdened with mining permits, while more than 800 abandoned acid-filled mining pits (many originally illegal) occurred across the province (Hadin and Oemar 2020). Meanwhile, coal mines were also established in the northern part of Central Kalimantan, particularly Murung Raya and Katingan. However, the transportation routes are still being developed, probably by rail, to gain access to ports for export through the nearby rivers (Alamgir et al. 2019). The main company in Murung Raya, PT AKT in Tuhup, lost its permit in 2017 due to maladministration. It produces high-carbon metallurgical coal, which is highly prized and expensive (Harsono 2020).

Despite some calls for a greater emphasis on renewable energy (including from BAPPENAS, the influential government planning agency), the Jokowi government has been continuing to support coal, with many prominent political figures having links to the coal industry in Kalimantan (BAPPENAS 2019; Coca 2021). While the government has committed to building no new coal-fired plants after 2023, 117 new plants are presently under construction (Jong 2021a). However, ideas are changing. It has recently been reported that the Asian Development Bank (ADB) is working on a financing scheme to buy Indonesia's coal-fired power stations and retire them early, hoping to speed up the energy transition in one of the world's top emitters of greenhouse gases (Harsono 2021).

It has also been suggested that Indonesian government officials, in sketching out revised net zero emission targets for the power sector, are facing more public pressure to modify their commitments to coal in favour of renewables (Hamdi and Adhiguna 2021). However, the renewables selected—cascading hydropower development through five dams on the Kayan River in North Kalimantan and "co-firing" with large amounts of wood pellet biomass or palm kernel shells—also come with potential environmental and social risks. The suggested use of carbon capture and storage technologies for massive gas consumption ignores the fact that those "new" technologies are still unproven (Rochmyaningsih 2016; Hamdi and Adhiguna 2021).

Construction of the Million-Hectare "Rice Estate" in
Central Kalimantan

Meanwhile, a project called the Mega Rice Project (MRP), or in Indonesian "Pengembangan Lahan Gambut (PLG)", literally "peatland development", was launched in 1995 in Central Kalimantan. The project was created to boost Indonesia's rice output by draining and cultivating 1.4 million hectares of peat forest in Central Kalimantan. It was accompanied by the transmigration programme, already in full swing under the Suharto government during the 1980s. Due to decreasing land availability for rice in Java, the government was motivated to develop new rice fields in the "empty" parts of Kalimantan, especially the swamp areas, by using Javanese transmigrants who have experience in wet rice production.

While some experts expressed doubt that rice could grow in the deep peat, McBeth (1995) concluded that "political considerations totally eclipsed technical planning". The project proceeded, quoting McCarthy (2013), "without cost-benefit analysis, engineering studies, or effective environmental impact assessments". More unfortunately, the initial opening of the project in 1997 coincided with a lengthy El Niño drought. It was not possible to irrigate the land during the drought, the soil quickly became acidic and rat plagues infested the crops. As the peat dried out enormous fires raged through the area, consuming the farms of both local people and transmigrants. The amount of carbon released into the atmosphere in the fire in 1997 was estimated to be more than the total emission by the EU in a year (Page et al. 2002).

The project was finally cancelled in 1999. After a decade of neglect, the Yudhoyono government issued Presidential Decree No. 2 of 2007, designed to rehabilitate the MRP. This brought several international consortia to attempt to restore the drainage, through rewetting and blocking the drainage canals and conserving the forest and wildlife, specifically the orangutans. To date, rice production in Central Kalimantan is low, forcing the province to rely on imports from Java (Octania 2021). When Potter visited in 2011, the transmigrants at the MRP site had given up trying to grow rice and were trying to negotiate with an oil palm company, but there were many issues over land rights. By 2012, only about 8,000 out of the original 15,600 households remained onsite (Radius 2012).

There has recently been considerable discussion between the concepts of "food security" (especially rice policies that necessitate importing some of the staples, particularly in bad years for local harvests), and "food sovereignty", preferred by President Joko Widodo. This entails setting up large-scale rice estates, for example, in part of the former MRP site in Kalimantan to try to ensure national self-sufficiency. In 2020 the Indonesian government decided to revive the MRP and drafted a plan to grow rice in 770,600 ha of degraded peatland (Jong 2020e). The reason given by President Widodo was to prepare the country to face an "impending global food crisis" triggered by the COVID-19 outbreak.

However, the plan has not come up with any feasible solutions to the same issues encountered in the past and the risk of repeating the same mistakes is very high. As this plan is working against other ongoing transformations in the land-use sectors, it has caused great concern among the people and observers, especially regarding the role of the army in its implementation, which was being rushed through (Jong 2020d). How this will span out requires close monitoring from various stakeholders and sectors to ensure the deplorable history of this project is not repeated.

Rapid Oil Palm Expansion, 2000–20

Alongside the mega land-based projects, oil palm (*Elaeis guineenis*) has become the new economic paradigm, expanding explosively throughout Borneo in the 2000s (Casson 2001; Suwarno, Hein, and Sumarga 2015). Oil palm is a perennial oil crop that originated in West Africa, growing wild in secondary forests and village groves. It is the most high-yielding oil crop with a productive lifespan of twenty-five to thirty years. Oil derived from palm fruits can be used not only as a cooking oil but also as raw material for a wide range of additives and non-edible products like detergents and cosmetics. Oil palm was developed into a cash crop in Southeast Asia, with the first commercial plantations established in North Sumatra and Aceh, Indonesia in 1911 and Peninsular Malaysia in 1917 (Tan 1965). By 1966 Malaysia had eclipsed Nigeria as the world's leading palm oil producer, a position the Malaysians held for forty years until Indonesia took over in 2006. Palm oil from Malaysia and Indonesia is now leading in the global vegetable oil supply with close competition from soy oil.

Sabah, with a history of plantation agriculture (e.g., tobacco, cocoa), was the first Bornean territory to plant oil palm, already having 36,000 ha under the crop by 1970, about ten years before Sarawak began establishing its industry (Avé and King 1986). By the end of the 1990s, around 1 million ha of oil palm were already planted throughout the state. However, it was not until the 1990s that oil palm began to expand across all the Bornean territories, though low prices dampened the enthusiasm during the Asian Economic Crisis of 1998. Surging prices after 2000, accompanied in Indonesia by regime change, decentralization, and privatization of the industry, induced a real boom in planting and production throughout Kalimantan. The local districts began using their new freedom since decentralization in 2000 to issue permits for oil palm. According to official statistics, the total oil palm area in Kalimantan was about 5.07 million ha by 2019 (Figure 2.8).

In Sarawak, the proliferation of oil palm occurred at almost the same time as in Kalimantan. Oil palm was regarded as the new economic engine for the state together with hydropower. This led to delivering large tracts of land to private companies under the name of development, especially the "big six" timber tycoons mentioned earlier who intended to convert their core business from logging to oil palm. As a result, the total area of oil palm plantations in Sarawak reached nearly 1.59 million ha in 2019, overtaking Sabah (1.54 million ha) as the largest producer among the

FIGURE 2.8

Changes in Oil Palm Area in Borneo Excluding Brunei Darussalam

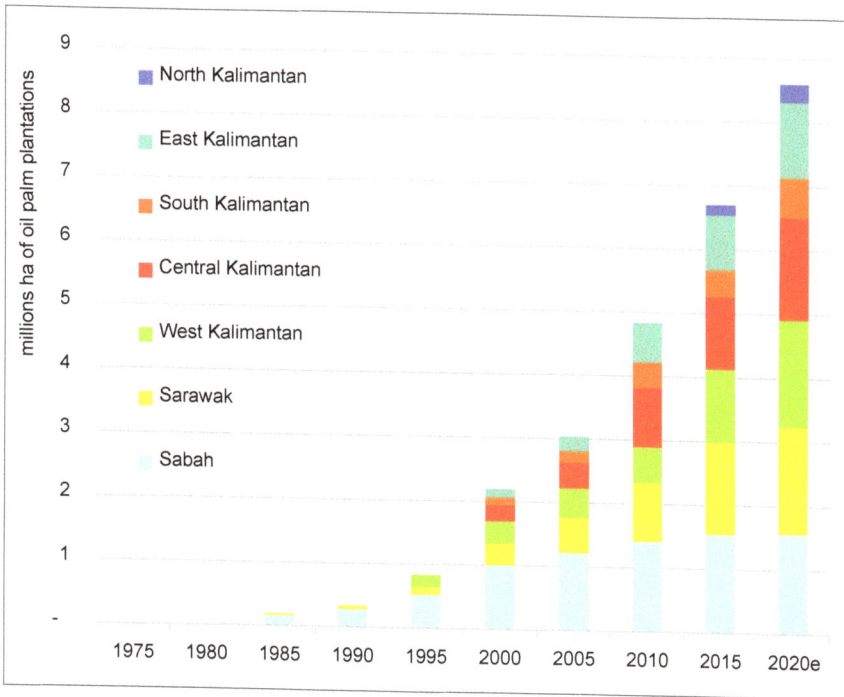

Source and Note:
1. Oil palm: MPOB (2021) for Sabah and Sarawak; (DG Estate Crop Indonesia 1996) (DG Estate Crop Indonesia 1996, 2012, 2016, 2018) for Kalimantan in 2011–18; BPS (2007) in 2001–7; missing years were interpolated.
2. Extrapolation for 2020.

FIGURE 2.9
CPO Production in Borneo in 2019

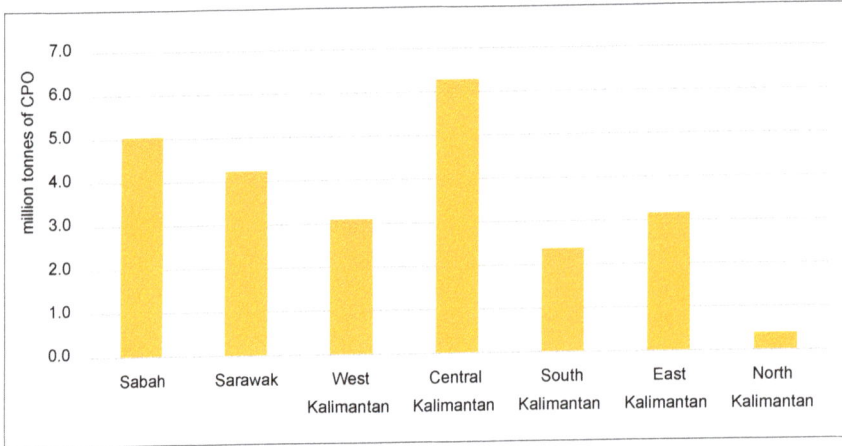

Source: DG Estate Crop Indonesia (2019); MPOB (2021).

Malaysian states (MPOB 2021). By 2019, Sabah and Sarawak had more than half of Malaysia's planted oil palm, while the Kalimantan territories planted about one-third of Indonesia's total (BPS 2020; MPOB 2021). The total production in Borneo reached almost 25 million tonnes of CPO, with Central Kalimantan leading at 6.3 million tonnes (Figure 2.9).

While the expansion of the cash crop has brought in significant revenues for the states and provinces, it also involved large-scale conversions of forests and peatlands. There are various estimates of the area of forests converted to oil palm, ranging from 4 per cent (Gunarso et al. 2013) to 90 per cent (Carlson et al. 2012) depending on the assumptions made, with the conversion processes being complex and involving earlier conversions. For example, some forests may first degrade into disturbed forests through logging and then be turned into scrubs and grasslands by fire before being converted to oil palm plantations. An ongoing study by CIFOR (2020), with all the maps available to the public on the online atlas, shows that close to one-third of the plantations in 2018 were established on recently deforested land, i.e., land which was still forested in the year before the oil palm was planted. Figure 2.10 illustrates the stark difference between land cover in 1973 and 2018 based on satellite images captured for Borneo.

Critically, many oil palm plantations were established on peat swamp forests in 2000–18. In Sarawak alone, at least 34–39 per cent of oil palm plantations are cultivated on peat soil, according to CIFOR (2020) and Wan

FIGURE 2.10
Borneo: Land Cover Map 1973 and 2018

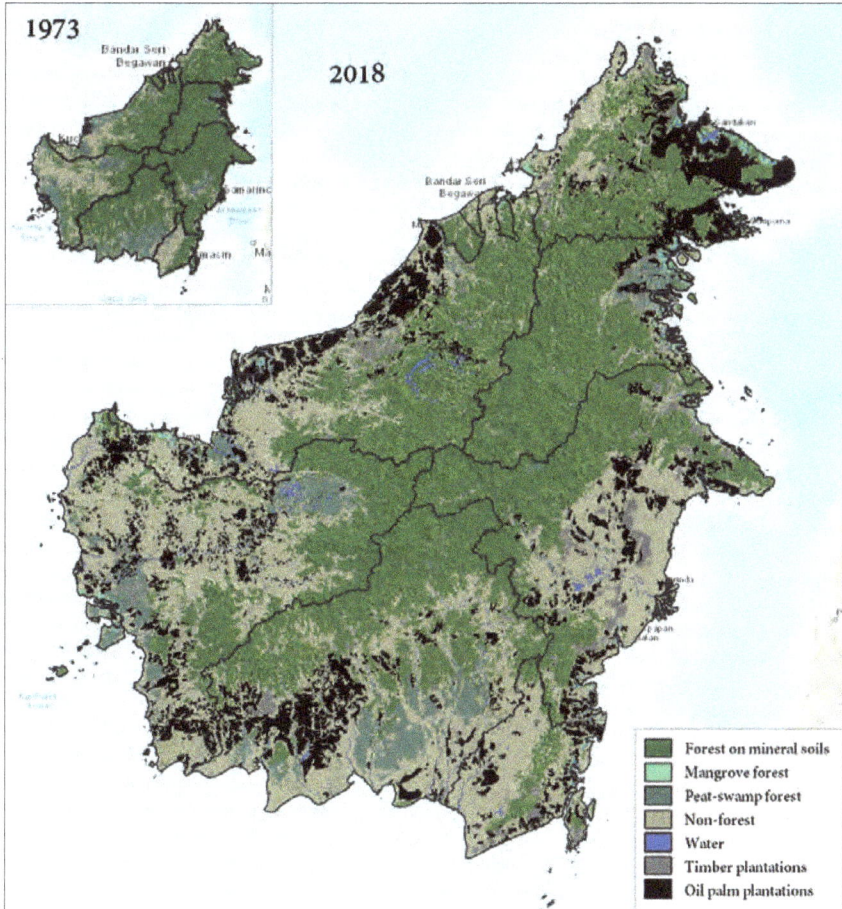

Source: CIFOR (2020).

Mohd Jaafar et al. (2020). About 124,000 ha of peatland in the ex-MRP area is now also planted with oil palm, with about two-thirds containing a deep peat layer (Dohong, Aziz, and Dargusch 2018). The conversion of peatland has exacerbated the spread of fire across Central Kalimantan during severe droughts. It was also one of two Indonesian provinces (the other one being Riau in Sumatra) with serious periodic land fire events in the past two decades (Syaufina 2018). It was suggested that many of the forest fires that erupted in Indonesia in the drought of 1997 were deliberately lit by logging companies wanting to plant oil palm (Dauvergne 1998). The level of carbon emissions from these events in just one month in 2015 was estimated to be comparable to the annual emission of developed countries like Japan (Field et al. 2016). The peat fires also triggered transboundary haze that caused further health impacts and economic loss in the entire region (Glauber et al. 2016). As an indication, Figure 2.11 shows the estimated amount of carbon emitted to the atmosphere from land fires in Southeast Asia (mostly in Sumatra and Borneo) against the total annual emissions of the UK.

One interesting question, given the prevalence of oil palm planting on peat soils in both countries, is why there did not seem to be the same burning problem in Sarawak as in Indonesia. It would seem to be explained by the generally heavier rainfall in Sarawak, especially in the area south of Miri, where much of the oil palm has been planted—see rainfall map and graphs for Sarawak, Kalimantan, and Sabah or Figure 2.3 in De Koninck, Bernard, and Bissonnette (2011). Fewer droughts would lessen the likelihood of fire in the peat. There is also less scrutiny of the Sarawak plantings, with fewer NGOs in action (with Greenpeace, for example, being excluded).

The expansion of oil palm has also led to "land grabbing" by private companies under the name of development and triggered many unwanted

FIGURE 2.11

Emissions from Land Fire in Southeast Asia (mostly in Sumatra and Borneo) Compared to Total Annual Emissions of the UK

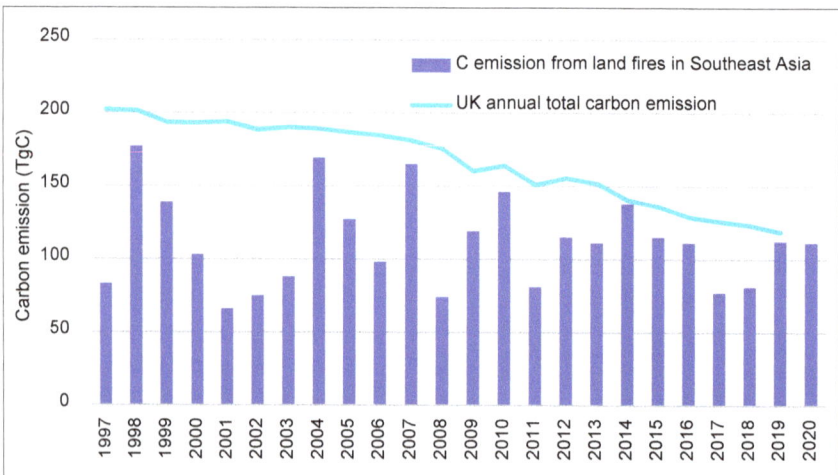

Source: BEIS (2020); GFED (2020).

social issues. Many conflicts have ensued as oil palm companies began taking over land from the local people, whose legal tenure is weak (Galudra et al. 2011; Abram et al. 2017; Sanders et al. 2019). Land grabbing was conducted in various modes, such as the seizure of native customary land in Sabah and Sarawak through unfavourable joint venture arrangements (Majid Cooke 2002, 2012; Cramb 2016). Also, many of the oil palm plantations operating in peat areas in Kalimantan are illegal as they are located on deep peat (Dohong, Aziz, and Dargusch 2018). Box 2.1 provides an example of how complex the situation on the ground can be.

BOX 2.1
The MRP, Oil Palm Plantations, and Fires

In its survey of plantation involvement in the fires, Greenpeace (2020) listed the top ten oil palm companies in Indonesia ranked according to the total burned area mapped in their concessions from 2015 to 2019. Four of the "top ten" were located in the former MRP. Following the 2015 fires, Minister Panjaitan, then Coordinating Minister of Political, Legal and Security Affairs, admitted the mistake of distributing peatlands to plantations and attempted to revoke the plantation permits of companies that failed to prevent their concessions from burning (Greenpeace 2020). Unfortunately, this did not happen and in 2019 the burning occurred again, with extreme impacts on air quality in Palangkaraya and further afield, but almost no action was taken against the offending companies. While the Indonesian Government recently won lawsuits against ten companies for setting forest fires, only one has paid a fine, with lawsuits dragging on for years (Greenpeace 2019; Jong 2019d).

Third on the Greenpeace list for the total burned area mapped in their concessions in 2015–19 was PT Globalindo Agung Lestari (PT GAL), a Genting company (therefore Malaysian in origin). The company's response to Greenpeace about the burning was to assert that the NGO had used an incorrect map. However, given the area occupied by PT GAL and its subsidiaries, Greenpeace's "burn scar" data had a good chance of being correct. [See Greenpeace (2019) photographs (with GPS verification) and video: "Documentation of Forest Fires Investigation in PT GAL concession (Genting) Central Kalimantan, 2019"]. PT GAL had taken over land from the original transmigrants in the MRP, provoking many complaints. It subsequently expanded its holdings very considerably, the suggestion being that this expansion was accompanied by the burning of the existing scrub, enough to set fire to the underlying peat.

As explained by Meijaard et al. (2020), the sustainability issue of palm oil is highly complicated when it is put into a global context, considering the surge in demand for vegetable oils. In addition to being an important food source, palm oil is also a major feedstock for chemical products like detergents and cosmetics. Considering the shifts of export-oriented agricultural expansion from one region to another, the governance of palm oil has become highly complicated as it involves local, national, and international stakeholders. With greater calls for sustainability, the region has moved on to a transition, albeit slow, in the late 2010s to a more sustainable mode of land-based development.

Transition to Sustainable Development, *circa 2010–Present*

While various conservation efforts had been initiated previously, more changes in the adverse trends were observed in the 2010s, when Borneo started more seriously to address the concept of sustainable development. Sustainable development was earlier defined as "development that meets the needs of the present without compromising the ability of future generations to meet their own needs" based on the 1987 Brundtland Commission Report. In acknowledging and embracing the principle of "sustainable development", the Malaysian and Indonesian governments as well as companies and various organizations are seeking more ways for reducing the unwanted consequences while generating new economic opportunities. For Borneo, the emergence of sustainable development to replace exploitative land-based development can be especially traced to three lines of inquiry: sustainability of cash crop production, climate change mitigation, and transboundary haze.

First, as oil palm development in Borneo is highly export-oriented, the growth in foreign consumers' awareness of the need for social and environmental sustainability, has strong implications for the industry. The growing concerns for wildlife, with the orangutan frequently used as a symbol of endangered animals in Borneo, have greatly changed consumer behaviour, especially in Europe and North America. Oil palm companies and farmers in Borneo have been confronted by pressures from the big buyers and consumers to enhance environmental and social sustainability.

This resonates with the global call for mitigating climate change. Borneo is in the limelight as a major contributor to this source of emissions if not the biggest among the other subnational regions of Indonesia and Malaysia. More than 50 per cent of the national greenhouse gas emissions of Indonesia in 2016 came from the AFOLU sectors, i.e., agriculture, forestry, and other land use (AFOLU). Kalimantan and Sumatra are the two regions in Indonesia that contributed most to the emissions especially due to deforestation and peat fires (Krisnawati 2015; MoEF Indonesia 2018).

Additionally, as described in the previous sections, the recurring transboundary haze events resulting from peat fires, especially the two serious episodes in 2015 and 2019, are also pushing the governments to understand the urgency of making a shift towards more sustainable development pathways (Nguitragool 2010). Haze affects not only those living closest to the fires but may travel great distances across boundaries. The accompanying health impacts and regional economic losses have caused multiple conflicts between countries, with both local operators and foreign investors involved in agricultural expansion in Borneo increasingly coming under the spotlight.

These three issues are closely intertwined but were governed separately in the past two decades. However, the stakeholders have started to realize that all these issues must be collectively addressed with more coherent policies. Gradually, the concepts of social and environmental sustainability have been ingrained into different aspects of economic development at different levels. At the subnational level, the two Malaysian territories have become more cautious in issuing timber licences and provisional leases for new plantations and have made multiple serious efforts to eradicate illegal logging (*Borneo Post*, 13 February 2015). At the national level, Malaysia pledged to keep at least 50 per cent of its land forested (Corley and Tinker 2015). Meanwhile, Indonesia introduced the moratorium on primary forests and peatlands in 2011 (which was first extended annually and later indefinitely extended from 2019 by the Jokowi government) as well as the oil palm moratorium for three years from September 2018. These restrictions suspended the issuance of new logging licences and oil palm concessions, respectively (Tacconi and Muttaqin 2019).

However, except for the restriction on the depth of peatland which may be exploited, the pledge and moratorium are not legally binding (Chain Action Research, 2021). For Indonesia, the moratorium on oil palm concessions was due to be extended in September 2021, which environmentalists (including some government officials) were hoping would occur, though so far there has been no indication of this (Jong 2021c). At the regional level, Indonesia eventually ratified the Transboundary Haze Agreement in 2014, about twelve years after it was signed. Varkkey (2018) has argued that this agreement, one of the few legally binding agreements to be enforced by ASEAN, was nevertheless "a seriously watered-down document

… that continued to protect current national economic interests" and has not been adhered to by Indonesia. Varkkey has suggested that the ethos of ASEAN, of non-interference in the policies and behaviour of member states, has been a disincentive to implementing regional environmental policies, including international policies on sustainable development, which have been formulated outside the region.

On the international platforms, Indonesia and Malaysia have committed to reducing their greenhouse gas emissions, especially from the land-use sector, by announcing their Nationally Determined Contributions (NDC) via the United Nations Framework Convention on Climate Change (UNFCCC) in 2015 (UNFCCC 2016b, 2016a). Both countries also engage in biodiversity management and policy development through the Convention on Biological Diversity (CBD) framework (Han et al. 2020). These national commitments have strong implications for Borneo as it has been the frontier of land-use emission and environmental degradation for both countries. Influences from various international organizations and civil society have also grown stronger, and their continuous pressure on both the governments and the big oil palm companies has resulted in the creation of platforms such as the Roundtable on Sustainable Palm Oil (RSPO) and the Heart of Borneo (HoB) (Pye 2019).

These efforts have started to see some results although not all have been successful. In the mid-2010s, oil palm expansion slowed down significantly, due to both market downturn (low prices of palm oil) and continuous pressure from the international communities and civil society. Although periodic peat fire remains an issue, the island has observed a reduction in deforestation (Carmenta et al. 2017). Especially, deforestation in wood fibre concessions has declined dramatically (Trase 2022). Governments have shifted some of the focus from primary extraction to secondary sectors like oleochemicals and bio-based industries as well as tertiary sectors like eco-tourism.

This was also accompanied by various funding opportunities from overseas, such as the (REDD+) schemes financed by several developed countries. REDD+ goes beyond simply reducing emissions from deforestation and forest degradation and includes the roles of conservation, sustainable management of forests, and enhancement of forest carbon stocks (Venter and Koh 2012) (see Chapter 9). However, there are still reports of breaking commitments to end deforestation by some companies, such as the secret sourcing of timber from East Kalimantan by large pulp companies (Jong 2018). There is still much to be done to fully transform the island from land exploitation to a more sustainable model of development.

The seventeen "Sustainable Development Goals (SDGs)" framework may become a guide for Borneo to move forward. The framework embraced in September 2015 by the UN General Assembly in New York has started to gain momentum in Malaysia and Indonesia in the last few years. As the seventeen goals are intended for global action, there is no mention of palm oil as such, but it is clear that there is much here under the SDGs that is relevant to both Indonesia and Malaysia and specifically to Borneo. While it is the main responsibility of the national governments to work towards meeting these goals (and both countries have set up structures to do that), more regional and local jurisdictions are also expected to assist, as well as non-government organizations, international agencies, and private companies. This process is termed "localization" and is particularly relevant to Sabah, Sarawak, and Kalimantan. Some of the goals are directly linked to the land-based sectors in Borneo, and they are also interlinked:

- Goal 1, "Zero poverty" is linked to the land-based sectors in Borneo as a means to increase the income of the population. However, it is not just met by reducing the proportion of the population below the poverty line; it also includes levels of social protection and rights to economic resources such as land (with secure tenure), together with a reduction of vulnerability to social and environmental shocks and disasters, including climate-related extreme events.
- Goal 2, "Zero hunger" is expanded to achieve food security: aggregated food availability, household food access, and individual food utilization with improved nutrition (ending all forms of child malnutrition including stunting) and promotion of sustainable agriculture. Details are sought on the productivity and incomes of small-scale food producers, especially women and indigenous people. Beyond local food production, the goal also includes ensuring the proper functioning of food commodity markets on a global scale—in the case of Borneo this would be its role in supplying vegetable oils to the world's population—with the elimination of extreme food price volatility.
- Goal 3, "Good health" for Borneo specifically targets improving air quality (and haze) and reducing water pollution, aspiring to "substantially reduce the number of deaths from hazardous chemicals and air, water and soil pollution, by 2030".
- Goal 12, "Responsible consumption and production" mentions encouraging companies "especially large and transnational companies" to adopt sustainable practices, and there is mention of sustainable tourism "that creates jobs and promotes local culture and products"

(also noted under goal 8 "Decent work and economic growth"). There is a call for the rationalization of inefficient fossil-fuel subsidies that encourage wasteful consumption and harm the environment, which is directly linked to the coal mining sectors in Borneo.

- Goal 13, "Climate action" is highly relevant to Borneo as the land-use sectors are the biggest contributor to the greenhouse gas emissions of Indonesia. Borneo is a key region for urgent actions to combat climate change and its impacts.

- Goal 15, "Life on land" may be the most important goal for Borneo with a focus on managing forests, halting land degradation, biodiversity loss, and deforestation as well as securing resources for conservation and reforestation.

- Goal 16, "Peace, justice and strong institutions" addresses the land conflicts and limited access to justice throughout Borneo due to weak governance and institutions. Immediate concerns include freeing people from all forms of violence in the land-based sectors, and long-term needs include strong institutions in land governance to protect the land and human rights of all.

The development narratives may be further altered with the spread of COVID-19 over the island since 2020 and the arrival of the digital revolution driven by the pandemic. Few could have appreciated the implications of the digital revolution in Borneo until then. For example, the Sarawak state government has expanded the Mobile Bank Branch Services in rural areas to ensure people receive financial aid provided by the state and federal governments during the period of the movement control order (MCO) (*The Star*, 8 May 2020). Substantial societal changes can be seen on the ground with the rapid improvement in digital connectivity in the 2010s. While the digital revolution spurs the emergence of new businesses and economic opportunities, it also changes lifestyles in both urban and rural areas. In terms of conservation efforts, unsustainable land-use practices and violations of human rights are also increasingly exposed through social media on a global scale. While the impact of the pandemic on sustainable development in Borneo remains unclear at the time of writing, the digitalization progress will likely be accelerated throughout the island as seen in both Indonesia and Malaysia.

Borneo in this period can be considered entering a new phase of development. Given its relatively short history of modern development, how Borneo can move towards sustainable development would be a compelling case in the modern history of land-based economies.

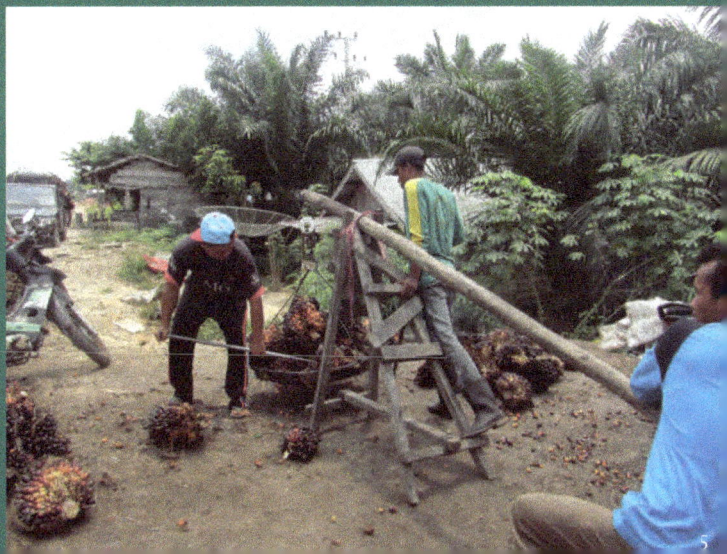

PART II

BIO-ECONOMY: PRODUCTIVITY-ORIENTED STRATEGIES

Road building activities connecting the remote areas resume in 2022, near Sapulut (Sabah) (taken by Goh in 2022).

Photos on previous page

1. Oil palm plantations on peat: trees are liable to fall over! In Sebabi, Kotawaringin Timur (Central Kalimantan) (taken by Potter in 2010).

2. Samalaju Port, Bintulu (Sarawak) (taken by Goh in 2016).

3. New farmers receiving instruction, Sintang (West Kalimantan) (taken by Potter in 2018).

4. Low carbon land, Gunung Mas (Central Kalimantan) (taken by Goh in 2014).

5. Oil palm smallholders weighing fruit at roadside Indragiri Hulu (West Kalimantan) (taken by Potter in 2014).

3

Boosting Upstream Productivity of Cash Crops

The great yield breakthroughs are a chief reason for the past century's population boom and economic growth (McArthur and McCord 2017). These were achieved through improving plant varieties, increasing mineral agro-inputs, upgrading irrigation, and intensifying animal farms. At the same time, demand per capita has also been growing significantly. Global per capita food supply increased from 2,196 to 2,929 kcal/day between 1961 and 2018. The United States is leading with 3,782 kcal/day, while China has doubled its average to 3,203 kcal/day. Both Indonesia and Malaysia, however, stay close to the world average (FAOSTAT 2021).

Nevertheless, yield breakthroughs have not taken place evenly. In reality, the continuously surging demand for agricultural products has triggered both abandonment of low-yield cropland and massive conversions of forests to new cropland across the world. Improving land-use efficiency through intensification has been deemed by productivists as a direct measure to reduce unsustainable expansion, forming the basis of a bio-economy (Garnett et al. 2013). An ambitious estimate made by Tilman et al. (2011) shows that moderate intensification of existing low-yield croplands is sufficient to reduce potential cropland expansion from 1 billion ha down to 0.2 billion ha by 2050, indirectly preventing global deforestation.

In Borneo, the tightened control over land concessions by the governments as well as the rising land cost is gradually shifting the trend from rapid expansion to the intensification of existing oil palm cultivation (Varkkey, Tyson, and Choiruzzad 2018; Yusuf, Roos, and Horridge 2018). Private plantation companies, supported by both federal governments are significantly investing in improving their productivity (Bernama 2020). While oil palm is already regarded as the most productive oil crop in terms of land area used, theoretically the yield can still be further boosted by narrowing the gap between actual and attainable yields. Timber plantations have also received considerable attention for intensification but more on the aspect of long-term productivity and sustainability. The effectiveness of this strategy thus lies within the question of how much palm oil and timber can be further produced from the existing plantations without triggering unwanted environmental consequences.

This chapter explores two premises of this question: (i) the agro-ecological; and (ii) the socio-economic aspects of the intensification of agriculture and forestry in Borneo. For (i), the current status and technical challenges in closing palm oil and timber yield gaps at the plantation level are identified. For (ii), the perspectives of small farmers and labour force issues are specifically discussed.

AGROECOLOGICAL PERSPECTIVES

Oil Palm

Both the large industrial players in Malaysia and the public agricultural entity, namely the Malaysian Palm Oil Board (MPOB), have been continuously investing in boosting the upstream productivity of oil palm, largely motivated by the limited land availability in the country for future expansion as Malaysia pledged to keep at least 50 per cent of its land forested (Corley and Tinker 2015). In contrast, expansion had been more attractive than intensification in Indonesian Borneo due to the lower cost (Varkkey, Tyson, and Choiruzzad 2018). However, intensification has been getting more attention in Kalimantan in recent years with the extension of the forest moratorium in 2017 as well as the introduction of the new oil palm moratorium in 2018 that calls for boosting the productivity of existing oil palm plantations (Tacconi and Muttaqin 2019).

With substantial investment in upgrading crop breeding and genomics as well as improving plantation management, a breakthrough in crude palm oil (CPO) yield has been reported from time to time—the most recent peak was 12 tonne CPO/ha/year in experimental plots. Theoretically, the yield of oil palm can go up as high as 18.5 tonne CPO/ha/year, pushing to the biological limits under the best possible agroecological conditions, with optimal management in terms of planting density, canopy management, pollination, and harvesting practices. This is six times higher than the current average yield of around 3 tonne CPO/ha/year (Woittiez et al. 2017).

Yet, the data in Borneo through recent years shows no significant improvement if not decline. The overall CPO yields from mature plantations were found to fluctuate in the range of 2.5–4.5 tonne CPO/ha/ yr in 2011–17 (Figure 3.1). The crop's performance is also highly uneven

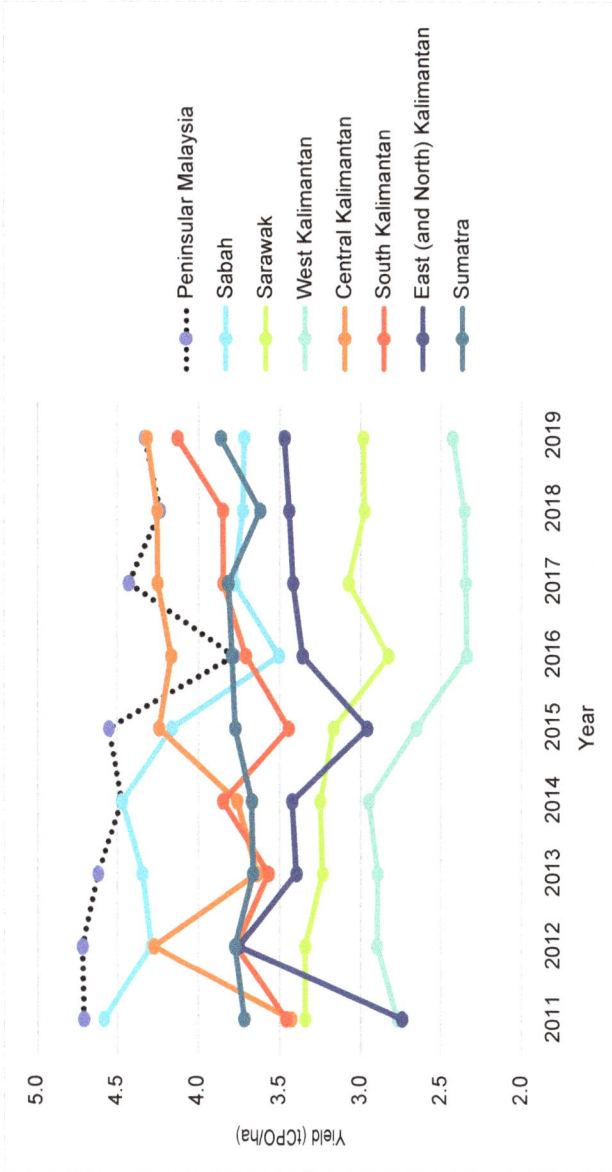

FIGURE 3.1

Yield of Mature Oil Palm Plantations in Borneo Compared to Peninsular Malaysia and Sumatra in 2011–19

Source: DG Estate Crop Indonesia (2012, 2014, 2016, 2018); MPOB (2021).

across the island. A key reason is that agroecological conditions such as soil type, water availability, latitude, radiation, temperature, atmospheric CO_2 concentration, and other factors vary from place to place. Some oil palm plantations were situated in very unfavourable locations, such as deep peat (especially in Sarawak and Central Kalimantan), flood-prone riparian areas (Abram, Xofis, et al. 2014), or infertile sandy areas (Fairhurst, McLeish, and Prasodjo 2010). Although in certain cases the economic outcome of oil palm cultivation in marginal areas can still be significantly improved from very poor to satisfactory with intensive agro-inputs and proper mitigating practices, the yield can hardly grow further as compared to those planted on better soil. A trial in Central Kalimantan reported by Tao et al. (2018) demonstrated that doubling fertilizer frequency to four times a year on an oil palm plantation in a dry, sandy area for two consecutive years did not further improve the annual yield of fresh fruit bunches (FFB).

Also, reducing factors like droughts, fires, and diseases is critical to overall productivity. Especially, high water stress can substantially reduce the potential yield. In Figure 3.1, the decline in 2015–16 is largely the result of the severe water deficits caused by El Niño, a routine weather-producing phenomenon due to the abnormal warming of surface waters in the eastern Pacific Ocean (Oettli, Behera, and Yamagata 2018). Unforeseen circumstances like the spread of pests and diseases also threaten the efforts in yield improvement, such as the Basal Stem Rot (BSR) disease which can only be visually detected at the late stage of infection (Alias et al. 2017). Oil palms planted on peatland are likely to be more susceptible to BSR due to a higher tendency towards nutrient deficiency, particularly micronutrients like copper and zinc as observed by Rakib et al. (2017) in Sarawak.

Analysis of the yield gap is a very complex task, as it involves accommodating carry-over effects (i.e., effects carried forward from previous years), actual harvested fruits, age effects, and scale of assessment. These require an enormous amount of data across a long period, not to mention the potential changes in climates from year to year. An attempt to do this by Hoffmann et al. (2017) based on data collected in Sabah, Central Kalimantan, and North Sumatra estimated the exploitable yield gaps for commercial oil palm plantations at 5–7 tonne FFB/ha/year, representing approximately 25 per cent more than the current average yield. As oil palms are planted in blocks for commercial plantations (approximately 1 km × 0.3 km), these yield gaps may be narrowed with fine-tuning of site-specific strategies at the block level, e.g., canopy, nutrient, and harvesting management (Tao et al. 2017) as well as soil maintenance (Pauli et al. 2014).

Another critical question is what the thresholds for intensification are before they trigger a significant alteration of the natural ecosystem. First, the use of N-fertilizer will increase the emission of nitrous oxide through nitrification and denitrification. Nitrous oxide is a potent greenhouse gas with a heat-trapping impact 300 times that of carbon dioxide (Chaddy et al. 2019). Furthermore, the application of herbicides, pesticides, and fertilizers on plantations may also pollute water sources through leaching (Tokuchi et al. 2020). Even with careful considerations to improve carbon storage and water yield, the intensification may generate some environmental trade-offs and reduce the quality of surrounding habitats. How to balance these trade-offs, especially in comparison with the business-as-usual scenario that involves forest conversion, will be a key consideration for the intensification strategy (Sharma et al. 2019).

Considering the aforementioned challenges in both agroecological and socio-economic aspects, the intensification of oil palm cultivation is unlikely to meet the high potential expected from the yield breakthrough shown in various field experiments. Rather, it seems to be more about combating the multiple emerging problems to prevent yield from declining in the future (Rasmussen et al. 2018).

Timber

Timber has been a major commodity in Borneo, though attention has been largely shifted to oil palm since the 2000s. Since the 1970s, timber products from Borneo have been a major source of building and industrial materials in Japan, Korea, Taiwan, and recently China (FAOSTAT 2021). Although its relative economic importance is decreasing, it is still a billion-dollar business that generates a substantial amount of revenue. Forestry in Borneo has been widely perceived as an unsustainable business due to large-scale environmental degradation that occurred in the past decades.

Some have argued that productive forestry with proper management can play a positive role in replenishing degraded forests in Borneo, as abandoning inactive concessions may increase the risk of illegal deforestation as observed by Burivalova et al. (2020) in North and East Kalimantan. Careful landscape planning for production and regeneration may better protect these forests from being cleared for agriculture (Fisher, Edwards, and Wilcove 2014). The Grand Perfect project in Sarawak which covers 490,000 ha is a prominent case for such a debate. The area was planned as an unusual mosaic—about one-half was set for *Acacia mangium* monoculture, one-third for biodiversity conservation, and the remaining area for indigenous people (Cyranoski 2007). However, the project has failed to meet its objectives. Based on

Goh's personal communication with some of the stakeholders, most of the acacia plantations, if the trees were ever planted properly, remained largely underutilized for various economic and political reasons.

Involving small farmers in tree planting may also be a potential option, provided that proper planning of infrastructure and market access were put in place (Kallio, Kanninen, and Rohadi 2011). To ensure long-term productivity, an overhaul of existing forestry models is inevitable but may need to be carried out gradually. This means that compromises like trading-in productivity at the early stage of transformation may have to be made for long-term, sustainable production.

From the technical point of view, the urgent task ahead would be transforming conventional logging to reduced impact logging (RIL), integrating with enrichment replanting, and eventually creating a sustainable timber production landscape. It can be deemed an intermediate stage on the pathway to Sustainable Forest Management (SFM), possibly banking with carbon compensation schemes (see also Chapter 9) (Galante et al. 2012). Griscom et al. (2019) reported that it is possible to reduce forest reference emissions by up to 33 per cent or about 43–87 tonne CO_2 per ha harvested by modifying harvesting practices. The emission reduction can be pushed further to 66–111 tonne CO_2 per ha by keeping lower commercial quality trees onsite and avoiding the use of bulldozers. Edwards et al. (2012) and Imai et al. (2012) also indicated that RIL can maintain more biodiversity benefits than conventional logging. One should note that logged-over forests still accommodate diverse flora and fauna, and proper management of these forests has strong implications for conservation (Jati et al. 2018).

Practising RIL requires proper monitoring of forest inventory and extensive knowledge of realistic forestry models to predict the dynamics of production forests. A case study in Sabah by Lussetti et al. (2019) identified a set of practices developed over eighteen years that improved the regrowth rates (basal area development) of commercially valuable dipterocarp species while reducing the competing establishment of the pioneer *Macaranga spp.* Instead of conventional logging, the foresters used supervised logging with directional felling, pre-aligned skid trails, and pre-harvest climber cutting. Two case studies in East Kalimantan revealed that the recovery period of forest biomass and phylogenetic structure can be shortened up to twenty years (Butarbutar et al. 2019) and ten years (Mahayani et al. 2020), respectively, with proper RIL practices in combination with post-logging silvicultural intervention. At a landscape level, relocating harvesting sites away from sensitive areas such as riparian habitats can also greatly reduce overall environmental damage. Furthermore, enrichment planting, i.e., increasing the diversity by (re)introducing different native species, can add further benefits to landscape sustainability. However, the financial implications of such silvicultural interventions, which vary from site to site, still need to be further examined (Ruslandi, Cropper, and Putz 2017).

Socio-economic Perspectives

Small Farmers
The general underperformance of smallholders has often been raised in the context of the productivity of oil palm. Currently, this group contributes to more than one-fifth of the total oil palm area in Borneo (Figure 3.2). It is a heterogeneous group that consists of farmers with different land areas, capabilities, and business models. For Indonesia specifically, the typologies of smallholders in Indonesia were reported in-depth by Jelsma et al. (2017), Glenday and Paoli (2015), Schoneveld, Ekowati, et al. (2019), and Schoneveld, van der Haar, et al. (2019). Basically, they can be divided into organized and independent smallholders which have very different characteristics. The discussion which follows will first start with farmers that were organized under various schemes and followed by those operating independently.

Organized Small Farmers
In Malaysian Borneo, about 21 per cent of the total planted areas of oil palm were associated with smallholders. In Sarawak, about 12 per cent of oil palm plantations were under managed smallholder schemes implemented by the Sarawak Land Consolidation and Rehabilitation Agency (SALCRA), the Federal Land Consolidation and Rehabilitation Authority (FELCRA), and the Land Custody and Development Authority (LCDA) (Sanderson 2017; SALCRA 2020). These lands were mostly native customary rights (NCR) land owned by indigenous people. At that point in time, joining the SALCRA scheme was perceived as the only way for customary landholders to obtain formal tenure.

SALCRA collectively managed these lands with loans from public funds and development financiers to transform the rural economies (Cramb 2011a). In 2009, the overall yields of SALCRA schemes were only about one-tenth of those achieved by private commercial plantations (Varkkey, Tyson, and Choiruzzad 2018). However, those yields have improved over the past decade. In January 2020, SALCRA yields were described as averaging 15 tonnes of FFB (fresh fruit bunch) per ha. The growers were exhorted by the state government to try to lift their yields to 20 tonnes, a level already being achieved in some areas (*Borneo Post*, 5 January 2020).

FIGURE 3.2

Percentage of Oil Palm Planted Area Managed by All Smallholders in 2017/18

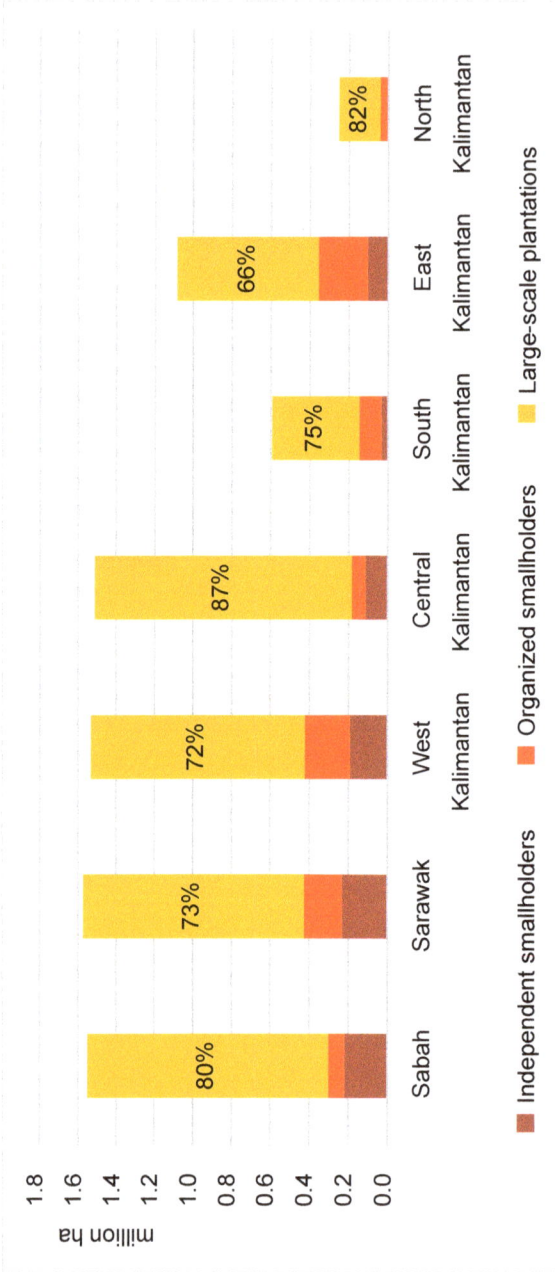

■ Independent smallholders   ■ Organized smallholders   ■ Large-scale plantations

Sources and Notes:

1. The independent farmers occupied around 106,000 ha and 29,000 ha in Sabah and Sarawak, respectively in 2007 (Ab Rahman et al. 2008). The numbers rose to 221,000 ha and 201,000 ha, respectively, in 2017 (Azman, Zulhusni, et al. 2018), while Kannan et al. (2021) (from the MPOB, with data for April 2019) increased that for Sarawak to 235,000 ha.
2. Cramb and Sujang (2016) provided an estimate of 118,000 ha for organized smallholders in Sarawak in 2011, while Sanderson (2017) suggested 190,000 ha in 2016, including 111,000 ha in managed small farmers schemes by SALCRA and FELCRA, and 79,000 ha in joint venture schemes by LCDA.
3. This is unclear for the case of Sabah as some smallholder schemes may have already turned into centralized industrial plantations (Khor, Saravanamuttu, and Augustin 2015). Roughly, the area may range between 56,000 and 69,000 ha for about 7,700 SLDB settlers from various sources, including SLDB (2020), Majid Cooke (2012), Majid Cooke (2013), Dalimpos (2020) with another 12,000 ha owned by FELDA settlers (Khor, Saravanamuttu, and Augustin 2015).
4. For Kalimantan, aggregated data of smallholders for the year 2018 was reported by DG Estate Crop Indonesia (2018). The areas for independent smallholders were roughly estimated using the result of the Agricultural Census in 2013 (BPS 2013).

While SALCRA was initially confined to the southern parts of Sarawak, it was subsequently allowed to expand into Kapit and Bintulu. This was seen by some officials as a mandate to take over after the failure of joint venture schemes operated by the Land Custody and Development Authority (LCDA) (Sanderson 2017). The LCDA had expanded the oil palm area to 79,000 ha by 2016 through joint venture schemes between private oil palm companies and indigenous landowners. However, these schemes have triggered sharp conflicts between the communities, the companies, and the authorities (Cramb and Ferraro 2012). In fact, with little or no knowledge about land law and land rights, the customary landholders were in a vulnerable position in the negotiations for the arrangements made through the schemes. Overall, they have largely failed to deliver expectations as a sound pathway for rural development (Cramb 2013).

For the case of Sabah, a similar scheme was initiated by the Malaysian Federal Land Development Authority (FELDA) in the 1980s with financial assistance from the World Bank. About 107,000 ha in the Dent Peninsula was put under FELDA's management. However, out of 64 proposed schemes, only 7 attracted smallholder settlers (1,665 settlers, each with 14 ha). The reason given by Khor, Saravanamuttu, and Augustin (2015) was that many locals had access to enough land of their own and were not keen to relocate there. While the guess was that about one-half of the settlers remained, the actual numbers of settlers were not generally known. FELDA was regularly accused by opposition interests of not being transparent in its operations, nor revealing how many settlers were still living on the scheme (*Borneo Post*, 13 February 2012).

Two joint venture schemes run by the state under the Sabah Land Development Board (SLDB) were Dalit (Keningau district) and Lalampus (Tongod), both located in the interior of Sabah away from the main plantation zone on the east coast. Studies by Majid Cooke, Toh, and Vaz (2011) and Majid Cooke (2012) suggested that customary landowners were persuaded to join such schemes to obtain a title for their land. In Lalampus, Communal Title (CT) had been adopted in what was described as an "Agropolitan" scheme. Although the schemes were rather different in their organization, the participants had been disappointed at a lack of transparency by the SLDB and rather low returns. In fact, the lands were worked by Indonesian labourers. Overall, the performance was not much better than in the case of Sarawak.

In Indonesian Borneo, smallholdings (both assisted or "scheme" and independent) form only 18 per cent of the total oil palm cultivation. The percentage is much smaller compared to 57 per cent in Sumatra (DG

Estate Crop Indonesia 2019). The first oil palm estates to be established in Kalimantan, on government-owned estates originating from Sumatra, used the Nucleus Estate and Smallholder schemes (PIR-NES) system with local Dayak smallholders in 1982 in West Kalimantan. Historically, the government-managed plantations only began including a smallholder component in 1979, with World Bank assistance. Plantations were arranged around PIR-NES, with smallholders cultivating 60–80 per cent of the plantation land, each family receiving a 2-ha plot, plus a food garden and house area while giving up 5 ha to the estate for the development. Once the trees were bearing, the settlers crushed their palm fruit in the estate factory, with 30 per cent being deducted to repay the cost of the smallholder plantation.

In the 1990s, more private involvement was encouraged using transmigrant labour (PIR-Trans), with the government facilitating the land acquisition and providing credit for estate development. In line with neoliberal ideas in favour of privatization, the government withdrew from funding the next group of schemes in 1995. These schemes, Primary Credit Co-operatives for Members (KKPA), were organized between a bank, a cooperative, the plantation, and the smallholders. Such schemes were widespread, with examples being studied in Parindu, West Kalimantan in 2002 by researchers Potter and Badcock (2006) and later by P. Gillespie (2011, 2016). The oil palm area began to grow rapidly in West Kalimantan in the late 1990s, partly a consequence of the Asian Economic Crisis in 1997, when several local companies went bankrupt, allowing Malaysian interests to buy up many properties.

PT SIA (owned by Sime Darby) was established gradually in Parindu and Bonti subdistricts between 1997 and 2000, being the first in the area to introduce the KKPA system. Farmers were expected to give up 7.5 ha in exchange for 2 ha of oil palm, unlike the earlier system, where only 2 ha of land had to be provided. They were not happy with this change (Colchester et al. 2007). However, PT SIA had an excellent cooperative that was favourable to the small farmers, with several being excused from giving up all of their 7.5 ha, but still receiving 2 ha of oil palm in return: an unusual situation (Potter 2015b). Most other cooperatives lacked legal and financial power, often being "just a tool for the company" (Gillespie 2016). In 2007, a "revitalization plan" was launched by the Government to help "plasma" or assisted farmers to replant their holdings when their trees reached an age of twenty to thirty-five years and were no longer productive. The original Dayak smallholders on government-owned estates like PTPN XIII, established in Sanggau District, West Kalimantan in the 1980s, did have ageing, unproductive trees, but had difficulty in raising finance for replanting (Potter and Lee 1998; Hideki 2018).

The expansion of oil palm in Kalimantan in the 1990s and 2000s was also a consequence of decentralization to the district level. Districts were forced to raise much of their own revenue and were keen to attract investment from oil palm properties (largely from Malaysia and Singapore) and to play down any problems (Varkkey 2012; Naylor et al. 2019). As oil palm prices rose in 2006–7, companies began lobbying for the "partnership" (*kemitraan*) schemes to control 80 per cent of their land, allocating only 20 per cent for smallholders, especially when smallholder farms were not very productive. These schemes which became compulsory for companies that had previously refused to accommodate smallholders, were much less favourable for the latter, especially with the "under one roof" arrangement, where the company worked the land on behalf of the smallholders, just paying them a nominal fee (Gillespie 2011; Levang, Riva, and Orth 2016).

In Central Kalimantan, Dayaks who were offered these kinds of arrangements tended to just sell their lands, especially as they had to wait for at least three years until their new "plasma" crops began to bear; most decided they could not wait so long. Unfortunately, many could subsequently only find employment as casual labourers on the plantations (Potter 2016a). A further change introduced in 2013 with Regulation 98/2013, in which the plantation would devote 20 per cent of its income to supporting smallholder co-operatives outside the plantation area, has not been widely accepted (Potter 2016b).

In the past two decades, as Naylor et al. (2019) have noted, a wide variety of systems have been developed, often mixtures of plasma and independent schemes. These include cases where plasma farmers bought more land which they farmed independently, or wealthy independent farmers bought up others' plasma land (Schoneveld, van der Haar, et al. 2019). In such cases, the farmers may deliver fruit to particular estate mills, but receive no other assistance (Potter 2015a). The plasma schemes, however, came to an end after the launch of the Jokowi government's "Omnibus Bill" in 2020 which removed the necessity for companies to reserve any land for plasma (Jong 2020d).

Independent Small Farmers

Different from organized farmers, independent farmers in Borneo emerged alongside the industrial plantations in a more dispersed manner but usually in reasonable proximity to processing mills. In Sarawak, the deployment of mills was a key reason for surrounding farmers to start planting oil palm, as observed by Cramb and Sujang (2013). In most cases in the Sarawak model, those farmers actively manage around 5 ha of land per household. All these independent small farmers share similar challenges. Compared to industrial plantations, they are short on agricultural inputs (seedlings, fertilizers, and pest control), machinery, and knowledge about best management practices (Ali Nordin et al. 2017). In Sabah and Sarawak, several schemes were introduced by the MPOB to technically support this group of farmers. For example, the Quality Oil Palm Seedlings Assistance Scheme (SBABB) implemented in 2006–10 helped thousands of smallholders to secure high-quality seedlings (Abd Manaf et al. 2013). Despite some positive cases reported, the overall adoption of effective practices and technologies by small farmers has been slow due to various socio-economic and institutional factors, especially the limited access to knowledge, information, and uncertainties of legal title (Majid Cooke 2012; Martin et al. 2015).

In Kalimantan, access to subsidized fertilizers and improved seedlings has also been problematic. Fake fertilizers and counterfeit seedlings were frequently found in the market. Those farmers in the interior who rely heavily on middlemen for supply were often the obvious targets. A case study in Pulang Pisau, Central Kalimantan found that some villagers would still fall for the trap as they simply did not believe that using more expensive seeds and fertilizers would result in higher yields (Goh et al. 2018). Woittiez et al. (2018) also observed that many small farmers still missed the balanced application of fertilizers despite training being provided. It was clear from the case report on Central Kalimantan by Goh et al. (2018) that small farmers located nearer to the cities enjoy a higher return per hectare compared to their counterparts in more distant areas.

Interestingly, the bottom-up consolidation of the independent small farmers in a loosely organized manner was observed in West Kalimantan. Community-owned cooperatives and credit unions (CU) were common throughout the province (Leonald and Rowland 2016). The CUs provide financial assistance to small farmers as an alternative to the major banking system (Kurniawan and Rahmawati 2018). These CUs are usually supported by external organizations and have strong Dayak ethnic elements, sometimes also called "the Dayak bank". Independent oil palm smallholders (Dayaks) in several districts of West Kalimantan are currently being assisted by international NGO Solidaridad in association with the large Credit Union Keling Kumang, providing field training, especially on aspects such as fertilizing, pest control, and harvesting, as well as potentially engaging them in the RSPO certification scheme (Potter 2016b; Solidaridad 2020). There are also active CUs in the oil palm businesses in East Kalimantan (Kawai and Inoue 2016). Meanwhile in Sarawak, the state government played a bigger role in this, creating the Sustainable Oil Palm Growers Cooperatives (KPSM) in Saratok, Sarawak (Ismail and Nazirah 2015).

In addition to these forms of consolidation, there are also local farmers or small private investors who have managed to privately accumulate larger tracts of land during the development of oil palm in the past two decades. As observed by Goh across villages in Central Kalimantan in 2014–15, the small landowners either hire external labourers to work on these lands or simply rent them out to the other farmers, but most of these relationships have been highly informal. These different forms of engagement, which often have strong communal contexts, are paramount in the expansion of small-scale oil palm cultivations throughout Borneo.

Schoneveld, van der Haar, et al. (2019) noted the different groups of independent smallholders in the Kalimantan context, with larger farmers more likely to cause environmental problems, such as deforestation and farming on peat. There are also ethnic differences, with indigenous elites (especially with public service experience), rather than first-generation transmigrants, often becoming more economically successful (sometimes through speculation), but also more likely to evade the standards imposed by the Indonesian Sustainable Palm Oil (ISPO). The study also identified the group of "migrant labourers" as better farmers, more focused solely on oil palm, more compliant, and more likely to benefit from government assistance. It was also noted that rates of peat conversion were rapidly increasing, possibly because large estates were prohibited from accessing peatlands due to the moratorium and so wealthier smallholders were filling this gap.

Despite the aforementioned progress and challenges, there are fundamental reasons why the productivity of independent smallholders remains lower. Improving productivity may not necessarily be a priority for all land users (and may not be in their interests) at least in the case of Borneo (Fraser and Campbell 2019). Given the low population density and a relatively large area of available land per capita, many small farmers can still operate their oil palm cultivations at a reasonably cost-efficient level compared to industrial plantations, i.e., with lower productivity but also low inputs (Ubukata and Sadamichi 2020). As observed by Goh in Pulang Pisau, Central Kalimantan, oil palm was generally planted by independent farmers as an additional crop (in combination with rubber and paddy) which generates "easy" income when the CPO prices are high. Although the productivity is relatively low compared to those under industrial management, it is still profitable from the perspective of these independent small farmers—these farmers would fall into the category of "subsistence farmers" according to the grouping of Schoneveld, van der Haar, et al. (2019).

Being small and independent allows the farmers to be also agile and adaptive to changes. They possess the flexibility in adapting and switching between diverse strategies that suit the agroecological characteristics of the landscape, such as tree planting and rubber tapping (Kallio et al. 2011), and taking up off-farm jobs, such as mining, as well as other employment opportunities instead of relying solely on farming. For example, gold mining remained the "safety net" for small farmers in many cases in Kalimantan during the financial crisis in 2008 (Potter 2010). A more recent case study by Soda, Kato, and Hon (2016) in Sarawak also provided a spatial account of how small farmers employed a variety of land-use options to survive during the depressed periods of the palm oil market.

More importantly, such a mosaic landscape also permits farmers to fulfil their daily needs from local products (such as bushmeat, if hunting is possible), significantly contributing to local food security (Santika, Wilson, Meijaard, et al. 2019). These livelihood strategies were made based on their characteristics, location, and interactions with other actors, and may change from time to time (Schoneveld, Ekowati, et al. 2019). Another interesting case study by Soda and Kato (2020) showed that oil palm planting was often perceived as a family or community activity that strengthened the social and economic ties between members spread across urban and rural areas while generating additional side income (see Chapter 12 for more elaboration on the differences between "traditional" small-scale farming with strong socio-cultural elements and the "Western", "modern" agricultural economic system that prioritizes productivity). In general, small farmers are very cautious with investment for intensification as they are unwilling to take the risk. Case studies in West Kutai and Paser in East Kalimantan revealed that unfavourable experiences in the past have substantially lowered the expectation and interest of small farmers in further venturing into such monocultural activities (Terauchi and Inoue 2016).

The heterogeneity of smallholdings in Borneo implies that strategies for boosting the upstream productivity of smallholders must be designed with a more realistic place-based approach based on contemporary socio-economic dynamics. Experience in Borneo has shown that oversimplifying the heterogeneity and complexity of smallholdings can trigger serious unintended consequences (Bissonnette 2013). This is not a unique problem in Borneo, as similar findings were also reported for cases in Sumatra (Jelsma et al. 2019). Although the smallholders in Borneo play a relatively smaller role in the production, their existence carries important social and political implications beyond boosting productivity. This also means that full utilization of all existing cropland to its biological limit is very unlikely in the current societal setting in Borneo.

The historical events show that further aggressive interventions to push smallholders into chasing higher productivity of cash crops may trigger various unwanted consequences, such as conflicts arising from company-community joint ventures or encroachment of unorganized smallholders into forested and protected areas (Resosudarmo et al. 2019). Such external interventions may also be entangled with political discourses, potentially intensifying inequalities and division within local communities (Andersen et al. 2016). Under these circumstances, fundamental policies like empowering rural communities with multiple financial and technological tools and knowledge may be more relevant in the context of rural transformation. Especially, the codesign of land-use strategies between local stakeholders and policymakers to reconcile the different interests is imperative to ensure the effectiveness of implementation.

Labour Force
Labour shortage is yet another factor that drags down the overall performance (Murphy 2014). Lack of labourers implies suboptimal management of plantations with longer harvesting rounds (Sheil et al. 2009; Sayer et al. 2012). Most plantations in Borneo, including small and medium holdings in Sabah and Sarawak, rely heavily on foreign (see Box 3.1 for the case of Sabah) or inter-island workers (e.g., via transmigration to Kalimantan) for daily operation. In the past two decades, the rapid development of the land-based economies in Malaysian Borneo was closely associated with the exploitation of low-waged workers. Their welfare, such as basic healthcare, safe shelter, and education opportunities for family members, has been largely neglected; see studies by Puder (2019) for Sabah and Sanderson (2016) for Sarawak. A significant percentage of this labour force is illegal and thus very vulnerable (Li 2017b; Allerton 2020). Such an exploitative development model may come with substantial social costs, such as the outbreak of malaria among the rubber tappers in Sabah (Jeffree et al. 2018).

The situation is much worse in smallholdings as the owners tend to hire illegal foreign workers and seldom adhere to minimal living and working standards. Dileep Kumar, Ismail, and Govindarajo (2014) described this with the term "precarious working conditions" based on their findings in a field study in Sabah. Things were also unfavourable for the accompanied

BOX 3.1
Migration for Plantation Jobs

There have been several studies on the organization of Indonesian workers to Sabah, which territory has a long history of such migrations. Because Sulawesi has been the main source of migrants, Indonesians in Sabah are routinely called "Bugis", even though many are also from NTT, especially Flores. Studies have shown that many migrants rely on previous contacts in Sabah (often from the same village in Indonesia) to find work for them and help them to fit in. "Semi-legal" and "illegal" channels, particularly using social networks, are cheaper and faster than strictly "legal" channels. One study found that 51 per cent of new migrants used family and relatives in Sabah to help them find accommodation. These networks also included various intermediaries, especially heads of villages, agents, boatmen, and employers. Migrants usually travelled in groups, especially Florianese, who, as Christians, were more likely to experience religious discrimination than the Islamic Bugis. More dangerous illegal routes undertaken by speedboats through mangroves at night took advantage of the proximity of coastal Sabah to North Kalimantan near Nunukan and Sebatik Island (Eki 2002; Mahadi, Hussin, and Khoso 2018).

One of the "localization" efforts of the Malaysian UNDP "ATLAS" project in Sabah (2018–19) in association with SDG 10 "Reduced Inequalities" and SDG 16 "Peace, justice and strong institutions" ("Leave no one behind and reach those furthest behind") was specifically directed to studying the significant number of people in Sabah who are undocumented and lack access to basic health and education, in support of Malaysia's trajectory for Sustainable Development. Census estimates (2010) suggested that migrant workers (mainly on oil palm plantations and in construction) formed almost 28 per cent of the population. Many undocumented minors grow up illiterate "street kids" as they have no access to education. The few schools operated by NGOs specifically for migrant children reach only 2 per cent of the total. While there is work for adults in the informal sector, it is insecure and deportation is always a threat, while negative stereotypes of the undocumented population are common. Medical and general health services are very limited, their position is one of extreme vulnerability, especially the group from the Southern Philippines, who constitute a kind of "shadow economy" (UNDP Malaysia 2018).

family members, as Hardi, Herbasuki, and Thalita (2018) reported the lack of access to formal education for children from migrant families. With the availability of other opportunities at home due to the booming economic development across Indonesia, plantation jobs in Sabah and Sarawak have become less attractive.

To address these issues, the Government of Malaysia announced a minimum wage of RM920 (about US$230) per month for East Malaysia in effect from 2016 (Kadir, Hussin, and Hashim 2019). However, this has raised objections from plantation owners, arguing that the minimum wage increased the financial pressure on operating plantations, given the problems of the palm oil market in recent years. The impact of a labour shortage has been much bigger for independent smallholders. Due to the lack of economies of scale, the labour required for operation on small plantations is higher per hectare compared to larger holdings. Azman, Ahmad, et al. (2018) estimated that the independent smallholdings in Sabah and Sarawak require nearly 8,000 and 5,000 workers, respectively.

As young local people tend not to get involved in agriculture, the farming communities in Sabah and Sarawak are ageing. Jobs on plantations were described as "dirty", "dangerous" and "distant". Especially for the last "d", working on plantations basically implies that one will be isolated from the "outside world" for a long period, as most plantations are located far from the urban areas (Govindarajo, Dileep Kumar, and Ramulu 2014). This reflects the previous false claims of job creation through conventional land-based development promoted by the state governments (Lim and Biswas 2019). Moving forward, a revamp of the current mode of plantation management is necessary to safeguard not only the environment and economic development but also humanity and social sustainability.

Final Remarks

While it seems important to push for higher palm oil yield, the immediate question is "to what end?". Competitors, especially soybean farmers, are also trying to boost their productivity. A big harvest of soybean in South America will drive the price of all vegetable oils down. Palm oil also faces market disadvantages with its bad reputation in terms of environmental sustainability. Boosting productivity with heavy agro-inputs makes no sense in terms of financial risk and resilience given the fluctuating prices, especially for small farmers who are much more vulnerable. The past experience thus suggests that stabilizing the price of palm oil and strengthening the financial resilience of the oil palm sector would be a more imminent issue in policymaking than boosting the yield.

In all, what the real objectives are of boosting the yield of cash crops should be carefully thought through. The key policy initiative should therefore be to institute a broad-based effort to address the price instability and marketing challenges. While rebranding palm oil is a necessary move (see Chapter 6), the incentive system may also be restructured to create a buffer for local production, e.g., incentivizing local uptake of palm oil for various end-uses (see Chapter 7). More importantly, Borneo needs to upgrade and diversify its downstream activities to establish a more stable, integrated value chain that is imperative for long-term development (Chapter 5). The results will hinge on both public and private efforts to gradually explore new industries that are suitable for Borneo. These strategies are all strongly complementary to upstream operation.

4

Activating Underutilized Low-Carbon Land

Diverting future agricultural production onto underutilized, low-carbon land with insignificant ecological services is deemed a better option than converting forests or other high-carbon lands for production, especially in the face of the growing demand for food and materials. This may effectively avoid carbon stock loss from forest conversion, in comparison to the expected business-as-usual scenario (Austin et al. 2015). Also, proper management of these lands may help to avoid further land degradation and replenish lost carbon stock. Activating underutilized low-carbon land is thus deemed a key strategy in establishing a sustainable bio-economy.

Various names, e.g., "abandoned", "degraded", and "marginal" land, have been proposed to quantify land available for future expansion. For example, the terms "*lahan kritis*" ("critical land") and "*lahan suboptimal*" ("suboptimal land") are used by the forestry and agricultural departments in Indonesia, respectively, to describe land that has experienced degradation. However, their definitions or criteria may be different, and some are not entirely clear, e.g., abandoned land is not necessarily degraded, and vice versa (Smit et al. 2013). A study by Gibbs and Salmon (2015) shows that global estimates of "degraded" land based on different databases and methodologies can vary widely from 1 billion ha to over 6 billion ha. Furthermore, the conditions of land may change significantly from time to time, complicating the monitoring efforts. At the moment, high-resolution monitoring on a landscape scale is still too costly to be implemented.

In the past, ambiguous definitions had created unrealistic expectations and unintended consequences in policymaking. In some cases, the classification of degraded land was used as an excuse for forest clearing under the guise of reforestation programmes, although the "degraded" land may still be rich in carbon stock and biodiversity (Obidzinski and Dermawan 2010). On this basis, it is crucial to understand how future expansion may take place on these lands, considering the multiple factors and perspectives of various stakeholders. This chapter explores this strategy in the aspects of agroecology, economy, society, and institutions.

AGROECOLOGICAL PERSPECTIVES

To be more explicit, land resources with the following criteria, or so-called underutilized low-carbon (ULC) land, may potentially be used where: (i) the lands are in non-ecologically sensitive areas; (ii) the level of carbon stock is low so that land utilization is unlikely to incur additional carbon stock loss; and (iii) the current economic productivity of the land is insignificant or low.

For (i), this may be deduced by excluding areas with "High Conservation Value" (HCV), i.e., "biological, ecological, social, or cultural values of outstanding significance" (Brown et al. 2013). HCV areas thus refer to areas that provide important ecosystem services or have exceptional value for biodiversity. Initially, the concept was applied mainly in the forestry sector. It was gradually broadened to other ecosystems and adopted in agriculture to widen the opportunities for conservation beyond forests and timber plantations (Filer, Mahanty, and Potter 2020). Excluding HCV areas from agricultural expansion like forest patches in an agricultural landscape and surrounded by non-timber crop cultivation like oil palm have strong environmental implications, not only in conserving the diversity of plant species but also in maintaining connectivity of habitats on a landscape scale. HCV has thus become a key concept in conservation priority setting to help decision-makers in land-use planning on both the farm level and the landscape level.

For (ii), some proposed to set the threshold value of above-ground carbon stock at 40 tC/ha, i.e., the average value of carbon sequestered in an oil palm plantation with a rotation period of twenty-five years to identify areas that can be used for future expansion (Khasanah et al. 2012). However, this must also consider the potential for regeneration and regrowth. One concept that has come to the fore in recent years with a clearer definition is "High Carbon Stock" (HCS) areas, which include secondary forests that do have scope for useful regrowth using carbon stock as an indicator. The term, originally coined by a major oil palm company Golden Agri-Resources (GAR) in association with an NGO, the Forest Trust, was seen as especially useful in "fragmented landscapes with moist tropical forests" (Rosoman et al. 2017). Such forests often occur outside the legal forest zone and are perceived to be "regenerating". They are also often found in patches on oil palm concessions.

The extent of ULC land, based on (i) and (ii), may be broadly accounted for through land cover maps. The Borneo Atlas produced by CIFOR (2020), now migrated to Nusantara Atlas by Gaveau et al. (2021), provides the latest land cover data for the entire island by territory which can be used as the base data. By integrating the official oil palm data and further distinguishing functional land classes, Figure 4.1 illustrates the distribution of different land covers in Borneo and the estimated area of low-carbon land in 2018. Based on this estimation, West Kalimantan has the largest area of such lands (6.5 million ha), followed by Central Kalimantan (5.8 million ha), East Kalimantan (4.4 million ha), and Sarawak (3.1 million ha). Concerning the size of the territories, only a small percentage of Sabah and North Kalimantan can be considered low-carbon (1.2 and 0.9 million ha, respectively) while nearly one-half of South Kalimantan can be categorized as that.

At first sight, it seems that the island still has massive areas of ULC land that might be potentially used for production if only the land cover and carbon stock are taken into consideration. However, such physical area estimations need to be further evaluated from various environmental and agroecological perspectives (Goh et al. 2017). While the mobilization of ULC land resources has been surrounded by debates over conservation versus production, some common grounds have been met. For example, ULC lands located just next to the remaining forest, or patches interwoven with forests and wetlands, should be prioritized for agroforestry or reforestation as buffers to avoid forest encroachment, especially in the absence of effective forest governance. An interesting comparison may be made with the study by Hadian et al. (2014) of WWF Indonesia that applied the EU Renewable Energy Directives (RED) sustainability criteria in mapping areas regarded sustainable for fuel crop expansion, as the demand for palm-based biofuel from Indonesia was spiking in the early 2010s. The result was significantly different from Figure 4.1 with only 14 million ha estimated for the entire Kalimantan region.

Few studies were made in the case of Sabah and Sarawak. For Sabah, the extent of low-carbon land was much lower compared to the other territories, with a significant portion located on hilly terrain in Kota Belud and Tuaran. For Sarawak, it could be challenging to distinguish degraded forests that resulted from intense logging activities and low-carbon land from satellite images. While the official government document to UNFCC by MESTECC

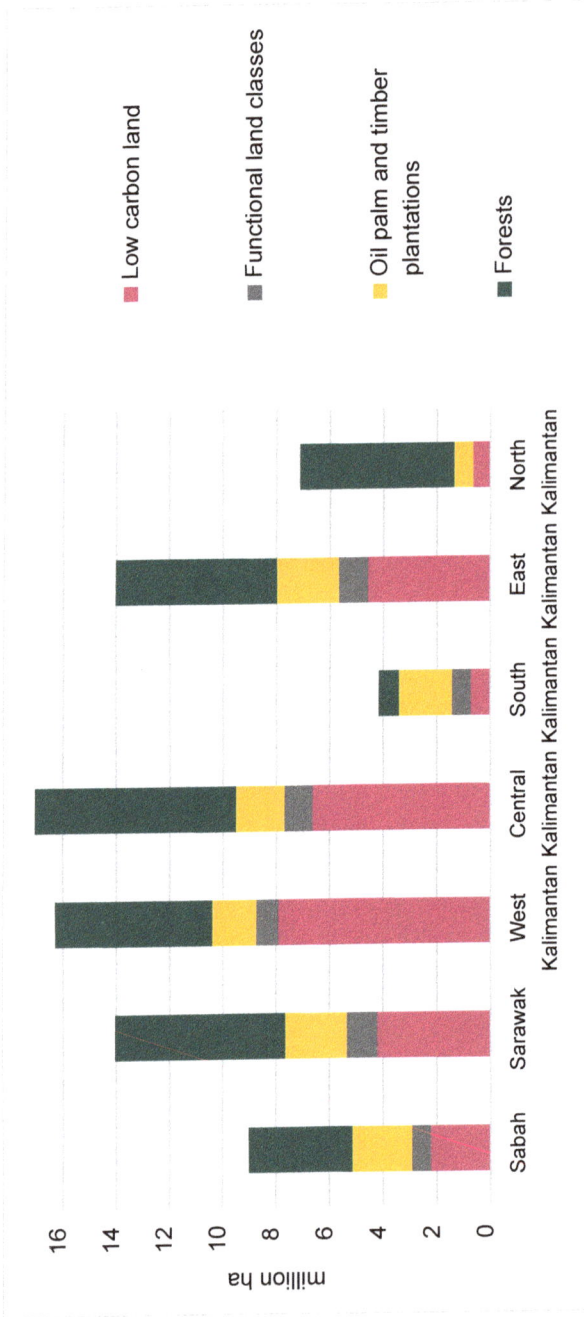

FIGURE 4.1
Extent of Low-Carbon Land in Borneo by Territories in 2018

Legend:
- Low carbon land
- Functional land classes
- Oil palm and timber plantations
- Forests

Y-axis: million ha (0, 2, 4, 6, 8, 10, 12, 14, 16)

X-axis categories: Sabah, Sarawak, West Kalimantan, Central Kalimantan, South Kalimantan, East Kalimantan, North Kalimantan

Sources and Notes:
1. All land classes were adapted from CIFOR (2020) except the following.
2. Oil palm data were adapted from DG Estate Crop Indonesia (2019) and MPOB (2021).
3. "Other functional land classes" which include settlements, mining, transmigration sites, non-forested wetland, paddy fields, and water bodies were adapted from Goh et al. (2017), assuming relatively insignificant changes in the area in 2010–2018 compared to the forest loss.

Malaysia (2018) reported that there was still 8 million ha of forest in 2014 (may include timber plantations), the atlas by CIFOR (2020) depicted only 6.9 million ha of Sarawak covered by forest and timber plantations in the same year (the figure remained relatively stable until 2018).

Considering these uncertainties, it is important to be careful with the estimation of available ULC land resources for future production. Instead of struggling with a simple dichotomization of HCV/HCS and non-HCV/ HCS areas, further classification based on suitability for different crops, considering both agricultural and environmental impacts may be a more practical approach. For instance, some land areas may not be suitable for cash crop cultivation due to water scarcity or soil features. This is especially important for water-intensive crops like oil palm (Safitri et al. 2018). For Kalimantan, multiple efforts have been made to examine the extent of low-carbon land area that can be deemed agroecologically suitable for oil palm cultivation. A number of studies estimated that about 11–13 million ha of the low-carbon land in Kalimantan may be deemed suitable for oil palm based on satellite images and biophysical models (Gingold et al. 2012; Mulyani and Syarwani 2013; Austin et al. 2017).

More importantly, the productivity of these lands may vary widely when considering factors like soil type (Afriyanti, Kroeze, and Saad 2016). Some ULC lands are considered "degraded lands" with a significant reduction in agroecological capacity to perform ecosystem functions and services, and have a lower environmental risk for future agricultural development compared to forest and peatland (Wicke et al. 2011). In some cases, hydrological changes (e.g., an increase in drought and floods) and poor water management (e.g., no irrigation) are also the main contributors (Goh et al. 2018). Further adding several environmental constraints, Smit et al. (2013) and Sumarga and Hein (2014) found that the area suitable for oil palm expansion was limited to 2.6 million ha for West Kalimantan and 1.8 million ha for East Kalimantan, respectively, i.e., only about one-third of all low-carbon land found in the respective provinces.

Other more flexible, versatile, and smaller-scale options may be adopted for ULC lands that are not suitable for large-scale oil palm plantations. For example, rubber is a familiar option for local communities throughout most parts of Borneo. In addition to monoculture, rubber cultivation is very often embedded in a complex agroforestry system called "jungle rubber" (Rahajoe et al. 2014). With such flexibility, it can play a role in restoration (especially in the areas where degraded forest patches are mingled with ULC land) while providing livelihood to local communities (see, e.g., a report by Hiratsuka et al. 2019) on South Kalimantan. Fast-growing exotic timber species like *Acacia spp.* and *Eucalyptus spp.* are also common options in Borneo, but they are facing problems like the spread of diseases and the threats of invading natural forests (Nambiar, Harwood, and Mendham 2018; Islam, Mohamad, and Azad 2019). While some reported that artificial plantations established on degraded grasslands can enrich biodiversity (see, e.g., Matsumoto, Noerdjito, and Fukuyama 2015) on butterfly assemblage, some others have suggested that monoculture tree plantations by themselves create various environmental problems, including soil erosion, water table and water quality change, reduced biodiversity, and pest attack (Potter and Lee 1998; Ueda et al. 2015).

In Sarawak, the more climate-resilient sago palm is deemed a potential cash generator after oil palm and has been promoted with multiple initiatives from the state government (Mohamad Naim, Yaakub, and Awang Hamdan 2016). Also, some other less well-known crops were proposed due to their particular characteristics. For example, Jaung et al. (2018) identified a variety of less common crops with a high energy content that can be utilized as biofuels, and attempted to quantify degraded land areas suitable for these crops. Agro mining, i.e., the process of extracting metal from the soil with plants, is another rare type of agriculture reported in Sabah where nickel was mined from certain degraded lands with a prospective "metal crop" species (Nkrumah et al. 2019). It has, however, yet to be realized on a large scale despite some successful experiments (van der Ent et al. 2015).

Unfortunately, despite several options proposed, accurate spatial matching of potential crops with local agroecological characteristics across Borneo is still largely missing. Even for oil palm, the aforementioned estimations were made based on rather coarse datasets. In any case, Borneo should avoid any kind of unsustainable plantation expansions that will cause adverse effects on the environment. This, however, must be built upon a detailed, transparent, and consistent spatial database on a landscape scale. This is further discussed in Chapter 8.

ECONOMIC PERSPECTIVES

Activation of ULC land is not favourable when the cost is too high. First, the land quality of some ULC lands may be too low to be used. This factor is a key reason why lands were underutilized or abandoned in the first place. Replenishing these lands may require substantial early-stage investments and may not be economically sustainable as ample supplies of agro-inputs and intensive management are required. For example, the attempts to replenish sandy soils in Central Kalimantan by large oil palm plantations have not met financial expectations (Fairhurst, McLeish, and Prasodjo 2010). Smallholdings have even more limited capability in intensive farming on degraded land (Ho, Wasli, and Perumal 2019).

Second, a majority of the ULC lands may be largely inaccessible in the current conditions. Poor logistics have prevented the productive use of these lands (Goh et al. 2018). However, the establishment of road networks may also trigger unwanted consequences, especially deforestation. In the past, roads constructed for logging were often followed by both local communities and migrants to expand their agricultural activities (Fox et al. 2009). Spatially explicit mapping of road distribution, road quality, elevation, and other factors that affect logistics can contribute to better planning of ULC land mobilization.

Labour scarcity was also found as a major barrier to mobilizing ULC lands in Borneo with a relatively low population density. For Kalimantan, Goh et al. (2018) estimated that based on the recent trend of population distribution and growth, a more realistic estimation for the land area that can be put under productive use is about 7 million ha by 2030, while 12 million ha will remain underutilized. Labour availability to mobilize ULC lands can be affected by (i) competition between agriculture and parallel off-farm income opportunities (e.g., mining), (ii) competition between different agricultural activities (e.g., working on industrial plantations instead of working on own farms), and (iii) uneven population distribution (e.g., preference to stay close to cities). In the past, the Indonesian government implemented transmigration schemes to redistribute and relocate the labour forces to open up lands in Kalimantan (Potter 2012). However, the transmigrants, as well as the spontaneous migrants, can have quite different land-use practices and lifestyles. Meanwhile, Sabah and Sarawak have long been relying on labourers from Indonesia (especially Sulawesi and Flores in the case of Sabah) to work in the land-based sectors (Majid Cooke and Mulia 2012) (see also subsection on "Labour Force" in Chapter 3). There can be considerable social risks associated with such migrations as serious ethnic conflicts have been reported in the past (Goh et al. 2018).

Due to a high proportion of land area to the population in many parts of Borneo, it has become a more reasonable option for local communities to keep most low-carbon lands underutilized in an economic sense, and only sporadically plant rubber and fruit trees to mark their ownership. Furthermore, speculative land trading has not been uncommon in Kalimantan despite uncertainties in land tenure. Goh et al. (2018) reported that in Palangkaraya and Kotawaringin Timur (Central Kalimantan), opportunities for local communities to sell their land at higher prices to extra-local buyers motivated the villagers to expand further into forests, especially those located at the edges of the city centre, roadsides, or an area that is expected to be converted to oil palm concessions. Many buyers do not intend to perform agricultural activities but plan to engage in speculation. Such speculative activities are a significant driver of the formation of ULC land in Kalimantan. This type of spillover and indirect risk has to be carefully accounted for when promoting the activation of underutilized land.

Finally, scale is a key economic factor that determines the use of ULC land. For industrial-scale oil palm plantations, large continuous concessions with an area >10 thousand ha (with 60-tonne FFB per hour mills) are more economically attractive than small concessions (with 30-tonne FFB per hour mills). This consideration thus limits the use of smaller, fragmented low-carbon lands for oil palm. Independent smallholders do have more flexibility in working on small patches of land, as discussed in Chapter 3, which gives them an economic advantage. However, their productivity by land area in economic terms cannot be comparable to the industrial plantations.

Social Perspectives

Social elements in characterizing "underutilized" land are much more subtle than the previously discussed agroecological and economic considerations. The term "underutilization" is a normative notion that can be interpreted differently depending on the perspectives of the stakeholders. In Borneo, a substantial area of land is occupied by local communities for small-scale farming. Land claimed by local communities may not be deemed "underutilized" by the occupants although it is not being used for intensive agricultural production. These lands may largely consist of dry-field agriculture that is being used in low-intensity areas and may not be considered HCV or HCS areas.

With limited data and resources, it is difficult to clearly capture the land-use activities of small farmers with remote sensing not only because of the small scale but also because many of them move and change their land use from time to time, involving the transition of shrub-fallow-agroforests in irregular patterns (i.e., swiddens). Lands that seemed abandoned may still be in use by local and also migrant communities. For example, Potter (1997a) observed a case in South Kalimantan where the villagers (in parts of the Riam Kiwa watershed) objected to the replacement of grasslands by acacia as these lands were being used, although in different ways. In the middle valley without any forest, Javanese settlers only had *alang-alang*

(*Imperata cylindrica*) grassland on which to farm. They used multiple ploughing with stall-fed cattle (some received through an ADB project) to prepare the grassland for cropping with peanuts, dry rice, and bananas. They also made irrigated rice fields in small valleys, a practice not copied by the local Banjarese, many of whom were Islamicized Dayaks, with more traditional systems.

Further up the valley, where grassland was mixed with forest and scrub, the Banjarese cut swiddens in the forest, though wealthier families did use the grassland by hiring Javanese ploughing teams to grow peanuts. Most were content with the yields from their forest farms, as they also engaged in collecting forest products and small-scale mining. Planting some of the grasslands with acacia was designed by the government, not only to reforest part of the watershed but also to persuade the swidden farmers to intensify their systems and not burn their fields. It meant that they had to go further from the village to find suitable land for swiddens and they were under constant pressure to keep the fire away from the acacia plantation. Unlike the Javanese, however, the Banjarese were not given any assistance in changing their farming patterns.

A large portion of such lands may fall under the existing local institutions embedded in the indigenous societies, i.e., traditional ways of governing land rights among the community members with customary law and traditional knowledge. However, most of these local institutions were largely undocumented, let alone have the boundaries accurately mapped. The terms "Native Customary Rights (NCR)" land, "Customary Forest", and "Community Forest" are used to describe the customary lands in Borneo. In Sabah, for example, many local communities are still struggling with land tenure issues due to ambiguity in determining the boundaries (Lunkapis 2013; Majid Cooke 2013).

In Kalimantan, the customary lands have been recognized as not forming part of the government-controlled "forest estate" through a landmark judgment of the Constitutional Court in 2013. To identify such lands more clearly, an NGO, the Ancestral Domain Registration Agency, working with AMAN (the Alliance of Indigenous People of the Archipelago), has assisted community mapping and submitted maps covering 4.8 million ha for inclusion in the official "One Map" initiative, with much larger areas scheduled to be added by 2020 (Fay and Denduangrudee 2016).

Similar to other types of land-based development in the past, the activation of the ULC lands can create substantial socio-economic changes in particular areas. For example, the building of roads to access these lands may potentially trigger land conflicts, migration, or unexpected deforestation, and exacerbate inequalities between different groups (Elmhirst et al. 2017; Permadi et al. 2018). Also, small farmers are generally slower in making changes, opting for practices that they are more familiar with (Artati et al. 2019). For example, the small farmers' timber planting scheme in West Kalimantan reported by Permadi et al. (2018) took more than ten years to be realized.

Ethnicity could be an important indicator when it is related to land-use practices. An example of distinctive practices can be observed between the Dayaks and the transmigrants. The former group prefers to practise rotational hill (dry) swiddens and sometimes "wet swiddens" (*padi paya*) in swampy areas, usually also with rubber or other cash crops such as rattan or pepper; the latter group tends to establish irrigated paddy fields, sometimes with cattle stall-fed with *Imperata cylindrica* (*alang-alang*), participate in small-scale oil palm plasma schemes or establish themselves as independent oil palm smallholders (Schoneveld et al. 2019b).

Agricultural practices are directly linked to societal structure and culture. For example, wet swiddens are formed in swampy areas nearer to the settlement site and are often worked by women—the water supply is not controlled, as in irrigated paddy, but yields are often higher than in the dry swiddens. However, usually, only dry swiddens can grow sticky rice (*padi pulut*), used for making wine, important for Dayak social activities. In Sanggau West Kalimantan, Dayaks also plant oil palm, and this involvement is increasing elsewhere, while the Jokowi government encourages various community tree-planting schemes on Dayak lands within the forest estate (Resosudarmo et al. 2019). Both groups have different interpretations of land ownership as well as economic visions. In the past, the ethnic distribution could be used as an important reference in characterizing human-environmental interactions in the ULC lands, though this is not quite as true today.

It is thus questionable for a simple idea of maxing out productivity from ULC land, considering the potential social risks. This complex situation points toward a key question—what models are suitable for activating underutilized land? A bottom-up approach with land-use plans integrating local social institutions and traditional rules, especially involving stakeholders in codesigning the business models may be more practical to ensure sustainable human-environmental relationships (de Vos and Delabre 2018; Meilasari-Sugiana 2018). This deserves greater scrutiny in the exploration of ULC land resources, not only in a quantitative manner but also using a narrative approach for collecting opinions from the different actors to understand the underlying socio-cultural implications which cannot be directly "measured". Particularly important is the analysis of these factors through the lenses of different actors, i.e., indigenous communities, (trans)migrants, industry, government officials, and civil society. The Free Prior and Informed Consent (FPIC) of local peoples was included in the "Principles and Criteria" of RSPO in 2018 to complement the HCV-HCS policy applicable to all large-scale oil palm plantations and in modified form also to smallholders (RSPO 2020b).

Institutional Perspectives

From an institutional perspective, the situation in Kalimantan has been more complicated than its Malaysian counterparts considering its rapidly evolving land governance system in the past two decades. The state governments of Sabah and Sarawak are the most powerful authorities in terms of land use as they retain a large degree of autonomy in land governance from the federal government while they have full control over local governments (Jomo and Wee 2003). In Kalimantan, rules and regulations were interpreted differently among the related departments at different levels, with a substantial risk of corruption and rent-seeking.

At the national level, the Indonesian Ministry of Forestry (now Environment and Forestry) has classified about 70 per cent of the total land area as "forest zone" and the rest as "other use zone (APL)". This legal classification, however, does not always correspond to the actual physical situation, i.e., the APL zone is not necessarily non-forested and thus cannot be simply assumed to be ULC land. In parallel, lands were also classified as timber, oil palm, and mining concessions by different ministries and departments. These concessions were not only located in the APL zone, but may intersect the "forest zone", complicating the mapping and characterizing of ULC land. Significant areas of low-carbon land were locked in the "forest zone" or on concessions. For example, Goh et al. (2017) estimated that about 32 per cent of the 0.7 million ha oil palm concessions in Kotawaringin Timur consisted of uncultivated land with sparse vegetation.

Meanwhile, since the implementation of decentralization policies in the 2000s, districts or regencies (*kabupaten*) and municipalities (*kota*) became the *de facto* decision-makers in terms of land-use policies among the authorities in the Indonesian hierarchy. In fact, deforestation in Kalimantan in the 2000s was largely driven by regency-oriented policies, which heavily promoted (large-scale) oil palm expansion, in some cases overwriting the national rules and policies (Barr et al. 2006). Between regencies, rules and regulations on land use can also be quite different and are enforced with varying degrees of stringency (Fairhurst, McLeish, and Prasodjo 2010). As such, land governance has been fraught with overlaps and uncertainties due to conflicting claims based on multiple concession issuances by different authorities, from national to regency level, not to mention the exclusion of customary land in the mapping (Rosenbarger et al. 2013). Releasing ULC lands from "forest zone" or concessions for more productive uses was very challenging due to the immense institutional complexity in Indonesia (Rosenbarger et al. 2013; Nurrochmat et al. 2020). While the districts initially had the power to issue oil palm, forestry, and mining permits, they did not always share this information with the provincial or national authorities, so the situation became very complex. That power was removed in the case of forest and mining permits in 2014 and returned to the centre (but retained for oil palm), with a "grace period" of two years (Afiff 2016).

This was exacerbated by the great uncertainties and confusion in land tenure as described in the previous section. Problems of displacement and forcible seizure of land from local communities have been reported in the past twenty years throughout Borneo (Cramb 2016; Levang, Riva, and Orth 2016; Li 2017a). Sorting out the complexity of land-use rights is of the highest priority to clarify if a piece of ULC land is considered "available" or not and to "whom" it is available. For small farmers, firm and clear land tenure is needed to enable and motivate them to utilize the land sustainably (Arvola et al. 2020).

To eliminate these disparities, efforts to create a unified national spatial database, namely the "One Map Policy (OMP)" have been made by the Indonesian government (BIG Indonesia 2020). The policy aims to consolidate and harmonize all official maps in one database to ensure legal consistency across different departments, with the first batch of maps published in 2018. While the OMP represents a substantial institutional improvement, the product is yet to incorporate customary territories into the database. As noted above, one exception is the rather small area of customary forests that have received legal recognition through participatory mapping organized by the Ancestral Domain Registration Agency. There was also a report in Sambas, West Kalimantan where the villagers attempted to collectively produce a spatial plan based on the "village law" in the face of encroachment of industrial oil palm plantations onto their customary land (de Vos 2018). Filling in this gap is particularly crucial for mapping underutilized land from a land user perspective, especially as AMAN has predicted that potentially, customary forests could be found to occupy about 400,000 ha or 30 per cent of Indonesia's forest area (Jong 2019a). Customary forests that are not mapped are likely to face encroachment by commercial interests, yet as Jong notes, the mapping depends on legal recognition, which is notoriously slow, complex, and expensive.

FINAL REMARKS

The various cases discussed in this chapter demonstrate that cash crop expansion may not be the best move even if ULC land is used. The complexity extends beyond agroecological characteristics, involving multiple economic, social, and institutional factors. From an economic perspective, further oil palm expansion may also not be the best move considering the vulnerability when palm oil prices become unfavourable. Supplementing the strength of upstream knowledge with upgraded downstream activities is probably a safer strategy to move forward (see Chapters 3 and 5). Also, adversarial relationships between local communities, private companies, and governments, especially in terms of land rights, have been frequently cited as one of the most serious problems discouraging the large-scale use of ULC land. The key question is how the different types of land use—from small household mixed farming to industrial monoculture—can coexist and interact.

Finally, restoring ULC land via reforestation or afforestation should also be part of the land-use portfolio for ULC land resources. This not only helps to tackle land degradation but also improves the resilience of the entire production system across the landscape (see Chapter 8). While legislation and subsidies could protect the remaining forest, alternative funding and long-term income sources are needed to restore degraded land. Potentially, this can be combined with, e.g., banking on the carbon credit system (see Chapter 9) and market premiums from sustainable product branding (see Chapters 6 and 11).

5

Upgrading and Diversifying Downstream Industries

Transformation of exploitative land-based economies to sustainable bio-economies entails boosting upstream productivity and production volume and, more importantly, driving structural changes. This implies the reallocation of economic activity across the broad sectors of primary agriculture and forestry, manufacturing, and services. Historically, countries would pull out of low-cost, unsustainable land exploitation when they were able to diversify away from primary production. As incomes from downstream expand, land-based economies may enter a transitional period towards a more advanced, and possibly more sustainable form of development, gradually increasing the efficiency of resource exploitation. Peninsular Malaysia is a remarkable example of a region that has experienced such a transition (Vincent and Ali 1997).

A dominant feature of Borneo's export profile is the extent to which a primary land-based product, i.e., palm oil, still looms large. Due to the growing pressures over land-use sustainability, Borneo is gradually losing its previous "comparative advantage", i.e., large tracts of cheap land, in furthering oil palm expansion. This mode of development has also suppressed other forms of land use and economic activities, as well as increased the risk of social conflicts. It is unlikely that Borneo will continue to see similar economic growth through low-cost expansion as in the past.

Therefore, creating and keeping added value in the territories is deemed essential to secure long-term economic interests. This has been regarded as a key step to transforming the Bornean territories from primary sector models to advanced bio-economies. It can be a turning point in moving the island away from rampant timber extraction and agricultural expansion while at the same time improving the welfare of the local population (Sadhukhan et al. 2018; Novindra et al. 2019). Shifting the local industries up in the commodity value chain requires advancement in manufacturing technologies, with products spanning from base oleo such as fatty acids to end products such as polymers and cosmetics (Salimon, Salih, and Yousif 2012). This chapter first elaborates on the downstream development in Borneo, particularly oleochemical industries and advanced biorefineries. Then the issues of infrastructure and investment are discussed.

OLEOCHEMICAL INDUSTRIES

As shown in Figure 2.4, territories in Borneo still rely heavily on primary production. Sarawak is an exception, leading in terms of manufacturing's contribution to the GDP, which doubled from 14 per cent in 1990 to 28 per cent in 2010. However, it then remained almost stagnant until 2018 (Drabble 2000; SPU 2016, 2019). It is not clearly known how much of this can be related to the value-adding of agricultural and forestry products, but a large portion probably comes from the oil and gas sector (also contributed as mining and quarrying) as well as aluminium smelting which relies on the state's cheap hydropower. The other territory that relies heavily on mining and quarrying, i.e., East Kalimantan, has a smaller general manufacturing sector with a much higher share of its GDP coming from petroleum products and gases, together with coal mining.

The risk from the absence of high value-added downstream to commodity-based economies in Borneo was exemplified alongside the booms and busts of commodity prices in the past. Especially, the export-oriented oil palm industry experienced profound financial impacts when the CPO price dropped sharply during the Global Financial Crisis in 2008. Growing a local palm-based oleochemical industry is necessary to boost economic resilience (Tong 2017). In 2019, about 48 per cent of global vegetable oil was used for technical purposes, with about 22 per cent from palm oil and palm kernel oil (Figure 5.1). Most were consumed in the chemical industry, with a relatively small amount devoted to biofuel production (Goh 2016). The contribution of the palm oil industry has doubled from 11 per cent in 2010. Particularly, non-food use in Indonesia has increased substantially.

Presently, the major oleochemicals produced are fatty acids, fatty alcohols, methyl esters, glycerine, and soap noodles. In the future, prospective markets include even highly-priced speciality oleochemicals like amino acid esters and β-carotene that have important applications in the cosmetic, pharmaceutical, and food industries (Mba, Dumont, and Ngadi 2015). These speciality oleochemicals are also considered better substitutes for fossil-based chemicals due to their bio-based nature (Basri, Rahman, and

FIGURE 5.1

The Global Share of Vegetable Oils Used for Non-Food Purposes in 2010 and 2019

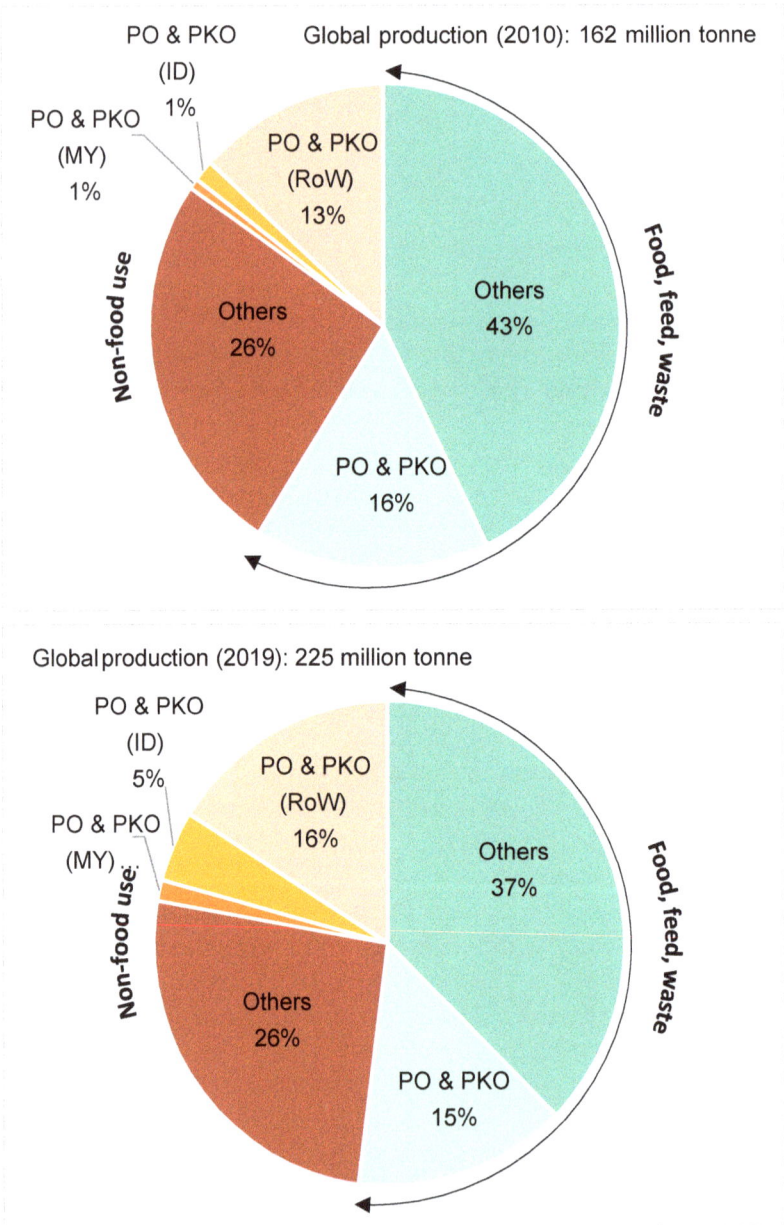

Note: Global production of vegetable oils in 2010 and 2019 were about 162 and 225 million tonnes, respectively. PO: Palm Oil, PKO: Palm Kernel Oil; MY: Malaysia; ID: Indonesia; RoW: Rest of World.
Source: FAOSTAT (2021).

Salleh 2013). Conceptually, vertical integration between primary producers and advanced manufacturers allows the opening of alternative, on-demand supply channels, especially when combined with technologies that can interconvert materials into a variety of chemicals, potentially optimizing the value chains. This allows broader access to different markets, especially those with high uncertainties like the EU-biofuel market (Schneider, Iaconi, and Larocca 2016).

The government of Malaysia has been continuously taking measures to stimulate the growth of local high-value-added agro-based industries through a series of industrial policies like high export duties on raw materials, tax benefits, credit financing, and other financial support. The New Key Economic Areas (NKEA) framework was implemented for palm oil, aiming to triple the sector gross national income (GNI) by 2020 (Jomo and Rock 1998; PEMANDU 2010). By 2019, Sabah achieved a refining capacity of 7.9 million tonnes, which exceeded its annual CPO production. Although its CPO production has caught up with that of Sabah, Sarawak is still behind with a total of 3.4 million tonnes of refining capacity (about 80 per cent of its annual CPO production) (MPOB 2021). Despite being among the largest oil palm-producing states in Malaysia, neither Sabah nor Sarawak has an advanced oleochemical plant despite the total national capacity which had grown up to 2.7 million tonnes by 2019 (MPOB 2021). Notable progress is the biodiesel plant established in Bintulu, the major seaport of Sarawak, in response to the national biodiesel policy promulgated in 2006 (Goh and Lee 2010). It was hoped that this might spur more initiatives for oleochemical development, creating more ambitious foreign and local investment opportunities.

Although a latecomer, downstream activities in Indonesia have been growing rapidly in the past decade with various incentive policies like a palm oil levy, tax allowances, and tax holidays, as well as lower energy cost for the industry (BPDPKS 2019). The refining capacity in Indonesia has been expanding in recent years. By 2019, about 74 per cent of the palm oil exported (~20 million tonnes) was refined compared to 44 per cent (~7 million tonnes) in 2011 (DG Estate Crop Indonesia 2012, 2019). However, there was no complete data about the distribution of refineries in Kalimantan which is publicly available. Table 5.1 shows the list of refineries collected by the authors through reports from the companies and various items of "grey" literature. A recent publication by Pirard et al. (2020) suggests a total of eighty-five refineries in Indonesia, without specifying their locations. There are obviously many outside Kalimantan. Wilmar was singled out as dominating Indonesia's refinery capacity; that company's "Supply Chain

TABLE 5.1
Palm Oil Refineries in Borneo

Territories	Description
Sabah	Two in Kinabatangan owned by IOI (Syarimo) and Musim Mas (the "PONGO" alliance" with Genting Plantations), respectively. Two in Sandakan owned by IOI and Wilmar. Five in Lahad Datu, owned by Mewah International, FGV Holdings, Kuala Lumpur Kepong, Kwantas, and Wilmar. There is one in Kunak owned by Wilmar and one in Tawau owned by FGV Holdings. Sources: (IOI Group 2019; KLK 2019; FGV Holdings 2020; Musim Mas 2020; Wilmar International 2020; Mewah Group 2021)
Sarawak	Five in Bintulu owned by Wilmar, Sime Darby, Rimbunan Hijau ("Borneo Edible Oils"), Sarawak Oil Palms Berhad, and BLD Plantation. There is another one in Kuching owned by Wilmar (SOP 2019; BLD Plantation 2020; Rimbunan Hijau 2020; Sime Darby 2020; Wilmar International 2020).
West Kalimantan	One in Pontianak owned by Wilmar (Wilmar International 2020)
Central Kalimantan	One in Bagendang (Sampit) and one in Kumai, both owned by Wilmar (Wilmar International 2020); one in Seruyan owned by Sime Darby (Sime Darby 2020).
South Kalimantan	Two in Kota Baru district. One owned by Golden Agri Resources through its subsidiary, and another one located in Pulau Laut owned by Sime Darby (GAR 2020; Sime Darby 2020).
East Kalimantan	One in Balikpapan owned by Apical-Royal Golden Eagle, and one in the Maloy Batuta Industrial Estate of East Kutai owned by KLK (KLK 2019). Pertamina is building a refinery in Balikpapan, due to open in 2023 (Bioenergy International 2020).

Map" (Wilmar International 2020) indicates several refineries in both Sumatra and Java.

Meanwhile, oleochemical industries are growing rapidly in Indonesia, reaching 11.3 million tonnes of annual capacity (BPDPKS 2019). However, no certain data is found for Kalimantan, although it is publicly known that Sinar Mas has long had a biodiesel plant attached to its refinery on Pulau Laut, South Kalimantan (Sinar Mas 2020). By 2014, the total capacity was about 1.4 million tonnes (Rofiqi, Maarif, and Hermawan 2016). The biodiesel industry in Indonesia is also growing, but the ambition to export palm-based biodiesel was hampered by the policy uncertainties in the EU market (Mintz-Habib 2016; Rahmanulloh 2020) (see Chapter 6 for more on biodiesel certification).

FIGURE 5.2
Export of Palm-Based Biodiesel from Indonesia and Malaysia by Region

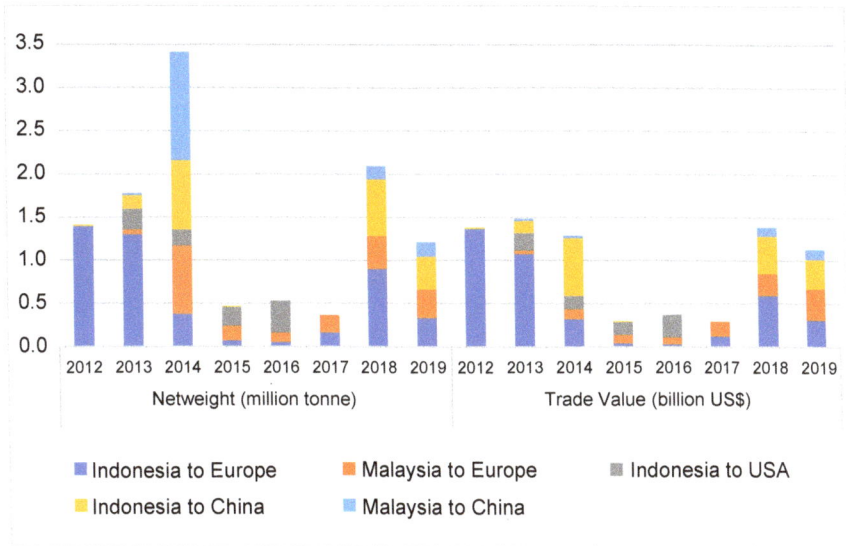

Netweight (million tonne) Trade Value (billion US$)

- Indonesia to Europe
- Malaysia to Europe
- Indonesia to USA
- Indonesia to China
- Malaysia to China

Source: UN COMTRADE (2021).

Figure 5.2 illustrates the export of palm-based biodiesel from Indonesia and Malaysia by region in 2012–19 based on data collected from UN COMTRADE (2021). China is an interesting case as both a big importer and exporter. In 2019, China imported 0.55 million tonnes from Indonesia and Malaysia but also exported 0.66 million tonnes of biodiesel to the world, especially to Europe. With these indirect linkages, Europe remains the most influential buyer due to its consumption volume—the total export of biodiesel from Indonesia and Malaysia dropped sharply in 2015 due to policy changes in Europe. In this circumstance, the demand gap is also partially compensated by the steadily growing local consumption of biodiesel as both the Malaysian and Indonesian governments increased the blending targets (see Chapter 7).

Advanced Biorefineries

Further extending the oleochemical industry to a broader concept of biorefinery has emerged as a development direction for Borneo since the mid-2010s, particularly in Sabah and Sarawak. An abundant amount of low-value bioresources are being generated in Borneo in the form of agricultural and forestry residues, such as empty fruit bunches (EFB) and palm kernel shells (PKS), the so-called biomass. Interests are growing in Europe, Japan, and Korea to import these biomass products as a potential substitute for fossil materials, such as solid fuel for power generation, second-generation liquid biofuels, packaging materials as well as drop-in and novel chemicals (Sheldon 2014; Mai-Moulin, Visser, et al. 2019). Furthermore, these biomass streams can be potentially converted into building blocks (e.g., sugars) for high-value chemicals or substitutes for fossil materials (e.g., bioplastics) (Zahari et al. 2015).

Figure 5.3 shows the estimated amount of biomass generated in Borneo. Sabah and Sarawak are among the territories that generate the most biomass,

FIGURE 5.3

Estimated Quantity of Biomass Generated Annually from Agricultural (2019) and Forestry Residues (2013)

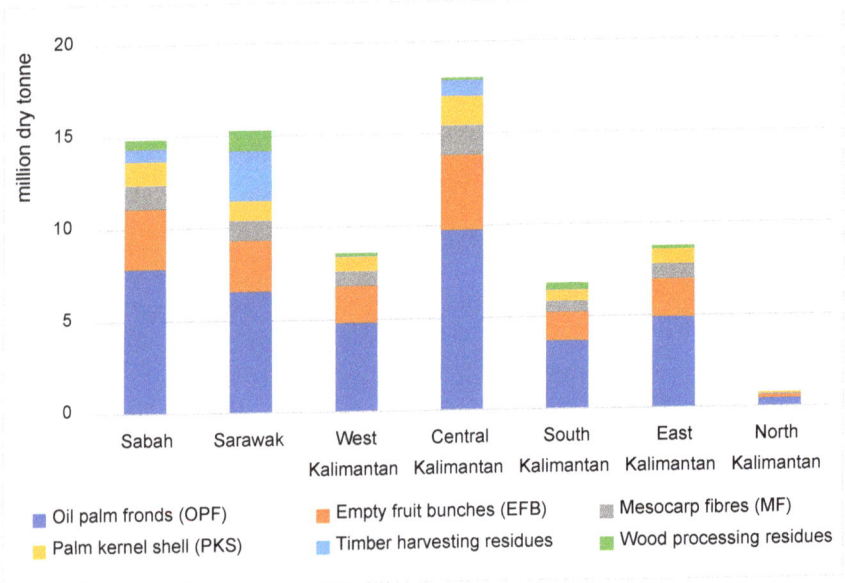

Notes and Sources:
1. Own estimation based on (Goh et al. 2010; Simangunsong et al. 2017; BPS 2020; MPOB 2021) and personal communication with government officials.
2. Data for 2019 was used except for timber, where only data for 2013 was available.
3. Oil palm trunks are not included here due to the dependency of their availability on replanting decisions with ageing plantations. A general trend is that tens of millions of trunks are generated from replanting every year. However, most plantations in Kalimantan and Sarawak may require replanting in the 2030s or earlier as the majority of the trees will become >25-year-old. This may lead to the generation of >50 million trunks a year (own calculation). See photo on p. 2.

amounting to about 15 million dry tonnes each, after 16 million dry tonnes in Central Kalimantan. For both, state-specific strategies were rolled out in 2016 under Malaysia's National Biomass Strategy (NBS) 2020 to develop domestic high value-added biomass-based industries by valorising the agricultural and forestry residues (AIM 2013). The plan was kickstarted by promoting energy pellet production for both local consumption and export, motivated by the Feed-in-Tariff schemes for bioenergy in both Malaysia and overseas markets (Garcia-Nunez et al. 2016). Especially for the latter, biomass from Southeast Asia is increasingly being explored as an alternative to coal for power generation and district heating in Japan and Korea (Goh et al. 2020).

It is thus interesting that Indonesia is now beginning to turn to cofiring biomass for power generation as part of an agreement to start phasing out coal under climate change commitments. The state electricity company (PLN) has organized tests cofiring with a range of biomass raw materials, including palm kernel shells in plants in Kalimantan and Sumatra and wood pellets in plants in Java (Adhiguna 2021). The plan is to extend the life of old and under-utilized coal units while claiming credit for increasing the mix of renewables. However, stable cofiring supplies of 4 to 9 million tonnes annually will be required. Adhiguna notes that Feed-in-Tariffs have been critical in the development of cofiring in other countries and so far, Indonesia has no planned policy incentives. PLN is looking for a cheap source of power, cheaper than coal. While Indonesia already exports both wood pellets and palm kernel shells (third in the world for exports of wood pellets after Vietnam and Malaysia), those sources are considered too expensive for day-to-day operations. Sawdust has been suggested but needs to be mobilized in large amounts.

This can be placed into a broader framework of biorefineries that also integrates the handling of other waste streams like palm oil mill effluents (POME) and municipal solid waste (MSW). POME is the liquid waste stream from palm oil mills. The treatment of POME is critical to the environment as it not only can severely pollute the water resources but also release large quantities of methane, a major greenhouse gas into the atmosphere. In Borneo, the low coverage, efficiency, and effectiveness of MSW treatment have also caused a major problem for the environment. Landfill was the main method if not open dumping (Pariatamby 2014). Similar to POME, improperly treated MSW not only pollutes the soil and water but also releases methane (Abushammala et al. 2011).

Converting these waste streams into, e.g., biomethane and biohydrogen, potentially combined with biomass processing, may significantly improve the economic feasibility of the treatment process (Lam and Lee 2011; Johari et al. 2012; Ali et al. 2015). This was once coupled with the extra revenue through participating in the Clean Development Mechanism (CDM) programme under the Kyoto Protocol, trading the carbon credit obtained from biomethane production primarily through the EU Emissions Trading Scheme (EU-ETS). However, the CDM programme expired in 2012 and the previous projects were only allowed to sell the credits until 2015 (this is further discussed in Chapter 9) (Chin et al. 2013). Hopefully, soon, with more big companies adopting the Roundtable of Sustainable Palm Oil (RSPO) scheme, the voluntary certification standard for the commodity may accelerate the progress in POME treatment and potentially the production of biogas from POME (see Chapter 6).

The large-scale conversion of biomass may create unwanted competition with existing users. For example, currently, a substantial amount of unused oil palm residues is returned to the soil to replenish carbon and nutrients through mulching (Tao et al. 2017). It is not clear what the impacts would be of diverting these biomasses for other purposes. Together with other economic constraints like logistical costs and market uncertainties, the large-scale mobilization of oil palm residues has only been partially realized in the past few years. There have been proposals for deploying decentralized or even mobile biomass processors in rural areas, but none have been realized due to unclear business models. The deployment of advanced POME and MSW treatment systems was also slow due to financial constraints, especially in the face of low CPO prices in recent years. In addition, other feedstocks like acacia, dedicated energy crops, and other solid waste were also studied, but remained theoretical or on an experimental plot scale (Amirta, Mukhdlor, et al. 2016; Amirta, Nafitri, et al. 2016; Ahmed et al. 2018; Jaung et al. 2018; Siti Maimunah et al. 2018).

Despite these existing economic barriers, the concept of biorefineries was not simply discarded. This was because it cannot be viewed solely from a pure short-term profit perspective. It carries more functions than conventional profit-oriented industries: the potential of decentralized energy systems in rural areas, the substitution of fossil materials, and solutions for waste management (Lanzafame, Perathoner, and Centi 2016). The anticipation of these multiple functions was reflected in renewable energy, agricultural, and waste management policies in the form of subsidies (e.g., feed-in-tariffs) and regulations (e.g., POME engineering to prevent methane emission). In a way, it was also deemed as a foundation for future development and innovation in the biotechnology industry.

INFRASTRUCTURE AND INVESTMENT

Realizing the potential of large-scale bio-based manufacturing requires substantial strategic investments, especially in infrastructure. Sarawak and Sabah were way forward with not only better infrastructure in place—both states have much larger and advanced seaports like Bintulu and Sandakan compared to Kalimantan (Soon and Lam 2013)—but also several master plans in promoting and accelerating the downstream industries. In Sarawak, the Sarawak Corridor of Renewable Energy (SCORE) was introduced in 2008 jointly by the federal and the state government as a major growth engine to boost job and wealth creation (RECODA 2016). The SCORE framework aims to integrate both existing and new physical infrastructure, e.g., roads, ports, power grids, and water supplies, across the state, tapping on the large-scale hydropower facility (Bakun Dam) completed in 2011. The Bintulu-Samalaju Ports are designed as a key growth node for advanced manufacturing.

In Sabah, a similar framework called Sabah Development Corridor (SDC) was also established in the same year, focusing on upgrading the state's agricultural-based economy with several integrative plans (SEDIA 2016). A prominent one is the Sandakan-Kinabatangan-Beluran Bio-Triangle. It covers the Palm Oil Industry Cluster (POIC) in Lahad Datu and Sandakan as well as the Wildlife Conservation Programmes. Particularly, the POIC is well equipped with facilities like purpose-fit storage and handling facilities to serve the refineries (Pang and Lee 2013). These corridors form the crucial basis for "bio-economy" as they can better attract and consolidate investment by integrating the emerging bio-based industries with the existing and new infrastructure surrounding the major ports.

While both Malaysian states have made strong attempts to create investment opportunities, the performance is dissimilar. In 2018, Sarawak ranked third among the other Malaysian states and territories in terms of total capital investment received (Table 5.2). Interestingly, compared to the other states, investments in Sarawak are mostly for big projects—the average amount is RM1.4 billion per new project in Sarawak, while the national average is less than RM0.2 billion. In contrast, Sabah received only RM0.2 billion, sitting in eleventh place.

Meanwhile, the Kalimantan provinces are far from venturing into high-value markets. Kalimantan in general is less attractive to investors other than in primary industries due to limited infrastructure and higher costs. Instead, most of the raw materials were exported overseas or fed into the downstream industries elsewhere in the region. Compared to its Malaysian

TABLE 5.2

Approved Manufacturing Projects by State in Malaysia

		2018				2017			
		New		Expansion/ Division		New		Expansion/ Division	
#	State	No.	RM million	No.	RM million	No.	RM million	No.	RM million
1	Johor	76	21,153	68	9,361	74	18,824	72	3,103
2	Selangor	138	13,522	103	5,424	104	2,566	98	3,027
3	Sarawak	6	8,625	5	34	7	9,430	13	1,104
11	Sabah	10	149	3	78	10	221	14	564
	Total	386	61,791	335	25,584	326	39,473	361	24,208

Source: MIDA (2018).

peers, the ports in Kalimantan are relatively small and less advanced. Only the northwestern part of West Kalimantan is considered close to the international waterway between East Asia and the rest of the world (Yan and Su 2018). Meanwhile, East Kalimantan still attracted considerable attention from investors due to its existing infrastructure for the petroleum industry, as well as the speculation about the opportunities that might arise from housing the country's new capital. Kutai Timur, the leading oil palm district in the province, may become a major industrial zone in this part of Borneo with the expansion of the "Maloy Batuta Trans Kalimantan Special Economy Area" (200 km north of Samarinda) (Rothenberg and Temenggung 2019). It is described as "a primary economic cluster in realizing East Kalimantan's development as the centre of oleo-chemical agroindustry and energy". The province is also forging a partnership with the Malaysian government to establish a Palm Oil Green Economic Zone (POGEZ) in the Berau district (Mafira, Rakhmadi, and Novianti 2018).

Another initiative is the planned construction of a series of five cascading dams on the Kayan River in North Kalimantan, to eventually provide 9,000MW of power. This Chinese-funded project will become the largest hydropower project in SE Asia. It would appear that some of the power will be sent to the site of the new national capital in East Kalimantan, as well as supporting a new port and industrial complex (Tanah Kuning Mangkupadi) south of Tanjung Selor. Observers such as Mongabay and WALHI have expressed concern for the indigenous communities along the river and the general environmental impact on this heavily forested region. Two villages will be inundated and relocated, but most will be affected, including important Kayan graves and historic sites (Rochmyaningsih 2016; CNN Indonesia 2019).

Regarding land transportation, many parts of Borneo still rely on rivers for transportation due to relatively poor road networks (Said 2015). A road-building project called the Pan-Borneo Highway stretching up to 1,060 km was launched in 2016, hoping to connect Sarawak, Brunei Darussalam, and Sabah (Sloan et al. 2019). Mirroring the development in the north, Kalimantan is also on its way to expanding its road network. The remaining sections of the Trans-Kalimantan Highway, stretching up to 3,316 km from west to east upon completion, will enhance connectivity between the Kalimantan provinces and are partly aimed to serve as an economic catalyst and decrease poverty in remote areas (Gokkon 2019). However, concerns have been raised about their environmental and social impacts, as several roads, radiating out from the town of Malinau in North Kalimantan, traverse some of the previously inaccessible forests and indigenous territories of the Heart of Borneo (MacInnes 2020) (Figure 5.4).

The continuity of all these projects has been interrupted by COVID-19 in the past two years. The first of the "border access" roads, from Malinau to Long Bawan in Krayan and then the Sarawak border has been prioritized, as the existing road on the Sarawak side has been closed and the people in Krayan have had problems in procuring necessary commodities. President Widodo visited the area in December 2019, when it seemed as though the project was well underway, but progress was interrupted by the COVID-19 outbreak. It is hoped it will be completed in 2023 (Kalimantan Utara, 2021). (See "Krayan" in Chapter 11, where the special "Aden" rice grown in the area is discussed.) One reason for the road into Krayan from Malinau is to provide access to Indonesia for this excellent rice, which has previously been sent across the nearby border to Malaysian markets. Another aim of some of the road projects in Kalimantan is to support eco-tourism. This aspect will be discussed further in Chapter 10) (Figure 5.4).

For Kalimantan provinces which have no comprehensive industrialization plans, promoting "border economies" with their wealthier Malaysian neighbours seems like a natural choice (Idris, Mansur, and Idris 2019). Subnational collaborations like the "Sabah–North Kalimantan Border Economic Area Programme" (Lord and Chang 2018) and "Malindo Socio-Economic Cooperation" between West Kalimantan and Sarawak (Karim 2019) were made. Ideas for regional cooperation like the Borneo-Wide Power Grid system were also promoted to share the excessive energy generated from the hydropower dams in Sarawak (Tabassum, Haldar, and Khan 2020; Tang 2020).

FIGURE 5.4
Existing and Planned Road Construction, Malinau, North Kalimantan

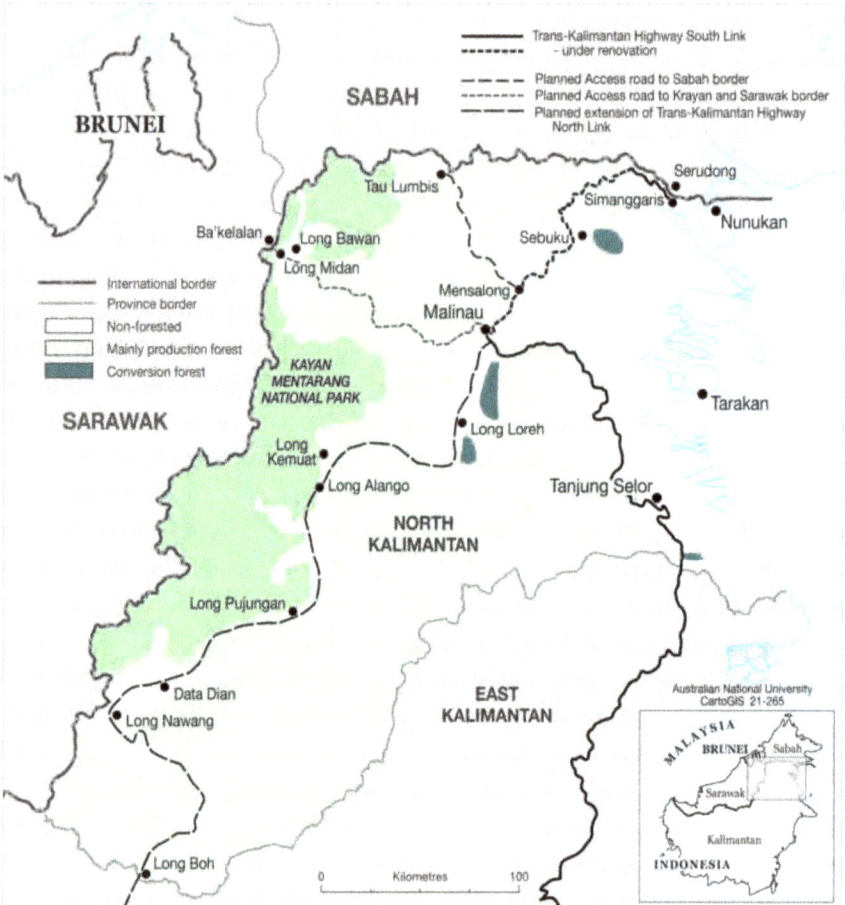

Sources:
1. The road "Planned extension of Trans-Kalimantan Highway North Link" is also called "Parallel border road" (Alamgir et al. 2019).
2. For the original map of the Trans-Kalimantan Highway, North and South Links, see Map 4.1 in Potter (2008).
3. The forest in this map which lies east and south of Kayan Mentarang NP is a mosaic, generalized here as "mainly production forest"; it also includes sections of "protected forest". See *Peta Kawasan Hutan Provinsi Kalimantan Utara* (2014). At that time the forestry office was combined with agriculture and food security. A generalized map of the road projects, which appeared in *Kompas* on 22 August 2016, has a similar background of forest types. The provincial forestry office, now an independent entity, has received training towards compiling a new map, but this has not yet appeared.

At the country level, a prominent collaboration programme is the Brunei Darussalam-Indonesia-Malaysia-Philippines East ASEAN Growth Area (BIMP-EAGA) initiative launched in 1994. It aimed to forge collaborations between the four countries in accelerating economic development mainly in Borneo, Sulu, and Sulawesi (Dent and Richter 2011). The Asian Development Bank (ADB) has played a major role in supporting the programme, especially the development of the West Borneo Economic Corridor that cut across Sarawak and West Kalimantan (with the recently completed power grid interconnection as the backbone), as well as the road link between Sabah and North Kalimantan (ADB 2014; Lynch, Perdiguero, and Rush 2017). The challenges of cross-border projects can be enormous, such as the harmonization of customs, security rules, procedures in ports, and border crossings. It may also trigger power struggles between central and local governments (Karim 2019).

Infrastructure development, however, can also pose new risks to environmental sustainability. Many of these industrialization plans are highly economically oriented. An analysis by Hughes (2018) shows that 99.9 per cent of deforestation occurs within 2.5 km of available roads. The potential environmental impacts of the construction of the Pan-Borneo Highway, Trans-Kalimantan Highway, and other major roads and railways are yet to be properly accounted for in the development plans (Alamgir et al. 2019; Alamgir et al. 2020). The extension of road networks may reduce the benefits of integrating the protected areas as the roads are likely to cut across ecologically important zones. While the state governments have come up with complementary plans for repairing ecological connectivity with forest corridors and highway underpasses, Sloan et al. (2019) warned that these plans are likely impractical from both an ecological and financial perspective. All these plans must be carefully managed with due consideration given to sustainability and safeguarded with strict regulation and enforcement. As noted by MacInnes (2020, p. 8), the result of this planned infrastructure is that the island of Borneo is being "sliced and diced in an effort to secure easy access to the rich natural resources that lie within the interior".

FINAL REMARKS

There is no doubt that climbing up the commodity value chains is desirable for land-based economies in breaking the bottleneck of economic growth. It can stabilize the economies from fluctuating prices of primary commodities and provide remunerative employment for local people. Importantly, this structural shift in growth may reduce considerable pressure on the forest, and thus contribute to overall sustainable development.

One key foundation for this course would be a more vibrant ecosystem of industrial development that extends beyond land-based activities, fostering close synergies with different industries, especially cross-collaboration with the energy, chemical, and food sectors. To this end, governments and industries must envisage the need to accumulate both skills and capital in terms of investment in education, training, technology development, and infrastructure. Technically, Malaysian Borneo can inherit Peninsular Malaysia's competitiveness in the oleochemical industry and biorefining by integrating and transferring technologies, research, knowledge, and marketing channels. Sarawak and Sabah also enjoy more advantages than their Indonesian counterparts due to more developed infrastructure. While things remain highly uncertain due to the COVID-19 pandemic, the moving of Indonesia's capital to East Kalimantan is likely to direct much attention to the Kalimantan provinces, with East Kalimantan possibly becoming the industrial powerhouse of Kalimantan.

While the island is not fully ready yet to see an expansion of its secondary sector, the extraordinary fluctuation of commodity prices in recent years makes immediate action desirable. If growth is what Borneo is seeking, this strategy is likely to remain the focus for development, unless the island discovers alternative economic opportunities.

6

Certifying Industrial Cash Crops
for Sustainability

Sustainable branding and certification of agricultural and forestry products, especially those produced on an industrial scale, is thought to be a key solution in addressing sustainability concerns in developing a bio-economy. Certification has increasingly become a prominent component not only for commercial branding purposes but also in non-state market-based sustainability governance. It involves sets of standards and instruments to regulate and monitor the sustainability of commodities from cradle to gate. A certification of approval which may also come in the form of a seal or label is given to a product that meets the standards, adding visible extrinsic information that underpins the "sustainability" attributes of the products.

Such endowment may enhance market access or even provide a price premium to the producers. For producers in Borneo, one potential strategy might be to increase economic output by gaining access to high-value markets in wealthier regions. This is built upon the premise that consumers in these regions are more likely to pay a price premium if the materials came from sustainable sources. For most cases of industrial cash crops, this is a "carrot" with a "stick", as producers do face enormous pressure from environmental NGOs to adopt more sustainable land-use practices (Gnych, Limberg, and Paoli 2015; Purwanto 2019). Actors along the value chain, especially large buyers of primary agricultural commodities such as food manufacturers, middlemen, retailers, as well as NGOs may also actively work with the producers in developing voluntary standards and certification schemes (Pye 2016).

However, such market-based tools may overlap with various legal frameworks in either producing or importing countries, causing unwanted competition between the public and private sectors in sustainability governance. Also, commodity-centred systems may significantly intersect with other regimes that focus on different lines of inquiry like climate change, biodiversity, haze, and economic development, forming a polycentric regime complex that involves a wide range of actors. The emergence of different standards, schemes, and legal requirements may stir confusion among the stakeholders and substantially increase transaction costs.

In Borneo, two important commodities, palm oil, and timber have been in the limelight. Many companies as well as smallholdings are in pursuit of various certification schemes to tap into price premiums, and more particularly, to gain access to the EU market. This chapter provides an overview and discusses the effectiveness of this strategy in achieving both its environmental and economic objectives. It is organized according to the types of major commodities, i.e., (i) timber and wood-based products (including woody biomass for energy purposes) and (ii) palm oil (including palm-based biofuels).

TIMBER AND WOOD-BASED PRODUCTS

Markets and Schemes

In the 1980s and 1990s, the appreciation of sustainable wood products started to grow globally with the emergence of campaigns against tropical timber. Especially, the major timber markets in Europe have increasingly demanded better governance of timber products. In 2003, the Forest Law Enforcement, Governance and Trade Action Plan (FLEGT) was made to address illegal logging by ensuring that timbers traded were produced according to the laws and regulations of the timber-producing country (Lesniewska and McDermott 2014).

Certification was then recognized as a useful instrument to monitor the sustainability of imported wood in terms of the standards of forest management and the origins of timber products. Certification systems like the Programme for the Endorsement of Forest Certification (PEFC) and/or the Forest Stewardship Council (FSC) were established. The quality of forest management is assessed against a series of agreed standards, now covering much more than just logging practices, including the environmental, social, and economic well-being of workers and local communities, transparency, and inclusiveness in decision-making. From a market perspective, it incentivizes the adoption of sustainable forest management by granting easier market access and price premiums. By 2019, a total of 430 million ha of forests were certified by PEFC and/or FSC (PEFC 2020). In 2016, about 23 per cent of global industrial roundwood production (excluding fuelwood) came from FSC-certified forests (FSC 2019).

For Borneo, Japan has been the most important market for its timber products (see Figure 2.6). The producers and buyers, especially the big players like Sumitomo Forestry have established long-term, cross-cutting relationships in the past decades. With such strong linkages, the changes in the Japanese market have a strong influence on the timber industry in Borneo. Despite the growing adoption of sustainable certification in Europe and North America, the uptake has been slow in Japan—for both local wood and imports from the tropics (Samejima 2020). In the coming years, the involvement of Malaysia in regional trade agreements like the Regional Comprehensive Economic Partnership (RCEP) may have considerable effects on wood production and consumption in Borneo. Trade agreements as such may stimulate and shift the trade patterns of forestry products through tariff elimination. Buongiorno and Zhu (2017) predicted that the involvement of China and Korea in a regional trade partnership will significantly increase the demand for roundwood, sawn wood and panels, and pulp and paper. However, the recognition of timber sustainability is still low in these markets.

Despite the lack of progress among the major buyers in East Asia, both Malaysia and Indonesia have taken initiatives in developing their own forest certification systems. In Malaysia, the Malaysian Timber Certification Scheme (MTCS) was established in 2001 and endorsed by the PEFC in 2009 (Shukri and Sam Shor 2015). By 2018 the total area of MTCS-certified forests in Borneo was about 1.47 million ha. Sabah is far behind with only about 0.15 million ha of natural forest certified. Meanwhile, Sarawak has about 1.32 million ha (MTCC 2020) (Table 6.1). The area of certified timber plantations is much lower, with 38,023 ha and 66,023 ha in Sabah and Sarawak, respectively.

In Indonesia, the Sustainable Production Forest Management or *Pengelolaan Hutan Produksi Lestari* (PHPL) was introduced by the government in 2002 and was then included in the legality verification system, namely *Sistem Verifikasi Legalitas Kayu* (SVLK) in 2009. The PHPL/SVLK certification has evolved into a regulatory instrument to resolve the problems of illegal logging. Its standard covers precondition (including FPIC by local communities for all forest management activities); production (including sustained yield, silviculture to maintain forest regeneration, and reduced impact logging); ecology (including set-asides for protected areas, and impacts on soil, water, and biodiversity) and social criteria (including the participation of local people in forest management, benefit-sharing, and conflict resolution). Although it was supposedly mandatory since 2013, only about 26 per cent or 18 million ha of the production forests were certified

TABLE 6.1

Production Forests and Certified Areas in Borneo as of June 2020

Territories	million ha					
	Total forested areas	Designated production forest	SVLK/MTCS-certified production forest	%	FSC-certified production forests	%
Sabah	3.57	1.65	0.15	8%	0.53	27%
Sarawak	6.15	4.21	1.32	31%	—	—
West Kalimantan	5.70	4.46	0.84	19%	0.17	4%
Central Kalimantan	7.32	9.74	3.69	38%	0.72	7%
South Kalimantan	0.73	1.04	0.28	26%	—	—
East Kalimantan	5.91	5.91	3.15	53%	0.54	9%
North Kalimantan	5.72	3.28	1.40	43%	0.20	6%

Notes:
1. "Production Forest" in Kalimantan may also include non-forested areas (previously deforested). Only certified natural forests are shown. Currently, Sabah and Sarawak have approximately 38,023 ha and 66,873 ha of MTCS-certified forest plantations, respectively. Permits issued for forest plantations of various types reached 5.1 million ha in Kalimantan in 2019 (CNN Indonesia 2021b), though information on certification is hard to find. East Kalimantan has the largest number of "wood fibre" concessions, in which the two major companies, Asia Pulp and Paper (Sinar Mas Forestry, APP) and APRIL (Asia Pacific Resources International Holdings Limited) with large pulp and paper plants in Sumatra, were well represented (Samsudin 2016). Those two companies have policies of zero deforestation, which they were using to attempt to restore certification that had earlier been removed due to poor environmental and human rights practices (the FSC had cancelled APP's certification in 2007). However, in 2018 the companies were found to have violated their zero-deforestation commitments by sourcing timber from a Djarum Group concession in East Kalimantan established in High Carbon Stock areas (Jong 2018; Koalisi Anti Mafia Hutan 2019).
2. All FSC-certified concessions are also SVLK-certified in Kalimantan, but this is not necessarily so for MTCS-certified concessions in Sabah and Sarawak.
3. Some FSC-certified forests in Sabah are currently pending recertification which was delayed by the 2020 pandemic.
Source: MoEF Indonesia (2019); FSC (2020); MoEF (2020a); MTCC (2020); Sabah Forestry Department (2020).

by 2015 (Maryudi et al. 2017). By 2020, East Kalimantan had achieved a relatively higher certification rate, where more than 50 per cent of the production forests were certified.

At the state level, as early as 1989, the Sabah Forestry Department started to explore a more sustainable system that could maintain the productivity of forests with minimal impacts on the environment, especially the adoption of reduced-impact logging (RIL). A remarkable example is the Deramakot Forest Reserve certified by the FSC in 1997. It is the longest-certified tropical rainforest in the world (Kitayama, Ong, and Lee 2013). By 2018, the FSC-certified forest in Sabah reached nearly 0.6 million ha (Naito and Ishikawa

2020). The state also developed its own Timber Legality Assurance System (TLAS) in close coordination with WWF Malaysia (NEPCon 2013).

Meanwhile, Sarawak has made multiple efforts to curb illegal logging in its expansive territory in conjunction with the implementation of its environmental regulatory system. Specifically, the Sarawak Timber Legality Verification System (STLVS) was established to ensure compliance with the state's regulations (Samejima 2020). There is no FSC- or PEFC-certified forest in Sarawak, but the MTCS area has increased substantially in 2018 from only 0.08 million ha to 1.32 million ha (MTCC 2020; Naito and Ishikawa 2020). Any certified Forest Management Units (FMUs) under the MTCS must also comply with legal requirements at the state level, i.e., TLAS and STLVS in Sabah and Sarawak, respectively. The FSC administration maintains a "post-1994 conversion" rule (excluding forests involving conversion activities after 1994), making it difficult for its uptake in Sarawak and Kalimantan as many forest plantations were converted or established after 2000. A revision of the FSC's rule has been ongoing to enable more participation in the scheme.

In Kalimantan, the NGOs play a big role in pushing for forest certification. A Dutch-funded NGO, the "Borneo Initiative", was established in 2012 to encourage and assist the logging companies in Kalimantan to obtain FSC certification. By 2017, the number of FSC-certified concessions had grown to twenty (Samejima 2020). It is estimated that at least about 1.6 million ha of natural forest in Kalimantan is FSC-certified (Table 6.1). Note that all FSC-certified concessions are also SVLK-certified in Kalimantan but not necessarily MTCS-certified in Sabah and Sarawak.

While familiar to Malaysia, the PEFC, a voluntary certification alternative to the FSC, was not widely known in Indonesia, its standards being only endorsed in 2014. However, it has since become quite popular in the country, by 2018 achieving coverage of 3.8 million ha, as opposed to the FSC's 3.1 million ha (Kartika, Hariyadi, and Cerdikwan 2020). While it seems rather more flexible in its standards than the FSC (perceived to be designed by environmentalists), it is also more market-driven and closer to the interests of the industries, though still aiming to strengthen sustainable forest management (Kartika, Hariyadi, and Cerdikwan 2020).

In addition to the conventional market, new certification schemes also emerged in European countries to ensure the sustainability of imported woody biomass consumed for heat and power generation. These schemes are voluntary but required to claim bioenergy subsidies. However, there are still substantial market uncertainties as the consuming countries have adopted different sustainability requirements (Mai-Moulin, Armstrong, et al. 2019). While it is unlikely that Borneo would venture into the EU's biomass market, it has been perceived as a potential major supplier for the Japanese and Korean bioenergy sectors in recent years. At the moment, both countries have not yet developed a sustainability requirement for bioenergy. This is similar to the trend in the conventional wood markets, reflecting the lack of awareness of sustainable consumption in the region.

Impacts and Challenges

Certification of timber products may help in improving the economic viability of conservation, provided market premiums are maintained. Abdul-Rahim and Mohd-Shahwahid (2012) found that upon the implementation of SFM practices, the overall production volume dropped, but the value per unit of timber increased significantly and market access was improved (Abdul-Rahim et al. 2012). A case study in Lower Kinabatangan, Sabah revealed that stakeholders were generally positive about the function of improving forest management in resolving environmental issues (Latip et al. 2013).

In Kalimantan, the analysis by Miteva, Loucks, and Pattanayak (2015) revealed that deforestation was reduced by 5 per cent with the application of the FSC standards from 2000 to 2008. In addition, although there are no statistically significant impacts on fire reduction, the certification scheme has contributed to reducing firewood dependence, air pollution (and so respiratory infections), and malnutrition. A study on FSC-certified forests in Berau, East Kalimantan that were selectively logged also showed that certification standards do have positive effects on biodiversity conservation (Arbainsyah et al. 2014). There are ongoing efforts to incorporate more robust and cost-effective methods into FSC, such as the attempt by Kitayama et al. (2018) with a method called "Biodiversity Observation for Land and Ecosystem Health" (BOLEH) to measure carbon stock and forest intactness in Sabah and East Kalimantan. One FSC-certified concession in East Kalimantan has passed its claim on biodiversity from the FSC Ecosystem Services scheme using the BOLEH method but is the only concession in Indonesia to have achieved that result.

However, the social impacts of forest certification can be uneven due to the different levels of standards applied, audit procedures, and stakeholder participation. When massive logging started to bloom in the 1970s, many indigenous communities took up jobs in logging companies and became involved actively in illegal logging. Logging (including illegal) was described by local people in a study by Goh et al. (2018) in Central Kalimantan as a very profitable business but it also commonly involved violent conflicts.

With the introduction of sustainable forest management and certification schemes in the 1990s, local people have faced many restrictions in accessing forest resources.

This exposed the shortcoming of environmental-oriented management—a lack of attention was given to ensuring the livelihood of rural communities that were lagging behind the transformation. While much of the literature suggests that sustainability certification helps to support local livelihoods, empirical evidence is mixed. By comparing cases in Kalimantan, Gabon and the Brazilian Amazon, Rana and Sills (2018) found that the effects of FSC certification varied considerably across space and time—this implies that a place-based evaluation is necessary, especially in key conservation spots. In this context, a greater variety of standards suiting local conditions may be needed, and long-term plans should be incentivized instead of seeking only immediate on-ground changes which are impractical in many cases.

While production forest management in Borneo has been evolving from "timber-corporate" management to "forest-multibusiness" management, one should not forget that politics plays a pivotal role in natural resource governance. The promotion of forest certification is politically sensitive in terms of influencing the attitude and mentality of local governments in enforcing environmental regulatory systems. The disparate on-ground performance between Sabah and Sarawak is a vivid example (Naito and Ishikawa 2020). The adoption of FSC in Sarawak has been limited partly due to the complexity in the area of indigenous rights. The determination of customary land has been a long-standing unresolved issue in the state. In contrast, the Sabah Forestry Department attempted to align both the state's laws and certification schemes in this aspect. It regards the high standard of FSC as an important factor in safeguarding the reputation of its timber products for entering the high-premium market. Meanwhile, certification politics in Kalimantan are more complicated as they involve power struggles at various levels, especially among central agencies like the Ministry of Environment and Forestry, the Ministry of Trade, the Ministry of Industry, and their relationships with industrial players, foreign governments (e.g., the EU), various NGOs, certification bodies and buyers (Dooley and Ozinga 2011; Wibowo and Giessen 2018).

In general, the integration of forest certifications into the broader socio-political framework that has specific local contexts is still limited throughout Borneo except for Sabah which has taken a more proactive approach. How to incorporate the interests of different parties and align voluntary schemes with national and local regulatory frameworks will remain the key challenge in the coming years.

PALM OIL

Markets and Schemes

The major cash-generating product from Borneo, palm oil, has been facing various barriers in entering the EU's markets due to a bad reputation from its historical links to severe deforestation. Resistance to palm oil in the EU has grown rapidly in the past two decades, fuelled by heavy criticisms from civil society and competitors' lobbying. However, imposing unilateral, universal tariffs or bans on palm oil has been controversial, as not all palm oil has direct links to environmental degradation. Monitoring and regulating the cross-border and cross-sector flows of palm oil through voluntary market forces has emerged as a logical way to influence the upstream activities from the EU perspective, assuming that informed consumers will prefer to purchase products that are sustainably produced (Goh, Junginger, and Faaij 2014). This can be especially effective for major markets with higher purchasing power like the EU. Figure 6.1 illustrates the differences in value per tonne of palm oil imported by the EU and Asia. On average, the value differed by >US$50/tCPO in 2001–18, remarkably boosted compared to 1995–2000. Such a price premium is an incentive for the producers to adopt more sustainable land-use practices to enter the EU market.

FIGURE 6.1

Differences in Import Value per tonne of Palm Oil between EU and Asia in 1995–2018

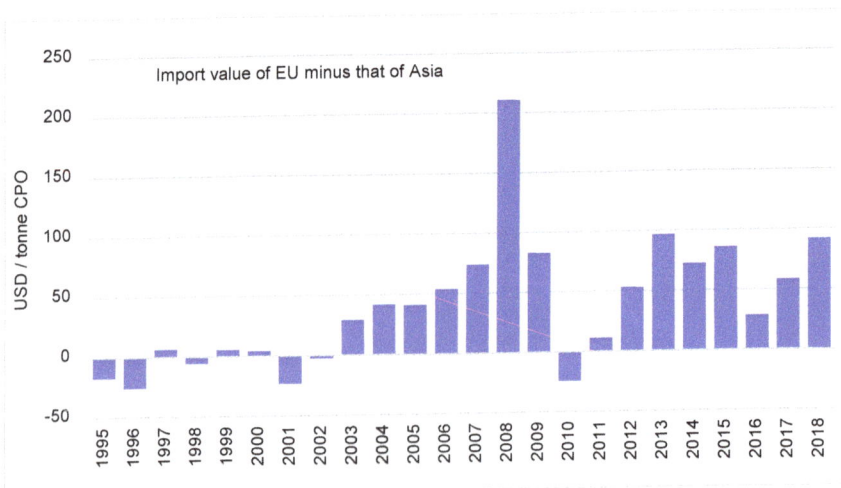

Source: FAOSTAT (2021).

The best-known and accepted certification scheme, the Roundtable on Sustainable Palm Oil (RSPO), was established in 2004 as a filter for consumers to separate "sustainable" palm oil from an "unsustainable" counterpart. Officially, RSPO is defined as "a not-for-profit that unites stakeholders from the seven sectors of the palm oil industry", covering oil palm producers, processors or traders, consumer goods manufacturers, retailers, banks/investors, environmental NGOs, and social NGOs. Companies that comply with environmental and social criteria set by the scheme would be granted certification. The "Principles and Criteria" of the standards are adjusted by country and revised centrally every few years, most recently in 2018. This mechanism motivates and advantages those who embrace more sustainable land-use practices by engendering confidence among consumers and adding premiums to the products (Gnych, Limberg, and Paoli 2015).

The certified area has been increasing but is far from catching up to the expansion of the total area. By 2019, about 2.1 and 1.2 million ha of plantations in Malaysia and Indonesia, respectively, were RSPO-certified (RSPO 2020b). These numbers are still small compared to their combined planted area of ~20.6 million ha (>8 million ha in Borneo) (DG Estate Crop Indonesia 2019; MPOB 2021). Sabah, West Kalimantan, and Central Kalimantan are among the territories that have the largest certified areas, while Sarawak is lagging. The reason for Sarawak's poorer showing in certification may relate to the fact that much of its more recent oil palm planting has been on peat.

Unfortunately, no provincial and state-level data on smallholders is made publicly available. The uptake of RSPO by independent smallholders remains very small even at a national level, recording only 36,313 ha by 2020. Meanwhile, a total of 418,227 ha of oil palm under organized smallholders has been certified. This figure may be compared with the area of independent smallholders certified in Malaysia by the MSPO by July 2020: 305,348 ha or 30.28 per cent of the total of just over 1 million ha (Kannan et al. 2021).

While the supply of certified sustainable palm oil has reached >18 MT globally (RSPO 2020b), the uptake is still limited by the demand in the EU market but not in the other regions. In 2017, the EU's total net import was around 7.3 MT, and possibly 83 per cent of that was certified (RSPO 2020b). By 2019, the uptake of certified palm oil by the EU may have risen to 7.1 MT (RSPO 2020b; FAOSTAT 2021).

While not all oil palm growers in Kalimantan actively seek voluntary certification, they must now comply with the Indonesian Sustainable

Palm Oil (ISPO) scheme founded in 2011. Compared to RSPO, the ISPO's regulations have been simpler, mainly based on compliance with existing Indonesian law. Free, prior, and informed consent (FPIC) from local landholders is missing, as is the need for specific protection of "High Conservation Value" (HCV) areas and "High Carbon Stock" (HCS) forests as in the RSPO framework (see Chapter 4). Even with a weaker standard, the latest figures suggest only about 37 per cent of existing companies have complied with the ISPO standards. However, the recent revision of ISPO in 2020 requires that all smallholders (with 25 ha or less) be certified within five years (Jong 2020b, 2020h).

The Malaysian Sustainable Palm Oil (MSPO) is the counterpart of ISPO in Malaysia, which shares the same issues of fewer environmental safeguards and lack of international acceptance. The mandatory implementation of MSPO for the whole industry was scheduled to take effect on 1 January 2020 (Senawi et al. 2019). It also carried an objective to transform the practices of independent smallholders in both economic and environmental aspects. The paper by Kannan et al. (2021) outlines some of the techniques employed to do this. SPOC or "Sustainable Palm Oil Clusters", placed smallholders into groups of 1,000–2,000, so all could be certified together after training by one extension agent. In April 2019, Sabah was said to have 29 SPOCS for 35,338 smallholders, the figures for Sarawak being 32 SPOCS for 41,418 smallholders (Kannan et al. 2021). While the Malaysian government had allocated sufficient funding to cover the certification costs of smallholders (defined in Malaysia as farmers having 40 ha or less), by July 2020, only 30 per cent of the independent group had been certified. Both Kannan et al. (2021) and Kaur (2020) quoting Ahmad Parveez, the head of the MPOB, noted the problem of the low numbers of extension officers to clients and the complexities of the certification process, though there was still a reluctance of many smallholders to be certified as it was not seen as providing them with economic benefits. Nonetheless, smallholders who had not started the certification process before the first day of 2022 were threatened with termination or suspension of their licences (Kaur 2020).

In addition to debates in the conventional food market, the dramatic changes in EU biodiesel policy throughout the past two decades have also played a role in accelerating the structural changes in palm oil value chain governance (Johnson, Pacini, and Smeets 2013). The EU's Renewable Energy Directive (RED) established in 2009 required biofuel to be certified based on social and environmental sustainability standards. Some companies such as Sarawak Oil Palms Berhad (SPOB) participated in alternative schemes like International Sustainability and Carbon Certification (ISCC) to gain entry into the EU's biofuel market (Ching et al. 2019). However, palm-based biodiesel, despite being derived from the same biochemically substitutable feedstocks as those used in the food sector, has been treated differently in trade policies. The policy on biofuel sustainability can also be quite different among the EU member states. These intertwined state-led and market-led developments have created market differentiation and potential leakage issues, causing substantial confusion among the stakeholders (Schleifer 2013).

The anti-dumping duty on Indonesian palm oil in 2013 marked the start of phasing out the use of palm-based biodiesel in the EU due to enormous pressure from both NGOs and politicians. A concept called "indirect land use change" (ILUC) was introduced in the debate on the sustainability of liquid biofuels. ILUC occurs when existing agricultural land is converted for biofuel production, leading to agriculture expansion elsewhere, which may involve deforestation, to fill the demand gap in the global market through market-mediated effects. However, previous works revealed that the forms and dynamics of ILUC related to cash crops like palm oil can be extremely diverse and open to alternative interpretations (Goh, Wicke, Verstegen, et al. 2016; Goh et al. 2018). While it is almost impossible to quantify ILUC, the EU's RED in 2018 ruled that the EU will phase out feedstock that may potentially involve ILUC by 2030, with palm oil included (Flach, Lieberz, and Bolla 2020).

Both Indonesia and Malaysia have protested, calling the directive discriminatory as oil palm competitors, especially soy oil and locally grown rapeseed and sunflower oil are treated differently from palm oil. In 2020, both Indonesia and Malaysia began taking legal action against the EU at the World Trade Organization (WTO) (*Edge Markets*, 1 January 2020). Two exemptions to the rule would be if the biofuels are produced on degraded or abandoned land or grown by smallholders (Flach, Lieberz, and Bolla 2020). The latter exemption partly explains the increased interest in both Malaysia and Indonesia in improving smallholder production and preparing them for certification under either the RSPO or the ISPO and MSPO alternatives.

Impacts and Challenges

Similar to many other certification schemes, compromises were made during the initial set-up of RSPO to rush for scaling up (Potts et al. 2014). The loosely designed principles and criteria and monitoring protocols have sparked criticisms of "greenwashing" among consumers. Although the

RSPO has been gradually improving the standards, the impacts have been uneven in terms of environmental sustainability, for which the RSPO was mainly established. While in some cases the environmental performance of RSPO-certified concessions in Borneo was reported to be better than those non-certified, in certain aspects the improvement was minimal if not non-existent (Cattau, Marlier, and DeFries 2016; Meijaard et al. 2017; Carlson et al. 2018; Morgans et al. 2018). For example, a study in Balikpapan Bay reported that a number of companies that are closely linked to the loss of the proboscis monkey habitat were discovered to be RSPO members (Toulec et al. 2020).

For RSPO-certified smallholders, a more recent report on Central Kalimantan in 2019 shows that they generally performed better in terms of agricultural practices and output, but there was no significant difference in the provision of ecosystem services (Suwarno et al. 2019). Moreover, other environmental impacts at the landscape level are still difficult to cover and monitor. For example, Larsen et al. (2014) reported a case in Central Kalimantan in which the water resources used by the local communities were affected by the establishment of plantations. In this case, the RSPO certification was found to be insufficient (or irrelevant) to address the problem of water distribution.

Another major concern is the financial feasibility. The main critique from the producers is that certification by the RSPO comes at a significant cost, mainly for verification (auditing) and administration, considering the complexity of the supply chain and the number of actors involved (Oosterveer 2015). The premium of RSPO is reportedly insufficient to cover the transaction cost and foregone economic opportunity cost (i.e., cost to conserve forests) (Ruysschaert and Salles 2014). The cost barrier was particularly critical for financially less capable independent smallholders (Glasbergen 2018). As a result, it has been mainly the large producers relying on European buyers, who have remained in the scheme to seek market penetration (Saadun et al. 2018). Such a system also seems to favour large-scale monoculture as it could be more easily monitored at lower costs (Azhar et al. 2015).

To increase the participation of smallholders, the RSPO scheme was expanded to allow the collective certification of smallholders in groups. However, the commitment of smallholders remains small. By 2019, the smallholders' certified area was only slightly above 0.4 million ha, or 15 per cent of the total certified oil palm areas (RSPO 2020b). Monitoring the smallholder expansion, which has much more complex patterns, requires enormous effort. This requires a thorough understanding of the heterogeneity of smallholders, as their land-use decisions are highly influenced by their characteristics, capability, accessibility (location), and types of plots (Schoneveld, Ekowati, et al. 2019). One key difficulty would be determining their role in peatland conversion and peat fire (Wijedasa et al. 2018). "Translating" conservation values held by international buyers to small farmers to encourage compliance with the standards can be an arduous task, requiring much time, effort, and creativity (Acciaioli and Afiff 2018).

Importantly, it has been very challenging to design the social criteria and monitor their compliance. Predation among locked-in oil-palm outgrowers by larger players was not uncommon throughout Kalimantan. For example, Li (2018) described a "mafia-style" system that was imposed on outgrowers in Meliau, West Kalimantan. Clerc (2013) reported a typical case of asymmetrical negotiation between the local communities and RSPO-certified plantation companies in West Kalimantan, which was exacerbated by the incapability (or lack of interest) of local authorities to intervene. Even though the company was committed to adhering to the RSPO standards, FPIC was not strictly followed in this process. One aspect that has often been overlooked is the welfare of labourers, many of whom are non-local, on the plantations (Li 2017b). As described earlier in Chapter 3, their working conditions can be very harsh. The most challenging part would be the monitoring of undocumented workers, especially those who moved illegally across the national borders from Kalimantan into Sabah and Sarawak (Puder 2019).

In the early 2010s, McCarthy (2012) noted that the RSPO generally had little influence at the district level in Indonesia, and there were few incentives to make sure the rules were followed. Moreover, corruption, regulatory evasion, and illegal practices are not uncommon among local entrepreneurs and elites (Schoneveld, van der Haar, et al. 2019). Nevertheless, there was also positive feedback like that reported by Kato and Soda (2020). Their case study in Sarawak revealed that participating in RSPO provided more opportunities for the smallholders to engage with leading companies and experts, especially in terms of gaining investment and technical support. A recent study by Santika, Wilson, et al. (2020) in Kalimantan shows that while oil palm certification has positive impacts on income in villages with market-based livelihoods, it did not help reduce poverty in places that have relied more on subsistence livelihoods in the past two decades.

The two national schemes of ISPO and MSPO are, however, troubled by their inability to convince the high-value markets in Europe (Hidayat,

Offermans, and Glasbergen 2018). These "brands" are largely disconnected between producers and consumers with great disagreement in terms of sustainability standards (Pacheco et al. 2017). The big corporations were just annoyed that the RSPO's principles and criteria were becoming stricter, especially the need to obtain FPIC from communities before planting began, instead of a few years later. They were happy to adopt the simpler and cheaper ISPO scheme, just based on Indonesian environmental laws, and to exempt smallholders (Filer, Mahanty, and Potter 2020). It was also argued that the auditing process required for the ISPO certification may be "woefully substandard", including collusion with plantation companies to disguise violation of the rules (EIA and Grassroots 2015). For smallholders, these government-driven schemes have inherited enormous challenges to handle the complex issues posed by their needs. While the MSPO schemes set a lower-than-optimum level to expand the coverage on smaller players (Senawi et al. 2019), until recently ISPO had little concern for smallholders.

However, things were no better in the past—the introduction of the two national schemes has indeed played a positive role in improving environmental governance. For example, the mandatory environmental impact assessment (EIA) report for oil palm plantations in Malaysia under the Environmental Quality Act Order 1987 was reported for its multiple weaknesses in terms of coverage, depth, and duration (Chew and Vun 2013). The involvement of governments in certification schemes may be seen as a key entry point to revamping the existing jurisdictional instruments.

On a global scale, the practical challenges to regain access to the high-value markets through the rebranding of palm oil are tremendous in face of the complex interactions between global actors with diverging interests, including strong competitors like rapeseed and soybean producers. More importantly, the fundamental issue of "market leakage" can greatly undermine the effectiveness of such certification schemes. In the case of RSPO, it means that the sales of palm oil were basically just rerouted and redistributed—low-risk stock was certified and channelled to the EU, while the rest of the palm oil was redirected to the rest of the world as in the past two decades (Goh, Junginger, and Faaij 2014; Goh, Wicke, Verstegen, et al. 2016; Wilman 2019). The net improvement in sustainability can be limited if major markets, especially those in South Asia, continue to favour lower-cost, uncertified palm oil.

Some advocated that transformation should be based on an appreciation of good values and trust-building beyond certification (Poynton 2015). The main argument is that the system of certification has been discouraging innovation and genuine changes in mentality. Within the private sector, some of the largest oil palm conglomerates and buyers voluntarily declared the "No Deforestation, No Peat, No Exploitation" (NDPE) policy in the early 2010s, and this stance has recently become very popular (Larsen et al. 2018). The findings of ten Kate, Kuepper, and Piotrowski (2020) suggest that 83 per cent of palm oil refining capacity in Indonesia and Malaysia is now covered by NPDE policies, making it "the strongest private instrument to cut the link between deforestation and palm oil". The report, however, also pinpoints suspicious "leakers" like FGV Holdings in Sabah, Best Group in Indonesia, and Kwantas and BLD (Sarawak) that do not really adhere to the NDPE policies.

Not surprisingly, the NDPE initiative has led to multiple debates and conflicts between stakeholders. In Sarawak, palm oil growers were very concerned when Wilmar released its NDPE policy in 2013 as many of them cultivated on peatland and used Wilmar's mills. In Indonesia, the biggest palm oil exporters made a move further with the push from the UN in creating the Indonesian Palm Oil Pledge (IPOP), a sustainability commitment signed in 2014. However, the Indonesian government rejected this initiative as it was deemed to threaten national sovereignty and constitute a cartel. IPOP was disbanded in July 2016 following threats of court action (Yusuf, Roos, and Horridge 2018). This showed the political complexity and challenges of having parallel governing systems that may not necessarily bring net positive impacts.

On the government side, Indonesia has made ambitious moves and targets. In the early 2010s, the Indonesian government decreed a moratorium on over 69 million ha of concessions, stopping the issuing of new permits to improve governance of primary natural forest and peatland (Murdiyarso et al. 2011). This moratorium was regularly extended every two years but made permanent in 2019. One of its deficiencies is that secondary forests are not included. In September 2018, President Widodo put in place a three-year moratorium on new permits for oil palm plantations and a review of long-standing unused permits (Purnomo et al. 2020) (however, this moratorium has now expired and was not renewed). In Malaysia, Sarawak had also declared that no more timber licences and provisional leases for new plantations would be issued (*Borneo Post*, 1 August 2015). Inevitably, such a hybrid public-private governance structure, considering also the failure of IPOP, will still largely be based on non-transparent negotiations and entangled with national-local politics (Orsato, Clegg, and Falcão 2013).

A Way Forward: Jurisdictional Approach

While the MSPO had become mandatory by the end of 2019, Sabah pre-empted this (despite an adverse reaction from the MPOB), having decided in 2015 to move the entire state to full RSPO certification, smallholders included, by 2025 (*Borneo Post*, 17 November 2018). This process, initiated here by the RSPO, is called the "Jurisdictional Approach" (JA). JA attempts to cover an entire administrative area, which can be a district or a province/state, cutting across multiple sectors and covering multiple commodities. It focuses on the political aspect of land-use decision-making, providing an official platform, facilitated by local governments, to align all stakeholders to work together on conservation and other development goals (Watts, Nepstad, and Irawan 2019). It has gained interest recently not only throughout Borneo but also in other parts of Indonesia as well as some other tropical countries (Stickler et al. 2018; Saragih 2019).

In this case, the "Sabah Jurisdictional Certified Sustainable Palm Oil" or JCSPO, is a commitment at the state level (initially from the Sabah Forestry Department), with assistance from NGOs (WWF, UNEP, LEAP) and contributions from foundations, organizations, and individuals. The four main aims were to: (1) transform Sabah's palm oil production and supply chains, (2) halt deforestation, (3) restore the ecosystems, and (4) secure sustainable livelihoods (Kugan 2018). In this approach, Sabah was acting as a pilot study for the RSPO, together with the Seruyan district (Central Kalimantan) and the Ecuadorian Amazon. By adopting the JA, the state government will develop statewide HCV mapping activities, reducing the financial burden of individual companies and farmers, especially smaller players in complying with the RSPO requirement (Wilson et al. 2018). After some uncertainty caused by a change of government in 2018, Sabah agreed to implement both MSPO and JCSPO concurrently, though perceiving the MSPO as only an initial step, with the JCSPO perceived as more likely to be accepted by the market. By that year, about 24 per cent and 22.4 per cent of plantations in Sabah were certified by RSPO and MSPO, respectively (Kugan 2018).

In the Seruyan district of Central Kalimantan, various actors along the value chain also play a role in accelerating the implementation of JA (Seymour, Aurora, and Arif 2020). In their useful graph of "Key milestones in the development of the jurisdictional approach in Indonesia" (Figure 2), the authors note that JA was first mentioned in 2013 when UNFCC defined REDD+ "at jurisdictional scale". The following year, the district head of Seruyan endorsed a jurisdictional palm oil programme and in 2015 the RSPO announced plans for jurisdictional certification. The Earth Innovation

Research Institute (INOBU) supported by Unilever helped establish the first Agricultural Facility (AF) in Seruyan in 2018 to assist smallholders with training, agricultural inputs, and financial instruments (RSPO 2018). INOBU also mapped and registered all oil palm growers, from plantations to independent smallholders in Seruyan to reduce uncertainties over supply chains and assist smallholders over legal issues in a program known as SIPKEBUN (Saragih 2019). This effort was also extended to the neighbouring district, Kotawaringin Barat in which there are many transmigrants with secured land titles (Suwastoyo 2019).

In the case of Sintang, the district government declared its ambition to be a "Sustainable District" in 2017 and further extended that in 2019 through the promulgation by Bupati's Regulation No. 66/2019 of a "Regional Action Plan for Sustainable Sintang", in which a key action is implementing a JA to develop a sustainable oil palm sector (Sukri et al. 2020). The district has conducted districtwide mapping activities to discover that about 1.1 million ha in the district can be considered HCV forests. These mapping activities also prevent overlapping land allocation and assist indigenous peoples and local communities in delineating their village boundaries. The other efforts include registering smallholders, providing them with training to obtain RSPO/ISPO certification, and encouraging income diversification away from palm oil and rubber.

Based on the ongoing cases in Borneo, the expected benefits of the JA for conservation are clear. First, it strengthens the enforcement of environmental regulations and cultivates appreciation and pride in the home region's sustainability among the local stakeholders. Second, a territory-wide mapping and monitoring activity may substantially circumvent the cost of identifying HCV and HCS areas by individual players. Third, a comprehensive HCV map with a formal jurisdictional basis will also contribute to spatial planning on a territorial scale, providing more opportunities in enhancing a territory-wide conservation landscape, such as building and connecting biodiversity corridors. This can address the technical issues in managing fragmented HCV areas in different concessions with the existing supply chain approach. Finally, it can also be effectively combined with other conservation strategies. In a report made for the Berau district government in East Kalimantan, where JA was adopted for the Berau Forest Carbon Partnership (BFCP), Mafira, Muluk, and Conway (2019) proposed that the district government could also apply the same approach to the oil palm sector to obtain a single certification for the entire district.

However, the implementation of the JA has been facing various challenges. First, the capacity of district governments (in the case of Kalimantan) is limited. They need substantial support on both the technical aspects and on-ground implementation (e.g., providing training). In addition, enforcing compliance with voluntary RSPO standards on non-RSPO members, especially in key issues such as FPIC could be a big challenge, such as in the case of the Seruyan district. Besides massive deforestation, there are over 300 land conflicts in Seruyan between companies and local communities, both indigenous and transmigrant. Third, friction among the different levels of government may occur (the push for ISPO/MSPO vs RSPO). While operating on a smaller territorial scale can be more pragmatic, it also implies competition between government departments and may spark localism. Furthermore, the implementation of the RSPO standards may conflict with existing laws and regulations, and thus may involve much longer procedures, e.g., through the State Assembly as in the case of Sabah. The legitimacy of the JA is also undermined by political instability, again the case in Sabah which has experienced political turmoil and changes in the ruling coalitions since 2018. A much longer time may be needed to build trust and sufficiently convince the various actors, especially the civil society organizations and consumers.

Overall, things have moved rather slowly for the implementation of JA due to the ambitious targets to be achieved. The Sabah JCSPO Initiative was claimed as the most advanced Jurisdiction Initiative globally with the completion of the statewide Forest Carbon mapping (for HCS forests) and near completion of the HCV map (Kugan 2018). The state-specific FPIC guide was also developed with a further pilot cataloguing smallholder progress to be conducted in the Telupid, Tongod, Beluran, and Kinabatangan districts (Kugan 2018). There is a plan to extend the study area to Sugut, Lahad Datu, and Tawau landscapes, with a focus on the integration of production by growers with middle-sized holdings (Colchester 2020).

However, it was also acknowledged that a statewide implementation can be too ambitious, and hence the concentration was shifted to priority landscapes (Colchester 2020). This is true, especially considering the challenges faced by the smallholders revealed by field studies of the NGO "Forever Sabah" (FS) in 2018: poor agricultural practices, legality issues (lack of land title), and lack of financial management skills. Considerable resources would be required to make the villages "RSPO-compatible" (Wilson et al. 2018). A similar situation was observed in Seruyan, where the RSPO cautioned officers to just begin with subdistricts as they were ready and eventually expand the coverage (Suwastoyo 2019). Having said that, the JA provides a means to consolidate efforts made in addressing sustainability issues in different lines of inquiry. More lessons may be drawn from other cases that focus on, e.g., REDD+ and sustainable forest in Berau (see Chapter 9) or sustainable rubber in Kapuas Hulu (assisted by GIZ-FORCLIME and WWF) (Brede 2018).

Final Remarks

While market differentiation can serve as an instrument to govern sustainable agricultural production, the biggest shortcoming of the market-based strategy is the implicit assumption that action can be standardized, which is made without accounting for on-ground heterogeneity on both the supply and demand side. Past experience in Borneo offers several critiques of such an approach.

First, market fragmentation creates uncertainty and inflates costs. This further increases the complexity of the already complex, pluralistic governance system in the oil palm sector, imposing high transaction costs and unnecessary burdens on the transformation of land-based economies. Also, while much of the literature suggests that sustainability certification helps to support local livelihoods, empirical evidence is mixed. It seems that the effectiveness of certification schemes varies considerably with individual market characteristics and producers, highly depending on scales and local conditions.

Furthermore, crop- and market-based approaches cannot provide full solutions to changing the land-use systems at the root of the problem, as economic, environmental, and societal impacts traverse farm boundaries. Rather than concentrating narrowly on what is happening within a restricted monoculture (and hence indirectly promoting it), the focus may be broadened to ensure sustainability on a landscape scale. Chapter 8 provides further discussion in this direction.

7

Creating New Domestic Demand for Cash Crops

Malaysia and Indonesia have been relying on the export of cash crops for revenue and, in exchange, the import of other food products to meet local demand. Especially, Borneo is a prominent region for such a model of development—it has relatively limited rice production (the staple food throughout Borneo) but extensive export-oriented oil palm plantations. This model, unfortunately, has proven to be highly risky to both the economy and food security when prices of commodities drop substantially (Figure 7.1). After enjoying almost a decade of growth in the 2000s, the palm oil sector

FIGURE 7.1
Price Trends of Crude Palm Oil in 2000–20

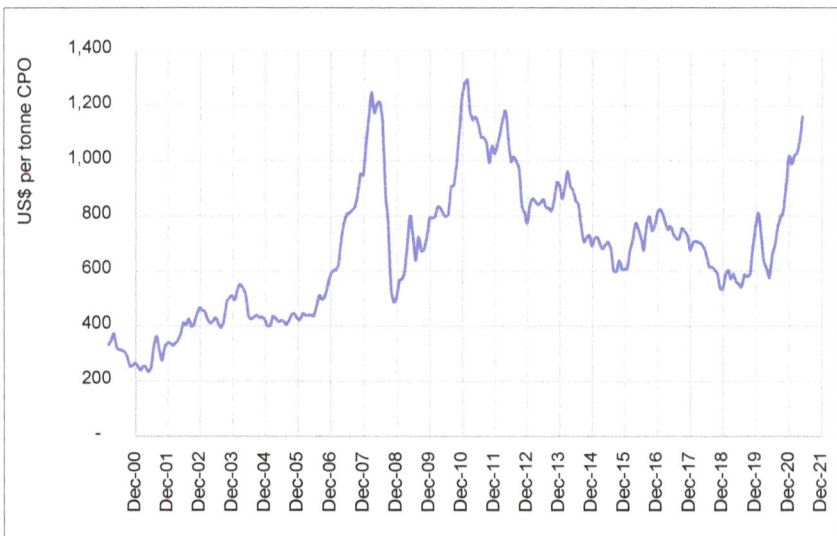

Source: IndexMundi (2021); MPOB (2021).

was hit by several market shocks with the greatest one in 2009. The global economic instability in recent years, especially the US-China trade war, the Saudi Arabia-Russia oil price war, and the global COVID-19 pandemic have imposed serious risks on such export-oriented economies. A few times, fresh fruit bunches were left to rot on smallholdings when prices were too low and unattractive; so plantations refused to accept the fruit and farmers had no alternative market.

Creating new local demands to take up the excessive stock as a buffer for sudden price dips has been a strategy adopted by the governments in the face of great economic uncertainties. In addition, domestic markets for various bio-based products, including those made of waste materials, may also help to stabilize local economies and farmers' incomes. This is tagged along with the multiple objectives of replacing fossil-based with bio-based materials and establishing a self-sufficient circular economic ecosystem. It can also stimulate the growth of local bio-based industries. Several successes observed around the world are often cited, such as the case of Brazil (sugarcane ethanol) and Sweden (woody biomass for heat and power) (Silveira and Johnson 2016). This strategy closes the loop of a bio-economy from supply to demand. To do so, proper policy directives and incentives to boost local demand would be necessary.

This chapter provides an overview of two categories of potential markets in Borneo as well as on a broader national scale in Malaysia and Indonesia: (i) the food sector, and (ii) the non-food sector. This chapter mainly uses a country perspective as this strategy relies on policies at the national level. However, the situation in Borneo is discussed wherever applicable or data is available.

FOOD SECTORS

One way to address the potential stockpiling of CPO due to low prices is diverting the stock to the local market by substituting it for imports of vegetable oil. Figure 7.2 displays the trade balance of both countries in 2014–17. Theoretically, there is still room for import substitution in Malaysia, where imports of both fatty acids and palm oil from Indonesia are two major contributors, followed by other cooking oils like soy oil and sunflower oil (FAOSTAT 2021). One possible explanation is that certified palm oil produced in Malaysia may be sold at higher prices in the high-end markets, while the gap in the local market was filled by non-certified, lower-priced palm oil from Indonesia. This implies that implementing this strategy may face competition not only from other vegetable oils but also more competitive (in terms of price) Indonesian palm oil.

FIGURE 7.2

Oils and Fats Trade Balance of Malaysia and Indonesia in 2014–17

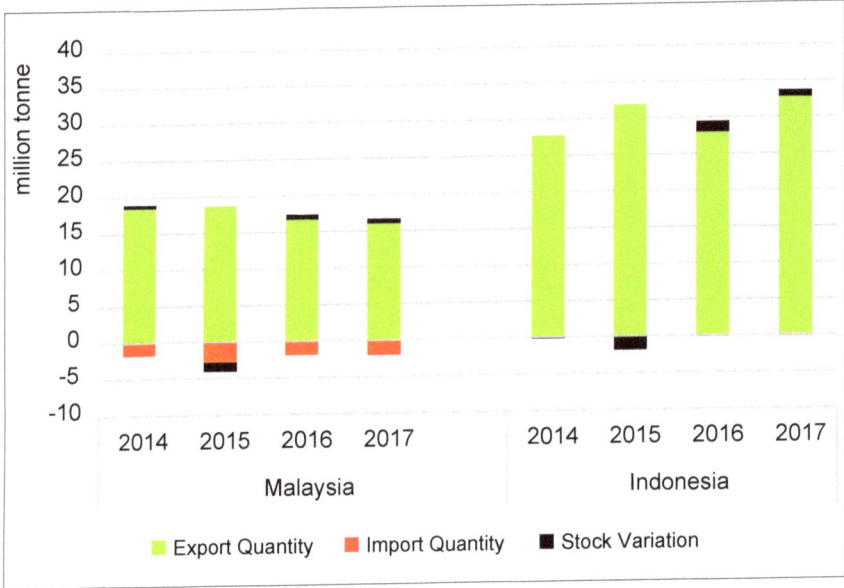

Source: FAOSTAT (2021).

It is clear that Indonesia has always relied on its own palm oil in the past few years, and therefore import substitution is less relevant. However, one should note that there is a remarkable gap in fats uptake per capita between Indonesia and Malaysia, not to mention with world-leading consumers, i.e., the US and the EU. The per capita fat supply from vegetable oils and animal fats in Malaysia and Indonesia are about 49 and 27 g per day, respectively, while the numbers in the US and the EU are about 78 and 53 g per day, respectively (FAOSTAT 2021). Considering these gaps, the potential of palm oil in the local food sectors remains significant, especially in Indonesia.

There might also be a shift from the use of animal fats to plant-based oils in the future, but the amount of total consumption of animal fats is relatively small. Figure 7.3 takes a closer look into the use of vegetable oils for different purposes in both countries. For food use, Malaysians generally consume less palm oil directly by proportion, but it is mainly used in processed food. It may be expected that the future growth of palm oil consumption in Indonesia may concentrate on the food processing sector if it follows the trend in Malaysia. One can also clearly see that vegetable

FIGURE 7.3
The National Share of Vegetable Oils Used for Non-Food Purposes in 2017

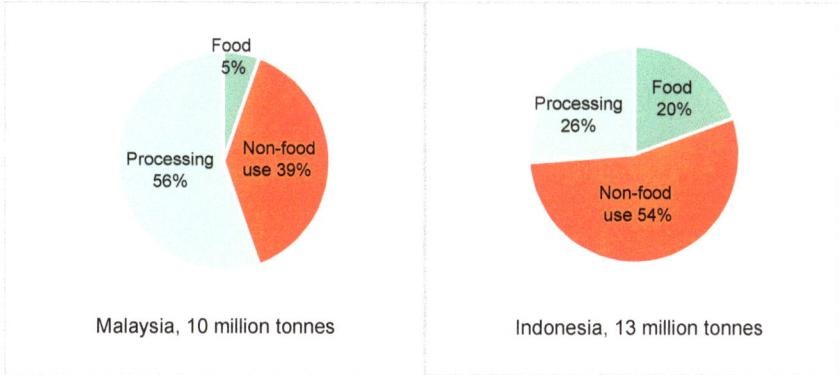

Malaysia, 10 million tonnes

Indonesia, 13 million tonnes

Note: National production in 2017 is about 25 and 46 million tonnes for Malaysia and Indonesia, respectively.
Source: FAOSTAT (2021).

oils play a very important role in non-food use—this is elucidated in the next section of this chapter.

NON-FOOD SECTORS

Liquid Biofuels

Since the 2000s, biofuel production, particularly biodiesel from palm oil, has been a popular topic in Malaysia and Indonesia. In 2006, the blending of biodiesel became mandatory in both countries, under the National Biofuel Policy (Malaysia) and Presidential Instruction on Biofuel Supply and Utilization (Indonesia), with a gradual annual increment target (Abdullah et al. 2009; Caroko et al. 2011). These policies carry the objectives of reducing reliance on fossil diesel and boosting energy security.

However, export to Europe has been the major focus in the early days. Large volumes of biodiesel were sold to the EU Member States to fulfil the blending target in the early 2010s. While the export business flourished for a few years, it has now run into a dead end. In 2018, the EU Renew Energy Directives (RED) ruled that the EU will phase out feedstock that may potentially involve indirect land-use change (ILUC) by 2030 (European Commission 2019). Although the mechanism to quantify the impacts of ILUC remains questionable, palm oil (and only palm oil) was included in the high ILUC category. Based on the new directive, from 2020 until 2023,

EU member states' maximum share of palm oil-based biodiesel that can be counted towards the EU renewable transport targets (and thus eligible for subsidies) will be capped at the 2019 levels. It will then be progressively phased out of renewable targets to 0 per cent by 2030 (European Commission 2019). This is not much of a surprise with the continuous strong objection to palm-based biodiesel throughout the EU.

In this regard, domestic consumption has become increasingly important for the industry. A domestic biodiesel market can act as a buffer for excessive stock in certain years resulting from the fluctuating CPO prices throughout the cycles of the commodity market (Goh and Lee 2010). Figure 7.4 illustrates the consumption, production, and export of palm oil and diesel in both countries with Borneo specially indicated. Palm oil biodiesel may replace a considerable amount of diesel even taking the blend wall, i.e., engine compatibility for a high blend rate, into account. In 2019, the blend rate reached 20 per cent in Indonesia but only 10 per cent in Malaysia. The adjustment of blend rates provides flexibility to strategically

FIGURE 7.4

Production, Consumption, and Trade of CPO in Comparison to the Consumption of Diesel for the Year 2019

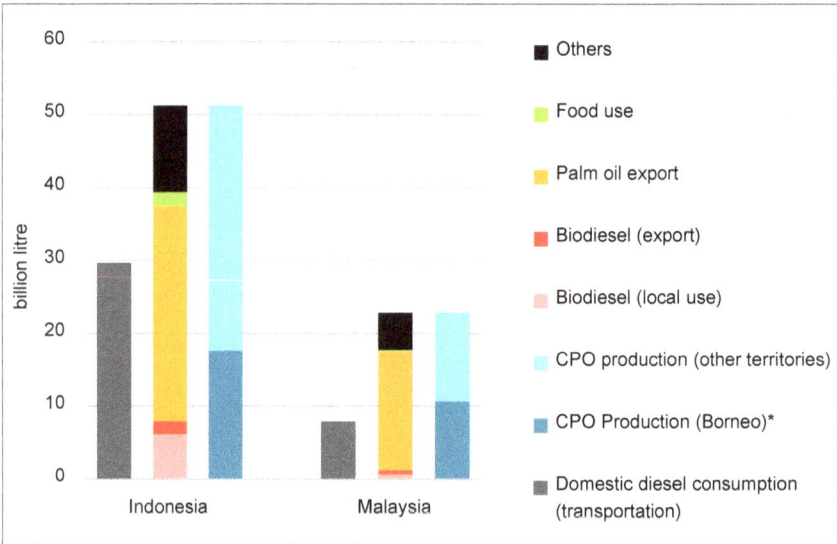

Note: *Sabah and Sarawak for the case of Malaysia, Kalimantan for the case of Indonesia.
In 2019, the actual blend rates are 20 per cent in Indonesia and 10 per cent in Malaysia.
Source: DG Estate Crop Indonesia (2019); Rahmanulloh (2020); Wahab (2020); FAOSTAT (2021); MPOB (2021).

manage the available resources (export for revenues during high prices, consume domestically during low prices), especially considering that both countries are also major petroleum producers.

In Malaysia, biodiesel consumption was promoted as early as the 1980s under the Promotion of Investment Act 1986 and incentivized with a tax allowance, but the progress was insignificant (Abdullah et al. 2009). In 2005, the National Biofuel Policy was introduced with a more comprehensive framework, including planned subsidies to blend processed palm oil into diesel. Its focus on the plantation industry was clear as the Ministry of Plantation Industries and Commodities was assigned to spearhead the implementation. The first target was set to 5 per cent by 2009 (B5 biodiesel), and some government departments and government-linked agencies were instructed to be the first few buyers.

As mentioned earlier, export to the EU was the main focus initially. Domestically, the biodiesel policy was shadowed by uncertainties in markets and subsidies, a vague governing framework, poor coordination among the ministries, and overly high expectations (Rahyla, Radin Firdaus, and Purwaningrum 2017). However, full implementation was achieved in 2014 (with Sabah and Sarawak included), and the blend rate reached 10 per cent by 2019. This may be largely attributed to the plunge in palm oil prices that allowed more uptake by the transportation industries (before 2019) as well as the decline in export to the EU (after 2019) (Wahab 2020). Instead of making it mandatory, the government adopted a more flexible approach, combining an automatic pricing mechanism (Hanafi and Raj 2011) and a voluntary blending rate that permits the fuel users to decide according to market prices.

In Indonesia, the early government target set under the biofuel promotion policy in 2006 was to achieve 10 per cent of fossil fuel substitution in the transportation sector within five years. The state energy company, Pertamina, was instructed to mix at least 2 per cent of biofuel into diesel fuel (Zhou and Thomson 2009). However, with the soaring price of palm oil in that period, the plan failed dismally (Goh and Lee 2010). A whole new mechanism was implemented in 2015 when the palm oil price dropped to the lowest level in the past 8 years. Subsidies were reallocated to the transportation sector using the revenues collected from a palm oil export levy.

In this context, Indonesia launched an ambitious blending rate for on-road transport of B30 in January 2020. This was three times higher than the next highest rate, B10, for any other country (Rahmanulloh 2020). By 2019, the palm oil consumed domestically as transportation fuels reached

6.4 billion litres with a blend rate of 20 per cent despite the huge decline in the exported volume of biodiesel. This was a big leap compared to 13 per cent in 2018. The 30 per cent blending target may be achieved in 2020 with 7.7 billion litres of biodiesel, owing to the reduced total consumption of diesel during the pandemic year (Rahmanulloh 2020). However, to further maintain the 30 per cent blend rate in the future, higher volumes may be needed. This raised the question of how Indonesia could meet the blending target while at the same time providing palm oil for food consumption and reserving a proportion for the export of palm oil (Khatiwada, Palmén, and Silveira 2018). As the CPO price has recovered substantially in 2021 (see Figure 9.3), it would be more logical to export for revenues instead of domestic consumption. Ideally, this strategy should be complementarily implemented with the strategy of boosting the productivity of smallholders (see Chapter 3) to achieve both energy security and rural development. However, the implementation is likely to be slow due to the low global cost of fossil diesel and reduced transport use by Indonesians during the COVID crisis.

In any case, liquid biofuels remain controversial with numerous sustainability and technical challenges encountered since the early days, especially the land-use impacts, food-fuel debates, and blend wall (Ashworth et al. 2012; Johari et al. 2015). Especially, the blend wall becomes a major concern with Indonesia's new achievement of B30. In terms of air pollution, a problem that concerns citizens the most, the contribution of biodiesel may not be significant in comparison with the other cleaner fuels, e.g., "low sulphur diesel" (Searle and Bitnere 2018). This makes them less attractive in competition with the electrification of the public transportation system (especially buses on diesel fuels) as a better option to reduce air pollution in urban areas. The biodiesel may also increase the corrosion of various metal components in the vehicle and plugging of filters and seals, necessitating frequent replacement, and increasing vehicle maintenance costs.

In terms of greenhouse gas emissions from the entire production chain (e.g., land use, milling, processing, and transportation), Harsono et al. (2012) estimated a range of carbon payback time from eleven to forty-two years for the case of Indonesian palm oil depending on the different types of land conversion. This has not included potential emissions from indirect land-use change (ILUC), e.g., the conversion of forests elsewhere to produce more vegetable oils for covering the demand gap in non-fuel sectors (Goh, Wicke, Faaij, et al. 2016; Goh, Wicke, Verstegen, et al. 2016). While the carbon balance issues have effectively blocked the entry of palm-based biodiesel into the EU market, the domestic biodiesel policies have not taken these into account.

An exotic species, namely Jatropha (*Jatropha curcas*) or *Jarak pagar* was also regarded as a potential fuel crop in both countries due to the expected low input and the possibility of it being cultivated on degraded land. In Sarawak, jatropha was aggressively promoted by some companies as an option to mobilize native customary lands (Mintz-Habib 2013). However, almost all of the plans fell apart due to unrealistic expectations. Fatimah (2015) used the term "fantasy" to describe such expectations, which were largely based on normative values (e.g., beliefs in technocracy) and personal interests instead of scientific analyses and understanding.

Other types of biofuels, e.g., bioethanol, were not competitive compared to palm-based biodiesel. Bioethanol from lignocellulosic biomass (especially oil palm residues) has been studied for decades, but no commercial production has been realized (Goh et al. 2010). There are no extra incentives given to second-generation biofuels as in the EU and US.

Bioenergy and Biomaterials

Bioenergy and biomaterials have been gaining attention among policymakers and stakeholders in recent years. This is in line with the emerging concept of "circular economy" that aims at keeping products and materials in use for a longer period, optimizing the resources in different forms and for different purposes. It minimizes pollution and creates new value from waste streams. In the context of the land-based economy, this means converting low-value bioresources, especially various types of residues from agriculture and forestry to higher-value energy carriers and biomaterials.

As previously described in Chapter 5, an abundant amount of agricultural and forestry residues is being generated in Borneo. Incentives are given to stimulate the use of biomass for power generation locally, as part of the national energy policies in reducing emissions and improving energy security, in the form of Feed-in-Tariffs (FITs) with prices fixed by the government since 2014 in Malaysia (rolled out to Sabah in 2014 but excluding Sarawak) and Indonesia, respectively (Bakhtyar et al. 2013; Umar, Jennings, and Urmee 2014). The use of local bioresources for energy purposes is not only perceived as an option to ease the stress of energy security in low population density areas due to high fuel cost and limited accessibility, but also an opportunity to create new jobs and income for the rural population (Pang and Lee 2013).

Without considering the mobilization costs, the theoretical potential of bioenergy is enormous in Borneo as shown in Figure 7.5 which has not

FIGURE 7.5
Potential Bioenergy for Electricity at 30 per cent of Conversion Efficiency,
Excluding Biogas from Palm Oil Mill Effluents

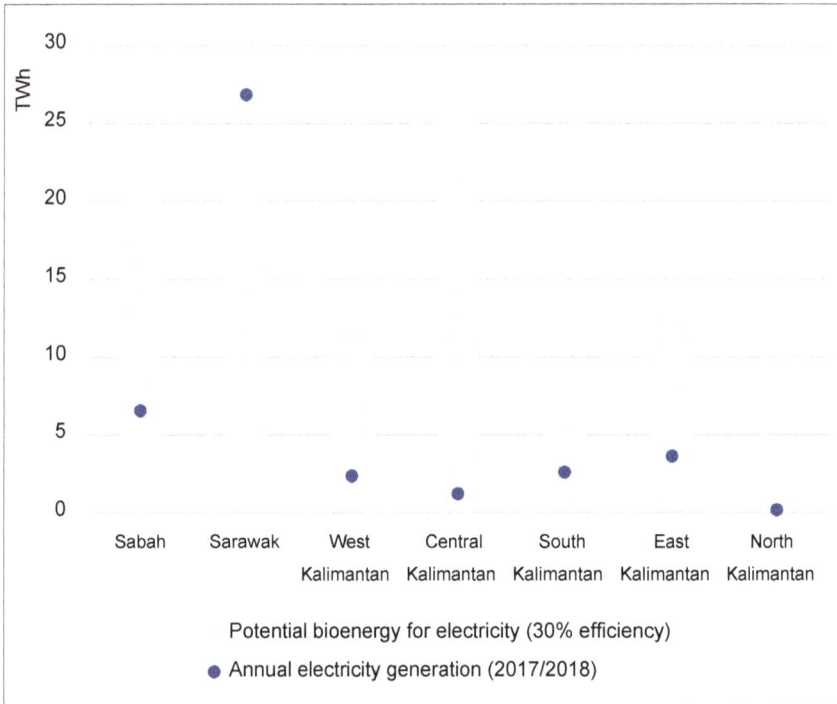

Potential bioenergy for electricity (30% efficiency)
● Annual electricity generation (2017/2018)

Notes and Sources:
1. Potential bioenergy for electricity: Own estimation based on (Goh et al. 2010; Simangunsong et al. 2017; BPS 2020; MPOB 2021) and personal communication with government officials.
2. Annual electricity generation data: 2017 for Malaysian states and 2018 for Indonesian provinces (BPS 2020; Malaysia's Energy Commission 2020).
3. The estimated primary energy from biomass for Sabah, 257 PJ, is close to the 267 PJ estimated by Suzuki et al. (2017).

yet included biogas from palm oil mill effluents (POME). By 2017, total electricity generation from bioresources, mainly on-site at palm oil and paper mills, has reached 0.7 and 9.7 terawatt hours (TWh) in Malaysia and Indonesia (mainly in Sumatra) (IRENA 2020). In Malaysian Borneo, there are nine bioenergy plants in operation on the east coast of Sabah with a total capacity of about 100 MW. Most of these plants are small with a capacity of <10MW but contribute to about 4 per cent of the total electricity generation of the state (Suruhanjaya Tenaga 2014). For example, Ngan et al. (2019) reported a case of converting palm-based biomass to energy by QL Tawau Palm Pellet Sdn Bhd (Malaysia) in Sabah. However, in Sarawak, only a small amount of biomass is used (mainly internally by palm oil mills) as the state is already largely powered by cheap hydroelectricity with the existence of mega hydropower facilities (Shirley and Kammen 2015). Also, the state is yet to be covered by the FIT scheme. In West Kalimantan, the first biomass power plant (15 MW) by the state-owned power company started operating in 2018, aiming to consume about 100 tonnes of agricultural residues (*Jakarta Post*, 25 April 2018) (and see the recent strategy by PLN to move some old coal-fired plants to co-fire with biomass, as noted in Chapter 5).

Overall, the progress to date is still slow throughout Borneo due to the high cost of mobilizing the widely dispersed biomass resources and inadequate grid connection (Aghamohammadi et al. 2016). This corresponds to the root causes of energy poverty in rural areas—the population is widely dispersed across the interior, including areas with difficult terrain and thick rainforests. A more efficient grid integration, such as the Sabah Green Grid proposed by Hashim, Khairuddin, and Ibrahim (2015), may allow further mobilization of previously inaccessible biomass resources. However, a small-scale bioenergy system is also deemed a potential option to be combined with other renewable energy sources like solar power and micro-hydropower for villages spread widely in the interior where the grid extension is not financially feasible (Izadyar et al. 2016). Such a hybridized renewable energy system requires a close understanding of how these systems can be integrated with the biomass supply chain, including local agriculture. Experience, e.g., in Ba'Kelalan of Kelabit Highlands, Sarawak shows that non-technical challenges like providing technical training for villagers should be carefully considered too in this kind of decentralized and diversified setting (Murni et al. 2013).

Meanwhile, wood-based biomass is also still largely used as cooking fuel throughout Indonesia and possibly the interiors of Malaysian Borneo (IRENA and ACE 2016). This type of traditional cooking system may impose negative impacts on both health and the environment when used excessively. While replacing these traditional fuels with natural gas is less practical in the near future considering maintaining a continuous, long supply chain, upgrading them to a cleaner system with advanced stoves and modern biofuels like biochar from local bioresources may be a potential solution (Rambli et al. 2019; Reza et al. 2019).

One should also take note of alternative uses of biomass. In places with poorer soil quality like Central Kalimantan, agricultural residues are largely used for mulching, i.e., returned to the soil as fertilizer (personal communication with industrial informants). Other agricultural residues can also be potentially used as composting materials (Wahi et al. 2019). The potential of oil palm residues, especially fronds and trunks in making composite boards was also explored (Rasat et al. 2011). These alternative uses (especially mulching) may significantly reduce the amount of biomass readily available for energy.

Meanwhile, a proposal frequently discussed in the oil palm industry is upgrading conventional palm oil mills to modern biorefineries with clean power generation from methane released from POME. Untreated POME releases a great amount of methane, one of the most potent greenhouse gases into the atmosphere. At the moment, many mills in Borneo still do not have proper treatment systems for POME. Regulations of all the RSPO, ISPO, and MSPO insist on the reduction of greenhouse gases from POME. Nasution et al. (2020) and Rana et al. (2017) explore different techniques for securing this result, with the former concluding that open lagoon technology, together with biogas technology and composting were the most suitable environmentally friendly treatments. However, there is presently no marketing channel for the biogas produced, as although mills may not be too far from population centres, securing a power and gas grid connection is usually difficult and electrification of nearby villages is slow to develop. How to combine environmental legislation (make POME treatment compulsory) and economic incentives to make this happen is still a challenge to policymakers (Loh et al. 2017).

In the case of Indonesia, Harahap et al. (2020) take this topic much further by examining the potential of advanced biorefineries that convert various feedstocks to a range of energy carriers to optimally meet demand locally and elsewhere in the country. Suitable locations of these mills in Sumatra and Kalimantan are suggested, to reduce the length of the supply chains. Based on the analysis, specific locations for the biorefineries in Kalimantan, nearest to Java, would be predominantly in Central and to a lesser extent, South Kalimantan. Similar efforts were long made for Sabah and Sarawak in the framework of the National Biomass Strategy but materializing such advanced biorefineries remains challenging (AIM 2013).

Final Remarks

The creation of local markets for bio-based products may provide a buffer to contain the risk of relying on export-oriented monoculture. While both countries have achieved relatively impressive growth in the agriculture sector, the general productivity level of advanced bio-materials remains low and domestic markets for bio-based products remain underdeveloped. Malaysia and Indonesia are only midsize economies and do not have much flexibility to accommodate more costly biofuel, bioenergy, and bio-based materials.

The latecomer status, however, allows both countries to emulate the examples of pioneers like those in Europe, which have learnt many lessons in the past two decades. This implies a greater role for governments in enhancing the capacity of local industries to respond to the uptake of bio-based products in substituting for fossil-based materials. The key challenge will be in channelling resources in the requisite directions to address coordination problems that cannot be adequately solved by the individual sectors. For example, the incentives allocated to the agricultural, food, industrial, and energy industries may be reshuffled to more effectively respond to the global market to optimize economic opportunities and minimize the risks. As rightly pointed out by Umar, Urmee, and Jennings (2018), effectively consolidating the various incentives scattered in different sectors and forms (from upstream to downstream, from land use to energy) is necessary to optimize the deployment of bioenergy. Only with innovative integration of value chains between agriculture, forestry, energy, and food sectors, this strategy may remain a potential option to reshape the supply-demand dynamics and thus land-use strategies in both countries.

PART III

ECO-ECONOMY: CONSERVATION-ORIENTED STRATEGIES

Longhouse, Toba (West Kalimantan) (taken by Potter in 2013).

Photos on previous page

1. Forest fruits, Toba (West Kalimantan) (taken by Potter in 2013).

2. "Heart of Borneo" advertisement board (Central Kalimantan) (taken by Goh in 2014).

3. Batu Punggul, Sapulut (Sabah) (taken by Goh in 2022).

4. Orangutans at Tanjung Puting National Park (Central Kalimantan) (taken by Potter in 2007).

5. Mt Kinabalu (Sabah) (taken by Ang Seong Chen in 2009, with permission).

8

Enhancing Landscape Resilience

Resilience to agroecological disturbances, i.e., the capacity of the land-use systems to anticipate and adapt to environmental changes in a timely and efficient manner, has gained more and more attention not only for its environmental implications but also for socio-economic importance. A resilient production system is able to absorb shocks and stresses like droughts, floods, pests, and diseases while maintaining production. Some shocks and stresses can be predictable, but some can come at unexpected times. Coping with these is therefore critical to protect the economies (Walker et al. 2010). This requires rethinking and redesigning the existing production systems from a conventional economy that focuses on maximizing short-term production to an eco-economy that considers long-term resilience.

The recurring droughts and uncontrolled peat fires throughout Borneo are prominent examples. In 2015, the direct economic loss due to peat fire was estimated to be US$16 billion for Indonesia alone (Glauber et al. 2016) and the amount of CO_2 released into the atmosphere in one month was more than the annual emission of Japan (Field et al. 2016). Not yet included are indirect health impacts and ecological damage, e.g., increased tree mortality (Kumagai and Porporato 2012). Neighbouring countries, especially Malaysia and Singapore have experienced tremendous economic losses due to transboundary haze (Nguitragool 2010).

One of the key factors is the large-scale degradation of peatland as a result of the Mega Rice Project (MRP) by the Indonesian government in 1995 which aimed to convert 1 million ha of peatland for rice production (see Chapter 2). Not only did it fail to achieve its objective of rice production, but it has also drastically exacerbated the impacts of droughts and fire. In addition to protection, careful restoration of degraded peatland and damaged ecosystem services are necessary to ensure the long-term resilience of not only Borneo but also the entire region (Possingham, Bode, and Klein 2015). However, reversing the natural systems that have been altered for decades is a very challenging task (Laurance 2016). The rising temperatures and extreme precipitation regimes due to global climate change may further increase the frequency, duration, and severity of the drought and fire events in Borneo.

To effectively enhance resilience to the upcoming pervasive threats, an integrated approach that covers both the agroecological and socio-economic systems is required. This chapter reviews the efforts made in Borneo in the past two decades from (i) the agroecological perspectives in terms of landscape planning and peatland restoration and (ii) the socio-economic perspectives in terms of landscape governance as well as technical and financial support.

Agroecological Perspectives

Landscape Planning

Enhancing resilience requires system thinking that considers various drivers, impacts, and feedback nested in multiple levels across a landscape (Berkes and Ross 2013). A diverse landscape that can supply a broad range of functions, products, and ecosystem services is less vulnerable to external shocks (de Vos 2016). The rapid decline of ecosystem services due to excessive land exploitation will substantially cripple agroecological resilience, such as the deterioration of water quality, fish, vegetable, animal resources, and non-timber forest products (Rahajoe et al. 2014; Safitri et al. 2018; Wilkinson et al. 2018). Alarmed by the decline in agroecological resilience, benefits apart from the economic output, such as food security, health and well-being are increasingly recognized by land users and governments (Fidiashtry et al. 2017; Sang et al. 2018). A holistic management that forges synergies between different land uses and ecosystem services throughout the landscape, or so-called a "landscape approach", may avoid unwanted environmental impacts and also create opportunities for restoration (Sayer et al. 2013).

The shift of perspective to the landscape level leads to a debate over the concepts of "land sparing" and "land sharing". The former advocates a clear separation of conservation areas and productive areas, while the latter suggests an integration of both. Land sparing was reported to be more advantageous for optimizing logging operations and monoculture plantations (Edwards, Gilroy, et al. 2014), but it can also be difficult to implement effectively, considering the sporadic use of land by the local communities. For example, Santika, Meijaard, and Wilson (2015) reported that forests surrounding commercial concessions were more likely to be cleared by the communities.

Importantly, some areas should be given top priority for conservation. Borneo has been in the limelight of this development. It is hoped that by adopting the "High Conservation Value" (HCV) concept described in Chapter 4, the island may see new opportunities for conservation in a landscape that is already dominated by oil palm. For example, riparian buffers are necessary not only to mitigate land conversion impacts on biodiversity (Chellaiah and Yule 2018b) and water quality (Chellaiah and Yule 2018a) but also to ensure the long-term viability of agricultural activities by slowing rates of riverbank erosion and lateral channel migration (Horton et al. 2018). Watersheds with greater tree cover are also less prone to flooding compared to those exposed to mining or oil palm plantations (Wells et al. 2016). These measures may significantly reduce flood frequency in Borneo which was found to be on the rise in the past few years in areas with extensive land-use activities (floods affected possibly as many as 5–10 per cent of the total population in Kalimantan in 2013–16) (Wells et al. 2016). Recently, severe floods in South Kalimantan in January 2021 killed twenty-one people and affected 256,000 ha. Deforestation in the Barito watershed, together with extensive mining and plantation development has been blamed for the extent and severity of the flooding, according to environmentalists, although the government has denied such claims (Jong 2021b).

Restoring patches of non-forested land surrounded by ecologically important areas (see Figure 8.1 for examples) may substantially improve habitat connectivity and hence the resilience of local flora and fauna (Proctor, McClean, and Hill 2011). For example, reconnecting forest patches to recover access to large water bodies can be critical for the survival of many species as demonstrated by the cases of the proboscis monkey and Bornean banteng in Sabah, documented by Boonratana (2013) and Lim et al. (2019), respectively. Understanding the diet of animals is also important for landscape planning to avoid human-animal conflicts (Suba et al. 2017). Reconnecting those once contiguous ecosystems can also reduce the risk of fire due to edge effects (Qie et al. 2017). Based on the evidence in the Lower Kinabatangan Wildlife Sanctuary, Sabah across seventeen years, Evans, Goossens, and Asner (2017) found that the regrowth areas have attracted Bornean elephants to establish corridor habitats from previously isolated patches. Including connectivity as a major target in landscape planning will generate large benefits for conservation (Williams et al. 2020).

FIGURE 8.1

A Snapshot of Heterogeneity of Land Cover in Borneo

Forest on mineral soil
Mangrove forest
Peat-swamp forest
Non forest
Smallholder oil palm plantation
Industrial oil palm plantation
Industrial pulpwood plantation

Source: CIFOR (2020).

Various studies have shown that setting certain areas within oil palm plantations for not only conservation but also enrichment planting would effectively improve the ecosystem services and carbon stock of the agricultural landscape (Fleiss et al. 2020). Some areas located next to the plantations, especially those within oil palm concessions, may have undergone natural regeneration, and require further protection from plantation expansion to ensure their full recovery (Scriven et al. 2019). In addition, some areas may have important agroecological functions for local communities, such as *pulau* (the Malay word for island) in Sarawak, and the isolated forest reserves that were traditionally maintained as seed orchards (Takeuchi et al. 2013). A series of studies in Sabah suggested that keeping forest remnants mingled with oil palm plantations may facilitate productivity through, e.g., pest control (Gray et al. 2014; Lucey et al. 2014). However, other researchers found no evidence of either positive or negative impacts on oil palm yield or pest control by nearby forest fragments (Edwards, Edwards, et al. 2014; Gray and Lewis 2014).

A key concern is the determination of the HCV areas in terms of the size and distribution of the fragmented patches across the landscape. While particularly larger patches contribute significantly to biodiversity, smaller ones may be artificially connected if they are close to each other. How these areas can be conserved and managed in smarter ways is the main question for the idea of conservation inside oil palm plantations. Past experience shows that the effectiveness of a mosaic landscape in maintaining ecosystem services is difficult to monitor and measure (Sayer et al. 2016).

However, a monocultural landscape clearly has major drawbacks. For example, the monospecific acacia plantations throughout Borneo are highly susceptible to pests and diseases, despite acacia trees being more competitive over some native species (Lee 2018b; Le et al. 2019). For certain parts of Borneo, the reactivation of abandoned monocultural timber plantations by introducing native species in combination with natural forest regeneration may be a practical strategy (Brockerhoff et al. 2008; Crouzeilles et al. 2017). Many *Acacia mangium* industrial plantations in Kalimantan (as well as in other parts of Indonesia) are required compulsorily to incorporate "green belts" of natural forest as habitat corridors, though these have sometimes become the target of illegal loggers (Potter and Badcock 2001). Some suggested that with proper management, larger continuous forest landscapes may be better maintained by combining protected areas with production forests, preventing natural forests from being converted to monocultural plantations (Gaveau et al. 2013).

Some also proposed incorporating drought-adapted genotypes into restoration programmes to cope with anticipated climate change, as drought can significantly slow down or even reverse regeneration (Axelsson et al. 2019; Qie et al. 2019). This method, however, shares the same risk as introducing exotic species that may potentially compete with and displace native species (Döbert et al. 2018). The invasion of heath forests in Borneo by acacia trees is a clear lesson (Le et al. 2019). In any case, trade-offs have to be made and "restoration" may not produce the same ecosystem as previously existed as the composition and conditions will likely be significantly altered (Page and Hoscilo 2018).

Instead of struggling with dichotomized land-use strategies in terms of land sparing and land sharing, the analysis by Law et al. (2017) on Central Kalimantan shows that flexible combinations of both gave the best overall performance. Considering the spillover effects, sustainable use of forests, based on a better understanding of local socio-economic dynamics with more flexibility in land-use planning may provide larger conservation gains in the long term (Runting et al. 2019). A quick start would be to eliminate bad land-use plans that make little financial sense but cause serious environmental impacts, such as expanding oil palm on flood-prone riparian areas or in deep peat (Abram, Xofis, et al. 2014).

For Borneo, the adoption of the JA approach described in Chapter 6 may be the biggest "experiment" in integrated landscape planning that is worth careful observation and evaluation. The excellent survey of the JA approach in Indonesia to more sustainable and equitable land use by Seymour, Aurora, and Arif (2020) has identified major progress since its inception in 2014. Within Kalimantan, there have been initiatives in several provinces and districts. In East Kalimantan through its governor's ambition for low-carbon development and especially the example of Berau district, assisted by The Nature Conservancy. In Central Kalimantan, the move was led by the previous governor, developing a Roadmap to Low-deforestation Rural Development, then through INOBU, working at the district level in Seruyan, Kotawaringin Barat, and Gunung Mas to achieve sustainable palm oil, together with Unilever, which has committed to preferential sourcing from jurisdictions moving towards sustainability.

Peatland Restoration and Fire Management
Uncontrolled peat fire has been a major threat to the agro-production system in Central and West Kalimantan, and a lesser extent in the other Bornean territories. Peat is an accumulation of partially decayed vegetation or organic matter. The total peat area in the Kalimantan provinces is reported

FIGURE 8.2
Distribution of Peatland and Burnt Areas in Borneo

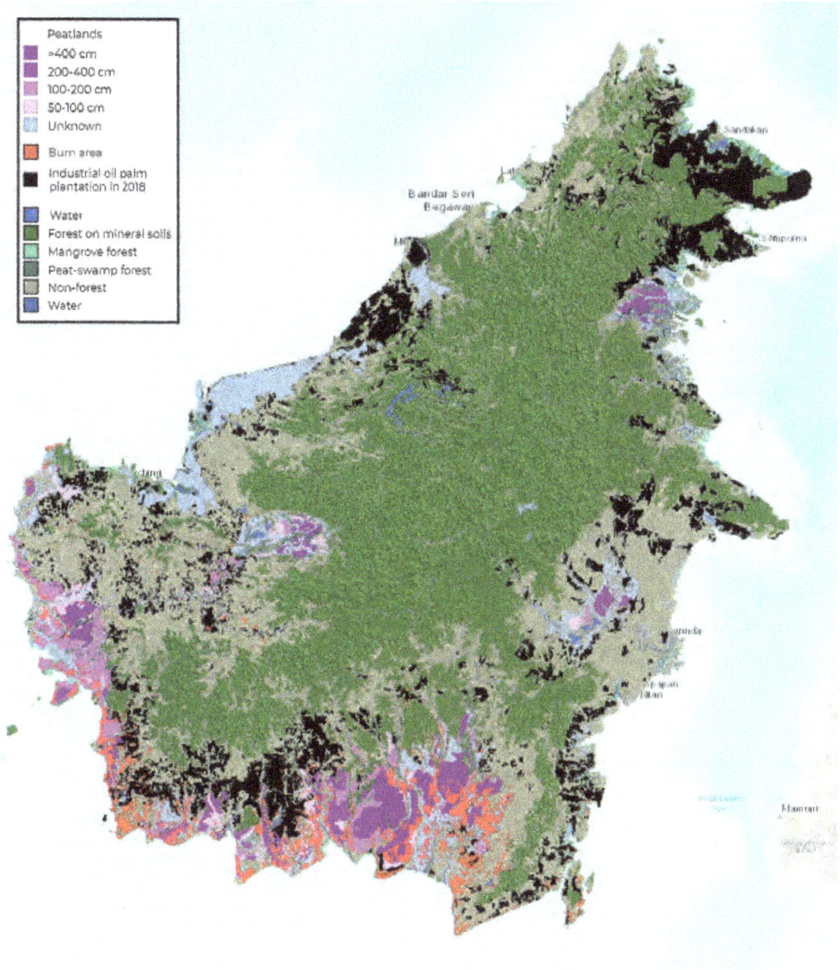

Note: Burnt areas were captured in 2019; only available for West, South, and Central Kalimantan.
Source: CIFOR (2020).

in a wide range from 4.8 to 8.4 million ha (mainly in Central and West Kalimantan), while Sarawak has about 1.6 million ha (Melling 2016; Osaki et al. 2016; MoEF 2020b) (see Figure 8.2 for the distribution of peatland in Borneo). Despite its ecological importance, tropical peatland in Borneo is still considered understudied. The failed Mega Rice Project (MRP) in Central Kalimantan in 1995 exposed the lack of knowledge on peatland hydrology and management problems (see Chapter 2). Overdrainage of peatland in the province greatly accelerated peat decomposition and increased land vulnerability to fire especially during dry seasons. The uncontrolled burning of peat not only releases an enormous amount of terrestrial carbon into the atmosphere but also destroys farms and forests, changing soil characteristics and reducing plant diversity (Agus, Azmi, et al. 2019; Agus, Ilfana, et al. 2019).

The sources of fire can be multiple, including deliberate burning for large-scale land clearing and slash-and-burn practices by the local communities. Following the fire incidences in 2007, the Indonesian Ministry of Forestry reported that about 64 per cent of the hotspots were linked to the communities, while the rest were found in industrial plantations (25 per cent) and forest concessions (11 per cent) (Saharjo 2014). In their comprehensive section on the management and rehabilitation of peat ecosystems, the Department of Environment and Forestry in *The State of Indonesia's Forests 2020* divided such systems into those in concession areas (industrial plantation forests, mainly in Sumatra, and oil palm plantations) and those on community land (MoEF 2020b). Following inventory and detailed mapping, they suggested the relative proportions were 21 per cent in concession areas and 79 per cent utilized by communities. There were again very serious fires in Indonesia in the dry El Niño season of 2015 and also in 2019. The latter year was not under El Niño influence, but temperatures were high, causing the overheated peat to burn. Many small farmers suffered badly from the rampant spread of fire, having their farms (and sometimes houses) destroyed.

In 2009 the Indonesian government first introduced the concept of peatland restoration, followed by the 2014 regulation on peatland protection and management. The latter banned the conversion of peatland to plantations and encouraged peat restoration. Despite these measures, the 2015 fires are considered one of the biggest environmental disasters of the twenty-first century. Following the 2015 fires, the government launched an initiative in 2016 to restore 2.6 million ha of degraded peatland over seven priority provinces (three in Kalimantan) through the Peatland Restoration Agency (BRG).

Responding to possible legal challenges to restricting the activities of oil palm and plantation companies, a new regulation limited the area that must be protected to the actual peat domes, the area where the peat is thickest. Observers described this regulation as "dangerous", countering that entire peat landscapes must be conserved and not drained (Jong 2019b). It was argued that draining (in preparation for planting) would lead to subsidence, with massive carbon emissions and a dry and inflammable peat layer (Wetland International and Tropenbos International 2016).

In 2019, a "Peatland Water Level Information System 0.4 m" (to ensure water levels do not drop more than 0.4 m below the surface) was installed by the Ministry of Environment and Forestry to monitor data continuously online from 10,690 water level monitoring points and 792 rainfall stations. An Information System will integrate various data on water availability, potential vulnerability to drought and fire, and GHG reduction from increased peatland moisture. Unfortunately, this system, internationally recognized as "the world's most massive groundwater monitoring system", was not functioning soon enough to have an impact on the 2019 fires (MoEF 2020b). While the idea was to persuade companies to install these groundwater level monitoring devices and rainfall monitoring stations, as well as the construction of rewetting infrastructures, such as canal blocking, and vegetation rehabilitation, less than one-quarter of forest and oil palm plantations were fully compliant in these activities by 2019.

Nevertheless, the BRG claimed that by the end of 2020 initial efforts were made to rewet 94 per cent of its targets outside concessions. The MoEF claimed that between 2015 and 2019 it had restored 3.47 million ha of peatland (68 industrial forest concessions and 212 oil palm plantations, largely self-reported). There has been some scepticism among environmental NGOs concerning the validity of the figures for restored peatland, particularly for peatland located in concessions, especially as different (and much smaller) figures were reported in the National Medium-Term Development Plan (2020–24) (Greenpeace 2021).

To restore the peat ecosystem on community land, in 2016 the Ministry of Environment and Forestry, in collaboration with local governments, universities, and private interests, developed a programme to encourage community involvement, with concepts such as "bring back the water", "bring back the vegetation", and "improve community livelihoods". It includes rewetting and water level monitoring, revegetation, and planting agroforestry plots with suitable commodities, together with fish farming in some areas. The BRG also developed a "Village Peatland Awareness Programme" with more rewetting activities.

Despite multiple regulations such as the ban on using fire in agricultural practices, the situation has not significantly improved. While the low enforcement capacity is a major challenge, one fundamental issue is the different perspectives of stakeholders on peatland management. A more holistic understanding of the human-peatland relationship is required to strategize peatland restoration. Throughout Kalimantan, some communities still rely heavily on peatland for their livelihoods, including degraded peatland in the ex-MRP site. These include the remaining transmigrants from the original population sent to the ex-MRP site in the 1990s (Medrilzam et al. 2014), a new group sent to Dadahup more recently (Potter 2012), and the Ngaju Dayak villagers whose original livelihoods were sustainably adapted to the peat swamp conditions but were destroyed by the MRP. The Dayaks have now changed their system as they survive in the new circumstances, planting mainly rubber as well as rice, the latter relocated in mineral soil along the banks of the larger drains.

Recognizing the rights of peatland-based, marginal communities is essential to effectively address the issues of peatland degradation. How to maintain community livelihood, improve welfare, and address local politics are among the critical questions in resolving the risks of fire (Law, Bryan, Meijaard, et al. 2015). These questions were often overlooked not only by the governments but also by international organizations which initiated various conservation programmes (Jewitt et al. 2014). Controlling the use of fire and the "3R-approaches", i.e., rewetting, revegetation, and revitalization are technically the keys to peatland restoration. However, sustainable ways to utilize peatland for local food security and livelihood, especially with the right business models, are also necessary to reduce fire risks and facilitate restoration (Giesen and Nirmala 2018; Surahman, Soni, and Shivakoti 2018b; Surahman, Shivakoti, and Soni 2019; Silvianingsih et al. 2020).

Some have attempted to rank the sustainability of different cropping systems on peatland, suggesting that rice farming can be a better option than oil palm or rubber (Surahman, Soni, and Shivakoti 2018a). Others instead, proposed that different species, such as sago, banana, pineapple, and many other fruits may be better suited in different modes, depending on the spatial characteristics of the sites as well as scalability and market potential (Law, Meijaard, et al. 2015; Uda, Hein, and Adventa 2020). For example, many local communities in West Kalimantan practise traditional dry or wet swidden agriculture for a mix of maize, pineapple, various vegetables, rubber, and oil palm as described by Agus et al. (2012). While sago palm was often mentioned as a prospective crop in swampy areas, Ming et al. (2018) reported that, based on the experience in Sarawak, it is largely not feasible on peatland except in areas with very shallow peat, as the trees are not suited to the conditions.

Potential bio-energy crops were also studied, such as the case of *Reutealis trisperma* (Blanco) (*kemiri sunan*) and *Calophyllum inophyllum* (*nyamplung*) in Pulang Pisau, Central Kalimantan (Siti Maimunah et al. 2018). Both were found to perform well in terms of growth and productivity when integrated with agroforestry instead of monoculture. However, the bio-energy plans remain only proposals as the financial feasibility is not clearly understood. Carbon management has been used as a major indicator of sustainability, but it was not always proportional to economic output (Nahrawi, Husni, and Radziah 2012). Possibly, combining these different options with careful choices of native species like *Shorea banageran*, *Alstonia pneumatophore* and *Dacryodes rostrata* for enrichment planting may be able to achieve the dual targets of livelihood and restoration (Blackham et al. 2013; Blackham, Webb, and Corlett 2014; Lampela et al. 2018). However, no grounded evidence of successful paludiculture has yet been reported in Borneo despite various attempts (Tata 2019).

While cultivating crops on peat under wet conditions may be promising, it is crucial to avoid repeating the problems created by planting oil palm on peat as in the past (Wijedasa et al. 2017). Detailed topographic mapping and soil classification are, however, the foremost kinds of information required to design holistic planning across the entire peat-based landscape (Veloo, Paramananthan, and Van Ranst 2014). To date, the knowledge needed for peatland restoration is still considered limited despite the urgency. Especially, enormous resources (e.g., large-scale land surveys) are needed to capture accurate spatial information on peatlands.

Socio-economic Perspectives

Landscape Governance

Large-scale land-use planning in Borneo commonly involves cash crop monoculture as the core component and private companies as the central actors. In this setting, landscape governance seems to be straightforward with clear divisions between intensified agriculture and conserved areas, i.e., land-sparing (Van der Laan et al. 2017). Conventionally, conservation focuses on the demarcation of large national parks and protected areas, with a simplified, binary categorization. Later, the mainstreaming of the HCV/HCS concept by RSPO in the context of oil palm development (see Chapter 6) provides a more advanced framework to identify areas for conservation. It covers various sizes of areas distributed across the landscape for conservation, including those that exist as "islands" within plantations and concessions.

However, such a binary land-sparing approach may become very challenging for complex mosaic landscapes occupied by loosely organized and independent small farmers. These farmers rely not solely on non-forested land but on various resources for living with their activities which may span across forests, mangroves, riparian and other areas (Sopian et al. 2019). In addition to biophysical considerations, managing these landscapes demands a thorough understanding of people-place and human-environment interactions which can be complicated by different values, beliefs, economic status, and socio-political networks (Berkes and Ross 2013). It is thus not a simple question of how much land is needed per household (which is always debated among the productivists as in the land-sparing scenario), but how to construct a resilient landscape with a "bricolage" of land-use options for local livelihoods. Landscape governance, as Puspitaloka et al. (2020) rightly pointed out for peatland restoration, should be "defined through multi-stakeholder collaboration within social-ecological contexts".

Interestingly, the concept of "moderate industrialization" was once introduced in the 1990s in Kalimantan for such a mosaic landscape. The concept promotes dispersed but modern high-yield smallholdings of rubber, coconut, forestry, and swidden in individual project management units (PMU). Unfortunately, the plan has never been realized due to unrealistic assumptions and expectations (Kawai and Inoue 2016). Since the collapse of the Suharto regime in 1998, shifting control over land resources from Jakarta to the districts and local societies was perceived as a solution to anchor fairer and more efficient land governance (Marshall 2009). In the 2000s, many district governments aggressively undertook large-scale land development for quick revenues, particularly from logging and oil palm expansion, taking advantage of legal uncertainties caused by decentralization (Barr et al. 2006; Setiawan et al. 2016). Abuse of power, corruption, and collusion among the local elites (including tribal leaders) and companies have remained common practices (Smith et al. 2003; Leonald and Rowland 2016).

Later in the 2010s, agrarian reform has been undertaken to redistribute land resources more justly to local communities. One type is in the form of several programmes known collectively as "social forestry" (Resosudarmo et al. 2019). The total area of one of the schemes, the village forest (*hutan desa*), was tripled to 0.25 million ha from 2012 to 2016 (Santika et al. 2017). Ambitiously, the government aims to put 12.7 million ha of land under the social forestry schemes by 2021 (Rakatama and Pandit 2020). In their paper, Resosudarmo et al. (2019) indicate that the actual implementation of the social forestry schemes, at least in their field area of Central Kalimantan, could hardly be worse. Mentioned are ambitious targets and rushed distribution, inappropriate site allocation and forest types, an imbalance between allocated resources and their translation into actual livelihoods, and a lack of attention to community capacity and local governance. The field research was carried out in various locations in Central Kalimantan, with several different types of social forestry schemes (6 in all) being studied.

While the social forestry programmes appeared to guarantee tenure security, questions remain about the production systems and available inputs, given problems of resource allocation and inappropriate forest types. There is no information about the protection of the growing trees from risks, especially from fire, a very serious hazard in Central Kalimantan, particularly as the plan is to plant some forests on deep peat. There is also very little information about the market or tree types (except for *sengon* [*Paraserianthese falcataria*], for which there is some demand in Java, though this was not explored). One interesting aspect in the detail of all the schemes is that while planting oil palm is not permitted, existing oil palm trees would be allowed to grow for up to twelve years. Whether farmers would then turn to other types of "forest" is not known. Note that the social forestry schemes were separated from agrarian reform (called TORA), which seemed to apply more to land redistribution to small-scale or landless farmers outside the forest estate and had fewer restrictions on farmers' behaviour.

The core argument from a conservation perspective is that granting more autonomy to the communities would allow them to consciously protect forests from being overexploited and maintain local ecosystem services. Eghenter (2018) illustrated an example of how this can be achieved through maintaining a community land-use tradition among the Dayak Kenyah people in North Kalimantan. This, however, is quite a different story among a much smaller group, anxious to maintain cultural control of specific forest patches (*tana ulen*) originally reserved for aristocrats and now amazingly diverse (see the example of the *tana ulen* in Setulang village [near Malinau] in the discussion on Eco-tourism, Chapter 10).

In general, the results of increasing local autonomy at district and subdistrict levels in Kalimantan have been mixed in terms of socio-economic and environmental progress (Palmer and Engel 2007). Purnomo et al. (2019) found that the frequency and abundance of fire events are closely related to local elections, as local politics regularly involves land transactions between local elites, and fires were an easy way to increase land value. This can be further complicated by the introduction of large-scale plantation development by the district governments, creating urgency and competition among the communities to control more land, as observed by Thaler and Anandi (2017) in East Kalimantan. Edwards et al. (2020) also revealed that the creation of new districts has triggered more frequent use of fire, as the sudden changes in governance have intensified the contests over land.

Sometimes communities, of their own will, opt for quick money instead of conserving their traditional lifestyles and the environment, as reported in the literature (Potter 2016b; Urano 2020). In Kotawaringin Timur, Central Kalimantan, studied by Potter (2016b) Dayaks have been unable to continue their traditional lifestyles as their land is occupied by oil palm companies. Some were offered "plasma" plots on one plantation but would have had to wait at least three years before their palms began producing. Being desperate for money, they just decided to sell their land. In this district, which is now very full of oil palm, their options have become increasingly limited. The case of aquaculture in the Mahakam Delta, East Kalimantan is a different kind of example. Since the fall of the Suharto regime, the region was turned into a new frontier of land-use change that was "free" from any formal governance. By 2010, about 21 kha of mangrove land in the Mahakam Delta was deforested and converted into highly profitable shrimp ponds (Rahman et al. 2013). Arifanti et al. (2019) estimated that such conversions resulted in a carbon stock loss equivalent to 226 years of soil carbon accumulation in natural mangroves. While the provincial government has been trying to improve the situation, attempts to close the gaps between formal and informal governing systems, with the latter dominated by powerful and wealthy locals, have not been very successful (Persoon and Simarmata 2014).

It is important to recognize that people may hold very different views on "livelihood" even within the same village, and not all members share coherent interests. Some may choose more traditional lifestyles; some may opt for more changes—whether gradual or radical. Studies have shown that factors like age, gender, and occupation significantly affect the attitudes of community members toward land use (Shuib, Yee, and Edman 2012; Permadi et al. 2017; de Vos and Delabre 2018; Permadi et al. 2018). Especially, a profit-chasing mindset can rapidly and widely spread among the communities, as shown in the recent land-use history of Borneo. When conditions allowed, such as access to affordable fertilizers and markets, it is reported that Indonesian smallholders predominantly opt for more lucrative options, especially oil palm and rubber monocultures, even though these can lead to negative ecological consequences (Clough et al. 2016). The authors' recent visit to West Kalimantan (Sanggau, Sintang, and Sekadau) in late 2018 revealed that some villagers who were once strongly against oil palm have started planting the crop themselves after observing the successes of their peers. This corresponds well with the observation of Langston et al. (2017) in Sintang where the landscape has been on a trajectory towards the dominance of monoculture.

Crucially, the inequality among the community members should not be neglected. Autonomy at the district or community level does not necessarily equal fair and just land governance, not to mention its low transparency and difficulties in monitoring (Urano 2014). For example, a case study in Sarawak shows that the wealthier families actually consumed more non-timber forest products than the poorer members (Sakai et al. 2016). In Kalimantan, the power voids in land governance created during decentralization were filled by informal management by local elites who generally have close relationships with the district governments. The disparities in social and economic status may lead to social injustice and land conflicts between and among the communities, e.g., the case of land grabbing by local elites in West Kalimantan (Semedi and Bakker 2014) and the case of competition among the Dayak Modang community in East Kalimantan (Fujiwara 2017). Inequality can be further entrenched by uneven development (e.g., access to knowledge and proximity to infrastructure) (Santika, Wilson, Meijaard, et al. 2019).

Since the colonial era, the disparities among local people were being manipulated by external actors to exploit the land resources throughout Borneo (de Vos, Köhne, and Roth 2018). In Sarawak, it was deployed by the state government to implement the so-called "land reform" known as *Konsep Baru*, which aimed to substitute traditional agriculture with large-scale industrial plantations (Bissonnette 2011). The "land reform", or as suggested by scholars as land grabbing, was driven mainly "by the exercise of state power to maximize opportunities for surplus extraction and political patronage" (Cramb 2016) and was regarded as "a useful strategy for establishing control over rural communities" (Majid Cooke 2002).

Ethnicity is also a major factor to consider in understanding the local human-environment relationships (see more in Chapter 12). While the notion of indigeneity was often used in collectively claiming autonomy and rights over land and resources, it is imperative to recognize that there is a wide range of ethnic groups in Borneo who can have very different land-use traditions (Rye and Kurniawan 2017; Großmann 2019). Politically, alliances were also commonly constructed based on ethnicity. Looking closely into local political struggles over land control in the Malinau district of East Kalimantan, Moeliono, Wollenberg, and Limberg (2009) revealed that such political alliances and ethnic affiliations can have a pervasive influence on land and forest governance. This is not unique to Kalimantan—ethnicity (and religion) has also been a core element of the political scenes in Sabah and Sarawak (Prasad 2015; Mersat 2018).

The aforementioned challenges expose the credibility and capability of local institutions when it comes to establishing sustainable land-use governance. It is crucial not to simply assume that the landscape will be automatically managed and governed sustainably by the local people without considering local socio-political dynamics and capabilities. In the case of Kalimantan, Resosudarmo et al. (2019) rightly pointed out that the Indonesian government lacks long-term land-use strategies to empower local communities. The concept of land sharing with multifunctional landscapes does not fit well into the existing governing framework, which was described as "sticky" by van Oosten, Moeliono, and Wiersum (2018). How to creatively reconcile the various opportunities and challenges that arise from different land-use options in designing a resilient landscape with cross-scale and cross-sectoral governance has been a challenge with the precondition that the interests of various stakeholders are taken into account (Nugroho et al. 2018). However, it is also necessary to raise local awareness over sustainability issues on various scales, including the impacts of regional pollution and global climate change in achieving a stakeholder agreement on local landscape management.

International Cooperation and Initiatives
At the international level, various supports and funding for landscape conservation and restoration in Borneo have been introduced by external parties. The initiative that covers the largest area, namely the Heart of Borneo (HoB) programme that involves all three countries in Borneo as well as a range of international organizations was created to tackle conservation and development issues with a transboundary approach (Yanindraputri 2016; Firdaus, Wibowo, and Rochmayanto 2017). The edited volume *Reflections on the Heart of Borneo* includes the following "vision statement" of the WWF:

> At the very heart of Borneo, there lies a uniquely rich largely forested landscape. It straddles the transboundary highlands of Brunei, Indonesia and Malaysia, and reaches out through the foothills into the adjacent lowlands. Our vision for the heart of Borneo is that partnerships at all levels ensure effective management and conservation of a network of protected areas, productive forests and other sustainable land uses. Borneo's magnificent heritage is thereby sustained forever (WWF 2005).

In the same volume, Eghenter (2008) suggested that there were three major groups involved: campaigners and conservationists; politicians and public figures, advocators of local development; and forest communities whose livelihoods were dependent on access to and exploitation of local resources. She concluded that success could only come through consultation and genuine local participation, with tangible and sustainable incentives for local people to be rewarded for contributing to the conservation and sustainable management of the Heart of Borneo. Although this is a commendable aim, sadly there is little evidence that it was pursued by representatives of the other two interest groups.

Most importantly, very little actual "transboundary" work was carried out, defeating the original purpose of the initiative which aimed to take conservation to a scale that covered as many elements as possible across the landscape beyond political borders. Most Bornean territories involved worked on their own, with most initiatives eventually not working as expected. Progress was more notable in Sabah. As the large central part of Sabah's territory (away from the east coast oil palm belt) fell within the HoB boundaries, the powerful Sabah Forestry Department under its Director Sam Mannan took the HoB initiative seriously, using it as a framework for statewide sustainable development plans. In its first Strategic Plan of Action (2008–13) the protected area was increased from 939,000 ha to 1,300,000 ha. The new protected areas increased the connectivity of Sabah's forests, benefiting the endangered wildlife. State Action Plans were developed for the three totally protected species: orangutan, Bornean elephant, and Sumatran rhino. A revised Strategic Plan of Action (2014–20) had begun to examine the HoB and green development objectives, comparing them to current national policies (especially the State Structure Plan 2013–33). The WWF 2018 report on the HoB indicated that its main purpose back in 2013 had been to intervene to have conservation included in Sabah's State Structure Plan 2013–33, which was successful (Tai 2018).

However, the Forestry Department had also noted the potential for conflict as well as synergy. A lack of communication and collaboration among and between institutions, gaps in knowledge and awareness, and a lack of funding were some of the weaknesses identified. Threats to a "Green" Sabah included habitat loss, degradation and fragmentation, pollution (including oil palm mills and untreated waste from villages and cities), invasive species (including acacia), wildlife poaching, and trade in both animal and plant species and human-wildlife conflicts. It was pointed out that the state's forests had been so heavily exploited that their timber had no economic value: although forest restoration was being attempted it was estimated to take decades (Sabah Forestry Department 2013).

Meanwhile, the recurrence of transboundary haze events in the 2010s and the accompanying health impacts and economic loss are also pushing the governments to envisage the urgency of changing the status quo (Nguitragool 2010). The Association of Southeast Asian Nations (ASEAN) is one of the key platforms for regional cooperation. The ASEAN haze regime, including the Cooperation Plan on Transboundary Pollution, the Regional Haze Action Plan (RHAP), and the Agreement on Transboundary Haze Pollution, was established after the transboundary haze events in the 1990s resulted from peat fire in Sumatra and Borneo (Nguitragool 2010). However, it was not until 2014 that all ten ASEAN countries ratified the haze agreement with Indonesia as the last country on board. Unfortunately, the treaty has not been very successful in coping with the haze issues as peat fires in Indonesia still occur from year to year.

While domestic complexity is a major challenge in addressing peat fires in Indonesia (Carmenta et al. 2017), ASEAN as a platform to negotiate and resolve transboundary issues has a rather limited role as it holds a principle of "non-interference", i.e., member states do not interfere with each other's "domestic affairs" (Varkkey 2018; Zhang and Savage 2019). Nevertheless, it remains a platform for collaboration with external parties that share the concerns about peatland conservation. The German government has commissioned the "Sustainable Use of Peatland and Haze Mitigation in ASEAN" (SUPA) programme that runs from 2018 to 2023. The programme aims to strengthen ASEAN cooperation in implementing a peatland management strategy by generating pilot experiences in Indonesia and Malaysia (GIZ 2020).

Community Empowerment
Community empowerment is a crucial component in building landscape resilience. This requires identifying, activating, and strengthening the capacity of local communities in dealing with potential changes, and their understanding of the diverse mechanisms in establishing resilient agroecological systems. On many occasions, the stakeholders lack enough knowledge, technical support, and financial means to equip themselves with the proper tools to counter unforeseen changes. Implementing sustainable landscape management in Borneo requires substantial external support (Ortiz et al. 2018).

In the past two decades, numerous efforts have been made to transmit scientific knowledge about ecosystem services to local communities. For example, Suwarno, Hein, et al. (2018) established a landscape zoning model in the Kapuas Protected Forest Management Unit, Central Kalimantan by involving the local stakeholders to jointly discuss the concept of ecosystem services and their implications to the local society as well as associated rights and responsibilities. On disaster prevention, especially fire management in Kalimantan, Kieft et al. (2016) documented a collaborative attempt by Columbia University and the IPB University to install an early warning system for fire in Central Kalimantan and Riau. Various innovative solutions were also proposed and tested to boost the capacity and effectiveness of local firefighting squads, e.g., the "smart" designed firefighting system that optimizes the use of water resources (Takahashi, Jaya, and Limin 2015), the use of smartphone application for reporting and validating fires (Aditya, Laksono, and Izzahuddin 2019), and the crowdsourcing of GIS data for landscape monitoring (Ioki et al. 2019). These efforts can be potentially integrated with fundamental modelling of agroecological and climatic characteristics, e.g., changes in rainfall and the sea-surface temperature to form the knowledge basis of landscape management (Sa'adi et al. 2017; Oettli, Behera, and Yamagata 2018).

However, long-term financial measures for sustainable livelihoods, which remain the primary consideration of the communities, have to be also put in place as mentioned earlier. The case of a reforestation programme in Gunung Palung National Park, West Kalimantan shows that economic incentives can be more effective than forging "perception change" in addressing illegal logging by local communities (Pohnan, Ompusunggu, and Webb 2015). For example, Fawzi et al. (2020) reported an interesting programme where some funds are allocated for former loggers to launch their own businesses in combination with voluntary chainsaw buybacks. More direct incentive mechanisms are needed to effectively motivate the adoption of sustainable land-use practices (Herawati and Santoso 2011; Noojipady et al. 2017; Watts et al. 2019).

In terms of financing support, one example is the microcredit loan scheme introduced by the Indonesian government to support a smallholder programme, aiming to establish a million hectares of timber plantation in Kalimantan by 2016. However, the programme has been suffering from poor management, particularly the mismatching of the loan scheme with borrowers without careful consideration of the conditions and needs of the small farmers (Nugroho, Dermawan, and Putzel 2013).

Meanwhile, there are also homegrown initiatives by concerned activists among educated Dayaks in Kalimantan to support marginalized community members in the form of credit unions (CU). This type of cooperative emerged in 1987 as the PancurKasih organization, with a philosophy developed by the Dayak farmers themselves, following a failed group of credit unions introduced by the Catholic Church in Pontianak in the 1970s. Its objective has been to decrease the socio-economic inequalities faced by the indigenous Dayak people, especially through funding education loans and alternatives to the banking system for those in remote areas. They strongly discourage Dayaks from gambling and selling their land (Bamba 2010). The CUs now have an extensive network especially in West Kalimantan, establishing themselves as strong agents in social transformation. Nevertheless, some have been intertwined with local political struggles and they strongly emphasize social and cultural aspects, with fewer concerns over environmental issues and landscape resilience (Kurniawan and Rahmawati 2018). The CU with whom we interacted in Sintang and Sekadau in 2018 (Keling Kumang), seemed to have become a largely commercial organization. It was offering fertilizer and herbicides for sale to Dayaks being trained to become independent oil palm smallholders by the international NGO, Solidaridad.

Some internationally funded conservation organizations have also launched livelihood projects in Kalimantan. However, they often struggle to find a balance between development and conservation. The less successful *Gaharu* nursery project for the Punan Murung community in Central Kalimantan is a neat example—the funding conservation organization and the communities have failed to come to a consensus over priorities of carbon stock and economic gains (Großmann 2018). This is in contrast with the national social forestry schemes, which were criticized for a narrow focus on poverty alleviation and inadequate attention to environmental impacts (Rakatama and Pandit 2020).

Interestingly, the plantation industry may play a key role in supporting the communities, as local prosperity can also be in their interests. Taking the case of Unilever plantations in Borneo as a case study, Williams, Whiteman, and Kennedy (2019) showed that forging positive cross-scale socio-ecological feedback is important for long-term profitable operations. Different business models are required to establish strong, long-term partnerships with small farmers, where trust and tolerance will be core elements as shown by Obeth (2013) in the case study in East Kalimantan. Jupesta et al. (2020) also reported a case in West Kalimantan where cooperation between a major oil palm company and local communities has managed to reduce the hotspots from 158 in 2015 to only 7 in 2017. Apart from these, an interesting case in Sabah was reported by Hance (2020) where a small swath of private land planted with oil palm was purchased by a small NGO for forest restoration. This piece of land was selected for its strategic importance in connecting two major protected areas, forming a wildlife corridor for endangered species like Bornean elephants, storm storks, and Bornean banteng.

Finally, leveraging and integrating local strengths with these external supports may further close the technical and financial gaps in landscape management. For example, traditional ecological knowledge that the communities learned from decades of human-environmental interactions can enrich the "knowledge bank" or "toolbox" for improving agroecological resilience (van Oudenhoven et al. 2011). An interesting case is the traditional rattan management by Ngaju Dayak in Katingan, Central Kalimantan documented by Schreer (2016). Understanding the dynamics of traditional shifting cultivation by the Dayaks is also imperative as it is a key component that affects the entire landscape—nutrient regulation, fallow length, adaptation to the soil, climatic conditions, etc. are all important items of information (Funakawa 2017). In general, farmers have for many years creatively incorporated cash crops into their traditional farming systems, such as those observed by Cramb (2007) in Sarawak, Daisuke (2018) in East Kalimantan, Goh et al. (2018) in Central Kalimantan, and Potter (2015b) in West Kalimantan, especially Sanggau District (see also Chapter 2). Protecting the traditional diversification of livelihoods, such as hunting, gathering, and fishing is essential to enhancing resilience, especially in the face of changing environments (Liswanti et al. 2011).

Final Remarks

Enhancing resilience gives no development promise but a way to create a healthy environment and society for the long-term benefit of all parties. The Bornean territories may incorporate resilience in their land-use strategies as a key consideration over short-term economic achievement, acknowledging potential environmental risks that will incur even higher social and economic costs, especially in the event of worsening regional climatic conditions. Large-scale land exploitations in the past decades have significantly altered Borneo's landscape. Both restoration and protection are needed, but what is imperative now is avoiding further degradation, especially where it is largely irreversible.

Furthermore, sound landscape management can only work effectively when a system-oriented view that accounts for both social and biophysical elements is adopted. Despite the emergence of multitudinous conceptual frameworks, onground implementation of large-scale landscape planning remains an arduous challenge for Borneo. For example, a lack of coordination between conservation strategies and community development by different agencies was deemed a key factor that undermined the success of conservation strategies as reported in West Kalimantan (Kubo, Wibawanto, and Rossanda 2019) and Sarawak (Pandong et al. 2019). Putting the various puzzle pieces together on a landscape scale requires very careful planning considering the complex interactions between different land-use components as well as different stakeholders.

In addition to stricter environmental regulations and enforcement, incentives need to be restructured in a way to motivate stakeholders with different perspectives. A better-diversified portfolio of financing is needed, including not only public funds and international aid but also private investment and various credit schemes for smaller actors. One critical move will be shifting the focus of financial communities from short-term monetary benefits to long-term inclusive benefits with careful consideration of environmental conservation. This leads to the idea of commodifying ecosystem services which is discussed in the next chapter.

9

Commodifying Ecosystem Services

To facilitate the conservation of natural environments, some economists have proposed to include environmental goods and services in financial accounting. It is argued by the advocates that putting environmental goals explicitly into the economic dimension can help decision-makers in designing and implementing interventions in environmental management. To this end, the concept of "natural capital" was created to explain the spatio-temporal interactions between man-made economies and natural ecosystems (Guerry et al. 2015; Polasky et al. 2015). It regards "natural capital" as the stock of natural ecosystems that may be somehow expressed in monetary terms. Natural capital provides various ecosystem services (ES) to human society. In agriculture and forestry, ES provided by soil and water are among the most conceivable in terms of economic consideration as land price is largely correlated to fertility and productivity (Robinson et al. 2014). It is, however, more complicated to link some ES to productivity in the short term, such as regulating services provided by carbon sequestration and biodiversity, although both have long-term effects on agriculture and the overall ecosystem.

Following this direction, a strategy that advocates incorporating ES with the contemporary market economy through monetizing "nature" with economic accounting practices has emerged as a means to address unsustainable land-based economies (Missemer 2018). This forms the basis for developing a conservation-oriented eco-economy. Commonly, the term "payment for ecosystem services" (PES) is used to describe such a strategy. More specifically for the case of Borneo, it proposes the creation of compensation schemes for landholders who choose conservation over intensive cash crop cultivation (especially palm oil) or logging. In a broad sense, the landholders will be paid a certain amount of money for some sort of ES provided by their land. Logically, the amount should be more or less equivalent to net benefits, in all aspects, received in other less sustainable land-use scenarios.

This requires linking natural capital to human benefits on a monetary basis. In any case, the precondition is a standard mechanism to quantify ES so that there are manageable attributes of natural capital stocks for interventions to take place (Maseyk et al. 2017). The next challenge is creating schemes to monetize the ES and platforms for the transaction (Gunton et al. 2017). This is then followed by the question of how to implement these schemes as a new form of environmental governance in Borneo.

In this chapter, the first section describes how environmental changes can be linked to economic impacts. Then, it takes a close look at past efforts in quantifying ecosystem services in Borneo from a technical point of view. Following this, it examines the compensation schemes promoted in Borneo to understand the concept and setup. Finally, the actual implementation is discussed in the context of localization and institutionalization.

Linking Environmental Changes to Economic Impacts

The disruption of ES can bring a variety of damages to the economies. Peat fire is among the most vivid examples in the case of Borneo with its economic impacts on a massive scale. The economic loss caused by the great fire in 2015 is estimated at around US$16 billion for the whole of Indonesia (Purnomo et al. 2017). The most recent figures from the World Bank for the 2019 fires, which might be triggered by the rise in temperature, are US$5.2 billion from the agricultural and environmental sectors—this is yet to account for the health-related effects. The worst-hit provinces, Central and West Kalimantan, incurred losses estimated at 7.9 per cent and 6.1 per cent of their respective GDPs (Jong 2019e). Conceivably, the economic damages due to widespread fire on farms can be pernicious. But more drastically, the damage can be transboundary due to the dispersion of haze that contains carbon monoxide and particulate matter, mainly across Indonesia, Malaysia, and Singapore (Tan-Soo and Pattanayak 2019). The account includes not only direct costs like additional burdens in healthcare, flight cancellation, and disrupted business operations, but also costs that cannot be directly quantified such as life expectancy, premature death, climate change, disruption of lifestyles, social unrest, and undiscovered mental health problems (Nguitragool 2010; Field et al. 2016).

In addition, there is a wide range of interlinked economic impacts due to various environmental changes. Especially, impacts on water resources are critical in the Bornean context. Past evidence shows that changes in forest cover have altered precipitation cycles, river flows, and water availability in Borneo (Herawati et al. 2018; McAlpine et al. 2018). Ironically, one of the biggest drivers of deforestation, oil palm plantations, is among the biggest victims as their productivity heavily depends on water availability (Safitri et al. 2018).

Public health is another key dimension. Multiple research studies in Borneo reported that deforestation has triggered outbreaks of malaria, hyperthermia, dengue fever, and other human disease risks (Jeffree et al. 2018; Ahmed et al. 2019; Husnina, Clements, and Wangdi 2019; Stark et al. 2019; Suter et al. 2019). These examples are yet to include more long-term, subtle impacts such as increasing local temperatures (Wolff et al. 2018; Masuda et al. 2019; Sa'adi et al. 2019), as well as the complex feedback loops in connection with multiple systems, e.g., flowering and fruiting (Ushio et al. 2019).

Interestingly, the actual protagonist in the wave of commodifying ES in Borneo is none of the above, but the climate regulation service provided by carbon stock has insidious but not immediate local impacts. Carbon stock embedded in terrestrial biomass is a key indicator in monitoring climate change mitigation, playing a major role in the global carbon cycle. Incentive schemes have been created mainly for carbon, driving the conservation activities in Borneo towards the theme of global climate change. In this context, the Reducing Emissions from Deforestation and Forest Degradation (REDD+) framework, which is explained in detail in the later section, plays a dominant role.

In addition to carbon, biodiversity in Borneo also receives enormous attention from the global communities, which are the key funding sources for compensating conservation. It has close linkages to carbon stock management and in many cases, both are assessed together, see, for example, a case study in East Kalimantan by Verstegen et al. (2019). There have been extensive discussions about how biodiversity conservation can be incorporated into the carbon-based framework (Ansell, Edwards, and Hamer 2011). As these two dimensions are closely linked and have been rigorously examined in Borneo, they remain the focus of the rest of this chapter.

Quantifying Ecosystem Services

Carbon Stock

Carbon stock is regarded as the "most measurable" element and is widely chosen as a key indicator for environmental impacts due to its link to climate change. The Intergovernmental Panel on Climate Change (IPCC) created in 1988 has spent decades establishing standard methodologies for estimating carbon stock and carbon dynamics. The guidelines were first published in 2006, namely the *2006 IPCC Guidelines for National Greenhouse Gas Inventories* and have been constantly reviewed with the latest refinement published in 2019 (IPCC 2019). Carbon stock can be estimated with default factors documented by IPCC, by complex biophysical and biogeochemical modelling, remote sensing, field measurement, or combinations of the above. The first approach is very coarse, while the combination approach can provide the best possible estimates. As it is not possible to carry out accurate field measurements throughout the entire landscape, modelling is frequently adopted to integrate and scale up field measurements although accompanied by significant uncertainties.

Across different types of land covers in Borneo, numerous studies have been conducted to measure tree-level and plot-level carbon stock, e.g., Khoon et al. (2019); Besar et al. (2020); Syahrinudin et al. (2020). To further quantify carbon stock on a landscape scale, remote sensing and aerial mapping are among the most important tools. Various efforts have been made to map the land cover and aboveground carbon stock in Borneo on various scales, e.g., river basin mapping by Vijith and Dodge-Wan (2020), region-wide mapping by Ferraz et al. (2018), and islandwide mapping by Gaveau et al. (2018) and Gunarso et al. (2013). In addition, oil palm companies that claim "no deforestation" have also been investing in mapping the carbon stocks. Apart from the "High Conservation Value" (HCV) forests, other areas of forests, especially remnant forests and secondary regrowth could be identified as having important levels of carbon, namely "High Carbon Stock" (HCS) forests and needing to be set aside to further justify "no deforestation" claims (see Chapter 4).

However, forest gradients must also be considered in measuring carbon stock as forest degradation has been a key contributor to carbon stock loss. To capture forest degradation, Darmawan (2012) demonstrated with a case in East Kalimantan to estimate the level of forest degradation based on Landsat data and MODIS data in 2003–9 through differentiating patch, perforated, edge, and core forest, while Kiat, Malek, and Shamsuddin (2020) attempted to address this through measuring carbon embedded in wood removals from the forests in Sarawak based on forestry statistics. Technological breakthroughs may allow more accuracy in capturing the carbon gradient at a higher resolution and on a larger scale, such as the use of unmanned aerial vehicles (UAV) (Fawcett et al. 2019) and airborne laser scanning (Wong and Tsuyuki 2017; Jucker et al. 2018), in combination with continuous improvement of carbon stock models and application of various digital technologies (Berninger et al. 2019). Combining ground measurement with large-scale mapping technologies allows more accurate estimation by taking the carbon gradient and heterogeneity of forested areas into account, particularly in logged and disturbed areas. Ground measurement may include important characteristics which may not be easily detected off-ground, such as the distribution of tree species, see e.g., the study by Samejima et al. (2020) on the Anap-Muput Forest Management Unit in Bintulu, Sarawak.

For below-ground carbon stock, studies have also been conducted to produce empirical data on soil carbon, especially carbon in peatland, and its changes caused by the conversion of land cover and forest degradation (Rahman et al. 2018; Agus, Ilfana, et al. 2019; Borchard et al. 2019; Hairiah et al. 2020). The carbon dynamics of tropical peatlands, which account for 8 per cent of the global peatland, are still considered understudied in comparison with those in the temperate areas. The very first challenge would be a rigorous classification of peat soil which remains a debatable topic (Veloo, Paramananthan, and Van Ranst 2014).

Finally, the most difficult task would be integrating these different carbon pools and various flows, e.g., dissolved organic carbon from peatland to ocean or end-use wood products, under different types of land uses and disturbances (Harun et al. 2016; Indrajaya et al. 2016; Martin et al. 2018). This is a highly complex task and comprehensive, accurate field measurements are extremely difficult to conduct. Much discussion has been concerned with the differences between a whole host of biogeochemical models, the assumptions made, and their uncertainties. This has to take into consideration various scenarios of productive use, restoration, and degradation, especially for critical areas like degraded peatland (Konecny et al. 2016; Basuki et al. 2019; Butarbutar et al. 2019; Hattori et al. 2019; Murdiyarso, Saragi-Sasmito, and Rustini 2019; Saragi-Sasmito et al. 2019; Wong et al. 2020).

Biodiversity

Quantifying biodiversity is much more challenging, and there are no "standard" methodologies like the IPCC framework. In past decades, different concepts, methodologies, or frameworks were invented to measure biodiversity in Borneo. For research purposes, various studies were performed on certain species in Sabah like monitoring proboscis monkey with unmanned aerial vehicles (Stark et al. 2018) and gibbons with semi-automated vocal fingerprinting (Clink, Crofoot, and Marshall 2019). On a larger scale, proposals to measure biodiversity were also made to evaluate the effectiveness of various conservation programmes, e.g., the "ecological health" indicators proposed by Wulffraat and Morrison (2013) for the Heart of Borneo (HoB) programme or the common framework of biodiversity accounting proposed by Khan (2014) for REDD+.

A platform similar to IPCC, namely the Intergovernmental Science-Policy Platform on Biodiversity and Ecosystem Services (IPBES) was established in 2012. Clearly, the experts and researchers from IPBES concluded that there are no simple ways of valuing biodiversity and other ecosystem services as it can be highly subjective depending on the place, time, and people (Pascual et al. 2017). Technically, the choice of base cases for comparison will have a profound impact on the measurement. For example, a logged forest may show relatively low species richness compared to a pristine forest but may be much higher in species richness than a plantation (Edwards et al. 2011).

Moreover, structural changes in biodiversity cannot be simplified into a few indicators when different land covers are interconnected with gradual transitions. The mosaic may also change with time due to forest growth, regrowth, and degradation. The case study in the ex-MRP site in Central Kalimantan by (Blackham, Webb, and Corlett 2014) may reflect some of these complexities. They found that although unassisted regeneration may happen in degraded peatland, some wind-dispersed species will have dominating advantages in the aftermath of deforestation and fire, resulting in a landscape with low species diversity. The environmental gradient, e.g., from pristine forest to severely logged forest must be taken into account and a more thorough understanding of the spatio-temporal dynamics is needed (Struebig et al. 2013). More importantly, any indicators to measure biodiversity should not be used independently for land zoning and land-use decisions, as a degraded forest may still provide important functions in biodiversity conservation (Woodcock et al. 2011). The perspectives of indigenous forest-dwelling people can be essential in understanding the dynamics across the landscape, as they have the most direct experience with changes in plant diversity and patterns (Sheil and Salim 2011).

COMPENSATING CONSERVATION

Schemes and Pricing

Borneo became a primary location for PES schemes in the 2000s due to the serious environmental degradation that had occurred throughout the island. REDD+ has been the major programme under experimentation in

Kalimantan. The programme aims to compensate land users who avoid degradation and deforestation for the opportunity costs of converting the land for agricultural production (Sills et al. 2014). The compensation is measured against carbon sequestration services of the land that can be paid for through financing from international donors and hopefully banking on the carbon credit systems. At the moment, several foreign governments like Norway (the biggest donor), Australia (minimally), and Japan as well as several international organizations operate as donors under the REDD+ framework. Norway has pledged up to US$1 billion depending on actual levels of emission reduction through declines in deforestation. Indonesia was due to receive the first payment in 2019–20, amounting to US$56 million (Jong 2019c, 2020f).

An array of projects was launched as shown in Figure 9.1. Three out of the five projects reported by Sills et al. (2014) of CIFOR were located in Central Kalimantan, with the rest in West and East Kalimantan: Kalimantan Forests and Climate Partnership (KFCP), Katingan Peatland Restoration and Conservation Project, Rimba Raya Biodiversity Reserve Project, Ketapang Community Carbon Pools (KCCP) and the Berau Forest Carbon Program. Among these projects, the KFCP funded by Australia covered 120,000 ha of the MRP area in Central Kalimantan and was regarded by some observers as the most established REDD+ programme in the country (Atmadja et al. 2014). However, the KFCP was withdrawn in July 2013, without having accomplished many of its objectives (Olbrei and Howes 2012).

In addition, Howson and Kindon (2015) reported another REDD+ project in Sungai Lamandau in Central Kalimantan funded by the Clinton Climate Initiative's Forestry Program. It was Indonesia's first "community-based" forest carbon finance initiative with autonomous land management, but to date, the anticipated well-operating REDD+ project has not yet materialized. There were also initiatives to develop REDD+ projects in North Kalimantan, but the progress remained similarly slow (Pramova et al. 2013; Komalasari, Peteru, and Atmadja 2018).

On the Malaysian side, the Sabah-EU REDD+ project was also launched in Sabah in 2014 (Sabah Forestry Department 2018). While it leverages the carbon banking system and funding from the EU, it also emphasizes the importance of developing other livelihood strategies for local communities. Besides carbon, Brock (2015) reported a market-based scheme for biodiversity, namely Biodiversity Conservation Certificates by the Malua BioBank in Sabah. It was opened to logging companies, palm oil corporations, and even responsible citizens who were offered an opportunity to compensate for their biodiversity impacts. It was a joint initiative of the

FIGURE 9.1
Location of REDD+ Sites

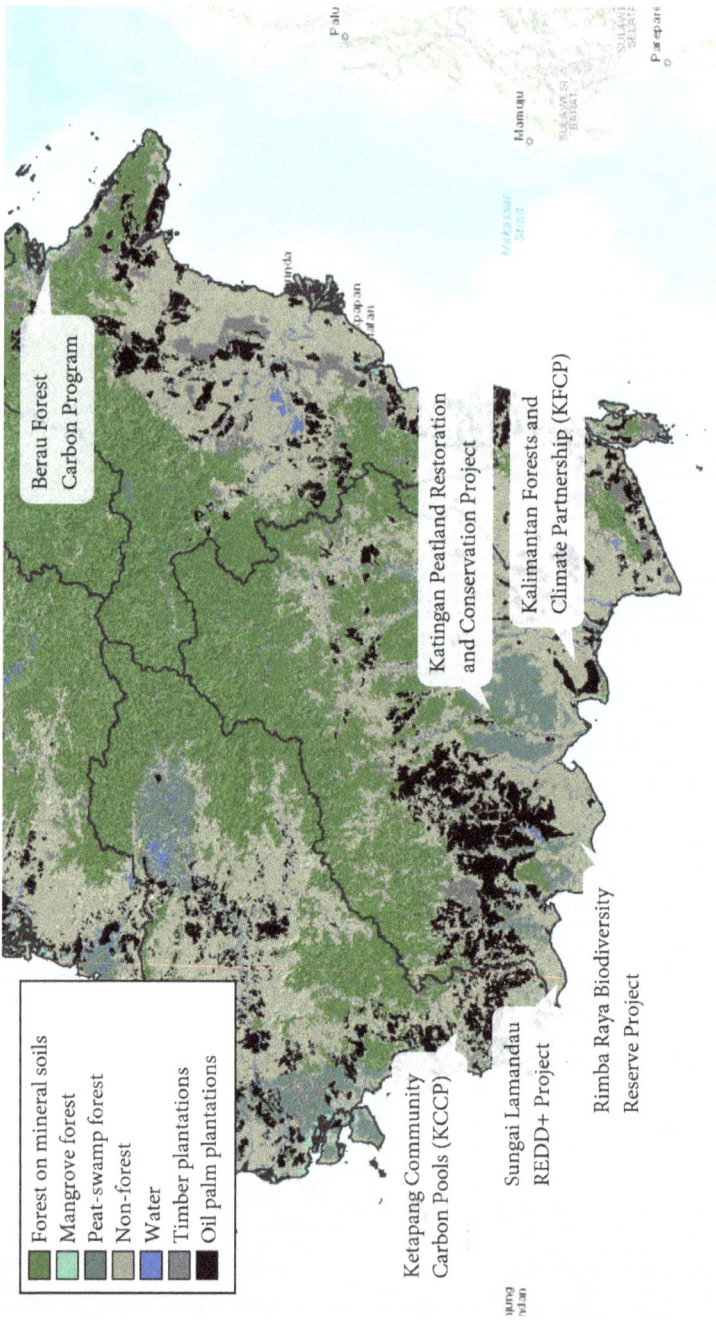

Note: Sabah-EU REDD+ Project is different from those in Indonesia and not shown on the map.

Sabah Forestry Department, Yayasan Sabah, and an Australian-registered company, New Forests Pty Ltd, using it as an instrument to govern Sabah's forests and operate conservation policies (see also a later section "Institutionalization").

Initially, it was hoped that these projects would be supported through participating in carbon credit systems, i.e., systems invented to "trade" emission savings in the form of certificates through market mechanisms. There were proposals to include REDD+ within the clean development mechanism (CDM) under the Kyoto protocol, which was established to allow developed countries to achieve their emission-reduction targets through developing "green" projects outside of their borders, especially in the developing countries (Bhullar 2013). In short, a "carbon market" is created by capping the overall emission of a country, forcing the emitters to either reduce their emission or purchase "carbon credits", such as from conservation projects, to compensate for their emissions. The original idea was to let market mechanisms trigger innovation in low-emission technologies.

However, such a plan was never realized. The world's largest carbon trading scheme, i.e., the EU Emission Trading Scheme (ETS) does not accept credits generated from afforestation or reforestation activities (European Commission 2011). The EU ETS, however, did accept credits from POME-biogas projects as mentioned earlier in Chapter 7 (Chin et al. 2013). However, jurisdictions around the world are also developing various domestic carbon pricing initiatives (World Bank 2020a). New opportunities may arise from emerging countries such as China which have started to adopt more ambitious mitigation targets. An unofficial estimate by the World Bank (2020a) shows that the upcoming national ETS of China in combination with the sub-national schemes may surpass the EU ETS in terms of the share of global annual GHG emissions covered (Figure 9.2).

In any case, to compete with oil palm, Hein and van der Meer (2012) estimated that REDD+ needs to ensure a net revenue between US$3 and US$7 per tonne of CO_2 to conserve forests on peat and mineral soil, respectively. Yamamoto and Takeuchi (2015) provided a slightly lower number for the peat case in Central Kalimantan, see also Yamamoto and Takeuchi (2012). During the CDM implementation period of 2008–12, the potential profits from the carbon trade fell short of foreseeable revenues from timber extraction and oil palm expansion in Borneo (Fisher, Edwards, Giam, et al. 2011). To give an impression, Busch et al. (2019) estimated that globally 55 or 108 billion tonnes of CO_2 emissions from terrestrial carbon stock loss can be avoided at a carbon price of US$20 or US$50

FIGURE 9.2

Share of Global Greenhouse Gas Emissions Covered by Carbon Pricing Initiatives

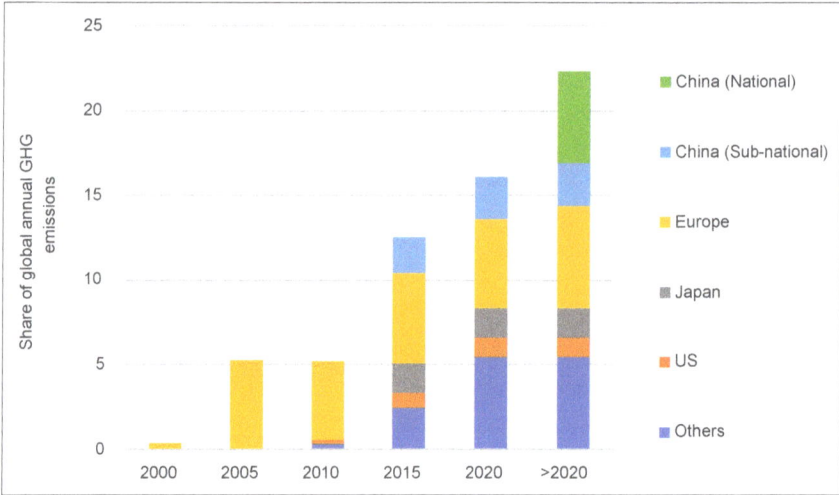

Source: Reproduced from World Bank (2020a).

per tonne of CO_2, respectively. For comparison, the CO_2 emissions from land fires in Indonesia in 2015 amounted to 1.5–2.0 billion tonnes CO_2 (Field et al. 2016).

Putting this into a landscape perspective can potentially change the game. A case study of about 30 kha of forest in the Lower Kinabatangan in Sabah by (Abram et al. 2016) shows that fine-scale planning across the spatially heterogeneous landscape can greatly improve the financial feasibility of REDD+ and allow it to outcompete oil palm. By more accurately identifying patches for conservation, considering spatially explicit characteristics like elevation, slope, aspect, soil types, distance to road, distance to rivers, etc., a price of US$3 per tonne CO_2 may be sufficient to secure 55 per cent of the forest. This can be further tagged along with other efforts and incentives in biodiversity conservation. For example, protecting degraded logged forest patches with a lower carbon stock and lower commercial value that play critical roles in connecting primary forests can be an easy goal for conservation (Fisher, Edwards, Larsen, et al. 2011).

These financial assessments are highly sensitive to the prices of crude palm oil (CPO) and carbon credits (Lu and Liu 2013). However, in reality, they do not necessarily correlate with each other. Figure 9.3 shows a comparison between CPO and the EU-ETS as a very rough example. Things

FIGURE 9.3
Prices of EU Allowances (EUA) and Crude Palm Oil (CPO)

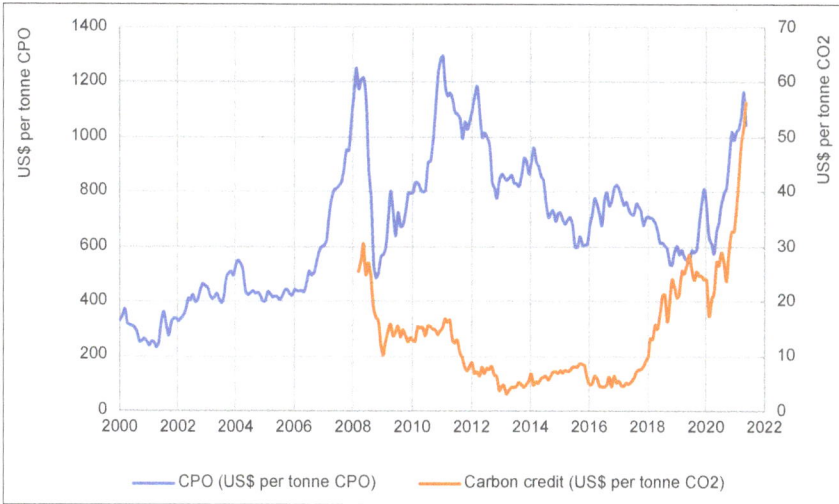

Note: A carbon credit represents an emission saving of one tonne of carbon dioxide (CO2e). These carbon credits are traded on exchange platforms like a stock exchange.
Source: Ember (2020); IndexMundi (2021).

would be more complicated with the mushrooming of numerous carbon pricing systems and the associated policy uncertainties. This implies that the financial feasibility of a REDD+ project in Borneo can be highly unstable as nobody can predict the future prices of both CPO and carbon. Worse still, these compensation mechanisms are troubled by carbon leakages. Local leakage may happen when deforestation is shifted from REDD+ areas to non-REDD+ areas. Similarly, global leakage may happen in countries and regions with no carbon trading in place, considering the expanding cross-border trade of food and fibres (Lu and Liu 2012; Goh, Wicke, Faaij, et al. 2016). Unless PES or regulatory instruments are widely applied throughout all high-risk countries and regions as suggested by Roopsind, Sohngen, and Brandt (2019), these leakages are hard to avoid and can fundamentally undermine the objectives of REDD+.

Beyond Carbon

Importantly, incentivizing only carbon stock conservation may trigger unwanted consequences on other ecosystem services. For example, focusing solely on carbon stock accumulation may not only lead to neglect of high biodiversity areas but also deprivation of biodiversity as reported in East Kalimantan (Budiharta et al. 2014)—note that a high carbon area may have low biodiversity, and vice versa (Harrison and Paoli 2012). Although co-benefits can be more accurately detected with high-resolution and locally validated data, as shown in the cases in West Kalimantan (Labrière et al. 2015) and Sabah (Deere et al. 2018), the current mechanism does not guarantee the protection of other ES when maximizing profits from carbon stock accumulation. Offsetting biodiversity losses would cost 2.5 to 10 times more than restoring carbon stock in all of Kalimantan's peatland (Budiharta et al. 2018).

Theoretically, to create a combination of mechanisms that avoids all these leakages and trade-offs, the ES have to be measured, valued, and compared in the same dimension. This is in line with the concept of "inclusive wealth" that was proposed as a measure to quantitatively cover all these costs in one index (Managi and Kumar 2018). There are also other proposals, such as the concept of ecological supply by Yan et al. (2020), i.e., the ability of the natural environment to provide bio-resources and absorb waste for certain population sizes to measure the impacts of land cover changes on the environment. However, the assessment of Borneo is troubled with very coarse assumptions made for different land classes, leading to a biased result. Some other studies also attempted to integrate provisioning services (food, fibre, and cash crops), regulating services (carbon cycle), and even cultural services like nature recreation on a monetary basis (Sumarga et al. 2015; Sumarga and Hein 2016). However, any attempts to measure overall sustainable development in a harmonized term unavoidably run into substitutability issues, e.g., how much carbon stock is equivalent to the satisfaction from nature recreation is highly subjective and changes with time.

Another potential pricing mechanism would be correlating compensation amount with communities' livelihood for conserving certain areas. This is a non-market valuation compared to the market-based carbon credit. For an example of "willingness to accept", a case study in Lubuk Antu, Sarawak estimated that a monthly fee of slightly more than US$100 per household may be sufficient for the communities to forego slash-and-burn practices. Moreover, compensation may not be necessarily in the form of cash, but material and technical support for rubber cultivation (Phua et al. 2014). Meanwhile, Ota et al. (2020) described another example of "willingness to pay", where the swiftlet farmers are asked to pay a tax for using or affecting the ecosystem services based on their revenues. This may also potentially resolve the issue of inherent difficulties in valuing other ecosystem services, such as biodiversity. However, it also relies on community awareness and knowledge about tangible and intangible benefits (Shah et al. 2016).

Considering these drawbacks, a region-specific, impact-based compensation may be much more effective in ensuring overall sustainability than a universal carbon pricing system. Technically, multiple policy instruments like regulations and certifications would be needed to address the different externalities (Bataille et al. 2018). In that sense, PES and carbon pricing initiatives can be useful options for policymakers to include in development and conservation plans. This is particularly important when put into a local and regional context to minimize conflicts between development and conservation (Venter et al. 2013).

The case of peat fire in Central Kalimantan is a prominent example. From a carbon perspective, unprotected degraded peatland is a priority area as it is highly susceptible to large-scale uncontrolled fire which will emit huge amounts of carbon into the atmosphere (Law, Bryan, Torabi, et al. 2015). For local and regional populations, their livelihood and health are largely affected by the transboundary haze generated by peat fires. In this case, climate advocates and the donors should work closely with all affected stakeholders (especially from the key countries that participated in the ASEAN Agreement on Transboundary Haze Pollution) to consolidate funding sources and different policy instruments (including transboundary governance) in reflection of the actual economic damages including those stemming from health and societal impacts (Forsyth 2014; Glauber et al. 2016; McClure et al. 2019).

Seeing the urgency of avoiding further environmental degradation, different approaches that bring faster actions than "muddling through" strict technical quantification are worth exploring. Compensation schemes for conservation may need to be developed with more creativity and flexibility with a diverse suite of techniques and mechanisms that can work effectively in varying local and regional conditions.

LOCALIZATION AND INSTITUTIONALIZATION

Social Equity

Besides technical issues elaborated on in previous sections, these programmes were intertwined with various local issues. First, there has been stiff competition between productive use and the conservation of land. While prioritizing conservation may effectively prevent the unsustainable expansion of cash crops, it may also potentially block local people from their traditional use of forests when local human-environmental relationships are not properly accounted for. The ongoing debates over the sustainability of traditional practices like shifting agriculture involve not only environmental implications but also socio-cultural elements. These were demonstrated by the polarized views among villagers and villages and the inconsistencies in government policies as seen in the cases of Ketapang and Berau (Anandi et al. 2014; Intarini et al. 2014). The unsuccessful KFCP pilot project that covered about 120,000 ha in the Kapuas district in Central Kalimantan clearly illustrates how local disputes can bring down projects like this (Olbrei and Howes 2012; Lounela 2015). It has never worked as a measure to prevent the deliberate use of fire (Yamamoto and Takeuchi 2016).

The immediately following question would be: who has the right to benefit from the "sales" of "ecosystem services"? Who are considered "service providers"? These critical questions have distributional implications for local societies (Mauerhofer, Hubacek, and Coleby 2013). Boer (2017) suggested that schemes like REDD+ can be viewed as an environmental "welfare" system that involves restructuring and redistribution of benefits. However, the uneven distribution of benefits among the local people has been troubling the REDD+ projects in Central Kalimantan (Joshi et al. 2010; Howson and Kindon 2015).

The case of the REDD+ project in Sungai Lamandau is a prominent example. The project was able to make finance available to some local people, but some others also lost their lands and livelihoods, as the local communities are very diverse and were very mixed in their level of association with the forest, especially the transmigrant Javanese rice growers. Howson (2018b) described REDD+ projects as neoliberal, market-oriented, imposed by government or international conservation interests, focusing on "green development" and unlikely to benefit more than a wealthy subset of forest dwellers. In a strong tone, Howson (2018b) warned that the entire framework of REDD+ in this case "is accelerating the very violence and environmentally destructive behaviours it claims to discourage", though this was denied by the operating organization, Yayorin (Iman Sapari 2018). This is not a unique problem for REDD+ as conflicts between local stakeholders were also frequently reported in other development projects and compensation schemes (Lee, Viswanathan, and Ali 2015).

Rietberg and Hospes (2018) also claimed that such a top-down approach to some extent shared similar characteristics with land grabbing by oil palm companies in terms of obscuring and eroding local authority and institutions. For example, the Rimba Raya Biodiversity Reserve Initiative

(Seruyan, Central Kalimantan) which was dominated by a foreign company based in Hong Kong raised concerns about the real implications of such schemes for local people (Indriatmoko, Atmadja, Ekaputri, et al. 2014). It is reported to be the only forest carbon project that managed to profit from global carbon credit markets (Enrici and Hubacek 2018). The biggest drawback of this kind of for-profit carbon initiative is that it reports to the investors but not the stakeholders. It seems unfair to impose the burden of forest protection on local communities while they are not involved in any decision-making process, and potentially receive the least benefits out of the schemes, especially in places like the ex-MRP areas where people rely heavily on resources from degraded peatland for livelihoods (Jewitt et al. 2014). As reported by Howson (2020), while the Rimba Raya project has further advanced to trade forest carbon in cryptocurrency (which may potentially generate high and quick profits), the local office "remains uninformed" and there is "no plan to offer financial compensation to local people".

The presence of formal tenure is a key factor in determining the successful implementation of REDD+, but tenure uncertainties have been a long-standing issue. The Indonesian government itself has a lot of concerns in giving out the licence for managing a large area of land for REDD+ projects due to legal uncertainties and extreme difficulties in managing potential land conflicts, not to mention the underlying political complexity (Indriatmoko, Atmadja, Utomo, et al. 2014). While there have been strong pressures to hurry the process, the Indonesian government does not seem to have enough capacity in implementing land reform (Resosudarmo et al. 2019). Especially, granting legal certainty to customary systems seems so far to be intractable. In the case of Sungai Lamandau mentioned earlier, Howson and Kindon (2015) flagged the potential risk of widening inequality caused by the carbon finance initiative due to the absence of formal tenure, unequal access to knowledge, and relationship-based distribution of benefits.

Interestingly, based on three village case studies in Kutai Barat, East Kalimantan, Saito-Jensen et al. (2015) argued that REDD+ may be more effective by taking the community as a unit, in the form of small-scale, dispersed community programmes supported by communal forest tenure. Accounting for biophysical, social, and political characteristics of forest restoration at the community level may be more effective in designing and implementing PES schemes. The work by Budiharta et al. (2016) on a community-based forest restoration project in Paser District, East Kalimantan demonstrates that the socio-political context can be decisive in the design of conservation plans.

Co-learning and Co-design

Top-down approaches to global environmental goals are likely to end up in long "fluid" and "messy" communications and negotiations between a complex web of land users and actors (Sanders et al. 2019). Bridging the discursive divide between foreign, national, and local organizations, especially in terms of technical-traditional and national-local perspectives, requires enormous efforts (Gallemore, Rut Dini Prasti, and Moeliono 2014). Relatively high transaction costs also prevent collaboration among a broader network of stakeholders (Gallemore 2017). These are often accompanied by unequal access to information that can potentially foster new inequalities (Kallio et al. 2016). How to refurbish the existing framework to allow and encourage bottom-up initiatives that fit well into local contexts is likely a key to moving forward.

Creating space for local inputs in planning processes at various levels is a precondition for the emergence of bottom-up strategies. Local knowledge in understanding local ecology and land-use dynamics can be valuable, especially when coupled with technologies like remote sensing for more accurate mapping (Beaudoin et al. 2016; Bong, Felker, and Maryudi 2016). This has to be a multi-directional mechanism to allow stakeholders to learn from each other from different perspectives with continual engagement (Boer 2019). For example, Schaafsma, van Beukering, and Oskolokaite (2017) reported a case in Central Kalimantan where communications with communities in the form of focus group discussions and choice experiments to design the compensation schemes can attract communities to participate in peatland restoration programmes. The discussion can be further supported with statistical analysis of local data and information (Yoshikura, Amano, Supriyanto, et al. 2016; Jagger and Rana 2017).

In any case, the inherent difficulty for local stakeholders in understanding the complex financing mechanisms based on the investors' and donors' requirements remains a formidable barrier to overcome (Muttaqin et al. 2019). It was found to be a key reason underlying the hesitance of local stakeholders to get involved in PES schemes (Thompson 2018). Translating information, knowledge, narratives, and perceptions for the understanding of all can be a tough challenge. An attempt made by Koh et al. (2012) was to develop a spatially explicit tool that allows stakeholders to quantify the benefits of carbon conservation in comparison to the opportunity costs from, e.g., conversion to oil palm plantations. Nevertheless, models were seldom built openly and dynamically that could absorb feedback from local actors. This shows that capacity building, coupled with cost reduction and procedure simplification is necessary to ensure meaningful and effective community participation (Harrison and Paoli 2012; Sanders et al. 2020). The historical engagement of local people with other development and conservation projects also influenced the learning process of local actors (Mulyani and Jepson 2015).

In this context, co-learning and co-design are increasingly recognized as crucial components in transforming land-use governance. Importantly, this should be placed in a longer time frame to deal with the interests and goals of different stakeholders. Only with such a vision, policies and investments in capacity building can be made strategically in line with different short-term and long-term targets, especially attending to the needs of local people who will face long-term consequences from these policies and schemes. For example, field studies by Inoue et al. (2013) and Hiratsuka et al. (2014) found that villagers still prioritize traditional shifting agriculture and commercial agroforestry over REDD+ for livelihoods. The launching of multiple income-generation programmes accompanying REDD+ projects in Kalimantan reflects the risk of relying solely on donors and carbon markets for income, and the importance of diversity and flexibility in managing the land-use system (Sills et al. 2014; Yoshikura, Amano, and Anshari 2018). In this context, understanding both the financial and non-financial concerns of local communities by their socio-economic conditions is crucial (Terauchi et al. 2014; Yoshikura, Amano, Chikaraishi, et al. 2016).

While some have argued that a more open, heterogeneous regime can provide additional opportunities for local actors to claim political authority (Andrew et al. 2015), it is not without risks if not broad and fair enough to cover all groups of people. In some cases, REDD+ was reported to be exploited by certain powerful local actors, resulting in new enclosures of land that excluded the less fortunate (Eilenberg 2015). For example, the KFCP was criticized for undermining local values of equality and autonomy (Davies 2015; Lounela 2020). In her fieldwork in 2011–12, Potter was told by the local people in Mantangai village that the project, which had an office in the village, was very secretive and did not communicate with them.

It has also been appropriated by some ethnic-based movements as an instrument in their struggles in land claims with state and private interests (Astuti and McGregor 2017). For example, the above authors reported the movement of the Indigenous People's Alliance of the Archipelago (AMAN) in taking the REDD+ opportunity to push a land claim in Central Kalimantan. Ethnic-based movements like this often led to debates on definitions of indigeneity. The emphasis on ethnicity raises worries about "green grabbing" that may undermine the benefits and livelihoods of certain land users in the REDD+ schemes (de Royer et al. 2015). How to accommodate these different interests remains a prominent problem for the implementation of REDD+. Along this line of inquiry, participatory decision-making processes built into governmental institutions, with a long-term vision, clear mandates and specification of roles may be essential for the effective implementation of REDD+ activities (den Besten, Arts, and Verkooijen 2014).

Institutionalization
Many reckoned that the failures of REDD+ in Kalimantan could be largely attributed to the lack of an agency that could coordinate the fragmented stakeholders and incoherent policies (Ekawati et al. 2019). There was thus a proposal to establish a jurisdictional basis for REDD+ beyond project-based activities to harmonize policy direction and clarify different roles of authorities at multiple levels for ensuring coherence and consistency in implementing REDD+ (Irawan, Widiastomo, et al. 2019). It was hoped that integrating overlapping but disjointed environmental regulation and external incentive schemes like REDD+ could improve the effectiveness of both (Watts et al. 2019). In practice, this would not be an easy task as it would involve shifting policy priorities and redistributing power that may galvanize political struggles and conflicts (Galudra et al. 2011). The everyday work involved in the institutionalization of REDD+ was reported to be highly demanding and inherited the problems of low capacity and poor enforcement in existing institutions (Jespersen and Gallemore 2018; Uda, Schouten, and Hein 2018). The institutionalization of REDD+ in Indonesia has been a highly complex and confusing process, and difficult to be summarized in one or two paragraphs. The rest of this section provides a brief overview of this.

In 2010, Central Kalimantan was chosen as a pilot province to experiment with the institutionalization of REDD+ and to consolidate projects and funding throughout the province (Sanders et al. 2017). A joint secretariat that involved provincial and national decision-makers was established in Palangkaraya. It aimed to harmonize forest governance at the national and provincial levels. However, the involvement of district governments in this process has been limited. This indeed works against the trend of decentralization that started in 2000. The differences among districts in Central Kalimantan can be stark. Suwarno, Hein, and Sumarga (2015) reported that the districts have been performing differently in terms of forest governance since the 2000s, reflecting the complexities of local political ecologies throughout the province. In 2015, the supportive governor of Central Kalimantan, Teras Narang left office, the local secretariat closed and permanent institutional arrangements at the provincial level seemed unlikely to take place (Irawan, Widiastomo, et al. 2019). In the same year, the REDD + secretariat (BP REDD+) at the national level was also disbanded and absorbed into the Department of Forestry and Environment. This change held up payments from Norway for emissions reduction under REDD+ until suitable arrangements were found to manage such payments (Jong 2019c). As noted by Seymour, Aurora and Arif (2020), following that occurrence "the REDD+ agenda appeared to, at least temporarily, run out of steam, mirroring a decline in enthusiasm for REDD+ internationally".

In 2017, REDD+ had been included in national-level regulations related to climate mitigation. Forest reference emission levels (FREL) had been developed for provinces to assign quotas for forest conversion, but provincial and district governments had not been consulted (Irawan, Widiastomo, et al. 2019). Yusuf, Roos, and Horridge (2018) also pinpointed the issue of regional disparities—Kalimantan had been receiving much more attention and funding compared to the other islands—which undermined the legitimacy of institutionalizing REDD+. While Central Kalimantan had been more ready than the other two candidate provinces, Riau and Papua, the institutionalization of REDD+ had not yet been realized at the provincial level (Ekawati et al. 2019).

However, East Kalimantan was later selected as the location of the Forest Carbon Partnership Facility (FCPF) Carbon Fund REDD + pilot. It was hoped that that province would become the first to receive actual payment from such a PES scheme (Ekawati et al. 2019). The Berau district in East Kalimantan has been a pioneer among its peers. The district has demonstrated the use of a jurisdictional approach in the Berau Forest Carbon Partnership (BFCP) (Hovani et al. 2018). Local leadership played a key role in ensuring the implementation of such an approach throughout the district (see also Chapter 6 for the use of the jurisdictional approach for oil palm certification). The progress of this pilot would indicate the feasibility of such a conservation strategy in Borneo.

Sabah has also been attempting to use REDD+ as an instrument for conservation with financial support from the EU to conduct some small projects and assessments in 2014–19. Different from Central Kalimantan which has a relatively weak provincial government, the state government of Sabah has full autonomy in land and forest governance. The Sabah-EU REDD+ initiative was endorsed by the state cabinet and officially incorporated into state policy (Sabah Forestry Department 2018).

Nevertheless, it is uncertain how these initiatives may be continued after the end of the funding period. Overall, the progress in Borneo has not met expectations. More efforts are needed to find out the feasibility of the strategy of commodifying nature as a means to protect it, rethinking the opportunities and challenges in a geographical and territorial context (Lilleskov et al. 2019).

FINAL REMARKS

In navigating the potential of commodifying ecosystem services, experience in Borneo (specifically in Kalimantan) offers several lessons to guide further thinking. Foremost among these were the intricate challenges of quantifying and monetizing ecosystem services, i.e., the extremely high uncertainties in data and subjectivity in assumptions. Furthermore, any attempts to measure ecosystem services in a monetary term unavoidably run into substitutability issues, e.g., the issue of carbon stock versus biodiversity.

Alternatives are an impact-based approach and or a livelihood-based approach to compensation, but these are difficult to be "marketed"—how to combine these perspectives into the existing carbon credit system and reform the incentive system will be a difficult question. In addition, banking on carbon credit may not be a stable revenue source with fluctuating carbon prices, not to mention that land-based projects are not accepted in the existing compliance markets. Long-term economic development also cannot rely solely on voluntary payment from other countries, as such arrangements are easily affected by global economic and political changes. Integration with other income generation activities, by providing space for economic activities, is necessary to improve the financial resilience of PES projects.

Finally, external interventions must be implemented with care to prevent land disputes and ensure equitable benefit distribution. "Ecosystem services" are not a fixed feature related only to the areas, prices, and production, but must also be considered together with the societal dynamics. More nuanced understandings of complexities rooted in societal contexts are therefore required.

10

Establishing Eco-based Tertiary Sectors

Conservationists have long realized the importance and potential of binding conservation with service-based livelihood strategies for local communities. For regions suffering from unsustainable land-based development, establishing a prosperous tertiary sector can be a potential avenue for shifting the development pressure away from land exploitation to alternative eco-economic activities that prioritize conservation. Alongside primary and secondary production activities, multiple conservation-related economic opportunities like eco-tourism can be featured. This has been found to assist local development in many cases around the world and can be particularly instrumental in places facing imminent threats of resource extraction or agricultural expansion (Das and Chatterjee 2015).

In the case of Borneo, the service sectors contributed the highest percentage to the regional GDP in the past few years (except for East Kalimantan) as displayed in Figure 5.1. Specifically, the development of the tourism industry has been widely considered a useful policy instrument for achieving the dual goals of poverty eradication and conservation, especially for communities surrounding ecologically important areas. Eco-tourism businesses have always been important income sources for Borneo, especially Sabah, ranging from highly commercialized packages to rural homestay programmes (STB 2020). Notably, business opportunities that are labour-intensive, unspecialized, and take advantage of local natural assets are the major foci, including tour services, transportation, accommodation, food, handicrafts, and cultural performances. This strategy not only supports conservation by providing alternative income sources but also can instil a sense of nature appreciation and community ownership.

Further expanding the service sectors beyond eco-tourism and creating more "green jobs" in this space for local communities could be a strategy to steer rural development onto a more sustainable pathway. Opportunities include environmental restoration projects, agricultural and forestry services, as well as waste management businesses with new income opportunities that grow upon healthy landscape management. These services are important to repair previous damage and fix current unsustainable practices.

This chapter is divided into two major parts: eco-tourism and eco-based services. For each part, overviews of the sector are provided. These are then followed by a discussion about the infrastructure and investment required to develop specific eco-based service sectors in Borneo.

Eco-tourism

Current Status

A definition of eco-tourism that fits well into the objective of transforming land-based economies is probably the one given by The International Ecotourism Society (TIES) in 1990, i.e., "responsible travel to natural areas that conserves the environment and improves the welfare of the local people" (TIES 2019). Eco-tourism has been developed vigorously across Borneo in various forms of activities, including among others wildlife exploration, adventures, wellness, hiking, rafting, and tapping on different types of natural assets found in particular locations. These are often intertwined with its unique blends of cultural assets. Figure 10.1 shows the tourist statistics to Borneo from both domestic (including other parts of the countries) and foreign visitors. There is no clear distinction between sectors, but the statistics can give some impressions of the current situation of eco-tourism. The Malaysian states are leading with more than 12 million visitors in 2018, nearly double the states' population. Nearly 1.8 million have visited national parks in both states (Figure 10.2).

Besides rare wildlife and abundant rainforests, another reason for Sabah to be the leading tourist destination is probably the famous Mount Kinabalu, the highest peak in Southeast Asia (Saikim and Prideaux 2014; Sheena, Mariapan, and Aziz 2015). Kinabalu National Park, together with Gunung Mulu National Park in Sarawak are the two UNESCO World Heritage sites in Borneo. Highland tourism in Sabah has developed into a very mature tourism industry, consisting of a range of activities from highly challenging mountain hiking to brief excursions that accommodate different groups of tourists (Latip et al. 2020). Furthermore, both the east and west coasts of Sabah hold many touristic islands which host distinctive ecosystems and spectacular landscapes and seascapes and attract millions of visitors every year. Water sports like diving and snorkelling are among the main activities. The Sipadan Island to the east of Sabah is probably the most famous spot in the region for scuba diving (Haddock-Fraser and Hampton 2012).

FIGURE 10.1
Number of Visitors to Borneo in 2018

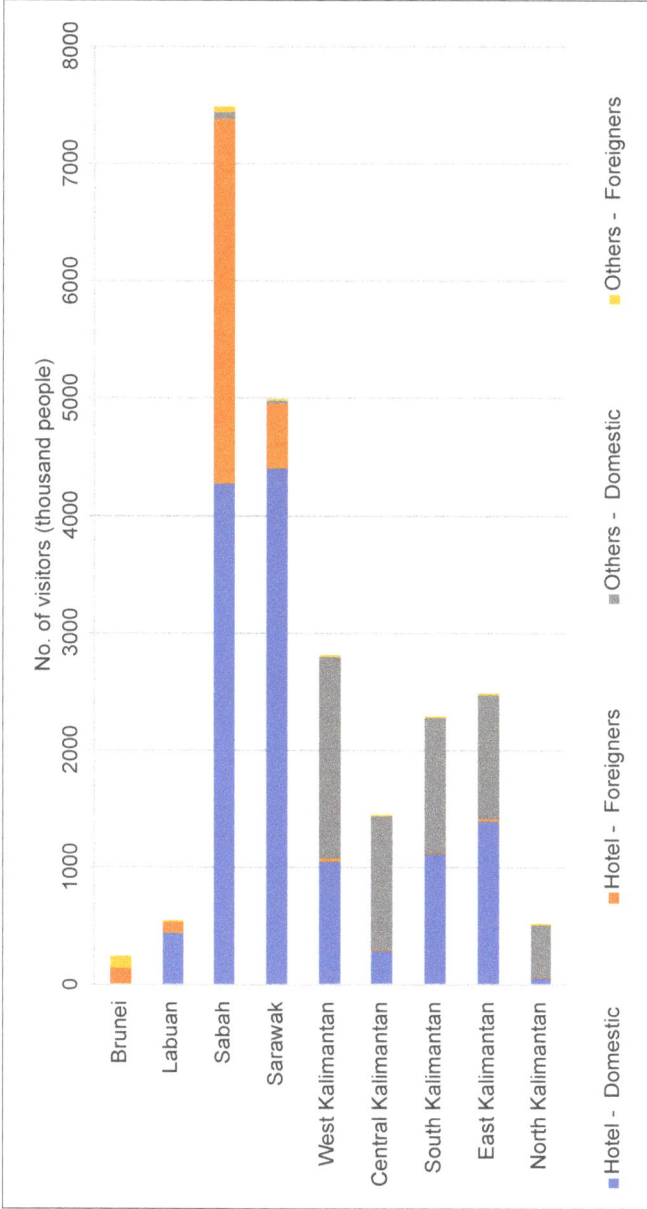

Note: These figures do not, however, distinguish between "mass tourism" and "eco-tourism" or simply visitors. Some of the Malaysian figures refer to urban activities which can hardly be considered "eco-tourism".
Source: Malaysia Tourism Promotion Board (2018); TDD (2018); BPS (2020).

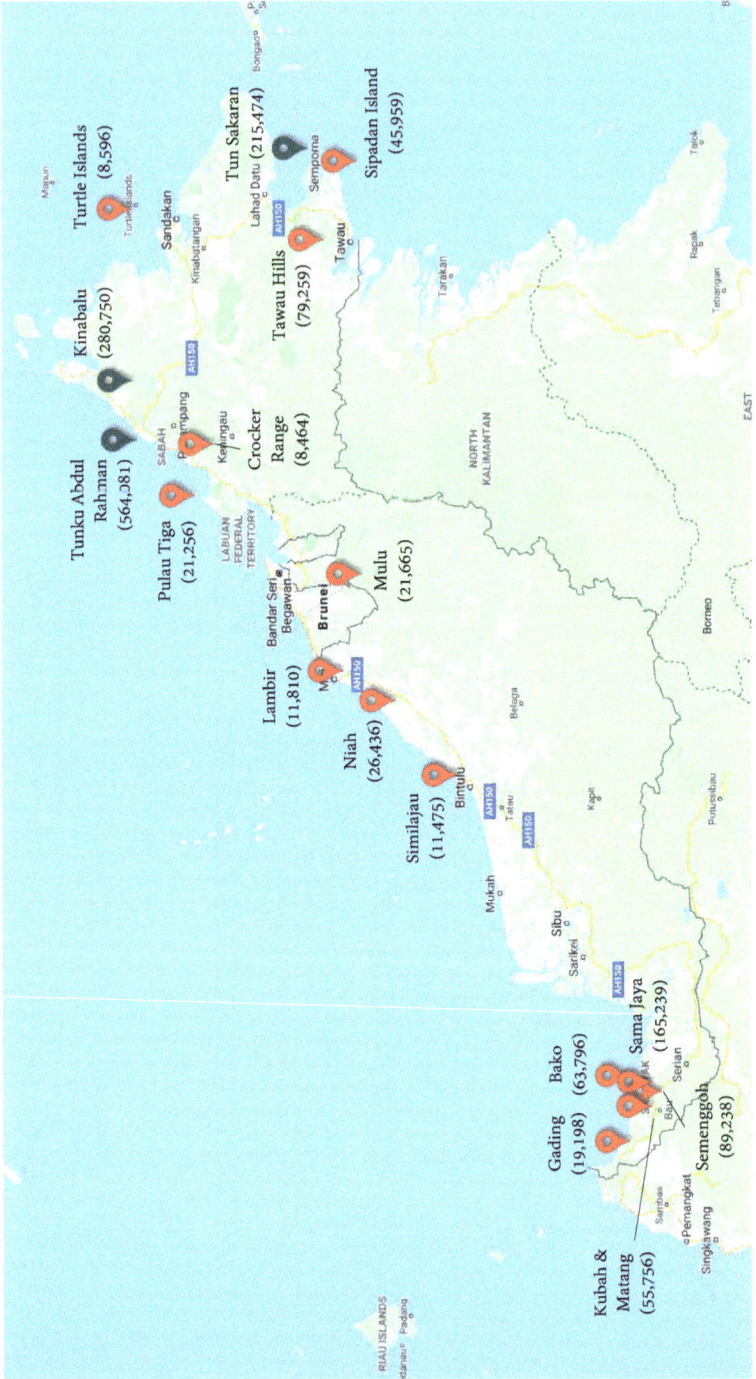

FIGURE 10.2

Visitors to National Parks in Sabah and Sarawak in 2018

Note: National parks with less than 2,000 visitors are not shown.

Source: Malaysia Tourism Promotion Board (2018).

Meanwhile, Sarawak, the "Land of the Hornbills", seems to be more popular among domestic tourists. While the state is also bestowed with natural wonders like Niah Cave (Hunt, Gilbertson, and Rushworth 2012), it is more famous for the culture of its people, such as the remarkable Dayak patterns, musical instruments (especially *sape*), longhouses, and adventurous stories captured by Western explorers in past centuries (Cramb 2007; Sweet and Kelly 2014). Records show that 16,456 tourists visited and stayed overnight at Iban longhouses in 1991 (Zeppel 1998). The Dayak culture is also closely linked to its nature and wildlife, reflected by the illustration of the precious Rhinoceros Hornbill in the state's emblem (Tisen, Kheng, and Gombek 2015). Tour packages often include river tours as longhouses are distributed alongside the riverbanks. Tours can also be combined with local agri-food products as in the case of the Kelabit Highlands which became a famous tourist spot through the branding of Bario rice, a very fine rice variety (see also Chapter 11).

Apart from the mushrooming of famous, starred hotels, a "homestay" as a new form of business has also emerged in recent years in Sabah and Sarawak, aiming to support local communities by tapping into their natural and cultural assets (Pengiran Bagul 2009). However, non-starred hotels, homestays, and other levels of accommodation are not very popular in these states compared to their Indonesian counterparts. The case study on the Dagat village homestay programme in Sabah by Kunjuraman and Hussin (2017) found that despite the concept having been promoted for years, it is still a challenging business due to a lack of infrastructure, marketing channels, and operating strategies. Another study of three villages in the same area near the Tabin Wildlife Reserve: Dagat, Parit, and Kampung Tidong (Saikim et al. 2016) identified a problem of lack of continuous support for international eco-tourism. The villages were initially given eco-tourism training and funding by the Japanese International Cooperation Agency (JICA) and attracted thousands of Japanese tourists for a few years, reorienting the villagers' main sources of income from illegal hunting and poaching the animals in the reserve (partly for the Chinese medicine market). But once the sponsoring agency handed over control to the local communities, tourism income began to decline. As they were unable to develop alternative income sources, many villagers were forced to revert to their previous practices.

Eco-tourism in Kalimantan is relatively underdeveloped compared to Sabah and Sarawak based on the indicator in Figure 10.1. This is also reflected in the number of tour books published in the market (especially those targeting foreign tourists, e.g., Lonely Planet). The gaps between the

Kalimantan provinces and their Malaysian counterparts in Borneo reflect the difficulties involved in opening up remote areas and providing adequate training and facilities in the "target" locations, but also the great potential of eco-tourism to be tapped. While many natural wonders are yet to be discovered by and promoted to foreign and local visitors, Tanjung Puting National Park in Central Kalimantan is already famous due to its importance for observing proboscis monkeys and conservation of orangutans and nine other primates "the highest concentration of primate species within a single park anywhere in the world" (quoted from Orangutan Foundation International n.d.). Another National Park in the province, namely the Sebangau National Park, was established in 2004 and has been slowly developing its eco-tourism (Russon and Susilo 2014; Yuyun, Kaarieni, and Sunaryo 2020). The National Park covers more than 0.5 million ha of forests and swampland that have experienced severe degradation. About half a million people depend on resources from SNP for their livelihoods. See Box 10.1 for the story of eco-tourism in Sebangau and Figure 2.1(b) for its location.

Kalimantan also has other unique cultural attractions like the floating market in Lok Baitan, South Kalimantan (Normelani 2016). Many cultural elements, which are yet to be widely known by outsiders, may attract certain groups of tourists seeking a deeper and possibly spiritual experience. For example, the blending of Dayak spiritual elements into Chinese cultural-religious rituals is a unique feature of West Kalimantan. The most famous touristic event is probably the Cap Go Meh festival in Singkawang, which is very different from the Cap Go Meh in Peninsular Malaysia, Taiwan, mainland China and other places with a Chinese diaspora with its unique Dayak elements (Ong, Ormond, and Sulianti 2017). Thanks to the digital revolution, now there are a handful of videos of such cultural events in Borneo available to the world on YouTube.

Besides nature-based and culture-based tourism, some other interesting forms of tourism may also rise as new opportunities for Borneo. Agri-tourism that allows visitors to experience farm activities may be a suitable option. An example is the dairy farm and tea garden in Sabah (Halim et al. 2019). Another form of tourism has educational and research themes, aiming to provide deeper insights into the knowledge of nature, culture, and human-environmental interactions, such as educational tour services provided in national parks (Goh and Rosilawati 2014). Synergistically, these activities may also be bundled with business and academic conferences, as is frequently done in Sarawak (BCCK 2020).

BOX 10.1
Eco-tourism in Sebangau, Central Kalimantan

While Tanjung Puting was declared a National Park in 1982, the Sebangau National Park was previously a production forest and only achieved park status in 2004. At that time almost half of its area was categorized as degraded and many human activities within the park (including logging) were declared illegal. Park zoning in 2015 allowed eco-tourism except in the core area, but the Sebangau National Park Authority had already begun developing eco-tourism to engage five of the forty-two village communities around the park and improve local livelihoods. Guesthouses and jungle tracks have been organized together with programmes on tourist guiding, homestays, food, and boat hire. Also, an art and culture studio focused on Dayak culture (including the Kaharingan religion) has been established. Nature-based tourism is planned to focus on fishing, orangutan observation, and forest adventures.

Agri-tourism, including jelutong resin harvesting, was also promoted. Jelutong is a wild rubber obtained from *Dyera costulata* trees. It was used as the base for chewing gum and mixed with poison in blowpipes. The tree grows wild in the peat swamps of Central Kalimantan and Sarawak and in the early twentieth century attracted hundreds of tappers in a "jelutong boom" (Potter 2005).

So far, the income received by the villagers is small and community participation remains limited, although visitor numbers have grown. However, eco-tourism in Sebangau is in a very early phase and its development is quite slow. Difficulties include the fact that orangutan observation (a core activity) can occur only in the rainy season through small canals, necessitating high costs for tourism operators (Meilani et al. 2019).

Transboundary or borderland tourism may also be a potential area to explore. This can be perceived in two forms. First, the Bornean territories may seek to strategically package attractions on both sides of the borders, like transboundary highland eco-tourism in Kelabit-Krayan—the Kelabit Highlands in Sarawak are connected by road with the Krayan Highlands in North Kalimantan. Due to its relative isolation, that area is less famous but possesses attractions like salt springs and Adan rice (Hitchner et al. 2009; Nugraha, Putri, and Suprihanto 2018). A road from Malinau town in North Kalimantan to Long Bawan in Krayan subdistrict is under construction but delayed because of COVID-19 restrictions. When completed, it will open the Krayan area to visitors from the Indonesian side of the border (see Figure 5.4).

A meeting for tour operators held in Jakarta in May 2019 by the Indonesian Ministry of Tourism launched a campaign to promote the Heart of Borneo as a tourism destination, under the heading "Visit the Heart of Borneo: An Ecotourism Promotion in the Heart of Borneo" (WWF 2019). By consolidating efforts from the three countries on the island, "Borneo" can be made into a brand to attract package tourists around the world. In this context, Heart of Borneo (HoB) is a collaboration between the three countries to achieve conservation and productivity together through a coordinated, transboundary approach to conservation and sustainable development, with a special emphasis given to eco-tourism (Firdaus, Wibowo, and Rochmayanto 2017), see also Chapter 8 and Figure 2.1(b).

Second, the Bornean territories can tap into the regular and continuous flows of people and goods across borders, forging closer regional economic cooperation at the local level (Muazir and Hsieh 2012; Muazir and Hsieh 2014; King 2016). Small-scale flows of goods and labour have been very active at the borders (Eilenberg and Wadley 2009). The Sarawak-West Kalimantan border, once famous for timber smuggling, is also widely used for legal trade. Potter observed evidence of the legal trade in 2007 when she walked across the border from the Sarawak side at Jagoi Babang (Bengkayang), a small crossing (one of five recognized crossings) that was still in the process of being opened up for larger traffic and more organized customs/migration between Pontianak and Kuching—see also Umahuk (2017). Indonesian farmers in Jagoi Babang village grow pepper to sell across the border, where prices are much higher; they also sell various handicrafts, such as bamboo screens and rattan baskets.

Impacts and Challenges

An anticipated benefit of eco-tourism is its synergy with nature conservation. Ideally, not only can it enhance visitors' awareness about conservation, but also educate local communities—revenues from tourism can only be sustainable if they follow sustainable practices. The promotion of eco-tourism in combination with programmes like REDD+ (mentioned in Chapter 9) provides new livelihood opportunities and creates awareness about sustainability. Box 10.2 provides an interesting example in Malinau, North Kalimantan where eco-tourism is promoted as an alternative to logging or oil palm.

BOX 10.2
Eco-tourism in Kenyah Oma Lung Village of Setulang

While access difficulties remain for the remote highland villages in the Kayan-Mentarang NP within the HoB, the Kenyah Oma Lung village of Setulang, only 29 km upstream from Malinau town has an ongoing eco-tourism programme. The people of Setulang migrated in 1968 from the upper Pujungan area, 125 km inland in the HoB, but are now permanently settled at the junction of the Setulang and Malinau rivers: while the riverside lowland areas are utilized for shifting agriculture and semi-permanent gardening, the forested uplands are relatively intact. This unique pristine forest (never logged) has the highest density of Dipterocarp species in Kalimantan and exceptional diversity. Part (5,300 ha) has been carefully nurtured by the village as a *restricted* forest (*Tane' Olen* or *Tana' Ulen*), to be used occasionally for hunting and extracting forest products and primarily for the security of water supplies.

Several attempts were made (largely assisted by CIFOR) to gain wider protection for the forest against various logging companies, including a failed Community Conservation Concession (Wunder et al 2008) and a REDD+ project (Pramova et al, 2013). In 2014, the Minister of Environment and Forestry granted Setulang Village full forest management rights. The new forest management plan "includes protection and sustainable landscape management through promoting non-timber forest products, environmental services, and eco-tourism activities" (FORCLIME 2016). The eco-tourist programme enables visitors to stay overnight in the forest and experience a wide variety of animal and birdlife as well as the vibrant local culture. There is even a book on Setulang, written with the assistance of the German Aid Agency GIZ, to celebrate the fifth anniversary of North Kalimantan in April 2018. The book explains the social and cultural traditions of the people in sustainable forest management, together with many illustrations (Ernawati 2017).

It is hoped that establishing "tourism concessions", i.e., legally delineating an area for tourism operations may contribute to sustainable financing of nature protection (MOTAC 2015). However, developing eco-tourism in conservation areas may generate negative consequences for the socio-ecological resilience of local systems (Bernard, Roche, and Sarrasin 2016). Macfie and Williamson (2010) rightly pointed out that conservation-based tourism may not be sustainably replicable in all places. There are significant risks to conservation when sound principles are not strictly followed from the start, harming the well-being and survival of the endangered species. For example, the booming business of proboscis monkeys viewing in addition to the massive clearing for oil palm in the Lower Kinabatangan has disturbed wildlife habitats (Boonratana 2013).

Numerous examples also show that responsible tourism awareness is still low among stakeholders, and in many cases, economic incentives from eco-tourism are not attractive enough to make an impact on pushing the conservation agenda (Ahmad 2014; Leasor and Macgregor 2014; Tay and Chan 2016; Tay et al. 2016). The efficacy of eco-tourism in poverty alleviation remains uncertain. Although household income has increased in general as reported by various studies in Borneo (Kunjuraman 2020), it remains unstable due to its seasonal nature. Jobs also remain mostly part-time and informal (Rasoolimanesh, Jaafar, and Tangit 2018). The sector has been facing stiff competition from other land-based development especially plantation development. Box 10.3 provides more insights into this example.

Exceptions can be those places that have really strong eco-tourism businesses like the Kelabit Highlands and Iban longhouses close to Kuching in Sarawak, where tourism has been closely interwoven with the social and cultural development of the communities, mutually reinforcing each other (Harris 2009). As landmarks of Sarawak, Iban longhouses have been hosting tens of thousands of tourists each year, not only creating a range of local tourism professionals but also making this part of their way of living (Zeppel 1998). However, that also implies potential alterations of and impacts on local culture through narrative engineering in advancing indigenous cultural and economic interests in partnership with the state's eco-tourism agenda (see Box 10.4) (Menon 2018). The traditional cultural industry in Sarawak has also been very active, especially traditional music. However, local artists and performers are often asked to relocate to major tourist spots, especially in urban areas (Haigh 2020). Such arrangements seldom bring spillover benefits to their home villages or communities.

An important question would be the adaptation and resilience of tourism businesses in a changing environment—how economically sustainable is eco-tourism in Borneo? Besides targeting wealthier countries, it is also strategic for Borneo to attract tourists within Indonesia and Malaysia (*Borneo Post*, 2 June 2020). This requires more careful designing of touristic activities based on an in-depth understanding of the characteristics of the tourists from different backgrounds and their experience in Borneo. For example, Sheena, Mariapan, and Aziz (2015) and Rasoolimanesh et al.

BOX 10.3
Eco-tourism or Plantation? The Case of Long Terawan, Sarawak

Long Terawan village is near the famous Gunung Mulu and offers eco-tourism. Kampung Sungai Melinau residents work in the tourism industry and are part of Long Terawan. They operate guest houses, work as guides and boatmen, or run small restaurants, but also farm and hunt. Resettled Penan live in Batu Bungan right next to the park. They rely heavily on the forest and its resources: sago palms, wild animals, timber, rattan, and medicinal plants.

A "land grab" by the company Radiant Lagoon Sdn Bhd for an oil palm plantation of 4,440 ha on "indigenous territory belonging to the groups Penan, Berawan and Tering", which includes part of Long Terawan, was reported by BMF (2019). Radiant Lagoon belongs to Mahmud Abu Bekir Taib, son of Abdul Taib Mahmud, former chief minister, and now governor of Sarawak. By 2019 the company had cleared some forest in the area. The environmental assessment of the project had never been revealed to the local people.

Villagers were divided about the project, but Penan unanimously opposed it. Penan and Berawan communities argued that the area was part of their traditional land, and they were angry not to have been consulted. Some gravesites had been destroyed and large amounts of timber illegally removed. The Penan-Berawan community filed a suit to stop the issuance of two provisional leases by the Sarawak Government for the company (*Borneo Post*, 6 August 2019). An update by Keeton-Olsen (2021) stated that the company has now withdrawn much of its machinery, with clearing halted since late 2019.

While the cessation of eco-tourism due to COVID-19 has hit the local economy, the establishment of an oil palm plantation may slow the resurgence of the industry there. Eco-tourism may be deployed as a strategy for income generation, but a larger question for Sarawak is the fragility of its national parks—even UNESCO-protected Gunung Mulu—if secretive oil palm land grabs can occur right on park borders.

(2019) found that more than half of the tourists from Malaysia to Kinabalu National Park, Sabah can be considered "soft" and "structured" tourists who prefer more relaxing and well-arranged, guided trips. Similar investigations were made on other locations, again Kinabalu National Park, three wildlife attractions around Sandakan (Corpuz 2017), and Bako National Park (Kamri and Radam 2013).

BOX 10.4
Narrative Engineering of the Heart of Borneo

An interesting cultural publication *Highland Tales in the Heart of Borneo* (2015) showcases indigenous oral histories and mythologies of some Upland Orang Ulu peoples: Kelabit, Lun Bawang and Lundayeh, in Sarawak and Sabah. It was published by the Malaysian section of *Forum Masyarakat Adat Dataran Tinggi* (FORMADAT), the leader of which stated that each group "has their own distinct dialects and cultural nuances yet rooted at the core with parallel mythology and oral history". He suggested that "this publication will serve as promotional material for eco-tourism at natural and cultural sites of the Kelabit and Maligan Highlands, a reference for nature guides to using and a way to document the history of the Kelabit, Lun Bawang and Lundayeh people in the Heart of Borneo" (WWF Malaysia 2015). One reviewer perceived this to be a very political document, quietly but firmly disrupting Sarawakian narratives of racial harmony and economic development by advancing indigenous cultural and economic interests, with a strategic partnership with state eco-tourism and even the Sarawak Forest Department (Menon 2018).

There are also studies on understanding the willingness of visitors to spend for eco-tourism and their loyalty towards the locations. Findings from the work of Emang, Lundhede, and Thorsen (2016) in Sipadan suggest that price discrimination among scuba divers can generate more income by estimating the willingness of different groups to pay higher user fees for environmental preservation. Some other works study the various factors that affect the decision-making of tourists, such as the paper by Rasoolimanesh et al. (2020) that investigated the engagement and loyalty of male and female tourists towards Kinabalu National Park.

Finally, transboundary collaboration in service sectors between Malaysia, Indonesia, and Brunei Darussalam can provide impetus to regional economic development, but it also faces some limitations. Nugraha, Putri, and Suprihanto (2018) found that as the Krayan Highlands is only easily accessible by ground transport through Malaysia, eco-tourism actually benefits Malaysia more than Indonesia. There was an interesting saying among the Krayan people, "Garuda in our hearts, Tiger in our bellies" (*di dada ada Garuda, di perut ada Harimau*) where Garuda and Tiger represent Indonesia and Malaysia, respectively (and see discussion on the new road project on the Indonesian side from Malinau to the Krayan in Chapter 5, which will be likely to change some of these relationships).

However, fruitful cross-national collaboration to take advantage of continuity and diversity is yet to be seen, and the actual development of tourism is highly uneven across the island (King 2016). In practice, most proposals remain conceptual, and more investment is still needed for on-ground implementation (Sloan et al. 2019).

Environmental Services

"Environmental services" may not be a common term in the literature. While "green jobs" may be more common to the general audience, some have criticized the concepts of "green jobs" and "green economies" due to their very broad coverage and ambiguity (Furchtgott-Roth 2012). However, there are indeed various new economic opportunities that have arisen from the push for environmental protection and restoration. In this context, the term "environmental services" may more precisely describe new jobs and businesses that provide services related to preserving or restoring the environment. According to UNCTAD (2003), environmental services include not only waste and pollution management but also nature and landscape protection services. The creation of income opportunities in the "environment industry" is touted as an important component of sustainable development.

A range of new jobs and businesses can be created in the direction of minimizing environmental impacts and optimizing economic output in the agricultural and forestry sectors. At the most basic level, the demand for agro services, like applying fertilizers and mechanization, is growing with the transition of small farmers from traditional to modern agriculture. It may be more economically feasible and more environmentally friendly if the farmers outsource these services to specialized external companies (*Borneo Post*, 9 January 2019). Goh has also observed this kind of business model in Central Kalimantan.

Knowledge-based services are also growing slowly in Borneo. These services cover various needs that have emerged with the advancement in agriculture, such as environmental engineering, laboratory works, regulatory compliance assistance, technology transfers, and consulting services, providing tailor-made solutions for customers both on paper and onsite management. Waste management is one of the key areas that require further attention to be in full compliance with legal requirements. In the agriculture sector, a prominent example would be the treatment of palm oil mill effluents (POME), which can be further integrated with biogas businesses (see Chapter 7) (Loh et al. 2017). Solid waste management is another critical sector in Borneo (Moh and Abd Manaf 2017). A landfill, if not open dumping, is the most common solution (Pariatamby 2014). In most cities in Borneo, badly regulated landfills and dumping sites have created very serious pollution yet received little attention to date (Abushammala et al. 2011). These aspects are also mentioned specifically in the SDGs, especially SDG 11 "Sustainable cities and communities" and SDG 14, "Life below water": plastic pollution in the oceans is very visible on many Bornean coasts and beaches, even in wealthy Brunei, and from cities such as Miri (Sarawak) and Kota Kinabalu (Sabah).

Conceivably, peatland restoration projects in Kalimantan can also create a spectrum of jobs, such as project facilitators, on-ground emergency squads, educators, researchers, translators, and coordinators between foreign funders and local communities. These opportunities are mostly grasped in the form of various local organizations. However, the allocation of funding can be highly complex and embroiled in political struggles as described in Chapter 9. Furthermore, such funding has been very limited given the amount needed for large-scale conservation. As such projects are highly dependent on external funding at present, they need to be integrated with other livelihood strategies such as the eco-tourism activities described earlier. Also, not empowering local people in more knowledge-intensive jobs (that are currently held by extra-local people) implies that some of the expected added value may remain a mirage. In the long term, how to create more high-end, not only low-end jobs for local people and how to stimulate innovation among local businesses are two aspects that require careful attention.

INFRASTRUCTURE AND INVESTMENT

The development of service sectors in Borneo has encountered multiple challenges. The isolation of the island from the core economic zones of Malaysia and Indonesia, as well as the lack of infrastructure throughout Borneo, have impeded the flow of tourists, customers, knowledge, and capital to and from their own countries.

First, inter-island and rural-urban linkages, i.e., transportation and communication will be the key to developing a prosperous tertiary sector (Abdullah 2016). Better connectivity in physical transportation enhances the mobility of people in providing and reaching services in both urban and rural areas. In this context, Sabah and Sarawak fare better than their counterparts due to higher investment in infrastructure in the past decades. As shown in Figure 10.3, Sabah's capital has the most international flight

FIGURE 10.3
Flight Connections of Borneo

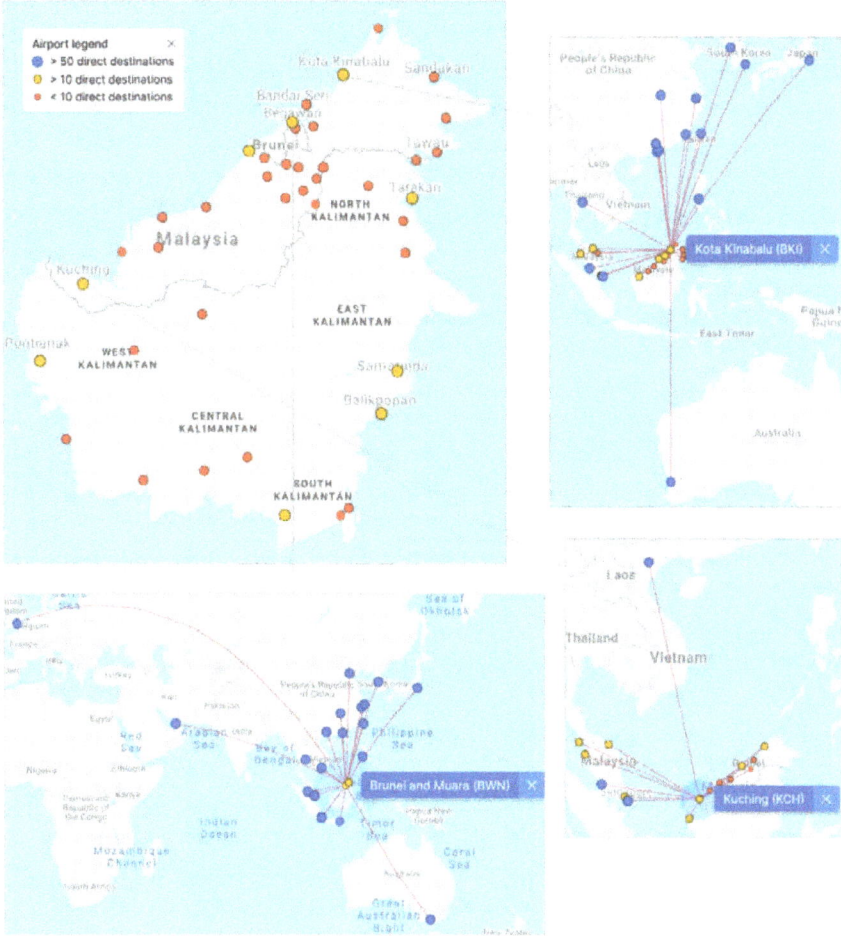

Note: Pontianak has flight connections to Kuala Lumpur and Singapore, while Balikpapan has one to Kuala Lumpur. No international flights to other cities.
Source: www.flightconnections.com (accessed December 2020).

connections after Brunei Darussalam. While Sarawak has a connection to Vietnam in 2020, the major cities in Kalimantan only have international flights to Kuala Lumpur and Singapore.

In addition, the availability of digital networks may allow effective marketing at much lower costs. The "tourism digital ecosystem" has been an important item on the agenda of the Malaysian government in promoting eco-tourism (MOTAC 2015). Two rural ICT projects in Sarawak, namely *e-Bario* and *e-Bedien*, are interesting examples (Gnaniah et al. 2005). The communities in the Bario Highlands and Long Bedian were largely isolated with no road connection and grid connectivity for both power and telecommunication. In the early 2000s when no mobile phones and data networks were available, these projects demonstrated that connectivity could bring important changes to remote communities. The promotion of the annual Bario Food Festival which celebrates the heritage and intact nature of the Bario Highlands was an example that leveraged the e-Bario telecentre facilities (Harris, Ramaiyer, and Tarawe 2018). The proliferation of digital technologies also has an important implication for socio-cultural preservation and research, such as the case of visualizing feminist epistemology reported by Spiegel (2019) for a village in Central Kalimantan.

Importantly, nurturing human and intellectual capital, as well as entrepreneurship among rural populations is a key to unlocking economic opportunities in tertiary sectors. A necessary precondition is equipping the local people with sufficient knowledge and skills to carry out environmental-related services instead of outsourcing them to external players. These include not only basic technical services like fertilizing but also high-end jobs like environmental engineering. Training and education are essential to overcome these barriers for indigenous people, especially in basic skills like ICT knowledge (Ahmad et al. 2016; Sada, Alas, and Anshari 2019). However, not much investment has been made in nurturing local intellectual capital as most decision-makers are looking for quick economic returns instead of long-term development in Borneo, which is often seen merely as a raw material production base (Mohammad and Bujang 2019). Governments may need to actively intervene in this aspect by strategically expanding training in secondary and tertiary education to attract more youths to take up professions in eco-tourism and agriculture with a sound knowledge basis in sustainability (Dhindsa and Md-Hamdilah 2015; Lee and van der Heijden 2019; Kasa et al. 2020).

Another critical element to eco-based businesses is their financial sustainability, especially those that were initiated by external donors or government funding. There are similarities with the problems faced by big programmes like REDD+ (see Chapter 9) or small programmes like financial aid for local communities. They are easy to start but not sustainable when unable to meet commercial viability. For local communities, these are often ad hoc projects that provide temporary or seasonal income instead of long-term business and career opportunities. In this context, governments need to play a more active role to forge a lively environment for local tertiary businesses to grow and thrive, such as facilitating investment and technology transfers through a partnership with extra-local companies and providing direct monetary support to motivate local communities venturing into new businesses (Hamzah and Mohamad 2012). While financial instruments to support small and medium start-ups are critical to boosting the service sectors, a critical issue to tackle is probably the lack of modern financial and business knowledge among rural communities. An investigation in Kinabalu National Park by Jaafar, Rasoolimanesh, and Lonik (2015) revealed that most entrepreneurs in the service sector were middle-aged or older females with poor education who often struggled with unstable income. Financial training for these local entrepreneurs is essential to improve the sustainability and resilience of their businesses.

At higher levels, economic clustering can be a way forward through fostering synergies with other parts of countries as well as among different sectors to create economies of scope, i.e., efficiencies formed by variety instead of volume, given that the production of one good reduces the production cost of another related good. The Malaysian governments have taken several measures with policy frameworks made at both national and state levels to consolidate efforts in promoting Malaysian Borneo for its attractions and various products (MOTAC 2015). Especially, symbols like Orangutan (an endangered primate species) and Rafflesia (the world's biggest flower) are used frequently to create both the brand of Borneo and Malaysia. The Kalimantan provinces have also devised some plans for tourism development, such as the Provincial Tourism Development Master Plan of Central Kalimantan 2013–28, and the Danau Sentarum Festival in Kapuas Hulu West Kalimantan each December (Timotius 2021), but they relatively lack attention from the national government and generally stay off-radar for foreign tourists compared to Sabah and Sarawak (Rhama 2019). Particularly, the Kalimantan provinces are less competitive when it comes to serving a wider group of tourists, including those who prefer "soft" eco-tours, as they lack hotels and restaurants that fulfil the needs of various types of tourists compared to their Malaysian peers in the north (Nugraha, Putri, and Suprihanto 2018).

Final Remarks

The situation in Borneo is not unique—the review by Das and Chatterjee (2015) showed that the results of eco-tourism across the world in 2000–13 varied greatly between remarkable successes and miserable failures. Eco-tourism is neither a panacea nor a predicament but should be designed and used strategically as part of the bigger plan for transforming the land-based economies (linked also to the SDGs). The emergence of the new demand for environmental services adds an interesting twist.

Clearly, education is the key to empowering local communities in grasping and creating new economic opportunities beyond labour-intensive and low-skilled jobs. Capacity-building may not be limited to only small, narrow, and short-term improvements, but be expanded with a revolutionary vision to grow local talents that can devise their own plans for long-term development and conservation. Additionally, geographical connectivity must be expanded if the Bornean tertiary sector is to become competitive. Besides physical connections that can be difficult to establish, deploying a wide coverage of digital connectivity allows quick flows of large amounts of knowledge and information to and from communities that previously had limited access, not only liberalizing them from intellectual isolation but also providing new business opportunities through lowering transaction costs.

11

Marketing Products from Smallholdings

Borneo is home to a wide range of natural products with various functions. While many of them are commonly used by local communities, these products may have potential in medium or high-end markets. Across the world agricultural and forestry products are marketed with names of regions or places for authenticity and exotics like "Thai rice", "Gouda cheese", and "Swiss chocolate", or with special labels like "organic" and "natural". The word "Borneo" itself also represents exotic and mysterious flavours to many foreigners. How to leverage this advantage to create new income sources and conserve nature would be a potential strategy for developing a sustainable eco-economy. In the past, the indigenous people in the hinterlands exchanged their forest products with extra-local traders through riverine hubs, such as trade-hub longhouses once found in Sarawak (Sakuma 2017).

The smallholder-centric approach is different from the large-scale certifications described in Chapter 6 which mainly focused on highly industrialized cash crops, as it seeks to connect the buyers more directly with the efforts of small farmers to improve their livelihoods. In other words, "small" itself can be a key branding element. This is bound to the enhancement of economic opportunities for a heterogeneous group of small farmers, with the ultimate goal to alleviate persistent poverty. Effective branding provides opportunities for not only upgrading the value chain but also improving the land-use practices of farmers, as securing livelihoods is a precondition for environmental conservation (Suwarno, van Noordwijk, et al. 2018).

Globally, products characterized by small-scale production systems have been receiving extra attention in the past few decades. Especially, the market share of those certified for sustainability has been growing (Willer et al. 2019). The presence of market differentiation for such products offers opportunities for small farmers to capture a better share of the selling price. The numerous successful branding and marketing stories of smallholders around the world, such as tea, coffee, and cotton with various certifications have reflected the potential of such a strategy to be adopted in Borneo. This chapter provides a brief description of a range of local specialities and geographical indications, as well as several potential niche markets for the small farmers in Borneo. Some thoughts on ways forward are also elaborated. Note that oil palm smallholdings are not included in this chapter but are discussed in Chapter 6 together with industrial plantations.

Local Specialities and Geographical Indications

Food Products

Local specialities can be marketed through Geographical Indications (GIs), a marketing approach that focuses on the embodied place-related value. A few agro-products in Borneo well known for quality and authenticity, such as Sarawak pepper, are among the examples that employ the GI approach. Pepper, sometimes known as the "king of spices", is a key speciality of Sarawak. Pepper gardens are a component of the income portfolio for many small farmers in Sarawak and to a lesser extent in West Kalimantan (Wadley and Mertz 2005). The pepper trade has had a long history in Sarawak since the 1900s under the rule of the White Rajah. The brand of "Sarawak pepper" was recognized in 2006 by the Malaysian Pepper Board through the use of GI (Sephton 2011). West Kalimantan is the current leader for Kalimantan in the area of pepper, followed closely by East Kalimantan, which obtains better yields (Dir Jen Perkebunan, 2018–2020). In East Kalimantan, a well-known and respected variety, namely Malonan Kutai Kartanegara White Pepper, with a particularly sharp aroma, was rewarded with a GI in 2019 (ASEAN GI Database 2019). This special pepper has evolved from plantings by Buginese migrants along the Balikpapan-Samarinda Highway from the 1970s. It is ironic that this industry was considered unsustainable in the 1990s (see Box 12.3 "Buginese Pepper Farmers", p. 548 in MacKinnon et al. 1996).

In Sabah, coffee beans from Tenom provide an example of a local speciality that is promoted using the name of the place. It contrasts with the long history of Sarawak pepper: "Tenom coffee" was only established as a "brand" in recent years (*Borneo Post*, 2 December 2017). Tenom itself has been famous not only for its agricultural products but also as a tourist spot with attractions like the Tenom Orchid Centre and the Murut Cultural Centre. Another popular beverage, tea, is also a potential commodity to be marketed through the GI approach in Borneo. It is just recently beginning in Sintang, West Kalimantan (*Pontianak Post*, 28 January 2020). Borneo's specialities may be famous in the region but also face fierce competition from neighbouring countries with similar products, especially coffees and peppers from Vietnam.

As Borneo has been a centre of diversity for many fruits, one potential product to be branded is Bornean cultivars of tangerine citrus (*jeruk siam*), a popular type of fruit in Indonesia, namely "Siam Banjar" in South Kalimantan (related to the name of the largest ethnic group) and "Siam Pontianak" in West Kalimantan (related to the capital city of West Kalimantan). These local tangerines are nutritious and delicious but are yet to be widely marketed in the region compared to the major competitors, oranges from the temperate zone. Improving the management of the supply chain, especially post-harvest handling can significantly improve the quality of fruits and compliance with trading standards (Hassan et al. 2013). Most of the tangerines in South Kalimantan are grown in low-lying districts like Barito Kuala; unfortunately, 4,662ha (30 per cent of the total) of tangerine trees were drowned in the serious floods in much of the province in February 2021 (Susanto 2021).

The yellow-fleshed durian, *Durio kutejensis*, is a widespread variety that grows wild in the forests of Kalimantan. It is known as *pekawai* in West Kalimantan, *likul* in South Kalimantan, *pampakan* in Central Kalimantan, *pulu* in Brunei and *rian isu* in Iban. Unlike durians found in other parts of Malaysia and Indonesia, this fruit lacks any unpleasant smell but has a sweet taste and good keeping qualities. Its chips also make a tasty snack that might be safe for diabetics (Lestari and Purwayantie 2018). A rather different example, one of the rarest mangoes, and now found only cultivated in gardens, is the small purple Kasturi mango. It is a mascot of South Kalimantan province, but it is listed as extinct in the wild by the IUCN. However, there is a risk that local knowledge of these rare fruits might be lost with time together with many marketing possibilities. A study in Sarawak by Faridah Aini et al. (2017) revealed that the knowledge about local, wild fruits has deteriorated among the younger indigenous people, especially given recent high urbanization rates.

In addition, other native products from rural areas, such as high-quality red rice (Masni and Wasli 2019), also have the potential to be marketed. These products can become famous for their health benefits or other specialities, filling in certain niche markets. Bario rice, a very fine rice variety from Sarawak, is famous for its sweetness and texture for the use of local cuisine (Harris 2009). Its authenticity is closely associated with the ethnic group and the place—Bario is the name of a major community of the indigenous Kelabit people in the Kelabit Highlands. Some have advocated the use of GI certification (which was obtained in 2008) in combination with its "organic" characteristics for better marketing of Bario rice (*Borneo*

Post, 22 October 2019). In recent years, "Adan" rice from Krayan Highland in North Kalimantan has become the major supplier although it is not grown in the Kelabit Highlands, as the brand of "Kelabit-Bario" is already well established. Even after Adan rice was listed in GI in 2012, marketing is very difficult: as there is no current transportation east to Malinau, but just west across the border in Malaysia lies the Kelabit village of Ba'kelalan, where the Adan rice can be sold (Antons 2017). The new road planned from Malinau to Krayan, hopefully, completed in 2022 (see Chapter 5 and Figure 5.4) should help to solve these problems.

Interestingly, promoting local specialities can synergistically help to support the efforts in conserving the genetic resources of local species. The Malaysian Agricultural Research and Development Institute (MARDI) has spent millions of dollars every year to keep genetic resources in *ex situ* "field genebanks", where plants are purposely cultivated in designated fields for gene conservation purposes. Encouraging on-farm or *in situ* conservation of native species like rare fruits by small farmers in their home gardens can relieve the financial pressure on conservation while supplying new income sources to the farmers (Abdul Shukor, Mohd Shukor, and Salma 2013). The term "community biodiversity management" (CBM) was used by Arsanti and Hardiyanto (2020) in their case study in South Kalimantan to describe how conservation of the genetic resources can be achieved by the community through valorizing and marketing of these species.

Non-food Products

Besides food specialities, Borneo is also endowed with various non-food products that have high market potential. Wild orchids are another natural wonder to be considered. Many Bornean orchids are precious, due to the difficulties of cultivating them in nurseries (Rozlaily et al. 2015). For example, the prices of *Bulbophyllum beccarii*, a Bornean endemic orchid protected by Indonesian law, were in the range of US$60–US$150 in Indonesia just prior to 2010. Unfortunately, smuggling and illegal trades have been taking place due to high selling prices. Turning this unfavourable situation into a sustainable business model for local communities can be a potential way forward with continued interest among orchid hobbyists around the world. A study by Prasetyo and Zulkifli (2010) in Danau Sentarum National Park, West Kalimantan, shows that the potential of orchid businesses had not been fully explored, as the conditions of wild orchid species in the park and the potential of orchid businesses were not then clearly understood. That paper noted the enthusiastic reaction of many local people in beginning to cultivate orchids. Most recently a new orchid was discovered in the Danau Sentarum National Park, called *Phalaenopsis kapuasensis*.

The aromatic, resinous heartwood of *Aquilaria spp*, namely *gaharu* or agarwood, is perceived as another potential luxurious product that may be suitable for smallholdings' operation. It can be exported at high prices for use in Middle Eastern perfumes and Chinese medicines (Paoli et al. 2001). It has become popular in Kalimantan since the 1990s, but as a wild forest product, especially in remote forest areas, such as the Kayan Mentarang National Park. One case reported was a failed *gaharu* nursery project run by a conservation organization in a Punan Dayak community on the Murung River, Central Kalimantan. The new business model introduced by the organization, which promoted cultivation instead of extraction of *gaharu* from nature, was not appreciated by the local communities. They considered such a model unsuitable for their traditional value and lifestyle. This applied more particularly to the young men, where finding wild *gaharu* was an important marker of an indigenous, masculine, semi-nomadic identity. The Dayak preference for collecting wild products resembles the early days of gutta-percha (a type of wild rubber), when young men asserted their identity by scouring the forests for the valuable commodity (Potter 1997b). This case reveals that it can be tricky to integrate conservation (in this case in the dimension of carbon stock) and economic opportunities when societal behaviour was not carefully considered (Großmann 2018).

As there has been no effective control or support from the governments, with *gaharu* prices shooting high, there have been cases of stealing by non-local collectors who arrive by helicopter, especially in the mountains. The report by Lim and Noorainie (2010) included many instances of collectors of various nationalities caught stealing *gaharu* from national parks and conservation areas, e.g., mainly Indonesians operating in Sabah (Maliau Basin Conservation Area, Crocker Range, and Mt Kinabalu National Parks); Sarawakians and Indonesians operating in Brunei (Kuala Belait forest reserve, Batu Apoi forest reserve and many other areas): Brunei seemed to be especially targeted; and Sarawakians operating in Indonesia (Taman Nasional Betung-Kerihun, West Kalimantan). There have also been trial plantings of *Aquilaria* by the Sabah Forestry Department and Yayasan Sabah and in Sarawak at Bario and Belaga.

In the future, combining advanced technologies with traditional knowledge and natural resources may be worth exploring. A noteworthy example is the discovery, refining, and marketing of forest-based medicines and perfumes in Sarawak by the Sarawak Biodiversity Centre (SBC) (Yeo, Naming, and Manurung 2014). SBC was set up by the state government to manage and seek new commercialization opportunities from the sustainable use of biodiversity, especially from local plant and microbial extracts, in conjunction with the Sarawak Biodiversity Regulations in 2004. Similar research efforts were also noticed in Kalimantan, albeit not as organized and formalized as in Sarawak, e.g., mapping and archiving medicinal plants of Dayak in the format of an ethnobotany database (Haeruddin et al. 2017); surveys of the practical uses of various medicinal plants (Qamariah, Mulia, and Fakhrizal 2020); as well as various items of laboratory research (Handayani 2019) (see more in Box 11.1).

Niche Markets

Organic Farming and Health Connotation
Besides local specialities, small farmers in Borneo may follow the footsteps of their peers in other parts of the two countries to tackle some of the potential niche markets to earn price premiums. This requires farmers to adopt certain practices to satisfy specific market needs. The demand for "organic" products that possess certain quality standards, particularly from a health perspective, is a small but growing market segment with higher prices. It was previously only common among high-end consumers in developed countries but has now become popular among middle classes

---

BOX 11.1
"Localizing" Sarawak for the SDGs

One interesting project undertaken by UNDP Malaysia was to mainstream biodiversity objectives, especially scaling up community participation in the "benefit-sharing" of biological resources with indigenous communities (UNDP Malaysia 2018). Two items have been identified for detailed study under SDG 15 (Life on Land):

1. An *Adenosma sp*, a natural repellent for lice and ticks, is a herbaceous plant grown by a Bidayuh village. The Sarawak Biodiversity Centre (SBD) will scale up the cultivation of the plant so the essential oil may be distilled and tested, the aim being eventual commercialization and benefit-sharing between SBD and the community.

2. *Daemonorops sp.* (*Wi Jerenang*) in the Bidayuh language; the plant belongs to the rattan family and produces a bright red resin (Dragon's Blood). It is used to dye baskets and as a component of Chinese medicine. The species has commercial value, and currently grows wild in forests: will be tested by SBD for use as an agroforestry crop. The plan is to establish benefit sharing with local communities to supply raw materials, and eventually cultivate the plant in villages.

including urban Malaysians and Indonesians due to increasing health concerns and purchasing power (Tiraieyari, Hamzah, and Samah 2017). There are no reliable statistics for organically produced goods in the region. As a reference, about 4 per cent of total US food sales come from organic sales (USDA 2019). In the case of Malaysia, less than 40 per cent of the organic food products are produced locally (Somasundram, Razali, and Santhirasegaram 2016). For Borneo, consumers in Singapore and Brunei Darussalam are also potential targets.

Organic products are promoted for their minimal use of external chemical inputs and hence there is a low risk of toxicity, involving practices and techniques like composting, no-tillage, and planting. They are also associated with nutritive value, freshness and taste, and in some cases animal welfare (Shafie and Rennie 2012). To be recognized by certifying bodies, the products must conform to a set of standards. However, as the rapid growth of this market has generated interest among small farmers in Malaysia, some local brands were established without going through certification schemes but instead self-promoted through social media. In reality, although the term "organic" was generally used, different producers and consumers may interpret them differently. In this context, the Malaysian government has taken initiatives to grow and regulate the sector with the introduction of the Malaysian organic standard MS1529 (Somasundram, Razali, and Santhirasegaram 2016; DOA 2020). Meanwhile, an initiative called "Go Organic 2010" was also promoted in Indonesia, but with limited impact (Mayrowani 2012).

The concept of organic farming is spreading slowly across Borneo, but the focus is mainly on upstream commodities, while the use of "organic" as a branding and marketing strategy is still very limited (*Borneo Post*, 9 January 2019). As the organic food market is not highly specialized, there are still chances for farmers in Borneo to enter the market. One possibility might be combining the local specialities with health connotations such as the example of Bario rice mentioned earlier. The concept of "slow food" may be something interesting to be explored, tapping on opportunities offered by initiatives such as the *Ark of Taste* organized by the "Slow Food Foundation for Biodiversity" which promotes and emphasizes the need "to prevent the disappearance of local food cultures and traditions, counteract the rise of fast life and combat people's dwindling interest in the food they eat" (see www.slowfood.com) (Milano, Ponzio, and Sardo 2018). While several products listed for Borneo are similar to those with the GI (such as Bario rice), there are many others of interest, some quite rare. One example is the forest honey in West Kalimantan, which contains enzymes and antioxidants, is used to prevent influenza and is consumed by pregnant women. In addition to its nutritional value, it also has interesting ecological and cultural elements. The honey is produced by the giant rock bee *Apis dorsata* (the biggest bee in the world) on tall trees. In the rainy season, these trees become partly submerged, so harvesting can only be done by boat. A song is chanted, asking permission from the queen bee to harvest the honey, in exchange for protecting the forest. Unfortunately, forest conversion is threatening the survival of the bee and honey industry.

A further example is Krayan Highlands mountain salt, originating from many salt springs. The mountain salt contains iodine, which prevents goitre among the population and also disinfects small wounds, as well as being used in cooking and preserving meat and fish. The Krayan salt has a long history and was a valuable trade product. Now it is equally valued for its purity using traditional techniques, being sold in small packages wrapped in palm leaves and tied with string. On the Sarawak side, products include Nipah salt (*garam attap*). The Nipah palm grows wild along the coastal areas where the leaves are bathed in saline water. The salt is extracted by boiling the dried and burnt leaves until the water evaporates, leaving a cake of salt at the bottom of the pot. While this salt used to be traded by the Malays with the Iban, who lacked a natural salt source, the availability of modern salt has meant that this traditional product is disappearing.

Tengkawang butter (*lemak tengkawang*) is the fat derived from the *tengkawang* or illipe nut tree (*Shorea Spp*, e.g., *Shorea stenoptera*), native to West Kalimantan, especially Sintang and Kapuas Hulu, but also found in Sarawak, where it is known as *engkabang*. The fat is obtained by boiling the nuts, extracted with a wooden tool, and stored in hollow bamboo reeds. It is used for cooking, especially flavouring rice, and in treating animal bites. The product can also be used in chocolate production, but its commercialization has never been successful, as the tree only fruits every three to four years, the large "mast fruiting" which is characteristic of Dipterocarps, but unpredictable. In Sanggau, the trees used to be planted near longhouses to ensure a supply of nuts, though as the timber is also in demand, in modern times tengkawang trees have sometimes been cut and sold.

Halal Products

The "halal" market is an interesting opportunity beyond sustainability and quality. Halal products are processed and prepared following Islamic requirements. The demand for halal products has grown rapidly in the past decades with an increasing Islamic population—at least close to a quarter of the world's population were Muslims in 2020 (CIA 2020). The demand has also been expanding from food to daily goods such as cosmetics and personal care. To enter this market, products must be processed following a set of standards to be officially certified as halal. This certification is especially important for Malaysia and Indonesia as both countries are dominated by the Islamic population. The halal certification systems in both countries are strictly regulated and enforced by the governments. Beyond dietary products, the halal cosmetics standard was also introduced in 2010 in Malaysia (Jusoh, Kamarulzaman, and Zakaria 2017).

Interestingly, countries with minority Muslim populations are currently the major producers of halal products (Asa 2019). In this context, the proliferation of halal certification in both countries can be comparatively advantageous in capturing new business opportunities, i.e., exporting their halal-certified products to other Islamic countries especially those in the Middle East. As consumers are more willing to pay a premium for halal products due to religious beliefs, the halal markets in these countries allow Malaysia and Indonesia to divert their less competitive products (in the global market) into these niche markets, such as coconut oil from Malaysia (Kabir, Shams, and Lawrey 2019). The "Halal Hub" programme in Tanjung Manis, Sarawak is a key location in Malaysia's global Halal Hub strategy, incentivized with tax breaks and other federal and state supports (RECODA 2016). A similar "Halal Hub" programme has also been introduced in Sabah Agro-Industrial Precinct (SAIP) (SEDIA 2016). On the Indonesian side, a "halal cluster" is being developed in the Surya Industrial Zone in Kumai, Pangkalanbun, Central Kalimantan (Winosa 2020). An offshoot of this company produces halal women's cosmetics in Kertak Hanyar village, near Banjarmasin, South Kalimantan.

Other places with large Muslim populations like South Kalimantan may be potential spots to implement halal-related development strategies. For example, similar to local specialities that can be well connected to eco-tourism, halal products may be connected to "halal tourism", a new trend among Muslim travellers (Budiman et al. 2019). The island of Lombok is a successful example in this sector (Khoiriati, Krisnajaya, and Dinarto 2018). Being close to Bali, Lombok has learned from the touristic example of that island. In Borneo, South Kalimantan stands out with its historical, cultural, and educational significance for Muslims, housing important graves in Martapura and an Islamic educational centre in Amuntai. Its capital city, Banjarmasin, is also famous for tourists as the "City of a

Thousand Rivers". However, South Kalimantan has not been selected by Indonesian officials as one of the eleven best provinces for halal tourism. Overcrowded Banjarmasin does not at present provide sufficient facilities and accessibility to easily develop as a "Halal city", while its officials lack international experience, as pointed out by Budiman et al. (2019). Facilities and Islamic sites are scattered through South Kalimantan but are not necessarily easy to access.

Sustainability Branding

The aforementioned selling points like local specialities, "organic", and "halal", have no guarantee in improving the sustainability of the land-use systems. To some extent, the use of local knowledge or the adoption of "organic" farming overlaps with sustainable agriculture with the minimal use of polluting chemical fertilizers and pesticides, but they may not be strictly in line with the mainstream framework of sustainability that is being promoted on international or even national platforms. From this point of view, the question is thus how the sustainability of small and medium businesses can be better governed with standard practices, and hopefully, the standard can evolve into a brand for gaining market premiums.

More progress was observed in Indonesia than in Malaysia, particularly in the coffee and tea sector with labels like UTZ, Fairtrade, Rainforest Alliance, and 4C. However, the socio-economic impacts are mixed. In terms of monetary gains, some reported that certified farmers perceive higher benefits than uncertified farmers (Ibnu, Offermans, and Glasbergen 2018), while some reported otherwise (Vicol et al. 2018). Also, while a system like Fairtrade covers both small producers and hired labourers in the agricultural sector, it has not been very successful in improving traditional employment modalities at the farm level, particularly part-time and informal waged labour on small farms which are very difficult to monitor. Adopting sustainability certification systems may further transform traditional small farms into highly organized cooperatives.

Past experience shows that rigid incorporation of sustainability standards into small businesses may unintentionally forge negative perceptions of "conservation", especially when implicit assumptions were made on local traditional beliefs, taboos, norms, and knowledge (Yuliani, Adnan, et al. 2018). Yuliani, Adnan, et al. (2018) argued cogently that the protection of endangered species such as the orangutan not only depended on preserving their habitat but also on the existence of fundamental beliefs and traditions about the animals by local people, including taboos on killing or disturbing them. Local people often had negative views about "conservation", as consisting of top-down restrictions imposed by government authorities without consultation, while their behaviour was in itself a more successful form of conservation. However, to receive support from governments or international funders, it is not unusual for local communities to selectively report on their production, practices, and livelihood (Rubis and Theriault 2019) (and also personal communications with local stakeholders in the field). Furthermore, crop-based schemes with rigid standards may drive the emergence of larger-scale monoculture, which is more easily monitored and organized, but not more flexible, than loosely organized smallholders. This may potentially rule out the possibility of sustainable landscape management that encourages a mosaic landscape with a diversity of crops, leading to overexploitation of the resources due to profit chasing (van Oosten, Moeliono, and Wiersum 2018).

For Borneo, the expansion of aquaculture in East Kalimantan that took place following decentralization can be a useful example that deserves further scrutiny. It demonstrates the complexity of governing the sustainability of a rapidly developing sector that is mainly occupied by small players. The conversion of mangrove forests in the Mahakam Delta into shrimp ponds started in the 1990s, but the rapid expansion occurred after the fall of the Suharto regime in 1998. The decentralized policy has created a power void, together with the growing demand for shrimps, attracting farmers and investors around the area to establish shrimp businesses on various scales. This resulted in great losses of ecosystem services and carbon stock. About two-thirds of the mangrove areas have been exploited for aquaculture (Arifanti et al. 2019). The aquaculture sector provides livelihood to many households, some of whom are the poorest in the province. However, it shares common problems with oil palm—unfair distribution of the newly created wealth, competing claims and land conflicts, corruption, and power abuse.

Transforming these unsustainable businesses into healthy modes of development requires the adoption of sustainable management practices which may potentially lead to market differentiation and price premiums. Several approaches were proposed and implemented. Notably, the Better Management Practices (BMPs) system was implemented by an NGO-led effort to assist the farmers with a set of standard guidelines for farm practices. This scheme also placed a special focus on environmental impacts (Kusumawati and Bush 2015). Some further suggested distinguishing ponds located on peat soils from those on other soils, so that specialized treatment could be made—either full restoration or transformation with technologies (Bosma et al. 2012). Nonetheless, the study by Kusumawati, Bush, and Visser

(2013) revealed that informal local patrons (*ponggawa*) who play the most critical role in influencing and regulating the entire shrimp value chain (sometimes with violence) may be the biggest challenge in improving the system. How to manage both the formal and informal governance of small businesses would be a crucial aspect to consider, especially in places like Kalimantan where local governance is less effective.

IMPACTS AND CHALLENGES

Markets for agricultural commodities from smallholdings are competitive with few dominant players that form complex supply chains on a global scale. Most consumers are not interested in spending time deciding which banana to buy except by checking the price. How to make a convincing brand with short and clear messages to attract consumers is essential for this strategy to be successful. This requires both an in-depth understanding of the market dynamics as well as creativity. Boosting the regional market for local bio-products, such as a "buy local eat local" kind of promotion may be an effective way to realize this strategy. This is not rare in developed countries like Japan where local bio-products by small and medium farms in rural areas are deemed among the highest quality with large premiums. Importantly, this can also boost regional pride and cultural identity. With increasing purchasing power from the urban population in the regions, especially in Kuala Lumpur, Jakarta, and Singapore, products with traditional flavours may have great market potential (see also Chapter 7).

However, gaps remain between the wishes of consumers and the actual uptake of these branded products due to their higher prices (Smith 2008). First, it is not easy for small farmers to compete in terms of pricing due to economies of scale, especially considering various costs incurred in branding. Additionally, there could be substantial competition between brands within the same market niche (Janssen and Hamm 2012). To reduce transaction costs in marketing efforts, a farmer may have to specialize in one or two brands or labels. Specialization may help the farmers to earn additional income from the premiums, but the overall production and sales may drop (Méndez et al. 2010). This may be a big disadvantage to the flexibility and resilience of smallholdings, especially for highly volatile markets.

To address these issues, collective branding may be achieved by building partnerships among and between small farmers, manufacturers, and traders, possibly with support from governments. These may also help to improve their businesses with better management practices tailored to a local context, including optimization of farm management with scale (e.g., lower cost for fertilizers), more opportunities for training and mutual learning, as well as stronger voices in price negotiation in face of commodity price fluxes (Blackmore et al. 2012). Through proper organization and cost reduction, this may allow the uptake of multiple branding for a single product, i.e., a product can obtain "organic", "halal", and also "sustainable" labels at the same time.

Furthermore, this may be expanded to collective geographical branding beyond just conventional GIs that focus on individual products to encourage a more diversified agricultural and forestry landscape. In this way, multiple synergies between different branding strategies can be forged, e.g., by binding cultural and traditional elements like music and arts to the sustainability of agricultural and forestry products. For example, the Kelabit Highland in Sarawak is famous for its culture and the fine rice of Bario, making the place itself a brand identity for both tourism and food (see also Chapter 10). The scope can be even broadened, e.g., to make Sarawak a brand to collectively promote products and eco-tourism from the territory, while pushing the state to adopt more sustainable policies in order to protect the brand.

Importantly, these branding efforts may also spur the development of inclusive, local small and medium-sized enterprises along the value chain, including storage, logistics, transportation, and wholesale and retail distribution (Vos and Cattaneo 2020). Interestingly, the study by Slamet, Nakayasu, and Ichikawa (2017) on Indonesia shows that the participation of small farmers in modern retail market channels like supermarkets has increased their income and their involvement has been growing. These opportunities are largely tapped by younger and more educated farmers or those who have better access to infrastructure, such as roads.

FINAL REMARKS

Practitioners may have to think carefully about how to materially maintain their businesses in the longer term while leveraging on their advantage of being small and agile. As smallholdings are naturally constrained by economies of scale, new business models to connect small sellers with buyers, such as virtual trade platforms, are highly desired. It may create new pathways to market smallholders' products and fundamentally change the entire supply chain with lower transportation costs and larger flows of goods between rural and urban areas. In the future, the deployment of digital platforms is likely a game-changer for small players, as one can observe in China (see Box 11.2).

BOX 11.2
"Tabao" Villages

"Tabao" villages refer to villages in China engaged in an e-commerce platform, Taobao, offered by Alibaba. The number of farmers venturing into e-commerce has been growing rapidly, especially among younger populations who have exposure to secondary education, urban experience, and knowledge of e-commerce, according to a report by the World Bank (Luo and Niu 2019). The report also indicates that e-commerce participation may have driven household income growth. The platform has evolved into an even more complex system with e-finance such as small loans across the entire supply chain (Zhou, Chen, and Li 2018). Martindale (2021) argued that such an e-commerce model is driven by both the need for land reform (in this case land consolidation) and food safety. It allows the reimagination of agricultural transformation that involves a large number of small and medium players from upstream to marketing. How China's e-commerce model will inspire neighbouring regions like Borneo will be interesting to observe as Alibaba and its competitor, Tencent, are expanding to Malaysia and Indonesia through their subsidiaries like Lazada and Shopee.

The Sarawak government has displayed a vision of promoting the application of digital technologies in agriculture to boost productivity (*Borneo Post*, 31 October 2017). This has been slowly growing during 2020–21 driven by the COVID-19 pandemic as observed by Goh, where people are now able to purchase farm produce directly from rural communities through the Internet. To realize such a vision, strategic investment in laying out the basic infrastructure and skill-building is needed. The opportunities and impacts of the digital revolution are further discussed in Chapter 13.

12

Encouraging Traditional Land-Use Systems for Self-Sufficiency and Sustainability

Malaysia and Indonesia have a rather skewed agricultural sector, as the national agriculture policy is shaped by export competitiveness with a specialized product: palm oil. This is especially applicable to Borneo as a major producing region; it produces more oils and fats than carbohydrates based on the current levels of consumption. In the past few decades, the model (export CPO and import cereals and other foods) worked reasonably well for both countries until the sharp decline in 2008–9 (see Figure 7.1). Another period of decline in 2015–18 clearly shows that such a model was no guarantee of food security in economic terms. The situation is severe in Indonesian Borneo, where per capita cereal supply has declined significantly throughout the major oil palm-producing sites in remote districts (MoA Indonesia 2018). This is reflected in the high prevalence of stunting (30–40 per cent) in many districts. While there are no comparable statistics in Malaysian Borneo, a similar trend of stunting (43 per cent) was found among the Penan groups in Belaga, Sarawak (Bong, Norimah A. Karim, and Noor 2018).

In this context, the concept of self-sufficiency has been frequently mentioned in land-use-related discussions with conservation also considered a core element. It is an alternative to the productivity-oriented mentality that essentializes development into economic outputs, especially in rural areas in the context of transforming land-based economies into eco-economies. It prioritizes food-fibre-fuel security and other provisioning services by creating a diversified agroecological and socio-economic landscape, which can sometimes be termed "neo-productivism" (Almstedt et al. 2014). Furthermore, it also advocates for the appreciation of the "traditional" way of living, in the hope of maintaining or regaining health and spiritual benefits through forging a healthy human-environmental relationship as in the past (Dounias and Froment 2011; Abram, Meijaard, et al. 2014; How and Othman 2017). This is not unusual in the developing world, where farming, hunting, and gathering are treated as integral parts of social life and not only for economic productivity (Hisano, Akitsu, and McGreevy 2018). Additionally, some have suggested that the preservation of indigenous agro-ecological and socio-cultural settings can enhance conservation efforts (Altieri 2004; Yuliani, Adnan, et al. 2018).

This does not necessarily mean that communities reject innovations that could contribute to improving their livelihoods and meeting their basic needs, such as the application of advanced technologies for irrigation, renewable energy, and clean water. Such an idea has been advocated elsewhere, e.g., in the rural areas of Japan where energy, security, and waste management are among the key issues (Goh et al. 2019). This also does not imply that farmers do not trade their produce but reduce their emphasis on cash crops and focus on more comprehensive management of local resources with diversification. Importantly, various ecosystem services are maintained and protected by and for local communities. It also emphasizes the social strengths that underlie human resilience to agroecological changes (Berkes and Ross 2013).

In a way, the narrative of self-sufficiency shares similar tunes with the Global National Happiness (GNH) index (as applied in Bhutan) that challenges the use of economic metrics, especially GDP, to measure development (Sears et al. 2017). It avoids the situation that all overarching changes are viewed in terms of how they will contribute to or impact economic growth. This chapter first provides an overview of the settlement patterns in Borneo, especially urban-rural transition and ethnicity, as a basis to explore the potential of this strategy. Then it discusses the concepts and practices of self-sufficiency, modernity, and sustainability in the Bornean context.

SETTLEMENT PATTERNS

Urban-Rural Transition

Human beings have been actively extracting their livelihoods from forests and lands on Borneo island for 50,000 years (Barker et al. 2017). Today, the lifestyles of the human population have changed drastically. "... civilization, modernity, progress, order and power, on the one hand, and the primitive, traditional, backward, nomadic, disordered, untamed and displaced, on the other."—This quotation from King (2017) illustrates how the mountain

Meratus Dayak people in South Kalimantan were perceived or looked down upon by both the Suharto government and the neighbouring Islamic Banjarese. To some extent, it may also represent the typical dichotomous perspectives of outsiders on local societies (especially those in interior Borneo).

In reality, it has been getting more difficult to clearly demarcate the circuits of "modern" and "traditional" parts of the continuously evolving society (Cleary and Eaton 1992). Industrialization and urbanization, which are often viewed as signs of development, have created complex urban-rural gradients that vary by the stage of transition (Topalovic 2016). The morphological characteristics of these gradients are yet to be fully understood, but one common scene across Borneo is the replacement of the "traditional" rural landscapes that consisted of longhouses, *tembawang* (and equivalents in local languages, meaning diverse fruit agroforest marking earlier longhouse sites), rice field, secondary forests of "jungle rubber" and closed forest (*hutan tutupan*) with unvarying oil palm plantations, mills, and rows of simple worker housing.

Besides oil and gas cities like Bintulu-Miri in Sarawak and Balikpapan in East Kalimantan, numerous towns and cities gradually emerged from and largely rely on various land-based activities, especially logging, oil palm plantations, and mining. This trend is very clear in towns in Central Kalimantan, such as Sampit and its surrounding area in Kotawaringin Timur with oil palm as the sole growth engine in the past two decades. It is clear that large-scale land-based economic activities have affected patterns of migration both out of nearby communities as well as across islands, but the patterns of population flows and the impacts on land-use changes are not yet fully understood (Kelley et al. 2020).

Based on the official statistics of big cities in Borneo, about 30 per cent of the population live in the core cities along the coasts, while most of the population can be regarded as living in a continuum of settlement types ranging from more densely populated suburbs to nomadic tribes. People living outside the core urban areas still rely significantly on forest and land resources for their livelihoods with a relatively low degree of industrialization across the island. A case study in Bau, Sarawak by J. Nelson, Muhammed, and Rashid (2015) may provide some impression over human-forest dependency in the 2000s, where households are commonly associated with <4 ha of land ownership, living within 50 metres of forests, the land utilization primarily for agriculture and monthly expenditure of <US$250.

The regions with the highest rural population in Kalimantan are the rice-growing lands of the Hulu Sungai (South Kalimantan) and Mempawah (West Kalimantan). They are also areas of cultural significance, the Hulu Sungai being the historical heartland of the Banjarese, with historical out-migration, most recently to Banjarmasin. Mempawah, a new district formed in 2008 from Landak, has a considerable remaining Chinese component, following the expulsion of Chinese from rural areas in Bengkayang and Landak. In contrast, the remote upland areas are of low population density and large sections are located in national parks, which characterize the "Heart of Borneo" (see Figure 2.1b). Out-migration from those areas towards the coastal lowlands has been especially notable in East Kalimantan, some beginning independently as early as the nineteenth century during Dutch times but subsequently "encouraged" by the Suharto government, which designated the inhabitants as *"suku-suku terasing"* (isolated groups, but also a rather insulting term, implying "primitive") (Avé and King 1986).

An urban-rural transition has been ongoing throughout Borneo, but the speed and degree of penetration in the past two decades have been momentous. Before this, urban-rural exchange was relatively limited with riverine trade playing a dominant role (Sakuma 2017). Today, the linkages between urban and rural areas in Borneo have become inextricable. Urbanization provides new jobs, modern food distribution systems, mass education, and health services to its surrounding areas. The improved urban-rural connectivity also opens up access to fertilizers, fuels, knowledge, and business opportunities for small farmers, bringing changes to land-use practices in surrounding areas (Smajgl and Bohensky 2012, 2013). As observed by Abdullah (2016) in Kapit, Sarawak, the source of rural income has gradually become more diversified due to improved connectivity.

The growing exchange and mobility transmit ideas, knowledge, and capital to rural areas, affecting communities' perspectives, lifestyles, land-use practices, and societal structure (Montefrio, Ortiga, and Josol 2014; Blanchet-Cohen and Urud 2017). Soda, Ishikawa, and Kato (2020) found that farmers in rural Sarawak can now quickly shift between multiple economic activities, including subsistence farming, plantation work, and urban jobs, taking advantage of the availability of both river and road transportation. Sarawak's Kelabit Highland, discussed in the latter reference, is an extreme example of the impacts of urbanization, with the longhouses almost deserted except for old people and the famous wet rice production being largely carried on by Indonesians from the Krayan uplands across the border, as already observed in the 1990s by Potter. Migration to urban areas, whether long-term, temporary, or seasonal, has been on the rise in general.

One interesting example of seasonal migration was the traditional movement in South Kalimantan of workers from the rice-growing areas of the Hulu Sungai (c200 km north) to the August rice harvest in Gambut village near Banjarmasin. This movement, largely of women with family connections in both areas, attracted 50,000 people in 1991 (Potter 1993). Now, in an example of "urbanization by decree", the village of Gambut (which still grows rice but is urbanized along the highway) has been classified as part of the Banjar-Bakula metropolitan zone, which constituted 9 per cent of the area of the province and more than half of its population (close to 2 million) in 2010 (Pusat Pengembangan Kawasan Perkotaan 2015). Comparatively, the greater Kuching-Samarahan area is either the largest or second-largest metropolitan area in Borneo with close to one million residents (about one-third of the state's population).

The increasing urban-rural exchange has also brought about manifold forms of impact on the environment. An interesting example is the changes in linkages between traditional medicines and biodiversity. On the one hand, the availability of public health services and modern medicines has reduced the use of traditional medicines from the forests by the rural population. On the other hand, the increasing demand for traditional medicines in urban areas has driven overhunting in rural areas as observed in Sarawak (Okuno and Ichikawa 2020). In turn, increased mobility has also exposed the population to the risk of zoonotic diseases, such as the cases of malaria infections reported in Sabah (Fornace et al. 2019; Grignard et al. 2019).

Rapid alterations in lifestyles, living standards, and conditions also trigger structural changes in rural societies, which may involve unpleasant social processes (Semedi 2014). Prostitution and gambling are reported to be widespread in Kalimantan, especially with the quick cash generated from illegal logging, as observed by both authors, and also a feature of "paydays" around large oil palm estates. Especially, inequality between different groups has been growing. Some have captured the opportunities offered by urbanization, while others have had their land rights eroded or have lost their livelihoods. Gender inequality is also a factor to be carefully considered. There is plenty of evidence reported throughout Borneo, such as the case studies in Sarawak by Hew (2011) and Lee (2018a), in West Kalimantan by Maharani et al. (2019) and Julia and White (2012), and in East Kalimantan by Elmhirst et al. (2017) and Toumbourou and Dressler (2020).

In the future, the planned move of the Indonesian capital from Jakarta to East Kalimantan is likely to drive rapid development of infrastructure on the island as well as (unplanned) massive inflows of migrants from Java and elsewhere in Indonesia. With the expansion of road networks and air transportation, as well as the proliferation of digital connectivity, rural change in Borneo will likely continue accelerating at an unprecedented rate.

It is worth looking more closely at the new land transport changes that were already being undertaken in the more northern sections of Borneo before being temporarily suspended due to the COVID-19 pandemic, for example, the new road network expected to radiate out from Malinau in North Kalimantan, mainly up into the mountains and the borders of Sarawak and Sabah (Figure 5.4). Maybe the impact of COVID-19 has reduced exchanges and activities in some areas, with local airlines bearing the cost, but alternatively, it has also accelerated the arrival of digital infrastructure, forcing people to adopt digital technologies (even elderly and rural people).

Ethnicity

Despite a growing trend of rural-urban differentiation with rapid urbanization and migration, the socio-cultural characteristics in Borneo are still largely ethnicity-oriented. Ethnic classifications have important political ramifications, and thus can be highly debatable (Prasad 2015; Alexander 2018). Although ethnicity itself is a fluid concept in Borneo, the population can be broadly referred to in several loose ethno-religious blocks with clear distinctions in land-use practices, lifestyles, territorial affinity, and spiritual connections to the land.

Dayaks, an umbrella concept for non-Muslim indigenous people who share many cultural similarities, can be regarded as the largest ethnic block in Borneo.[1] Roughly, there are more than 5 million non-Muslim indigenous people, including those not regarded or self-claimed as Dayaks, e.g., Kadazan-Dusun in Sabah. Today, many Dayaks in parts of Kalimantan and Sarawak still live in the *Rumah Panjang* or "longhouses" where several families live together. Many remote longhouses can only be accessed through river transportation.[2] Despite being ethnically and ecologically distinctive, most of the indigenous people in rural areas rely heavily on land for their livelihoods. Traditionally, shifting cultivation, also called swidden, remains the primary farming practice. It involves rotating cultivation between different plots of land, with some plots actively managed while others are left to regenerate. Hunting-gathering and fishing are also integral parts of traditional lifestyles, albeit practised now to different extents, see, for example, the case of Punan Tubu in Kalimantan (Guèze and Napitupulu 2016) and Penan in Sarawak and East Kalimantan (Koizumi, Mamung, and Levang 2012; Selvadurai et al. 2013).

The people engage in market and non-market exchange, and traditional riverine trade hubs can be found in many geographically important areas (Sakuma 2017; Lounela 2019). However, the land-use practices of many indigenous communities have shifted towards more commercial farming, like clonal rubber, which continues in many areas, despite the attractions of oil palm in the past two decades. That may depend on the relative prices of the two commodities, access to good planting materials and markets, and distance to commercial oil palm plantations (Kato and Samejima 2020). In certain areas, mining is also a major economic activity for the indigenous people. The cultural divide is clearer between the lowland and upland which is unnavigable through the major rivers, such as the Apo Kayan in North Kalimantan. The Penan group settled in the Belaga Area of Bintulu, Sarawak is among the few exceptions that keep their nomadic lifestyles in deep forests, largely excluded from mainstream market development (Selvadurai et al. 2013).

Meanwhile, the indigenous Muslims (Banjar, Malay, Melanau, Bajau, etc.) mostly settled in the coastal areas and along the rivers. The Banjarese, mainly resident in South Kalimantan are the major group in this block in terms of population (about 4 million).[3] They were historically known for coastal trading and once established a powerful sultanate in Borneo (Milner 2009). Today, Muslims still dominate the politics in most of the Bornean territories, even in Sarawak where they do not have a majority in population compared to non-Muslims (Chin 2014). These groups combine semi-subsistence and small-scale commercial farming practices but are not aggressive in agricultural expansion. Many also work full-time as fishermen, and some enjoy a living from trades.

This block is also joined by Muslim migrants from other islands especially Java, Madura, Sulawesi, and the southern islands of the Philippines. A substantial number of Muslim transmigrants live in former transmigration villages, usually not far from oil palm plantations. Due to the rapid oil palm expansion in the mid-2000s, the Suharto period's discontinued transmigration programme was revived in the form of district-to-district arrangements to fill the growing gap in the plantation labour force in Kalimantan. The programme ambitiously aimed to create new towns or cities, namely *Kota Terpadu Mandiri*, to integrate various functions and be "self-sufficient" surrounding oil palm plantations (Potter

2012). Another group of spontaneous migrants (not transmigrants) mainly work on the plantations with short contracts, with some of them choosing to stay longer or permanently (note that some of the Indonesian oil palm workers are Christians from Flores, West Timor or even refugees from East Timor) (Sanderson 2016). Despite the religious linkage, there are significant differences in terms of culture and origins among this population of nearly 10 million people.

The remainder is mainly Chinese descendants, made up of more than 1.3 million people, mostly living in highly urbanized areas in Sarawak, West Kalimantan, and Sabah.[4] They have played major roles in large-scale land-based economic development in these territories, from pre-independence mining and agriculture to post-independence timber extraction and oil palm plantations in Borneo, but now mostly residing in the cities (Heidhues 2003; Cramb 2011a). They are still involved in a wide range of agro-businesses but with relatively strong commercial mindsets and stay higher up in the value chain, see, for example, case studies in West Kalimantan by Chiang and Cheng (2017). Remarkably, most timber and oil palm tycoons and senior management of plantations in Sarawak are local Chinese descendants (Cramb 2016). In contrast, those Chinese Indonesians who became prominent in timber, plywood, later pulp and paper and oil palm during the Suharto era did not originate from Kalimantan, but from other parts of Indonesia.

Finally, there are also nearly 1 million non-citizen residents in Sabah based on the census in 2010, predominantly Indonesians and Filipinos (Dollah and Abdullah 2018; DOSM 2020). This has not yet included undocumented migrants and the second generation who were born locally in Sabah as well as in Sarawak. Many also travel frequently with or without documents across the porous borders between Malaysia, Indonesia, and the Philippines. There is little quantitative information in the literature about their distribution and activities, but it is believed that most of them work as low-wage labourers either in the cities or on the plantations (Pye et al. 2012; Dollah and Abdullah 2018). The latter group has been playing a key role in Sabah's land-based economy, albeit hidden from official statistics (see discussion on this topic in Chapter 2 especially the project by UNDP). Unfortunately, conflicts between immigrants and local communities are also no less reported in Sabah (*Borneo Post*, 2 June 2020). Recognizing the socio-cultural differences among different groups of people in Borneo is crucial to explore how applicable is self-sufficient land use as a strategy to overcome sustainability issues with land use across the island.

SELF-SUFFICIENCY, MODERNITY, AND SUSTAINABILITY

Subsistence and Commercial Farming

Historically, transitions between different land-use practices and crop systems have long existed in Borneo, and are not necessarily purely motivated by self-sufficiency or food security (Dove 2019). For example, the current food staple, rice, is prone to failure and low yield compared to other carbohydrates like sago palms but has been given cultural prioritization (Barton 2012). Indigenous people also adopted pepper gardens for cash income since the early twentieth century, especially in Sarawak and West Kalimantan (Wadley and Mertz 2005).

With the growing penetration of cash economies, many rural farmers have attempted to transform themselves into cash crop-oriented farmers in the waves of rubber and oil palm expansions. To give a quantitative overview, Figure 12.1 illustrates the land area used for agriculture per household on the district average for Kalimantan. Note that while there is a wealth of case studies of trends and patterns in land-use practices of local communities in Malaysian Borneo, no comprehensive and harmonized statistics can be found. Generally, people in the interior districts occupied larger areas of land for agriculture. In densely populated South Kalimantan, most households operated only less than 2 ha of land. Overall, the average farm size rarely exceeds 4 ha per household. A high percentage of the land was used for cash crops. In certain districts, the ratio of cash crops to other crops can be more than 90 per cent. This implies that most small farmers are likely actively involved in cash economies in general. This is complementary to the transitions from traditional food systems to emerging and diversifying ones with growing modern supply chains and long-distance trade for fresh and processed foods. A better distribution of food within the island and across the seas has been driving crop specialization to maximize productivity and profits.

What was observed is the co-existence of cash crop plantations, both large and small, with subsistence farming throughout the island. Many smallholders view cash crops as flexible livelihood options that can be combined with subsistence and other economic activities based on available manpower and financial situation (Kato and Soda 2020). The previous studies on Sabah provide some indications. While a range of community-based conservation projects has been deployed alongside oil palm expansion in the past two decades (Vaz and Agama 2013), as described by Lindsay et al. (2012) "for many residents of Sabah oil palm is very much part of their day-to-day reality; part of their connection to place."

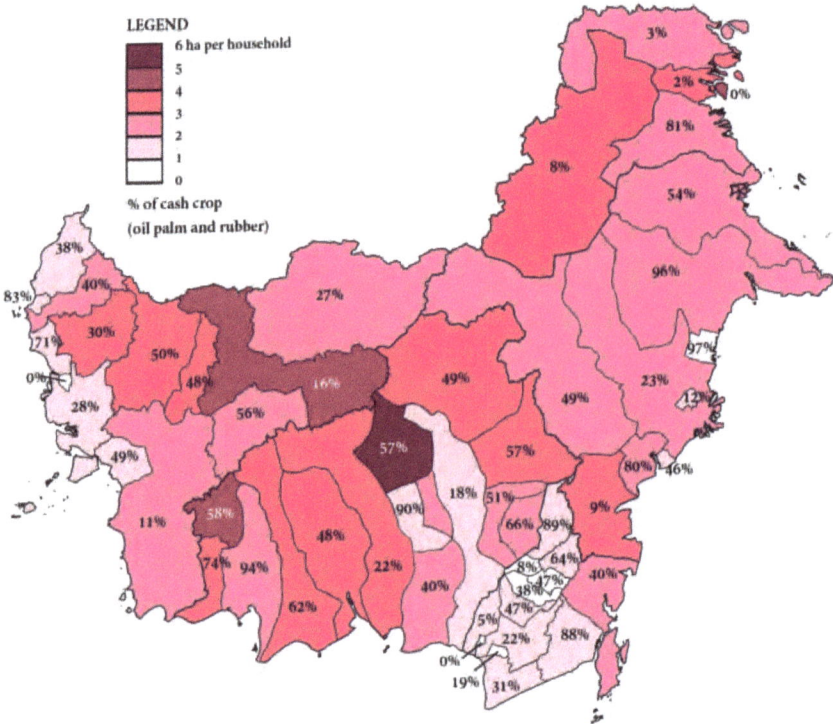

FIGURE 12.1

Land occupied for agriculture per household and the percentage of these lands used by small farmers for rubber and oil palm on district average in Kalimantan based on agricultural census 2013

Source: BPS (2013).

Several case studies also reported that the indigenous people can be very flexible in capturing various emerging economic opportunities depending on market prices and seasonality, adapting to the establishment of industrial plantations in the neighbourhood and expansion of road networks while keeping traditional subsistence farming (Gönner 2011; Kato 2014). While rubber is commonly planted by small farmers, many have further attempted to integrate commercial oil palm cultivation (Harrington 2015; Khasanah et al. 2020). One should also take note that small-scale mining, whether legal or not, has been an important income source in many parts of Borneo for many decades, such as gold mining in the north-western part of West Kalimantan (Peluso 2018) and interior of Central Kalimantan (Bruno et al. 2020), coal in Murung Raya of Central Kalimantan (Morishita 2016), and many more. For example, a case in East Kalimantan described how farmers may be able to take advantage of coal mining and the intruding market economy while balancing existing land-use practices and social relationships (Terauchi 2020).

However, the transitions from subsistence to commercial farming are uneven across the island. Many are not exposed to or do not have access to alternative economic opportunities mentioned above, still relying heavily on subsistence farming and hunting-gathering (Santika, Wilson, Budiharta, Law, et al. 2019). Also, while cash crops generate more income for small farmers, over-reliance on cash crops also exposes them to market volatility (Potter 2010; Bou Dib et al. 2018) (see also Chapter 3). This was observed by Goh and Potter during the visit to West Kalimantan in 2018, where farmers who initially rejected oil palm in the 2000s but converted their farms into oil palm in the 2010s, have been facing household economic crises due to the great fall of oil palm prices in that year. A case study by Purwanto (2018) in West Kalimantan also found that communities once actively involved in timber extraction until the early 2000s have now returned to the traditional way of life due to the shrinkage of the logging industry. Furthermore, a large group of people (especially the indigenous Dayak people) have been marginalized in such a monocultural economic setting (Semedi and Bakker 2014). These frequently come with social conflicts and political struggles, involving violence, bribing, and political threats, e.g., manipulating customary claims and land appropriation by the government (Peluso 2017; Prabowo et al. 2017) (see more cases reported by Dayang Norwana et al. (2011) in Sabah; Andersen et al. (2016) in Sarawak; Yuliani, de Jong, et al. (2018) in West Kalimantan; Goh et al. (2018) in Central Kalimantan; Haug (2014) in East Kalimantan).

In this sense, one should recognize that the indigenous people are not a homogeneous group and their mindsets change from time to time— communities and individuals can have diverse perceptions, ambiguous attitudes, and contrasting responses to changes in the farming systems (Haug 2018a; Dharmawan et al. 2020; Yuliani et al. 2020). While it is true that not all reject the idea of integrating into market economies to tap into the benefits of new income and wage labour, many may hesitate to embrace changes that are too rapidly impacting their lifestyles (Haug 2018b). Furthermore, some forest-dwelling communities like the Penan people may not be able or willing to fully adopt settlement in fixed villages and prefer, at least partially to maintain their nomadic hunting-gathering lifestyles (Koizumi, Mamung, and Levang 2012; Selvadurai et al. 2013; Yuliani, de Jong, et al. 2018). An edited volume by Sercombe and Sellato

(2007) *Beyond the Green Myth: Borneo's Hunter-Gatherers in the Twenty-First Century* provides much information about the adaptations of Penan/Punan in Indonesia and Sarawak to the changes and challenges presented by the modern world.

Settled Dayak agriculturalists becoming oil palm smallholders also experienced cultural problems, as they felt the need to continue to comply with customary norms, including rice planting in swiddens. Box 12.1 provides an example of such a dilemma in Parindu, West Kalimantan observed by Potter.

BOX 12.1
Bidayuh Oil Palm Villages in Parindu, Sanggau (West Kalimantan)

In Parindu, groups of Bidayuh farmers, or "assisted or scheme smallholders" (also known as "plasma") were attached to oil palm plantations, generally with 2 ha of oil palm per farmer. As summarized by Potter (2015b), there were extreme variations within the district, among the hamlets, and among households, as the Dayaks used their agency and resilience in adapting to the conditions. For example, despite rat infestations that reduced yields, most continued to grow small areas of rice in swampy parts of their holdings (*padi paya*), if there was no longer suitable land for hill swiddens. They did this largely for cultural reasons, as Dayaks without swiddens could hardly still be called Dayaks. The *padi paya* were "wet swiddens". If possible, they also needed to still be able to produce sticky rice (*padi pulut*) for *tuak* or rice wine, important for social activities.

The experiences with plantation companies varied widely, see for example, Gillespie (2011, 2016) and Semedi and Bakker (2014). There was a change in rules in favour of the plantations known as "kemitraan" in 2007. It was characterized by Potter as "onerous", as compared to the previous rather "generous" system: from an original 80 per cent of the land to the smallholders and 20 per cent to the plantation; by 2007 the reverse situation was being applied, as palm oil prices were high, and companies wanted control over more of their lands (Potter 2016b). Gillespie found the situation on one of these plantations very difficult for the Dayaks, many of whom just sold their lands.

In the 2000s, independent smallholders, who were very numerous in Sumatra, scarcely existed in Kalimantan. They have recently become much more visible in West Kalimantan and are making their own arrangements with the plantations, though they do not yet have independent mills, as exist in Riau (Sumatra).

Traditional Practices and Sustainability
As the transitions from subsistence to commercial farming especially the case of oil palm have brought substantial chaos and confusion in Borneo, Ong and Wilson (2020) identified and formulated the critical question: "How can we be more self-sufficient, and re-value traditional practices of planting food crops and farm produce, exchanges of planting materials, remembering how the ancestors prepared for unforeseen difficulties (like keeping salt in jars)?"

This question could be further integrated with the conservation agenda given the massive environmental degradation that has accompanied the transitions in the past few decades: Can Borneo maintain self-sufficiency with traditional practices while adopting the global values of sustainability? For conservationists, "traditional farming" may be regarded as a type of land-use system that can be well integrated with conservation. First, although fires and land clearing are involved, the impacts on the environment can be kept low if the scale is small and the frequency is low. Traditional shifting cultivation is also considered more sustainable due to its low level of artificial inputs. Importantly, it provides a good reason to conserve certain biodiverse areas which have important functions in shifting cultivation, where they may be regarded as communally reserved forests (CRFs) (Takeuchi et al. 2017).

However, these advantages have been compromised by various modern interventions. First, the use of modern agricultural inputs like chemical fertilizers and pesticides in "traditional" farming has proliferated (Padmanabhan and Eswaran 2011). What has also been observed is the shortening of the fallow period in shifting agriculture, i.e., the time left for abandoned agricultural land to regenerate into forests, resulting in more land clearing and use of fire (Hattori et al. 2019). Further clearing of forests for agricultural expansion may be tolerated by the farmers for their own interests (Meijaard et al. 2013). In this sense, the perception of "traditional agriculture and forestry" may be quite different among the local people as well as from the general understanding of conservationists (Hazard et al. 2018). For example, the ban on slash-and-burn practices in West Kalimantan has failed due to contradictions between the perspectives of different stakeholders on the relationships between fire, subsistence, and haze (Thung 2018).

Another stark difference in perspectives between conservation and traditional lifestyles is human-animal relationships, with the hunting of orangutans as a remarkable example. Capturing orangutans as pets by local people is not rare in Kalimantan. Such a practice was described as "illegal" by Sherman, Ancrenaz, and Meijaard (2020). Davis et al. (2013) documented that on average, one killed about ten orangutans in his/her active hunting lifetimes, based on a survey with over 5,000 respondents in the rural areas across Kalimantan. While human-orangutan conflicts were perceived as an important reason for orangutan killing (Abram et al. 2015), the main reason found in this study was something else—more than half of the respondents took orangutans as food. There are also differences in perspectives among indigenous people. In their study in Danau Sentarum, Yuliani, Adnan, et al. (2018) found that it was plantation people, not locals, who took young orangutans as pets, maybe after the mothers were killed as they strayed onto the plantation. Their study also found that the Malay fisherfolk would sometimes hunt orangutans, while the Iban swiddeners would not. Various Dayak groups have different traditional beliefs and taboos towards orangutans and other animals. For example, the Iban people regard slow loris as a sacred animal that brings good luck, while the Penan people consider them as food or pets (Miard, Nekaris, and Ramlee 2017).

In many places in Borneo, bushmeats remain important to dietary health among rural communities (Reyes-Garciá et al. 2018). Recognizing this fact, some conservationists and modernists have advocated the substitution of wild meat with poultry and other meat sources (Cheok and Mohd-Azlan 2018), but this also implies intervening and altering traditional lifestyles. In some cases, overhunting is driven by the overall trend of increasing consumption and access to urban marketplaces (Okuno and Ichikawa 2020). Some called for tightening control over local hunting and trading activities, and labelled them as illegal trafficking, but the situation remains tricky in the vast rural areas (Gomez and Shepherd 2019). Perhaps, more vigorous enforcement is likely to be seen after the global outbreak of the COVID-19 pandemic in the early 2020s.

A theoretically "sustainable" and "traditional" system recognized by extra-local conservationists may not be viewed as appropriate or attractive in the eyes of local communities. For example, the agroforestry system advocated as an alternative to slash-and-burn practices, ideally, should be able to provide sufficient food and some extra income through trading forestry products like rattan while maintaining other ecosystem services (Wulan, Budidarsono, and Joshi 2008; Rahman et al. 2016; Bakkegaard et al. 2017). Traditionally, it also carries cultural implications like ethnic identity and ancestral linkages (Afentina, McShane, and Wright 2019). However, not all indigenous people are willing or capable of actively engaging in forest management (Nelson et al. 2014). With decades of rapid socio-economic and environmental changes, perspectives towards human-environmental relationships may have changed substantially, as traditional ecological knowledge and values may have already been degraded among the younger generations (Siahaya et al. 2016). Traditional knowledge may play a role as a social instrument rather than a practical tool, and access to traditional knowledge may also strongly depend on social status and connections (Reyes-García and Gallois 2016; Reyes-García et al. 2018). In Sarawak, van Gevelt et al. (2019) only found weak evidence to support traditional knowledge related to climate based on a case study on Penan tribes.

Embracing traditional practices and values may indeed help to guide decision-making from an ethical viewpoint (Choy 2014). However, as pointed out by Rubis (2020), there is a risk of romanticizing traditional practices of indigenous communities without envisaging the fact that the group is constantly changing and adapting to new socio-economic dynamics brought by external actors. The changes may be driven by multiple forces and instilled in multiple aspects, from integrating into market economies through cash crop expansions to embracing modernity through large-scale conversion to Christianity (Low and Pugh-Kitingan 2015; Chua 2016). How to pragmatically integrate local interests and preferences with global conservation agendas considering a range of trade-offs will remain a key question to be tackled for a better overall outcome for both (Runting et al. 2019).

Autonomy and Heterogeneity
Conservationists deemed empowering local communities in Borneo a key move to protect their livelihoods and their surrounding environment, with a great emphasis on maintaining subsistence and self-sufficient land-use systems. Past failures in large-scale land-based developments have degraded people's trust in the governments and called for land reforms. Transferring more power to local governance may provide more space for local people to establish and configure ways to cope with changes and uncertainties ahead in specific spatial settings, regaining self-sufficiency as in the past. For Sarawak alone, about one-quarter of the land area is claimed by indigenous people as native customary land that must be preserved for traditional farming (Andersen et al. 2016).

Foremost among these is the bottom-up push for revitalization of local institutions, which in this context means traditional governing systems. For example, a system called "*kademangan*" has been practised in Central

Kalimantan by the Dayak communities, in parallel to the "village" system that is used across Indonesia (Yuliyanto 2017). Traditional institutions and customary laws have been gradually eroded and replaced by top-down legal systems in the past decades, degrading the identity of indigenous people. Especially, traditional land-use practices like shifting agriculture have received negative connotations from the state and national governments (a continuation of similar prejudices dating from colonial times) as obstacles to development (Cramb and Sujang 2016; Hattori et al. 2019). Numerous case studies by Lunkapis (2015) in Sabah, Nelson, Muhammed, and Rashid (2016) in Sarawak, Muhdar, Tavip, and Al Hidayah (2019) in East Kalimantan are fragmented accounts of such transitions.

Struggles of local people to (re)gain and safeguard their rights over land through the revitalizing of traditional institutions and customary laws have been mushrooming, such as the "*Dayak Misik*" movement in Central Kalimantan which aims to unite the Dayak communities in rural and interior areas of Central Kalimantan in defending their rights over land (Großmann 2019; Jarias 2020; Potter 2016b). However, such ethnic-based struggles may trigger competing claims over resource access between different communities, especially between "indigenous people" and "migrants" (Goh et al. 2018), or among "indigenous people" themselves who are made up of diverse groups with different statuses and power (Großmann 2019). Counterfeit claims of indigeneity and rights to land are widely reported in Kalimantan (Nugroho, Skidmore, and Hussin 2020).

In many instances, such ethnic-based, highly localized, and spontaneous institutional architectures are only temporarily effective in achieving desired outcomes when they coincide and interrelate with national or international agendas. When conditions change, their functions quickly fade away. The characteristics of "traditional governance" can be very different from place to place in Borneo. For example, Dayak Ngaju in Central Kalimantan value more autonomy and flexibility without strong chieftainship and a clear community hierarchy (Lounela 2020). In contrast, the study in Pakan, Sarawak by Rezaul Islam, Wahab, and Anggum (2020) illustrates the importance of leadership in determining the cohesion of indigenous tribes.

While elements in the Ministry of Environment and Forestry in Indonesia have been reluctant to recognize the rights of indigenous people to customary or *adat* forest by changing the status of such forests from state to community control, this is slowly taking place following the decision of the Constitutional Court in 2013 and the mapping activities led by AMAN (see discussion in Chapter 4). The paper by Nugroho, Skidmore, and Hussin

(2020), using a case study of deforestation by an *adat* forest community in Paser, East Kalimantan, concludes that the *adat* community manages their forest sustainably by adherence to *adat* law. They should continue to do so with the empowerment of and respect for customary law and *adat* institutions, land allocation to ensure tenure and livelihood security, and improvement of farming practices, but not by forcing them to convert from swidden to permanent agriculture. In migrant communities in parts of the same area, both local Banjarese and Javanese transmigrants are more likely to encroach on the forest as they extend permanent cropping, especially of oil palm.

However, ethnic-based identity politics may drive further polarization among the ethnically heterogeneous population and lead to unwanted consequences, especially considering the historical ethnic-based violent incidents, e.g., in West Kalimantan (Chen 2020). For decades, Indonesia suppressed ethnic-regional identification in politics, especially during the Suharto period (Ananta et al. 2015). The Indonesian government has also become more cautious about regionalism which may cause disjointed governance. The potential political anxieties between the pursuit of local well-being and national interest can be acute (McCarthy and Obidzinski 2017). There are also similar struggles in Malaysia between the Bornean states and the federal government, where the states demand more power in the name of protecting the interest of the indigenous people (Harding 2018).

Regionalism in Kalimantan also stems from uneven development between districts. For example, there was a recent push from some district governments to subdivide Central Kalimantan into smaller provinces, with the main proposal to make a new province of "Kotawaringin Raya", consisting of three major "oil palm districts", i.e., Kotawaringin Barat, Seruyan, and Kotawaringin Timur, together with two other smaller districts along the western border (Damara 2021). While there is probably not much chance of this subdivision getting accepted by the central government, it draws attention to the inequities in "development" across the province. The recent proposal to move the national capital to East Kalimantan displays the ambition of the government in strengthening its control over its large territory across three time zones and narrowing the gaps between different parts of the country (Maulia 2019), as well as the reality of the sinking of Jakarta city, which has exceeded its ecological limit as a population centre.

Most importantly, local autonomy does not automatically bring fairer and equitable outcomes for all. The inequality between and within the communities, i.e., economic gaps and social status, can be stark and must be carefully considered. As observed by Haridison, Sandi, and Retei (2019), the customary governance framework may also turn out to be an instrument for small groups of informal elites to formalize their power, and further widen the gaps within the communities. Moreover, history has shown that the struggles for land rights by indigenous people can be easily countered by short-term economic lures, especially with the traditional leaders as key targets. If the leaders have changed their attitude towards "development", the villagers are left with few choices. This is particularly prominent in Malaysian Borneo where economic development has been a central axiom in daily politics (Idris and Mohamad 2014).

As pinpointed by Chua et al. (2020), the word "local" should be used with care especially involving generalization to avoid neglecting the heterogeneity and complexity of the communities. In reality, sources of livelihood or occupations in a place, which are closely linked to the level of wealth and social status, significantly affect people's perceptions of sustainability. The cases in East Kalimantan reported by de Jong and Kuipers (2020) and Lukman et al. (2020) on the perceptions of people on water quality in the Mahakam Delta and seagrass ecosystems in Berau, respectively, provide evidence of this. For example, for those who have access to some benefits from commercial plantations, undermining the entire system may not be the first choice (Acciaioli and Dewi 2016). Those who do not may hold a very different view. Also, gender and gender equality are less discussed but should not be neglected as a factor that drives the changes in livelihood strategies, see, for example, the case study by Toumbourou and Dressler (2020) on Dayak Modang women in East Kalimantan.

The wave of development throughout Borneo has dragged the indigenous people into a race to be a "legitimate participant of modernity", whether they like it or not (Schreer 2020). Their worldviews and behaviours towards nature have changed significantly depending on the accessibility to the "outside world" and the level of socio-cultural assimilation (Nugroho, Skidmore, and Hussin 2020). As a result, inequality among the local people has grown substantially, with some enjoying the benefits but many being victimized along the "race". In Kalimantan, the combined effects of increasing income polarization and ethnic fractionalization have contributed to various social conflicts since the early 2000s (Indra et al. 2019). In Sarawak, the heterogeneity and inequality were reflected in the past election in 2018, when indigenous voters split into multiple camps, with some remaining supportive of the pro-development ruling coalition and some swinging to the opposition when their cultural and environmental concerns were largely side-lined (Mersat 2018).

Final Remarks

While the allure of harmonious human-environmental relationships in a "traditional", self-sufficient land-use system is enticing in a romantic context, one must note that the traditional society in Borneo has largely evolved due to rapid changes brought by the growing exchange and societal integration between rural and urban areas, as well as with the other parts of Malaysia and Indonesia. "The last swiddens of Sarawak", the title set by Mertz et al. (2013) in their paper reflects such a trend across Borneo.

The idea of returning Borneo to a decentralized, traditional governing system must be carefully thought through. Especially for Kalimantan, the central government of Indonesia would probably not want to see the country further beset by political fragmentation and economic disparities between regions (Indra et al. 2019). Even shifting to a local level, revitalizing traditional governance does not guarantee sustainability and equity in the eyes of modern society, as the groups involved are not necessarily unprejudiced, considering the societal heterogeneity and inequality embedded in traditional societies. Predominant framings of "self-sufficiency" may also overlook the specific issues faced by marginal groups who require external support.

This "strategy" in its current progress is more of a subtle form of promotion of environmental ethics and cultural values among decision-makers than well-defined actions on the ground, see for example, Choy (2014), if not purely an ideology. In the future, technological advancement in food production and provisioning services may provide new means of development, allowing the deployment of small, decentralized, self-sufficient settlements spread across the island (see Chapter 13). How to smartly combine sophisticated technologies with traditional lifestyles, especially to be supported by localized education (Halik and Webley 2011; Pellier et al. 2014), would be an interesting way to cope with unsustainable land exploitation as in the past.

Notes

1.   In Sarawak, about 0.8 million of Iban people (2018), the "Sea Dayak", mainly spread across the coastal districts and along the Rajang River. The "Land Dayak", Bidayuh people are mainly concentrated in Kuching and towards the west of it, with about 0.2 million (2018) of the population (Hata and Wahab 2018; SPU 2019). In Sabah, there are more than 1 million non-Muslim indigenous people (2010), but there is no consensus among them on whether they belong to the Dayak group or not (Cleary and Eaton 1992; DOSM 2020). The situation was less clear in Kalimantan as Indonesia was "suppressing ethnic-regional identification for decades" (Ananta

et al 2015). With the end of the Suharto era, the Indonesian census does try to list the various groups, with a much more detailed listing at the 2010 Census than in 2000. Based on the estimation of Ananta et al. (2015), there are roughly 1.5 million Dayaks in West Kalimantan (mainly Bidayuh, Iban, Ot Danum, Punan), 1 million in Central Kalimantan (mainly Dayak Ngaju, Ot Danum, Maanyan), more than 0.1 million in South Kalimantan, and 0.3 million in East and North Kalimantan (Kenyah, Kayan, Murut, Lawangan, Bahau, Maanyan) in 2010.

2. Although "*Rumah Panjang*" is technically correct in describing a longhouse, and in use in Sarawak [Iban: *Rumah Panjai* (Cramb 2007)], across West Kalimantan the traditional communal houses of Dayaks are termed "*Rumah Betang*". King (1993), noting that Ngaju Dayaks do not build longhouses, suggested that a *Rumah Betang* referred to the "great house" (two- or three-family residence) occupied by that group. In West Kalimantan, the Suharto regime attempted to destroy all longhouses in the early 1970s, arguing that they harboured communists, encouraged promiscuity and were a fire risk. By 1978, only eight longhouses remained in the Sanggau district out of more than 100 (Jenkins 1978). The only longhouse still standing in Sanggau is in the remote Toba subdistrict, (across the Kapuas River) where it is known as "*Rumah Betang Nek Bindang*" (Grandmother's longhouse). A second, larger longhouse previously existed at Kopar in Parindu but has now fallen into disrepair (see photo in Potter 2009a). In the more remote districts of West Kalimantan, such as Kapuas Hulu and Melawi, several functioning longhouses may still be found (Potter, field observations).

3. There are about 0.6 million (2010) Malay and Bajau in Sabah, 0.8 million (2018) Malay and Melanau in Sarawak, 2.4 million (2010) Malay, Javanese, Madurese, and Buginese in West Kalimantan, more than 1 million (2010) Javanese, Banjarese, Malay, and Madurese in Central Kalimantan, 3.4 million (2010) Banjarese, Javanese, Buginese, and Madurese in South Kalimantan, more than 2.5 million (2010) Javanese, Buginese, Banjarese, Kutai, and other Muslim groups in East Kalimantan, and 0.4 million Malay (2011) in Brunei (Ananta et al. 2015; SPU 2019; DEPS 2020; DOSM 2020). Note that "Javanese" include Sundanese in these tabulations.

4. About 0.3 million in Sabah, 0.6 million in Sarawak, and 0.4 million in West Kalimantan, mainly in the cities of Pontianak and Singkawang (Ananta et al. 2015; SPU 2019; DEPS 2020; DOSM 2020).

PART IV
CONCLUSION

Floods in Kapuas River, Sanggau (West Kalimantan) (taken by Pak Adi Susanto in 2021, with permission).

Photos on previous page

1. Fires (Central Kalimantan), especially peat fires, disrupt crops and animals, human health and transport, while haze drifts over neighbouring countries (taken by Potter in 2014).

2. Grid connection in Pagalungan, a remote border village in Sabah (taken by Goh in 2022).

3. Crossing the Sabah-Kalimantan border. Sabah's anticipation of potential impacts from the relocation of Indonesia's capital, putting the borderland in the limelight (taken by Goh in 2022).

4. Young women with their mobile phones in longhouse, Toba (West Kalimantan) (taken by Potter in 2013).

5. Periodic droughts suspended fishing in the Mahakam Lakes (East Kalimantan) (taken by Potter in 1991).

13

Venturing into the Era of the Digital Revolution

This book has so far described various ways or lines of inquiry to improve productivity and support conservation in Chapters 3 to 12, attempting to answer the three subquestions set in "Scope and Structure" in Chapter 1. Importantly, the chapters also invoked concerns about the immense challenges that come with these strategies, with monitoring and communication as the most prominent ones. This chapter suggests that the digital revolution, also called Industrial Revolution 4.0, may provide new solutions to overcome these challenges, and at the same time bring new options to the table for development planning. While there are studies that touched on the different aspects of the application of digital technologies in Borneo, an overview of the opportunities and impacts brought by the digital transformation of land-based economies of the island remains largely missing. How will the developing, land-relying populations in Borneo fare in their experiences with the digital revolution will be an important question for researchers in the coming years.

This chapter first illustrates the recent trends of digitalization in Borneo. This is followed by an overview of technological vectors in the context of land-based economies. With this basis, the chapter continues to explore how the digital revolution can be practically operationalized in Borneo, using the framework of ten strategies described in previous chapters, populating with cases found across the island or elsewhere but applicable to Borneo collected from literature, through personal communications, and from field observations.

RECENT TRENDS IN BORNEO

The digital revolution has become a major policy focus in Malaysia and Indonesia to ensure the nations survive and evolve in the face of disruptive changes in the global economy. Digital and smart technologies are perceived as key modular building blocks for sustainable development in the next few decades (Sachs et al. 2019). Transformative efforts and initiatives have been made primarily for urban areas, especially on integrating infrastructure and various services via digital platforms, with labels like "smart cities" or "digital cities"; see, e.g., Yau et al. (2016), Jurriëns and Tapsell (2017), and Beschorner et al. (2019).

It was in recent years that both public and private sectors in both countries have started to realize one thing: rural territories that traditionally rely heavily on agriculture and forestry are a key strategic area for digital transformation and investment (*Borneo Post*, 5 July 2020; *Jakarta Globe*, 6 May 2020; Shukri 2020). This is especially important for Borneo which has undergone severe deforestation and forest degradation due to large-scale land development activities. The digital revolution may enable various transformative strategies in the quest for more sustainable ways of development in these frontiers of environmental degradation.

From a productivity perspective, the emergence of digital and smart technologies may help push development off the agroecological limits, especially in terms of improving productivity and reducing the need to exploit more land. Such a productivity-oriented transformation forms the core of the "bio-economy" concept. The rapid advancement in connectivity and coverage in recent years, accompanied by the confluence of artificial intelligence (AI), Internet-of-Things (IoT), and robotics is redefining "productivity" on an unprecedented scale (Goh, Ahl, and Woo 2020). These technologies are poised to reinvent not only farm management but also supply chain operations, ranging from empowering farmers with tools for precision farming to optimizing the entire supply chain (Deichmann, Goyal, and Mishra 2016).

Meanwhile, digitization may also enhance conservation efforts and bring multiple socio-economic benefits (Watanabe, Naveed, and Neittaanmäki 2019). Digital innovations concerning conservation and production may significantly boost various alternative economic activities that prioritize conservation, which may be collectively, loosely framed as the "eco-economy". The digital revolution allows a narrative of decentralized but well-coordinated small-scale, grassroots innovations owing to wide connectivity and low transaction costs, with tools like real-time, spatially explicit forest monitoring or electronic marketing platforms. More importantly, the convenience offered by the digital revolution may redefine the urban-rural transition, permitting more sustainable alternative livelihoods and lifestyles for populations spread across rural areas instead of relying solely on land-based activities.

While governments have tried to spur investment and encourage innovation in these areas, significant changes have yet to be seen (Onitsuka, Hidayat, and Huang 2018). Few could have appreciated the implications of the digital revolution in Borneo until the spread of COVID-19 over the island. In Sabah, the story of a young university student who stayed overnight on top of a tree to ensure better connectivity for her online examination has gone viral on YouTube (*Borneo Post*, 17 June 2020). During the movement control order (MCO) period, many students were forced to return to their villages and faced difficulties in following online lectures and exams due to poor connectivity. Incidents like this have somehow accelerated the progress of digitalization in Borneo. Especially, Sarawak has been leading in the race to digitalization with visions and policies for crafting a digital economy. For example, the state government has expanded the "Mobile Bank Branch Services" in rural areas to ensure people receive financial aid provided by the state and federal governments during the MCO period (*The Star*, 8 May 2020). In the future, the state plans to extensively introduce electronic banking via mobile phones as a permanent solution to overcome the limitation in physical access in rural areas (*Borneo Post*, 8 February 2020).

Borneo is now in its third "oil palm" decade (broadly speaking—considering the rapid expansion in most territories started in the 2000s) in the age of the digital revolution. The past impediments to sustainable development may now be resolved with new means. While the idea of introducing advanced, futuristic technologies in a relatively underdeveloped region like Borneo remains speculative, exploring the opportunities and impacts can have important implications for steering the transformation. Improvement may revolve around a gradual rate of increase like growing productivity, but it may not be an understatement that Borneo may see a total disruption of existing land-use models.

Still, the digital transformation of land-based sectors remains poorly understood in the Bornean context, although it has been widely discussed and kickstarted globally. Sarawak with the strongest industrial foundations among the Bornean territories has taken bold steps to embrace the digital revolution in their land-use sectors. While the state is still far from spearheading the development of cutting-edge smart technologies, it has started to lay out infrastructure to capture the benefits of digitalization, especially in terms of connectivity and data governance (CMO 2020). It also sees the importance of connecting its comparative advantage, i.e., rich biodiversity and natural resources with the digital revolution. A noteworthy example is the investment of the state in digital documentation of indigenous medicine and perfumes through the screening of bioactive compounds extracted from tropical forests in Borneo, hoping to create new markets for traditional products and new income sources from conserving tropical rainforests (Yeo, Naming, and Manurung 2014).

The penetration of the Internet in Borneo has been growing rapidly. While the penetration of fixed broadband remains low in Sabah and Sarawak, the penetration of mobile broadband has achieved 81 per cent and 108 per cent, respectively (MCMC 2020). A major network provider in Malaysia, however, revealed that the two Bornean states of Malaysia have recorded the highest mobile Internet usage in 2018 as their data consumption doubled compared to 2017 (*Borneo Post*, 10 December 2018). Horn et al. (2018), however, revealed that there are still a small number of populations, especially those poorer and older, excluded from digital connectivity. For the Kalimantan provinces, the surveys by Asosiasi Penyelenggara Jasa Internet Indonesia in 2013 and 2019 show that the penetration of the Internet has risen from 17–24 per cent to 78–85 per cent. This is comparable to Jakarta, where the penetration grew from 43 per cent to 85 per cent (Marius and Pinont 2013; Irawan, Yusufianto, et al. 2019). While the penetration rate has generally surged throughout Borneo, one should also note that the quality and cost-effectiveness of connectivity are also greatly enhanced with the rolling out of the 4G technology in the past decade (Shayea et al. 2020). Clearly, Borneo is heading slowly but steadily into the era of the digital revolution. The island will likely continue to see rapid growth in digital connectivity, with broader coverage and lower cost, as well as digital literacy, especially among the younger generations.

OVERVIEW OF KEY TECHNOLOGICAL VECTORS

To provide a basis for more specific discussion in later sections, this section provides an overview of key technological vectors in the context of land-based economies. Table 13.1 lists the key technological vectors for the transformation of land-based economies based on the framework proposed by Siebel (2019). An important technology vector is IoT which can greatly improve the capability of monitoring, on both the farm and landscape scale. IoT represents a complex network of interconnected systems consisting of sensors and computing devices that permit the flow of data without human-machine interactions. The most foreseeable is the application of

TABLE 13.1
Overview of Key Technological Vectors for Transformation of Land-Based Economies

Vector	Functions Applicable to Land-Based Activities
Internet-of-Things (IoT)	• Complex networks of systems consist of sensors and computing devices that permit data flows without human-machine interactions. • Farm-scale and factory-scale monitoring with wireless network sensors, i.e., various biological, physical, and chemical sensors, controllers, computers, and mobile phones that can be connected through an electromagnetic transfer. • Landscape-scale monitoring with remote sensing, i.e., the scanning of the earth by satellite or high-flying aircraft for spatially explicit mapping and planning. • Automation with robotics, i.e., intelligent robots that can assist or replace humans in farms, forests, and industrial operations through machine-to-machine communication.
Big Data	• Voluminous, ever-growing data is collected from IoT platforms in digital formats, including various numerical databases, text, still images, audio, and video. • Growing digital libraries that contain, e.g., spatially explicit maps, socio-economic statistics, climatic changes, biological materials, genetic information, and enzymatic reactions.
Artificial Intelligence (AI)	• Computers capable of performing tasks that typically require human intelligence but with higher speed. • Improve automatically without human intervention, through machine learning and deep learning with Big Data fed into the machines. • Analysing digital images or videos, e.g., satellite images, and images of individual trees. • Predicting and optimizing complex operations, e.g., "smart" farming systems, landscape management, and "smart" factories.
Cloud technologies	• Provide on-demand data storage, exchange, and computing power without the need for physical possession and management of advanced computer system resources by the users. • Accessing shared pools of data and applications through cloud storage. • Digital platforms, e.g., trading, product marketing, communications, e-banking.

inexpensive wireless network sensors in farm management to allow real-time adaptive operation. This can be further enhanced with an intelligent automation system that can react promptly to changes in temperature and moisture, as well as detection of abnormalities and diseases.

Information systematically collected through digitization and virtual connection of land-based activities leads to the formation of Big Data, i.e., huge, ever-growing, comprehensive databases. Examples range from digital libraries of crop growth cycles under various conditions, biodiversity, and genetic information to large-scale biogeochemical processes. These form the basis to generate knowledge for a holistic understanding of the entire system. The availability of and access to this knowledge has important global implications for optimizing production, conservation, and supply chains in the increasingly connected world.

The most intriguing domain is probably AI which grows with "nutrients" from Big Data. The key feature is its ability to solve problems without human intervention. Pairing with IoT and Big Data, it can continuously learn to make decisions without explicitly being programmed. At the farm level, it can analyse, predict, design, and optimize operation and maintenance. This is not limited to direct numerical inputs but also digitized visionary information (e.g., real-time images of trees or land cover). At the landscape level, it can monitor and operate the management of the entire land-use system, not only based on information on the ground but also connected to the larger climatic system with complex mathematic models.

Finally, through digital platforms and cloud computing, communication between rural and urban areas will be greatly enhanced. Cloud technologies provide on-demand data storage, exchange, and much larger computing power without the need for physical possession and management of massive, advanced computer system resources by the users. These open a new door to small-scale, highly dispersed smallholdings by providing lower-cost access to and exchange of information, knowledge, services, and applications which were very difficult or expensive in the past. It potentially relieves rural farmers from information opacity and physical connectivity barriers, allowing them to acquire various services, subsidies, market information, and consultancy much faster. It also relieves governments from the need to invest heavily in building a costly and inefficient physical governance system—a foreseeable example is much faster paperless communication through various digital platforms like emails between mobile devices and various mobile apps.

A combination of these domains can create a powerful land management system to overcome some of the key binding constraints to accelerating transformation. All transformative strategies will likely greatly benefit from the deployment of these technological domains. The following sections more specifically identify the key technologies applicable to each strategy, with interesting case studies mainly found in Borneo, and if applicable some others from Malaysia, Indonesia, and elsewhere.

DIGITAL REVOLUTION FOR PRODUCTIVITY

Boosting Upstream Productivity of Cash Crops

Land intensification has been ongoing with biological (breeding) and chemical (agro-inputs) methods. Nevertheless, multiple challenges could not be effectively addressed by bio- and chemical-based technologies only. For example, the average yield of palm oil in Malaysia and Indonesia has been fluctuating if not stagnant for almost a decade due to a combination of management, socio-economic, and climatic factors. In this sense, digital and smart technologies offer new opportunities for breakthroughs.

First, the relationships between growth, yield, agro-inputs, climate, as well as inter- and intra-field variability can be better understood with more thorough and precise monitoring through the concept of "precision agriculture" or "digital plantation" with the IoT and Big Data analytics, coupled with robotics and farms automation (Feng, Yan, and Liu 2019). For example, real-time diagnosis can be done through large-scale screening of farms and plantations by sensors, airborne vehicles, non-invasive imaging, and high-performance computing. Examples include the case of smart compost monitoring in an organic farm in Serian, Sarawak reported by Siswoyo Jo et al. (2019), the case of smart farming of shiitake mushrooms in Mount Kinabalu, Sabah (Kassim et al. 2017), and the case of early-stage Basal Stem Rot (BSR) disease detection by using airborne hyperspectral imaging for a 5,000-ha industrial oil palm plantation in Sabah (Alias et al. 2017). The relationships between different factors and yield can also be better modelled by harnessing Big Data if the monitoring efforts were greatly improved by scale, frequency, and depth (Shanmuganathan et al. 2014).

In addition, the digital revolution may also take conventional marker-assisted breeding and field phenotyping to a new level. For example, researchers and breeders can better deal with the complexity of mislabelling during marker-assisted selection as reported by Javed Muhammad et al. (2017), increasing the chances of discovering and developing new plant materials with strong climate resilience and other desirable agronomic traits (Kushairi, Singh, and Ong-Abdullah 2017). The biological limits may be further uplifted with advanced genetic engineering assisted with high-performance computing (Long, Marshall-Colon, and Zhu 2015).

Beyond farms and plantations, productivity can also be greatly improved through supply chain optimization. For example, palm fruits can be harvested at optimal ripeness for higher oil extraction rates (OER) with the help of wireless sensor networks (WSN). A study in North and East Kalimantan estimated that 10 per cent of the total land demand for cash crops can be potentially fulfilled by improving the chain efficiencies and chain integration of by- and coproducts (Van der Laan et al. 2017). In the future, the application of digital trading platforms with AI and real-time tracking may change the business models, allowing the best matching of FFB delivery and mills, ideally within 24 hours of harvesting to minimize the generation of free fatty acid in the CPO. One can imagine the financial implications, especially for smallholders when low-cost transactions can be made without middlemen while ensuring the optimal output and prices.

For smallholders, digitization implies better access to information and technological advances, especially for those located in the interior and far from cities. In the past, small farmers at best could receive technical advice by phone (Cole and Fernando 2012). Communications among themselves are also less efficient. The availability of digital platforms especially mobile phones can open up new channels of information and knowledge. It facilitates the uptake of expert advice and also enables quick feedback from small farmers (Jiménez et al. 2019). Importantly, organizing large groups of farmers dispersed across a large area (including independent ones) is more feasible at much lower costs. This also means collective actions like the collective purchase of fertilizers at a lower price can be made possible. This can be further extended to e-banking applications for functions like microcredit and subsidy management with the remote assistance of financial experts and policy officers (Vong, Mandal, and Song 2016). Empowering small farmers in this way was unimaginable in the past, especially in underdeveloped regions like Borneo.

Furthermore, robotics and automation of the farming process may potentially address the emerging issue of labour shortage mentioned earlier. Increasing wages and partly substituting with machines are some immediate measures, but this largely depends on the overall profitability, i.e., the market price of CPO in the long run. In the future, revamping the current labour-intensive and low-wages model with more automation may be a solution. The progress has been impressive for annual crops, e.g., with controlled traffic farming systems (Lu et al. 2016), but lagged for permanent crops due to the challenging architecture and terrain of the plantations (Kushairi, Singh, and Ong-Abdullah 2017). For Sabah and Sarawak, the economic measure taken by the Malaysian government to reduce reliance on foreign labourers through the implementation of the minimum wage laws mentioned earlier, may motivate more innovations in this direction (Kadir, Hussin, and Hashim 2019).

Activating Underutilized Low-Carbon Land

The very basis to ensure sustainable use of underutilized low-carbon land is high-quality spatial data. Advances in remote sensing in terms of hardware, processing technologies, and data-sharing have made land surveys not only broader and more detailed but also easier and more affordable. Drone and intelligence-based forest- and landscape-mapping solutions are also being expanded commercially. Technology diffusion and widened access to a spatial database also encourage more mapping activities across Borneo, especially by local researchers. Multiple mapping and modelling exercises have been performed to identify and capture various properties of potential underutilized low-carbon land in Borneo. For example, Agustan, Mubekti, and Sumargana (2015) assessed the use of SAR data to extract soil moisture information to identify potential areas for paddy fields. Studies by Jaung et al. (2018) and Gingold et al. (2012) are the other two examples that attempted to quantify degraded land available for cash crop and biofuel production in Borneo. The study by Peter et al. (2020) demonstrates some of the latest advances in this direction, employing the open-access Google Earth Engine to visualize the agroecological information supported with an analysis of crop suitability. For example, one may zoom in on a specific location and compare crop suitability with rainfall, temperature, and other various biophysical characteristics. The beauty of such an online platform is that it utilizes cloud computing and server-side geoprocessing to allow agricultural professionals to analyse continuously updated data at much larger scales and faster speed than they can do on their own.

Furthermore, the digitization of existing maps from both remote sensing and ground surveys enables the harmonization of spatial information obtained from different sources. It permits the creation of a harmonized public database that will greatly improve the consistency and efficiency of land governance across sectors and levels, as attempted by the "One Map Policy" in Indonesia (Mulyani and Jepson 2016). Consistent maps are the key to addressing land disputes long troubled with immense legal complexity (Rosenbarger et al. 2013). This also creates opportunities for integrated land-use planning when socio-economic mapping, e.g., land occupancy and land-use history can be explicitly analysed together with biophysical and agroecological properties (Goh et al. 2017). Subtle institutional and cultural elements, such as fragmentation and uncertainties of land ownership have always been a big barrier to mobilizing underutilized land resources. Land tenure can be made more transparent and accurate with the use of drones for mapping smallholdings, potentially preventing land underutilization or overexploitation due to tenure uncertainties (Radjawali and Pye 2017). Such transparency is essential to avoid the history of injustice from being repeated, i.e., the seizure of land from indigenous people under the name of development.

The digital revolution may open a new way to address another barrier, i.e., labour availability which imposes a great limitation on the actual use of underutilized land (Goh et al. 2018). Creating new settlements in unfertile areas with low population density is not economically and socially attractive, not to mention the past failed transmigration schemes that triggered a multitude of social and environmental problems (Potter 2012). The application of a smart farming system that is remotely monitored, controlled, and partly automated can greatly reduce the required manpower on site. This can significantly reduce unnecessary social risks of moving extra labourers into the interior.

Upgrading and Diversifying Downstream Activities

The implications of IR 4.0 to downstream industrial operations are widely discussed with numerous ongoing experiments and evidence found around the world, such as the concept of a "smart factory" (Chen et al. 2018). Applications are wide, ranging from an IoT platform that ingests voluminous data from sensors to AI that runs complex algorithms for data analytics and optimizes operations. For the oil palm sector, this implies exciting possibilities for upgrading and diversifying downstream industries. An interesting prospect is the convergence of digital innovation and biotechnology. The application of sophisticated bio-processing such as enzymatic processes in producing oleochemicals is a core part of this strategy (Abdelmoez and Mustafa 2014). This is particularly vital for Malaysia which is among the leading countries in the oleochemical industry.

First, digital technologies bring biotechnology research to a new level through greater integration with engineering design. For example, the automation of iterative processes with machine learning greatly shortens the long test phase in research (OECD 2020). Also, technological feasibility, productivity, and product quality can be improved through smart operations with IoT and AI (Wang et al. 2016). This means that not only complex automation for most advanced bio-processing like protein- and RNA-sequencing can be realized (Boles et al. 2017), but the implementation of various types of bio-processing can be made more feasible and flexible, allowing the creation of tailor-made biorefineries based on local bioresources, supply chains and markets (Dragone et al. 2020).

Similar to the effects on productivity improvement, chain integration is another key benefit to be tapped from the digital revolution on downstream development. For example, flows and quality of feedstock, intermediates, and products can be automatically tracked and managed across the value chain, reducing transaction costs, delivery time, and unused capacities (Hirbli 2018). This offers new opportunities for more efficient cross-sectorial partnerships and business models if the strategic infrastructure was put in place. For example, the Bintulu Port in Sarawak, the Lahad Datu Port and the Sandakan Port in Sabah have deployed the concept of a Palm Oil Industry Cluster (POIC) to promote the integration of different industrial operations by providing on-demand and pay-per-use facilities, ranging from purpose-fit storage to smart grid (Pang and Lee 2013; Soon and Lam 2013). Such a model can potentially reduce capital, operation, and maintenance costs to attract more investment in bio-based industries in the region, as well as reduce greenhouse gas emissions and pollution.

In addition, the expanded use of advanced cloud-based technologies will redefine the modes of technology transfer and research collaboration between developed and developing regions, upstream and downstream, buyers and suppliers, as well as among different sectors (Scheitz, Peck, and Groban 2018). This can potentially narrow the gap between Borneo and other regions due to its physical remoteness in terms of distance to major industrial clusters in Peninsular Malaysia and Java.

Tracking and Trading Certified Products
Sustainable branding and certification of agricultural and forestry products are thought to be key solutions in addressing sustainability concerns, especially for those produced on an industrial scale. It will certainly be boosted with various digital technologies and cloud platforms. First, the sustainability of upstream production can be better monitored with improved spatially explicit information in terms of both spatial and temporal resolution. This is particularly important for the oil palm sector which has been suffering from data poverty when it comes to land-use monitoring.

For timber, Melendy et al. (2018) reported a case in which an automated algorithm was deployed to capture the changes in production forests caused by different logging methods. For oil palm, Gaveau et al. (2021) reported the development of an automated, near-real-time alerting system for forest loss within oil palm concessions.

Furthermore, the flow of agricultural products or timber can be tracked and traced from plantation to gate, with, e.g., radio-frequency identification (RFID) tags and cloud technologies (Guo et al. 2015) or the use of biomarkers (Vlam et al. 2018). Ng et al. (2016) reported a case in Sabah and Sarawak where genetic identification databases of timber with DNA markers were developed to block illegal logging and smuggling, safeguarding valuable species from being exploited. Synergistically, cost and emission reduction can also be achieved through the optimization of operation and supply chains with artificial intelligence, further enhancing the sustainability of products while delivering tangible benefits along the value chains. Time-consuming and error-prone complex management tasks that needed to be done manually by supply chain practitioners can be passed to much more efficient AI operating through cloud computing. The impact will be especially notable for a long-distance supply chain of bio-based products (Visser, Hoefnagels, and Junginger 2020).

Potentially, the use of digital platforms may greatly reduce the transaction costs of certification, and thus increase the uptake by financially less capable smallholders who are often blamed for their inefficient and unsustainable land-use practices. In the past, the price premium of RSPO-certified palm oil was reportedly insufficient to cover the transaction cost (Ruysschaert and Salles 2014). This may significantly contribute to addressing the long-lasting governance challenge of the oil palm complex (Carlson et al. 2018). In the future, this may potentially further be assisted with blockchain technologies. Blockchain, a decentralized digital ledger that immutably records all transactions, can enable more transparent tracking from production to end-use along the entire value chain. This prevents potential alteration of data and gains greater trust from the buyers. It can leverage the mass balance, and book and claim traceability models developed under a certification framework like the RSPO (Hirbli 2018).

Finally, more efficient chain monitoring activities will also indirectly contribute to the expansion of a global land-use database. As the world is increasingly connected through trade, a global understanding of land-use activities, consumption patterns, and various drivers and consequences is essential to effectively transform the world's land-use systems. The expansion and integration of multiple databases of land use, trade flows, and related activities can substantially improve various modelling efforts in coping with global environmental changes (Verstegen et al. 2016).

Optimizing Domestic Use of Bio-resources

A compelling feature of the digital revolution is enabling decentralization, i.e., empowering people or things in physically isolated areas by connecting them via virtual networks. For instance, highly dispersed biowaste streams like biomass residues from forestry and agricultural sectors can be optimally channelled to decentralized bioenergy systems scattered in rural areas through AI-powered logistic planning. With extensive IoT, biomaterial quality parameters can be automatically tracked and shared among the actors in the value chain, allowing real-time matching and informed decision-making (Ahl, Goto, and Yarime 2019). This can be integrated with other energy sources, e.g., solar power through a smart grid, i.e., an electrical grid equipped with IoT (can be millions of smart metres across the entire grid) and optimized with AI which evolves with continuous learning. With its aptitude for market decentralization, a blockchain-based distributed energy system would be an interesting model to be explored in the future to address intermittency and transparency (Ahl et al. 2019). This will meaningfully address energy security in low population density areas which are troubled by high fuel costs and limited accessibility.

The digital revolution may also strengthen the advantage of Malaysia and Indonesia as "prosumers" (producer + consumer) of their major commodity: palm oil. Both countries have designed their biofuel policies with the objective of creating a domestic biodiesel market as a buffer to relieve the excessive stock resulting from the fluctuating palm oil prices throughout the cycles of the commodity market (Goh and Lee 2010). The artificially created domestic demand functions as a backup for the oil palm industry, providing more economic flexibility, especially considering that both countries are also major petroleum producers. However, the wildly fluctuating prices in recent years have created many issues in policymaking and on-ground implementation, considering the time lag and flexibility of incentive schemes. In this context, AI may be employed to create a more robust mechanism for designing and integrating government interventions on local demand creation and export strategies, supported by Big Data from both the food and fuel sectors. A sophisticated monitoring framework of bioresources with timely inputs of data powered by digital technologies can make policymaking nimbler and with faster reaction to market changes (Goh, Junginger, and Faaij 2014).

DIGITAL REVOLUTION FOR CONSERVATION

Enhancing Landscape Agroecological Resilience

Digital innovations may overcome the technical constraints of precise large-scale mapping and monitoring across a multifunctional landscape. Interesting examples include the identification of movement areas of elephants (Evans et al. 2020), image recognition of plants with deep machine learning (Heredia 2017), and precise positioning and imaging using wireless devices (Liu et al. 2019). These mapping and monitoring efforts can be integrated with climate-smart technologies in adaptation to potentially severe long droughts, floods, and climate change, such as machine-to-machine (M2M) communication that facilitates autonomous interactions among machines, from sensors to robotics, in detecting and responding to changes on a landscape scale. In return, data collected from AI-powered monitoring and feedback systems can contribute to advancing the knowledge of uncontrollable climate factors such as severe droughts brought by El Niño and improving the accuracy of existing land-climate models to evaluate short- and long-term interactions between land use and climate change (Kwan, Tangang, and Juneng 2014; Chapman et al. 2020).

Importantly, real-time, spatially explicit monitoring and forecasting systems with IoT and AI can greatly improve the knowledge and capacity for the advanced planning of land fire prevention and mitigation in Borneo, such as establishing an early warning system (Kieft et al. 2016). For example, through a spatio-temporal data mining approach, Syaufina and Sitanggang (2018) found that real fire detection was indicated by three consecutive days of hotspot occurrences for the fire in Kalimantan in 2015. Another study by Sumarga (2017) examined the relationship between fire hotspots and human locations such as distance to settlement and river. The precision and frequency of hotspot monitoring can be greatly enhanced by integrating data from satellites, drones, and long-range wireless sensors installed in the field (e.g., monitoring water levels) as well as real-time participatory monitoring by farmers and the public through mobile apps (Stolle et al. 2010; Yoon et al. 2012; Kibanov et al. 2017; Aditya, Laksono, and Izzahuddin 2019; Kadir et al. 2019; Widodo et al. 2019).

Digital technologies also offer complementary solutions to bioremediation in recovering degraded land. Bioremediation can replenish ecosystem services in critical locations through the application of microbial partners, endophytes, and soil enzyme-mediated processes (Grobelak et al. 2018). Wireless sensor networks can be applied to monitor not only on-ground but also below-ground conditions, e.g., nutrients and water dynamics (Salam, Vuran, and Irmak 2019). For example, a dam equipped with a microcontroller board with sensors can be employed to artificially rewet dry peat areas (Hamzah, Jalil, and Suhaili 2018). This can be further integrated with spatial information of not only geophysical, climatic, and agroecological properties but also present and historical land-use activities of degraded areas which are important to understand carry-over effects and socio-economic influences (Zhou et al. 2019).

The diffusion of digital communication tools empowers local communities not only through expanding access to information but also by opening up new opportunities for more effective collaboration between different groups of people. Interestingly, it also increases communication between groups of people who are affected by transboundary environmental issues but are physically separated. For example, the author has witnessed growing discussions, or more often debates and arguments, between Malaysians, Indonesians, and Singaporeans on social media about transboundary haze and environmental issues in Borneo and Sumatra. This was unimaginable in the past when people knew little very about their neighbours across the South China Sea or the Malacca Straits let alone having (near) real-time discussions. Previously, the regional environmental cooperation among ASEAN countries to address transboundary haze has not been effective (Nguitragool 2010). It is unclear how social media will transform relationships, but it likely will affect societal perspectives in these countries and bring new progress in the future.

Expediting Commodification of Ecosystem Services
The application of enhanced monitoring tools like drones, wireless sensors, and shared databases may substantially improve the accounting of ecosystem services (Deichmann, Goyal, and Mishra 2016). For example, carbon stock data collected from wireless sensors in field measurement, integrated with information retrieved from both optical and radar remote sensing can greatly reduce data uncertainty (Langner et al. 2012; Marvin et al. 2016). The use of a Random Forest Machine Learning (RFML) algorithm can further enhance regional modelling through better recognition of land cover patterns. This was demonstrated by Asner et al. (2018) to examine spatial variation of carbon stock in Sabah by forest use, growth, degradation, and protection status. Other examples include the works by Cushman et al. (2017) and Pfeifer et al. (2016) on examining forest degradation gradients and drivers of deforestation, respectively.

In terms of biodiversity, monitoring of wildlife like the proboscis monkey with unmanned aerial vehicles has been ongoing in Borneo (see, e.g., Stark et al. 2018). Combined with camera-trap images and videos, large amounts of information can be employed for identifying various species, capturing their distribution, and estimating biodiversity in larger areas through "deep learning" in artificial intelligence (Christin, Hervet, and Lecomte 2019). More data can also be obtained through a participatory approach, encouraging local communities to take photos and videos with smartphones, noting the location, time, and conditions under which wildlife or vegetation is observed, and sharing that with researchers. This can potentially allow better safeguarding measures to be incorporated into the REDD+ scheme beyond carbon stock (Vijge et al. 2016).

The setting up of a global and national digital database, such as the One Map Policy in Indonesia explained earlier, can greatly improve transparency in monitoring (Wibowo and Giessen 2015). A consistent spatial database for clarification of land ownership is vital to resolve various conflicts arising from the implementation of REDD+ as described in Chapter 9, especially in determining the legal right to benefit from the "sales" of ecosystem services (Sanders et al. 2017). This can be further enhanced with a higher degree of participation and lower transaction costs with the proliferation of platform technologies. It also improves the reliability and reputation of payment for ecosystem services (PES) schemes like REDD+ to gain the confidence of (potential) donors and increases the chances of the outcomes being formalized and institutionalized (Salzman et al. 2018).

In terms of credit trading, blockchain technology can assure traceability and connect national registry systems, preventing double counting and ensuring consistency and transparency (World Bank 2021). One notable initiative is the introduction of VerdePay, a new form of payment method to offset the embodied carbon emissions of any purchases made with carbon credits generated from the Rimba Raya REDD+ project in Central Kalimantan via blockchain (Howson 2018a). In terms of carbon pricing, AI can be applied in forecasting carbon prices to provide a risk-mitigation mechanism and allow governments to design a more stable market instrument (Hao, Tian, and Wu 2020). Tools like these are important to ensure PES models can remain financially workable in the long run.

Facilitating Eco-based Tertiary Sectors

Traditional tourism businesses in Borneo rely heavily on government efforts for collective promotion, with a few locations being selected and prioritized. With platform technology, businesses can now pursue low-cost marketing strategies, targeting a wider range of customers. Urban youths with more opportunities to explore their own countries, especially due to the availability of budget airlines, are among the targets.

This can be a two-way thing, where the gap between consumers and service providers blurs (Buhalis and Sinarta 2019). For example, a group of young, adventurous tourists who visit interesting locations in Borneo may share their stories in the form of words, photos, and videos including live streaming thanks to advancements in connectivity. These have exposed places that were out of reach of the touristic radar in the past, attracting more young visitors, who will then further spread their experience virtually. Interestingly, some of them may also work closely with local guides to start new businesses, including making money through broadcasting on YouTube, Facebook, and other popular platforms. Goh has observed the rapid growth of such business models in recent years. There are numerous interesting examples that consolidate promoting efforts by individuals or small groups of tour service providers in various languages. Some of them may be viewed as a combination of service providers and consumers, or "prosumers".

Other tourists may also produce reviews or ratings on various platforms, making the process more transparent and increasing the confidence of potential tourists who have previously never thought of visiting Borneo. Collectively, these data can be analysed with AI, giving service providers unprecedented visibility into tourists' experience, and enabling them to improve their business models, including real-time pricing models powered by AI based on Big Data (Al Shehhi and Karathanasopoulos 2020). The Big Data here include information collected from flight companies, migration departments, fuel prices, and currency exchange, relieving service providers from making raw guesses and adjustments.

IoT can also be applied to promote sustainable tourism, such as estimating fuel emissions along the entire tour, monitoring the situation in national parks with sensors and cameras, and connecting climatic data for route planning, It is also possible to view tourists as part of the conservation web rather than being outsiders, i.e., communities and tourists can work together to virtually monitor conservation activities. For example, tourist-generated media published on the Internet can be harnessed through Big Data technologies as supplementary to enhance understanding of wildlife activities, as illustrated in the case of Borneo elephants by Walker (2018). Some "prosumers" business models mentioned earlier may also forge synergies with environmental and cultural conservation-promoting activities.

In aggregate, platform technologies may create a new form of economy in rural Borneo, namely the "gig economy". Gig workers are independent contractors who take up jobs through online platforms. The gig economy normally refers to urban applications like Uber, but in the future, it may be formed in rural areas as well due to the proliferation of smartphones and data connectivity (Robinson et al. 2019). This is not restricted to tourism-related services, but also other environmental-related or knowledge-based jobs. For example, motivated, self-learning indigenous people may now have opportunities to obtain new knowledge from digital platforms and forge new collaborations with external organizations or companies, e.g., river and water management, forest rangers, and sustainable farming practices.

While it seems to be a wild feat of imagination for that to happen in rural Borneo, local businesses may become digital-based as may be observed nowadays in the urban areas. Furthermore, the availability of other low-cost digital tools to assist local communities, like smart sensors and mobile apps to detect and manage water quality (Gallagher and Chuan 2018), will increase the chances of turning such an unlikely scenario into reality. In the past, the concept of a "smart village" was promoted in Sarawak, aimed to improve living standards and overcome the "digital divide" for populations in remote areas by providing access to information and communication technology. It was implemented (though not as impactful as expected) in the Kelabit Highlands town of Bario (*e-Bario*); in Long Bedian, a remote Kayan logging area 500 km from Miri (*e-Bedian*), and in Long Lamai, a Penan village in the Upper Baram (see discussion in Chapter 10) (Cheuk, Atang, and Lo 2012; Harris, Ramaiyer, and Tarawe 2018). The more recent impact of mobile phones has led observers to suggest that the digital divide has now been largely bridged so telecentres need to modernize the kinds of services they supply. During a field trip to Bereng Bengkel, Central Kalimantan in 2014, Goh observed a case where an individual learnt how to establish a more efficient aquaculture system in his own backyard through digital media and communication (through an old laptop and a smartphone) and was planning how to promote these results to his peers.

Marketing Products from Smallholdings
Similar to the service sector mentioned earlier, digitization may also effectively enable branding and marketing strategies for small farmers which were fraught with high costs and economic uncertainties. Through ICT innovations, real-time inventory tracking and pricing mechanism will

greatly facilitate the tracing of food from farm to consumer, reassuring the authenticity and quality of perishable products which can earn price premiums for the producers (Rana and Oliveira 2015).

Most importantly, the emergence of digital trading platforms and extensive delivery systems grant the small farmers market access, connecting them directly with buyers that are physically far away. Farmers can deploy multiple low-cost strategies to brand, promote, and trade their products through the use of digital platforms coupled with AI and Big Data, more precisely target potential customers. This allows a more flexible, diversified, and demand-based business model as small farmers can continuously adjust their production strategies to changing conditions, e.g., adopting AI-powered price settings, selling on multiple platforms with different labels or certifications, and engaging various distribution channels. This is not something new in the other parts of Indonesia, where collective farm management and marketing was set up by the Merapi and Merbabu Farmers Association and supported by the dedicated website Tanilink. com (Tanilink.com 2020). In the long run, this may spur the growth of rural entrepreneurship, especially among the younger populations (Zaremohzzabieh et al. 2016).

Interestingly, this may also allow the marketing of traditional knowledge and products which were previously less known. A noteworthy example is the digital documentation of indigenous medicine and perfumes through the screening of bioactive compounds extracted from forests in Sarawak (Yeo, Naming, and Manurung 2014). The programme aims to improve local livelihoods by digitally connecting traditional knowledge and biotechnology, hoping to generate new income sources from conserving tropical rainforests.

Financially, electronic banking and trading platforms reduce the cost of transactions via the elimination of intermediaries. These also give small producers more flexibility in making financial arrangements, e.g., quick approval of small loans through e-banking without physical appearance. Supporting policies of governments may also be better executed, e.g., farmers can now apply online for subsidies and access supporting programmes or consultations. This is critical to those located far away from urban circles who have no access to physical banking or government services.

Enabling Self-sufficient Farming

The digital revolution may turn out to be the key enabler in (re)adopting "traditional" ways of living, enabling rural settlements to also enjoy some provisioning services from conventional urban areas, ranging from education to healthcare. This trend has been accelerated during the coronavirus pandemic in 2020, such as online teaching and telemedicine (Smith et al., 2020). Interestingly, virtual hearings for court cases have been made an official option in Sabah for those located in the interior and unable to travel to cities (*Borneo Post*, 1 June 2020).

In terms of food security, self-sufficient farming may be facilitated with the use of digital technologies. In the coming decades, the ongoing changes in the urban-rural gradient may blur the line between urban farming and traditional farming. The former normally refers to farming occurring in urban and peri-urban areas and enjoys various advantages from the proximity to the urban centres (Carolan 2020). However, with the improvement in digital technologies, the incorporation of silicon-based hardware and technologies into small farms scattered throughout the greater rural areas may be further accelerated.

While there are plenty of new technological applications to boost productivity as described in the early section of this chapter, the important question for this strategy is how feasible it would be to apply these technologies to a stand-alone farming unit that aims to provide self-sufficiency at the household or village levels. Basic infrastructure and subsidies need to be strategically put in place to make technologies and assets accessible and affordable to rural communities. The application of smart farming on a moderate scale, such as those that can be optimally operated at the village or communal levels, has been widely discussed and studied. For example, Jo et al. (2019) reported a case design of IoT monitoring architecture for smart organic farming at Satoyama Farm 52 in Serian, Sarawak. Mustafa et al. (2016) from Borneo Marine Research Institute also produced a review of how smart aquaculture can be effectively implemented by an organized fish farming community despite its underlying complexity.

In addition, these technological advances may also be applied to address human-wildlife conflicts which may turn out to be a greater issue alongside urban-rural population outflow. For example, Fazil and Firdhous (2018) designed an IoT system to detect approaching elephants and alert the residents. Optimistically, the rapid development of digital technologies may further lower the cost of adopting smart farming by households. Just like the evolution of mobile phones, such smart farming systems are also continuously evolving in terms of user-friendliness.

One can imagine that this may not only bring enormous impacts on rural populations like those described by Horn, Philip, and Sabang (2018) but also trigger a significant outflow of urban dwellers, dispersed further away from the urban centres for more space and better environments. This implies that the urban-rural gradient will evolve to some new patterns, changing the landscape extensively as happens now in richer countries, where people opt for a "sea change" and relocate away from the city, for they can work quite satisfactorily from anywhere, as long as they have digital access.

FINAL REMARKS

Imagining what is going to happen in Borneo in the era of the digital revolution is an ambitious undertaking. This chapter is painted with an oversimplifying broad brush, but it gives an illustration of potential breakthroughs in the land-based sectors. While socio-economic transitions in Borneo in the past two decades occurred on an unprecedented scale and rate, the digital revolution may irreversibly disrupt the entire system. IoT, Big Data, AI, and cloud technologies are creating new ways of functioning in Borneo. On the one hand, conventional, highly centralized land-based businesses may gain more control over land with enormous amounts of data retrieved in unprecedented dimensionality and granularity. On the other hand, the possibility to operate in a decentralized mode may revive traditional values in appreciating human-environment relationships and reinventing new ways of living. While both seem to be going to very different ends, they may exist together if proper interventions are put in place, leading to improvement ranging from the prevention of illegal logging to the emergence of self-sufficient villages, in the hope of creating a more sustainable landscape.

As the land-based sector is increasingly entangled with how food, energy, education, and other services are delivered, top-down interventions can be designed coherently to tap potential synergies generated from the convergence of different sectors. There are a couple of clear common benefits for society through integrating multiple services on digital platforms. First, it improves living standards by making life more convenient and possibly lowering goods prices. Second, digital infrastructure improves governance and allows more participatory systems. It may greatly facilitate the efforts of nurturing and empowering rural communities. Third, it creates a basis for bottom-up innovation. Tools and expert knowledge are now available at a much lower cost than ever, with the island observing the mushrooming of bottom-up digital innovation across agriculture, conservation, eco-tourism, etc.

To achieve these promises, governments need to play an active role in establishing a common policy framework that cuts across all sectors, potentially linking land-based sectors with the others in the framework of, e.g., the "digital economy" or "digital society". The "digital economy" development framework introduced by the Sarawak government is a remarkable example (CMO 2020). The digitizing agenda has been further intensified across all sectors of Sarawak's economy after the COVID-19 pandemic in 2020. Interestingly, it is placed together with environmental sustainability as the two major policy directions of Sarawak in the future. Strategic investments can be made in key areas like upgrading ICT infrastructure, deploying platform technologies, restructuring financial and regulatory systems, and encouraging domestic research and education (OECD 2020). In East Kalimantan, this has been done in partnership with international organizations, where 1,700 smartphones loaded with various apps were distributed across 160 villages in 2017, to boost community engagement for conservation and livelihood improvement (Hovani et al. 2018). Importantly, attitudes towards new technologies as well as the readiness to exploit these technologies are vital to set the scene. This requires careful consideration of local or territorial particularities from a more holistic perspective to ensure revolutionary changes brought by digitization will not victimize certain groups of people.

Land-based economies often fall into a trilemma—it is very challenging to find a balance between economic growth, environmental protection, and social participation. Some even suggested that this can only be addressed with either radical degrowth, radical decentralization, or even uncivilization (Kallis, Kerschner, and Martinez-Alier 2012; Sconfienza 2019). These options are probably unfavourable or impractical to most of the human population. Can the digital revolution provide a breakthrough for this trilemma? The transformations induced by the digital revolution in regions like Borneo in the upcoming decades may supply new insights into this question. The upcoming decades will be an interesting period of change to be closely observed.

14

Moving Forward

The modern development of Borneo has so far been characterized by large-scale land exploitation, accompanied by the wax and wane of commodity cycles, economic polarization, rural-urban disparities, and environmental destruction. Especially in the past two decades, the island has been in massive disruption and constant change. It is not simply a series of land cover and biophysical changes but also societal evolution with deep implications for future generations. The transformation is still ongoing and hopefully evolving from large-scale land exploitation to more sustainable ways of development.

How to improve livelihoods without causing further environmental impacts but also repairing the damage done in the past? This book has been written to gather insights into the understanding of such transformation, walking through the changes from 2000 to 2021 using the framework of ten transformative strategies under productivity-oriented "bio-economy" and conservation-oriented "eco-economy". Generally, utility-based development strategies with wealth creation as the centre of policymaking may prevent further degradation but are inadequate to repair the previous environmental damage to the island. This can be especially observed in the case of Sarawak where no significant restoration initiatives were implemented in the territory in the past two decades. Similarly, strategies that emphasize restoration have shown a relatively limited contribution to economic progress as observed in the case of the Kalimantan provinces. The interconnected nature of economic productivity and conservation means that no single strategy is a perfect solution, although some can be more practical and effective than others in different places and periods, or more acceptable by multiple stakeholders. "Stepping outside rhetorical extremism is necessary", as Meijaard and Sheil (2019) justly summarized for the case of oil palm, "if we seek resolution and pragmatic advances".

However, formulating "pragmatic advances" with the right combination of strategies would not be an easy task considering the variation in places and the timing of implementations. For example, boosting upstream productivity of cash crops (Chapter 3) and enhancing landscape agroecological resilience (Chapter 8) can be contradictory or complementary under different conditions, such as the amount of fertilizers or water resources used (Rockstrom et al. 2017). In some cases, hard choices have to be made as there are no other better options available at a particular time, considering the socio-economic conditions and transition in a particular area. An interesting example to reflect such complexities is a case study on Mahakam Delta in East Kalimantan by Lahjie et al. (2019) where new income generated from sustainable wood production from mangrove forests may help to reduce overfishing and mangrove conversion to brackish ponds.

If things were to be done right, the potential of integrating economic and environmental planning of land-use systems in Borneo may be significant. Runting et al. (2015) showed that it was possible to keep about one-half of the island forested while maintaining a reasonable economic outcome compared to the business-as-usual scenario. A carefully crafted combination of strategies of activating underutilized low-carbon land (Chapter 4) and commodifying ecosystem services (Chapter 9), such as the scenario proposed by Killeen et al. (2011), with REDD+ combined with biofuel production on degraded land, may effectively finance the conservation efforts. The pairing of two strategies with a circularity characteristic, i.e., establishing new domestic demand (Chapter 7) and encouraging self-sufficient farming (Chapter 12), may make the economies more agile in handling market uncertainty, shifting from a linear economy to a complete "circular economy" and strengthening local food, fibre, and energy security (Kirchherr, Reike, and Hekkert 2017).

All these, however, must not be taken away from the larger contexts of global and regional changes. In this final chapter, the future perspectives of changes in Borneo are discussed against the major events that are taking place globally: the COVID-19 pandemic-endemic, global climate change, and the mainstreaming of the 2030 Agenda for Sustainable Development.

COVID-19 AND ITS IMPACTS ON BORNEO

At the early stage of this book, the difficulties which COVID-19 would bring for Borneo, especially the longevity and depth of the pandemic through 2020 and 2021, had not been expected. Both Indonesia and Malaysia experienced negative growth in 2020, bringing Indonesia's status back to that of a lower-middle-income country. The poverty rate in Indonesia rose from 9.2 in September 2019 to 10.1 in March 2021, being somewhat mitigated by the government's quite extensive social protection programmes. Both countries had shown signs of recovery by mid-2021 with high prices for palm oil products assisting their economies and in the case of Indonesia, thermal coal exports booming later in the year, towards the onset of the northern hemisphere winter.

Among the Malaysian territories, Sarawak has experienced high COVID-19 case rates, with 9 cases per 100 people by November 2021 compared to the national average of 8 (MoH 2021). While Sabah's all-time rate is lower at 6 per 100 people, there was a rapid surge in September 2020 when the state held an election in the middle of the pandemic. Although also due for an election, the Sarawak government had to postpone it to January 2022 due to a State of Emergency until November 2021 (*The Star*, 3 November 2021). Both states have been hit hard by the pandemic as their major source of revenue, the oil palm industry, could not be fully operated due to the institution of the Movement Control Orders (MCO).

The five provinces of Kalimantan have also suffered considerable numbers of COVID-19 cases (though generally lower than those in Sabah and Sarawak, at least on paper). East Kalimantan, with overcrowded urban areas like Balikpapan and Samarinda, was the fifth Indonesian province in the number of confirmed cases after Jakarta and the heavily populated provinces in Java. South Kalimantan, with the highly populated city of Banjarmasin being consistently mapped as a "red" zone, was another province with substantial cases reported (Antaranews.com 2021).

Climate Change and Borneo: What to Expect if Amelioration Is Not Sufficient

While the disruption brought by the COVID-19 pandemic was abrupt and radical, the threat of climate change to Borneo is relatively insidious. Nevertheless, potential changes in climate parameters and the impacts on communities, livelihoods, and economies in the next few decades are already well illustrated in the latest country reports jointly published by the World Bank Group and Asian Development Bank in 2021.

The climate of Borneo is tropical, with the highest rainfall in upland areas (which can reach up to 6,000 mm, compared to 1,800–3,200 mm in lowlands). There is little seasonal variation in temperature and relatively little by elevation, 23°C average in uplands and 28°C in lowlands. The tropical climate is primarily influenced by ENSO. There has been a consistent warming trend in temperatures since 1960. Warming by the end of the century under the highest model approaches +4°C through central regions of Borneo (with little seasonal variation). A heat index of 35°C is often highlighted as a threshold beyond which conditions become extremely dangerous for human health. Under the worst scenario, by the end of the century, Indonesia (and Malaysia) would experience such conditions almost every day.

Meanwhile, projections of future rainfall are more uncertain. Rainfall maps of Borneo (1991–2020) show heavier rainfall in the western part (especially parts of West Kalimantan, Sarawak, and western Sabah). Projections for the period 2040–59 show decreases, with drier areas in Sabah and everywhere except the uplands, to be replaced by heavier rainfall in most areas later in the century, but not in eastern Sabah (palm oil growing areas).

On the one hand, greater decreases in rainfall may occur in the dry season, making droughts more intense. In the past decades, drought associated with El Niño–Southern Oscillation (ENSO) has contributed to the extension of man-made fire events in Indonesia (e.g., in 1997 and 2015). Increased fire risk is not only associated with droughts but with temperature rise in non-drought years (e.g., 2019) (Fernandes et al. 2017). The economic impacts, as described in Chapter 9, can be up to billions of US dollars.

On the other hand, while Borneo is outside the general range of cyclones, with climate change there is a likely increase in flood risk due to extreme river flows. Together with the impacts of land-use change (Wells et al. 2016), the frequency and severity of flood events may increase significantly with climate change. The impacts could be especially profound in highly populated coastal areas and cities near the rivers. Major flood events in urban areas like Samarinda, Sibu, and Banjarmasin were reported across Borneo in 2020 and 2021.

While human development pressure is likely to remain the dominant threat to species richness and diversity, climate change presents new challenges. A key threat is a potential shift in suitable habitat ranges, as rising temperatures shift ranges away from the Equator, and upslope. One study based in Borneo suggested that 11–36 per cent of mammal species could lose over 30 per cent of their suitable habitat by 2080 because of climate change, driving significant population declines (Struebig et al. 2015).

Similarly, crops can be very sensitive to temperature and rainfall too. Risks to agriculture, in the context of Borneo, particularly include rice and oil palm. Rice production in the main growing areas of Java (still the most important source of supply to much of Kalimantan) is affected by changes in the onset and length of the wet season and ENSO droughts as well as temperature increases. While it may be possible to develop new rice varieties suitable to different environments, such as peatlands, the upland rice-growing areas of Sarawak and North Kalimantan are likely to increase in importance. The climatic suitability for growing oil palm in both Indonesia and Malaysia is also predicted to decrease by the 2030s, this decrease becoming more pronounced later in the century (Paterson et al. 2015). The likely changes in these two major crops will have enormous impacts on Borneo's economies.

Rising sea levels, with strong wave action, are likely to cause significant coastal erosion. High tides and land subsidence will affect settlements, rice fields, oil palms, prawn ponds, and harbours/airports. Salinization of coastal water resources is likely. The Indonesian provinces are disproportionately affected by land subsidence due to ecosystem degradation in the lowlands, especially in West and Central Kalimantan. In Sarawak, Hooijer et al. (2015) predicted that about 42 per cent of the 850,000 ha of coastal peatland would experience flooding in twenty-five years, affecting the communities that rely on these lands for their survival (see discussion in Chapters 2 and 8). Conserving coastal mangroves and corals is also important to shield low-lying coasts from erosion, e.g., in parts of East Kalimantan and Sabah. Sea level rise along coasts, which are often the location of tourist infrastructure, will also reduce the attractiveness of some prominent tourist locations. At present, measurement of the socio-economic effects of sea level rise at the local level has been identified as a key knowledge gap.

Borneo has been playing a major role in global greenhouse gas emissions, particularly with its emissions from the conversion of peatlands into agricultural plantations and the extraction of fossil fuels. While renewable energy is often highlighted as a remedy to climate change, unsustainable agricultural expansion and poorly managed mining will remain urgent matters to be addressed in Borneo in the context of climate change. In the past, the transformation of land-based economies has often been troubled by the issue of allocation and distribution of benefits among and between different groups. The urgency of mitigating climate change may provide an opportunity to build a broad coalition in achieving the sustainable transformation of Borneo in the coming decades.

MAKING PLANS FOR THE 2030 AGENDA

Amidst all the problems with COVID-19, the planning authorities in both countries took stock of the situation and proposed ways to implement a "sustainable and resilient recovery from the COVID Pandemic for the achievement of the 2030 Agenda". As President Jokowi noted on 17 December 2020 at the SDGs Annual Conference 2020: "The pandemic caused a health and economic crisis that hampered the achievements of our SDGs ... However, this challenge should not dampen our enthusiasm and should not lower our SDGs target. We have to find new ways, we have to find breakthroughs so that we can take a leap in achieving the SDGs targets" (SETKAB 2020). It is not so surprising as SDGs have been widely promoted in both countries as a succession to the Millennium Development Goals (MDGs) since 2015. Various plans have been made in accordance with the 2030 Agenda from the national level to the state or provincial level, aiming to steer the countries onto the pathway of sustainable development in the next ten years as anticipated.

Sarawak on the Way to Digital Transformation
Against the backdrop of COVID-19 and the 2030 Agenda for Sustainable Development, the Sarawak Economic Action Council, chaired by the Chief Minister, prepared a highly optimistic review of the state's plans and likely achievements from 2021 to 2030 (Economic Planning Unit Sarawak 2021). It states that Sarawak "aspires to be a developed state by 2030" with improvements in physical and digital infrastructure, science-based education, and "smart" farming. Digital transformation of all sectors is especially emphasized. The plan is also to move the economy further towards the manufacturing and services sectors.

For land-based sectors, developing a "bio-economy" through boosting productivity and added value remains a key feature. Oil palm obviously continues but was mentioned only twice—the construction of a palm-based oleochemical plant and the use of oil palm biomass in producing a "circular" economy. Forestry, on the other hand, is specifically identified as an increased income earner, from forest plantations plus new products such as bamboo and local plywood. Interestingly, the state is also looking into the potential of large-scale carbon credit programmes. The most ambitious (and difficult) activity, revealed near the end of the report, is the "restoration of more than 200,000 hectares of degraded forest", with carbon trading cited as a major financing mechanism.

There were two major surprises: the first was Sarawak's stated intention to become a net food exporter by 2030 and a food supplier to the region; the second was a return to the idea of exporting power by undersea cable across the South China Sea to Peninsular Malaysia, a plan dropped some years ago after completion of the Bakun Dam. With regard to agriculture, especially food crops, the plan seemed to require a shift to commercial farming away from subsistence agriculture. It is not known if "Native Customary Land", occupied by Penan, Iban, and "Orang Ulu", are parts of the plans, as what happened in the past with oil palm expansion. The revised intention to export power further afield may mean the continuation of new dam construction, always planned by the ruling party, but put on hold during COVID-19 and believed unnecessary by many observers, considering the inevitable disruption to local livelihoods on Native Customary Land and the fact that cheap power is already available.

Sabah's Plans for Sustainable Tourism and Jurisdictional Certification
Sabah had a bigger post-COVID-19 problem, compared to Sarawak which had more diverse revenue resources, due to its heavy reliance on tourism, especially mass tourism from China. It appears to have suffered the most economically as a result of the pandemic, especially with high unemployment (Nga, Ramlan, and Naim 2021). The pandemic may offer a chance for Sabah to rethink its development model, as proposed by Goh (2021), based on "a nexus mapping of tourism-poverty-environment". Sabah has just released a new development plan, covering five years from 2021 to 2025, the first under the new government elected in 2020, seeking to revive the economy. The Sabah Maju Jaya (SMJ) plan outlines three main thrusts, based on the SMJ slogan. "S" refers to the economic sectors of agriculture, industry, and tourism; "M" refers to human capital and well-being; "J" refers to green infrastructure and sustainability.

The SMJ received praise, including from major organizations like WWF Malaysia for its openness and efforts in collecting detailed information and feedback from the stakeholders. Following a recommendation from WWF Malaysia, the SDGs are listed at the front of the document. WWF also made suggestions for "sustainable tourism" and a "green" recovery as top priorities, in which investment decisions were integrated with climate considerations (Miwil 2021). For example, one planned "high-end" ecotourism site to be developed by a Taiwan agency (on Mengalum Island, not far from Kota Kinabalu), will only be released after the reforestation of barren sections and rehabilitation of the surrounding damaged coral reef (*Borneo Post*, 3 October 2021). An interesting comment concerns a focus on "strategic border towns with development potential, such as Semedong-Simanggaris" (North Kalimantan) (see Figure 5.4). This "takes into consideration the potential economic benefits that come with the shifting of Indonesia's capital to Kalimantan" (*Borneo Post*, 22 September 2021).

The concentration on palm oil, decried by some critics, has nevertheless enabled the WWF to claim Sabah as a global leader in sustainable palm oil, through its adoption of both the Jurisdictional Certification of Sustainable Palm Oil (JCSPO) and the Malaysian Sustainable Palm Oil (MSPO) within the state (see Chapter 6). The JCSPO has been described as a very important initiative to balance conservation and sustainable development. The Chief Conservator of Forests from the Sabah Forestry Department (Frederick Kugan) indicated that the Jurisdictional Approach (JA) "will not just support the sustainability of the palm oil industry, it will be able to address environmental and social issues faced by the sector" (WWF Malaysia 2021).

Central Kalimantan to Be a Leader in Food Estates?
With the onset of COVID-19 in 2020, one controversial activity, developing "rice estates" on peatlands in Central Kalimantan, was pushed by President Jokowi to start in 2020, as the President feared a food crisis during the pandemic (Rahman 2020). These shortages were largely due to the impact of the virus on the food distribution systems together with an unseasonal dry spell; Jokowi decided that additional plantings should go ahead, with a special emphasis on rice in Central Kalimantan. The initial 30,000 ha (pilot project) was to use existing rice fields planted by local farmers, 20,000 ha in Kapuas district and 10,000 ha in Pulang Pisau (Jong 2020e). Notably, the army has been involved in supervising the activities (Rahman 2020). All but 900 ha of the planned 20,000 ha (first phase) of rice in the Kapuas district had been planted by May 2021 (with some already harvested); an accelerated planting campaign for the balance was being assisted by the Central Kalimantan government and the Ministry of Agriculture in part of Dadahup (a former transmigration site on the ex-MRP) (Sutrisno 2021).

While there were worries that the use of peatland may exacerbate the fire events as in 2015, the government officers emphasized that these may be avoided with proper water management. This is coupled with the use of a special rice variety, the employment of Artificial Intelligence (AI) in the timing of fertilizing and water control, and the possible application of modern technology such as drones and "floating tractors" (Sutrisno 2021). However, there have been many critics of the involvement of (external) investors in the expansion plan for 2021–23. They appear to be replacing farmer landowners with corporate management, contradicting the "United Nations Decade of Family Farming, 2019–28", with Ben White at the International Institute of Social Studies at the Hague calling it "the colonial agricultural model" (Jong 2020a). Repeating the conflicts from oil palm expansion may not be wanted. The government will need to make sure it is not contradictory to the principles of the SDGs which cover more than just food security but also peace and justice.

East Kalimantan: Relocating Indonesia's Capital to the "Green Province"

The biggest, and probably the most controversial project to be observed in Borneo post-COVID-19 will be the proposed relocation of Indonesia's capital from Jakarta to East Kalimantan which will be continued in 2021. The more central location towards the eastern part of Indonesia is symbolic. Called the country's capital (Ibu Kota Negara, or IKN), its theme "*Nagara Rimba Nusa*" ("land of forests and islands") will represent all of Indonesia (CNN Indonesia 2021a). Among the Kalimantan provinces, East Kalimantan has the strongest claim to be "green" and would appear to be a fitting place for the development of the new capital. It declared itself a "green province" in 2010 with a pledge to reduce deforestation by 80 per cent and improve the quality of life of the population, reducing pollution and threats of climate disasters and raising awareness of using renewable resources.

The report *Visi Kaltim 2030* (Kaltim Vision 2030) revealed that the Governor envisaged such developments as gradual up to 2030 (Ishak, Rusmadi, and Yusuf 2013). They would start by limiting the production of fossil fuels, developing secondary industries based on those resources, extending agriculture beyond palm oil and developing industries based on agricultural products, and then eventually developing new and renewable energy sectors and infrastructure to support industrial needs. In 2016, a Green Growth Compact (GGC) was launched in partnership with the private sector, regional and national governments, universities, communities, and NGOs, together with international organizations. The plan was to use the GGC as a platform to transform the provincial economy (Komalasari et al. 2018) and achieve net zero deforestation by 2030. The province has its own jurisdictional REDD+ under the Forest Carbon Partnership Facility which is claimed to be the first large-scale green growth framework in Indonesia (Nofyanza et al. 2021).

The new capital will leverage the existing infrastructure in the coastal cities of East Kalimantan, i.e., Balikpapan and Samarinda, and be reached from the almost-completed toll road (Johansah et al. 2019). The toll road, which will reduce the travel time between those two large cities from 3 hours to 1 hour, will "accelerate access to the core area of the State Capital Region" (PT Jasa Marga 2021). The actual location of the centre will be on the highest spot above the small town of Sepaku, the capital of the Penajam Paser Utara (PPU) district. It is also very close to the border with the Kutai

Kartanegara district, so the new capital will likely spread over the two districts. While it is outside the main population hubs, there appears to be enough room for the city to grow as required: from 20 sq. km in 2024 to maybe 2,000 sq. km in 2045 (Gokkon 2019).

One feature of the new capital that has been frequently mentioned is its "greenness". However, it is likely that the main power source of the city's development will be coal, although alternatives, such as hydro power, may later be employed. The province has been unable to break its dependency on coal, which remains the largest contributor to the GDP (Nofyanza et al. 2021). A useful addition to the argument is the work of Toumbourou et al (2020), who documented the privileged political position of coal mining companies in the East Kalimantan mining and post-mining landscape, hiring thugs to defer criticism by attacks on NGOs and escaping demands for mine site remediation. The transitioning to a low-carbon economy in the province likely remains difficult even with the new capital aiming to embrace "green" objectives and grow as a modern "smart" city given the coal interests of some prominent government members (Nofyanza et al. 2021).

Furthermore, the land to be occupied by the capital is already given to many concessionaires. Logging interests are well represented and affiliated with timber tycoons in the country. It has been suggested that owners of these and other concessions may be allowed to swap their land for forest land elsewhere, such as Papua (Jong 2020g). In addition to the potential damage onsite (Teo et al. 2020), the indirect impacts on forests in places like Papua due to such swap deals have not been thoroughly studied. In addition to pulpwood, there are large numbers of coal mining concessions and a few for oil palm, which amounted to 162 concessions altogether (Johansah et al. 2019). Things become even more complicated when local people living near the site are worried that they might be pressured to give up their land, as speculation is rife in the area (Paturusi 2019). Rumours and speculations may persist until the full plan is revealed.

GOVERNING LAND-BASED ECONOMIES

Sabah and Sarawak: Gaining More Autonomy Amidst Political Turmoil

Compared to their Indonesian counterparts, the Malaysian states in Borneo have been retaining a relatively larger degree of autonomy from the federal government, especially the jurisdiction in land use and immigration policies (Jomo and Wee 2003). Within the states, power has been largely concentrated on the state government with the suspension of the local council election after the Indonesia-Malaysia confrontation in 1964 (Saravanamuttu 2016). Powerful (in the context of land use) state governments allow Sabah and Sarawak to implement their land development policies without needing many negotiations between governments at different levels (Cramb 2011b). However, both states were also stripped away much of their power in sectors other than land use and immigration, especially since the amendment to Article 1(2) of the Federal Constitution in 1976, demoting them from equals of Malaya to equals of the eleven states of Malaya.

In the past two decades, "state nationalism" has been the focal point in East Malaysia's politics. This term was used by Chin (2019) to describe the increasing demand from Sabah and Sarawak for their "lost rights" since the formation of the Federation of Malaysia, if not a secession from the Federation. Taking the advantage of political turmoil in the Peninsula, which has made Sabah and Sarawak the "kingmakers" in determining the candidate for Prime Minister, both states have been reinforcing their demand for autonomy and asking for a constitutional amendment to recognize their special status. Various proposals have been made by politicians, scholars, observers, and citizens. In Sarawak, politicians are scrambling to be champions in regaining the rights for its oil and gas resources. Meanwhile, Sabah's economic status as the poorest state in Malaysia has often been emphasized to portray the inequality between East and West Malaysia.

While a complete secession is unlikely, further autonomy may be wrested over from the Federal Government with the prolonged political instability in the Peninsula. Will the power be concentrated at the state level? Is further decentralization down to the municipal level, as proposed by Chacko (2021), a better option (considering the experience in Kalimantan)? How the shift of power structure in Sabah and Sarawak will affect the land use and land-based economies in both states will be something important to observe.

Kalimantan: Dealing with a More Powerful President and the Omnibus Bill

At the subnational level, the Indonesian provinces do not have a similar kind of power as the Malaysian states. Instead, the districts or regencies do enjoy a larger degree of autonomy in land-based development after the implementation of the decentralization policy in the early 2000s. In practice, there are significant overlaps and uncertainties in power distribution between and within the central, provincial, and regency governments (Sahide and Giessen 2015). In many cases, the attempts of the central government to implement provincial strategies clashed with the regency development plans which granted land-use permits for commercial plantations (Suwarno, Hein, and Sumarga 2015). In fact, this type of dual development has been observed throughout Indonesian Borneo in the past two decades (Anderson et al. 2016).

Things started to change when Indonesia's President moved to grab more power in his hands, claiming to "rescue" Indonesia from the problems of the pandemic. On 5 October 2020, the "Omnibus Bill" on job creation was passed by the Indonesian parliament. This massive law, which Jokowi first proposed in 2019, has been designed to attract foreign investment and make land acquisition easier by reducing regulations and environmental laws. Largely drafted by the business community, it weakens legal protection for indigenous groups, including their access to forests and customary lands, and reduces basic labour rights, including minimum wages, job security, and other benefits (Human Rights Watch 2020).

Some have reasoned this has made the country more authoritarian, less democratic, and less concerned with human rights or the environment. Demonstrations against the law were broad-based, with mounting opposition from labour unions, civil society, scientists, and religious groups, amid fears it will lead to further land grabbing and deforestation, therefore increasing emissions. Coal mining companies are exempt from paying royalties if they develop downstream facilities, such as power stations, even though there have been moves to minimize the number of coal-fired power stations in favour of alternative energy sources. A further problem is that the Amdal (environmental impact assessment document) no longer has an independent committee to review it, only those directly impacted (which tends to exclude NGOs), so public participation will be limited. The result may be that only "dirty" investors with little regard for environmental protection would be attracted to Indonesia (Jong 2020c).

Another trend that is worth noting is the two distinctive development narratives in Indonesia (Agussalim et al. 2018). One narrative, put forward by the President, is about "conventional", state-centric, infrastructure-led development. In the Medium-term Development Plan of 2015–19 published by BAPPENAS in 2014, investment in palm oil was regarded as a key strategy to strengthen the country's economy (BAPPENAS 2014). The President has also been pushing for more coal-fired power plants, hoping to tap into the advantage of the rich coal resources in the country. Another narrative, which came a few years later, concerns sustainable development using the SDG framework. In 2019, a new, well-argued, low-carbon development report was published by BAPPENAS for Indonesia, which would cut the country's greenhouse gas emissions, but would require the country to reduce emissions from the land-use sectors and its reliance on coal (BAPPENAS 2019).

It is clear that the "Omnibus Bill" could have severe ramifications affecting both human rights and the environment in Kalimantan, but public protests have so far been forcefully put down. The self-contradictory "dual-track" development plans made by BAPPENAS (comparable to the earlier "dual-track" development due to overlaps of power between districts, provinces, and Jakarta) have also made Kalimantan vulnerable to unsustainable resource exploitation. These changes seem to indicate a recentralization of power in the President and his administration, a "worrying trend" (Kurlantzick 2020), which is likely to be exacerbated with the relocation of the capital to East Kalimantan.

Final Remarks

With the pandemic beginning to lift across Borneo, pressures have been growing for "sustainability", "green" pathways, and implementation of the SDGs, against a background of uncertainties in the global economy and the looming risks of impending climate change, which is now very much under discussion. Governments in Borneo now have a unique opportunity to create economies that are more sustainable, inclusive, and resilient. The recent adoption of the Sustainable Development Goals (SDGs) framework by Malaysia and Indonesia marks a big departure from sectorial-based planning but an overarching vision for improving people's lives, prosperity, and well-being. The framework established by the United Nations (UN) aims to collectively reset conventional economic-oriented development thinking with a broader set of social, environmental, and economic targets. This implies that transforming land-based economies in Borneo would require a more holistic development thinking beyond just "land" but covering multiple aspects of the territory. The SDG's target in 2030, which does not seem very far away, may need to be extended due to the unexpected difficulties produced by COVID-19.

The ongoing digital revolution will add a completely new dimension to the transformation and lift it to a different level. Digital and smart technologies, which are perceived as key modular-building blocks for sustainable development in the next few decades, can be deployed as powerful tools in transforming land-use economies as explained in Chapter 13. The waves of changes brought by the digital revolution will affect not only the economy and environment but also the entire society with new dynamics, new rules, and new thinking. Furthermore, the travelling restrictions due to the COVID-19 pandemic in 2020 have accelerated the deployment of digital technologies and may also drive the creation of more self-sufficient suburban and rural settlement units, redefining the urban-rural gradients. The shifts in socio-economic relationships can be as significant as the previous displacement of subsistence farming by cash-crop agriculture. Optimistically, these changes may create tractable spaces within which stakeholders with different interests can work in achieving common goals.

How Borneo will fare in these sweeping waves of change will be an important question for development thinkers, researchers, practitioners, community leaders, and development institutions in the coming years. To examine more closely a range of possible future pathways for the island, one needs also to check what is being proposed by the political leaders in Borneo as well as in Putrajaya and Jakarta over the next five or ten years, when hopefully the economic and health situations will have improved. In any case, people in Borneo should be prepared for the upcoming disruptive changes and grasp the opportunities to transform its land-based economies and move onto a more sustainable track of development.

Bibliography

Ab Rahman, A.K., R. Abdullah, F. Mohd Shariff, and M. Simeh. 2008. "The Malaysian Palm Oil Supply Chain: The Role of the Independent Smallholders". *Oil Palm Industry Economic Journal* 8, no. 2: 17–27.

Abd Manaf, Z., A.K. Ab Rahman, N.A. Abd Halim, S. Ismail, and R. Abdullah. 2013. "Assessment of the Oil Palm Seedlings Assistance Scheme on Fresh Fruit Bunch Yield and Income of Smallholders". *Oil Palm Industry Economic Journal* 13: 35–44.

Abdelmoez, W., and A. Mustafa. 2014. "Oleochemical Industry Future Through Biotechnology". *Journal of Oleo Science* 63, no. 6: 545–54.

Abdul-Rahim, A.S., and H.O. Mohd-Shahwahid. 2012. "Sustainable Forest Management Policy and the Analysis of Convergence Effects on Timber Production". *Forest Policy and Economics* 22: 60–64. https://doi.org/10.1016/j.forpol.2012.05.002

———, H.O. Mohd Shahwahid, S. Mad Nasir, and A.G. Awang Noor. 2012. "Market and Welfare Economic Impacts of Sustainable Forest Management Practices-An Empirical Analysis of Timber Market in Sabah, Malaysia". *Journal of Tropical Forest Science* 24, no. 4: 440–54.

Abdul Shukor, A.R., N. Mohd Shukor, and I. Salma. 2013. "Current and Future Strategies and Practices in the Conservation and Sustainable Utilisation of Underutilised Fruit Genetic Resources in Malaysia". In *Acta Horticulturae: International Society for Horticultural Science.*

Abdullah, A.Z., B. Salamatinia, H. Mootabadi, and S. Bhatia. 2009. "Current Status and Policies on Biodiesel Industry in Malaysia as the World's Leading Producer of Palm Oil". *Energy Policy* 37, no. 12: 5440–48. https://doi.org/10.1016/j.enpol.2009.08.012

Abdullah, R.G. 2016. "Accessibility and Development in Rural Sarawak. A Case Study of the Baleh River Basin, Kapit District, Sarawak, Malaysia". School of Geography, Environment and Earth Sciences, Victoria University of Wellington. http://researcharchive.vuw.ac.nz/xmlui/bitstream/handle/10063/5556/thesis.pdf?sequence=1

Abram, N.K., D.C. MacMillan, P. Xofis, M. Ancrenaz, J. Tzanopoulos, R. Ong, B. Goossens, L.P. Koh, C. Del Valle, L. Peter, A.C. Morel, I. Lackman, R. Chung, H. Kler, L. Ambu, W. Baya, and A.T. Knight. 2016. "Identifying Where REDD+ Financially Out-Competes Oil Palm in Floodplain Landscapes Using a Fine-Scale Approach". *PLoS ONE* 11, no. 6. https://doi.org/10.1371/journal.pone.0156481

———, E. Meijaard, M. Ancrenaz, R.K. Runting, J.A. Wells, D. Gaveau, A.S. Pellier, and K. Mengersen. 2014. "Spatially Explicit Perceptions of Ecosystem Services and Land Cover Change in Forested Regions of Borneo". *Ecosystem Services* 7: 116–27. https://doi.org/10.1016/j.ecoser.2013.11.004

———, E. Meijaard, J.A. Wells, M. Ancrenaz, A.S. Pellier, R.K. Runting, D. Gaveau, S. Wich,

Nardiyono, A. Tjiu, A. Nurcahyo, and K. Mengersen. 2015. "Mapping Perceptions of Species' Threats and Population Trends to Inform Conservation Efforts: The Bornean Orangutan Case Study". *Diversity and Distributions* 21, no. 5: 487–99. https://doi.org/10.1111/ddi.12286

———, E. Meijaard, K.A. Wilson, J.T. Davis, J.A. Wells, M. Ancrenaz, S. Budiharta, A. Durrant, A. Fakhruzzi, R.K. Runting, D. Gaveau, and K. Mengersen. 2017. "Oil Palm–Community Conflict Mapping in Indonesia: A Case for Better Community Liaison in Planning for Development Initiatives". *Applied Geography* 78: 33–44. https://doi.org/10.1016/j.apgeog.2016.10.005

———, P. Xofis, J. Tzanopoulos, D.C. MacMillan, M. Ancrenaz, R. Chung, L. Peter, R. Ong, I. Lackman, B. Goossens, L. Ambu, and A.T. Knight. 2014. "Synergies for Improving Oil Palm Production and Forest Conservation in Floodplain Landscapes". *PLoS ONE* 9, no. 6. https://doi.org/10.1371/journal.pone.0095388

Abushammala, M.F.M., N.E. Ahmad Basri, H. Basri, A.H. El-Shafie, and A.A.H. Kadhum. 2011. "Regional Landfills Methane Emission Inventory in Malaysia". *Waste Management and Research* 29, no. 8: 863–73. https://doi.org/10.1177/0734242X10382064

Acciaioli, G., and S. Afiff. 2018. "Neoliberal Conservation in Central Kalimantan, Indonesia: Evaluating the Approach to Environmental Education of the Transnational Conservation Organisation Rare1". *Indonesia and the Malay World* 46, no. 136: 241–62. https://doi.org/10.1080/13639811.2018.1531968

———, and O. Dewi. 2016. "Opposition to Oil Palm Plantations in Kalimantan Divergent Strategies, Convergent Outcomes". In *The Oil Palm Complex: Smallholders, Agribusiness and the State in Indonesia and Malaysia*, edited by R. Cramb and J.F. McCarthy, pp. 327–53. Singapore: NUS Press.

ADB. 2014. "An Evaluation of the Prospects for Interconnections Among the Borneo and Mindanao Power Systems: Final Report". Asian Development Bank (ADB), November 2014.

Aden, J., T. Walton, G. Dore, and J. Vincent. 2001. *Indonesia: Environment and Natural Resource Management in a Time of Transition*. Jakarta: World Bank.

Adhiguna, P. 2021. "Indonesia's Biomass Cofiring Bet: Beware of the Implementation Risks". Institute for Energy Economics and Financial Analysis (IEEFA).

Aditya, T., D. Laksono, and N. Izzahuddin. 2019. "Crowdsourced Hotspot Validation and Data Visualisation for Location-Based Haze Mitigation". *Journal of Location Based Services*: 1–31.

Aeria, A. 2016. "Economic Development Via Dam Building: The Role of the State Government in the Sarawak Corridor of Renewable Energy and the Impact on Environment and Local Communities". *Southeast Asian Studies* 5, no. 3: 373–412. https://doi.org/10.20495/seas.5.3_373

Afentina, P. McShane, and W. Wright. 2019. "Ethnobotany, Rattan Agroforestry, and Conservation of Ecosystem Services in Central Kalimantan, Indonesia". *Agroforestry Systems*. https://doi.org/10.1007/s10457-019-00428-x

Afiff, S.A. 2016. "REDD, Land Management and the Politics of Forest and Land Tenure Reform with Special Reference to the Case of Central Kalimantan Province". In

Land and Development in Indonesia: Searching for the People's Sovereignty, edited by F. McCarthy and K. Robinson, pp. 113–40. Singapore: ISEAS – Yusof Ishak Institute.

Afriyanti, D., C. Kroeze, and A. Saad. 2016. "Indonesia Palm Oil Production Without Deforestation and Peat Conversion by 2050". *Sci Total Environ* 557–58: 562–70. https://doi.org/10.1016/j.scitotenv.2016.03.032

Aghamohammadi, N., S.S. Reginald, A. Shamiri, A.A. Zinatizadeh, L.P. Wong, and N.M.B.N. Sulaiman. 2016. "An Investigation of Sustainable Power Generation from Oil Palm Biomass: A Case Study in Sarawak". *Sustainability* (Switzerland) 8, no. 5. https://doi.org/10.3390/su8050416

Agus, C., F.F. Azmi, Widiyatno, Z.R. Ilfana, D. Wulandari, D. Rachmanadi, M.K. Harun, and T.W. Yuwati. 2019. "The Impact of Forest Fire on the Biodiversity and the Soil Characteristics of Tropical Peatland". In *Climate Change Management*. Springer.

———, Z.R. Ilfana, F.F. Azmi, D. Rachmanadi, Widiyatno, D. Wulandari, P.B. Santosa, M.K. Harun, T.W. Yuwati, and T. Lestari. 2019. "The Effect of Tropical Peat Land-Use Changes on Plant Diversity and Soil Properties". *International Journal of Environmental Science and Technology*. https://doi.org/10.1007/s13762-019-02579-x

Agus, F., Wahyunto, A. Dariah, E. Runtunuwu, E. Susanti, and W. Supriatna. 2012. "Emission Reduction Options for Peatlands in the Kubu Raya and Pontianak Districts, West Kalimantan, Indonesia". *Journal of Oil Palm Research* 24 (August): 1378–87.

Agussalim, D., A.R.M. Umar, K. Larasati, and D.H. Tobing. 2018. "Localizing the Sustainable Development Goals: Assessing Indonesia's Compliance towards the Global Goals". In *Sustainable Development Goals in Southeast Asia and ASEAN*, pp. 39–62. Leiden: Brill.

Agustan, Mubekti, and L. Sumargana. 2015. "The Utilization of ALOS-2 Data to Identify the Potential Area for Paddy Field". Paper presented at 36th Asian Conference on Remote Sensing 2015, Manila.

Ahl, A., M. Goto, and M. Yarime. 2019. "Smart Technology Applications in the Woody Biomass Supply Chain: Interview Insights and Potential in Japan". *Sustainability Science*. https://doi.org/10.1007/s11625-019-00728-2

———, M. Yarime, K. Tanaka, and D. Sagawa. 2019. "Review of Blockchain-Based Distributed Energy: Implications for Institutional Development". *Renewable and Sustainable Energy Reviews* 107: 200–11. https://doi.org/10.1016/j.rser.2019.03.002

Ahmad, A. 2014. "The Disengagement of the Tourism Businesses in Ecotourism and Environmental Practices in Brunei Darussalam". *Tourism Management Perspectives* 10: 1–6. https://doi.org/10.1016/j.tmp.2013.12.002

———, A.R. Che Omar, L.H. Osman, N. Alias, M.R. Che Abdul Rahman, S. Ishak, and M.A. Jusoh. 2016. "The Push and Pull Factors in Business: A Study on Independent Oil Palm Smallholders in Selected States in Malaysia". *Oil Palm Industry Economic Journal* 16: 9–18.

Ahmed, A., M.S.A. Bakar, A.K. Azad, R.S. Sukri, and T.M.I. Mahlia. 2018. "Potential Thermochemical Conversion of Bioenergy from Acacia Species in Brunei Darussalam: A Review". *Renewable and Sustainable Energy Reviews* 82: 3060–76.

Ahmed, K., M.S. Jeffree, T. Hughes, and P. Daszak. 2019. "Editorial: Can the Health Implications of Land-Use Change Drive Sustainability?". *EcoHealth* 16, no. 4: 585–86. https://doi.org/10.1007/s10393-019-01462-y

AIM (Agensi Inovasi Malaysia). 2013. *National Biomass Strategy 2020: New Wealth Creation for Malaysia's Palm Oil Industry*. Cyberjaya: Agensi Inovasi Malaysia.

Al Shehhi, M., and A. Karathanasopoulos. 2020. "Forecasting Hotel Room Prices in Selected GCC Cities Using Deep Learning". *Journal of Hospitality and Tourism Management* 42: 40–50. https://doi.org/10.1016/j.jhtm.2019.11.003

Alamgir, M., M.J. Campbell, S. Sloan, A. Suhardiman, J. Supriatna, and W.F. Laurance. 2019. "High-Risk Infrastructure Projects Pose Imminent Threats to Forests in Indonesian Borneo". *Sci Rep* 9, no. 1: 140. https://doi.org/10.1038/s41598-018-36594-8

———, M.J. Campbell, S. Sloan, J. Engert, J. Word, and W.F. Laurance. 2020. "Emerging Challenges for Sustainable Development and Forest Conservation in Sarawak, Borneo". *PLoS ONE* 15, no. 3. https://doi.org/10.1371/journal.pone.0229614

Alexander, J. 2018. "Migration, Imagination and Identity in Modern Sarawak". *Asia Pacific Journal of Anthropology* 19, no. 3: 264–280. https://doi.org/10.1080/1444 2213.2018.1458893

Ali, A.A.M., M.R. Othman, Y. Shirai, and M.A. Hassan. 2015. "Sustainable and Integrated Palm Oil Biorefinery Concept with Value-Addition of Biomass and Zero Emission System". *Journal of Cleaner Production* 91: 96–99. https://doi.org/10.1016/j.jclepro.2014.12.030

Ali Nordin, A.Z., S.M. Ahmad, A.S. Sahidan, N. Abdullah, and H. Ain. 2017. "An Economic Study on Technical Efficiency among Independent Oil Palm Smallholders in Sabah and Sarawak". *Oil Palm Industry Economic Journal* 17: 16–31.

Alias, M.S., A.M. Ismail Adnan, K. Jugah, I. Ishaq, and Z.A. Fizree. 2017. "Detection of Basal Stem Rot (BSR) Disease at Oil Palm Plantation Using Hyperspectral Imaging". 5th Workshop on Hyperspectral Image and Signal Processing: Evolution in Remote Sensing (WHISPERS), Gainesville, Florida, pp. 1–4, https://doi.org/10.1109/WHISPERS.2013.8080700

Allerton, C. 2020. "Stuck in the Short Term: Immobility and Temporalities of Care among Florenese Migrants in Sabah, Malaysia". *Ethnos* 85, no. 2: 208–23. https://doi.org/10.1080/00141844.2018.1543338

Almstedt, Å., P. Brouder, S. Karlsson, and L. Lundmark. 2014. "Beyond Post-productivism: from Rural Policy Discourse to Rural Diversity". *European Countryside* 6, no. 4: 297–306.

Altieri, M. 2004. "Linking Ecologists and Traditional Farmers in the Search for Sustainable Agriculture". *Frontiers in Ecology and the Environment* 2, no. 1: 35–42.

Amirta, R., A. Mukhdlor, D. Mujiasih, E. Septia, Supriadi, and D. Susanto. 2016. "Suitability and Availability Analysis of Tropical Forest Wood Species for Ethanol Production: A Case Study in East Kalimantan". *Biodiversitas* 17, no. 2: 544–52. https://doi.org/10.13057/biodiv/d170222

———, S.I. Nafitri, R. Wulandari, Yuliansyah, W. Suwinarti, K.P. Candra, and T. Watanabe. 2016. "Comparative Characterization of Macaranga Species Collected from

Secondary Forests in East Kalimantan for Biorefinery of Unutilized Fast Growing Wood". *Biodiversitas* 17, no. 1: 116–23. https://doi.org/10.13057/biodiv/d170117

Anandi, C., I. Resosudarmo, M. Komalasari, A. Ekaputri, and D. Intarini. 2014. "TNC's Initiative Within the Berau Forest Carbon Program, East Kalimantan, Indonesia". In *REDD+ on the Ground: A Case Book of Subnational Initiatives Across the Globe*, edited by E.O. Sills, S.S. Atmadja, C. de Sassi, A.E. Duchelle, D.L. Kweka, I.A.P. Resosudarmo, and W.D. Sunderlin. Bogor, Indonesia: CIFOR.

Ananta, A., E.N. Arifin, M. S. Hasbullah, N,.B. Handayani, and A. Pramono. 2015. *Demography of Indonesia's ethnicity*. Singapore: Institute of Southeast Asian Studies.

Andersen, A.O., T.B. Bruun, K. Egay, M. Fenger, S. Klee, A.F. Pedersen, L.M. L. Pedersen, and V. Suárez Villanueva. 2016. "Negotiating Development Narratives Within Large-Scale Oil Palm Projects on Village Lands in Sarawak, Malaysia". *The Geographical Journal* 182, no. 4: 364–74. https://doi.org/10.1111/geoj.12181

Anderson, Z.R., K. Kusters, J. McCarthy, and K. Obidzinski. 2016. "Green Growth Rhetoric Versus Reality: Insights from Indonesia". *Global Environmental Change* 38: 30–40. https://doi.org/10.1016/j.gloenvcha.2016.02.008

Andrew, M., E. Challies, P. Howson, R. Astuti, R. Dixon, B. Haalboom, M. Gavin, L. Tacconi, and S. Afiff. 2015. "Beyond Carbon, More Than Forest? REDD+ Governmentality in Indonesia". *Environment and Planning A* 47, no. 1: 138–55. https://doi.org/10.1068/a140054p

Ansell, F.A., D.P. Edwards, and K.C. Hamer. 2011. "Rehabilitation of Logged Rain Forests: Avifaunal Composition, Habitat Structure, and Implications for Biodiversity-Friendly REDD+". *Biotropica* 43, no. 4: 504–11. https://doi.org/10.1111/j.1744-7429.2010.00725.x

Antaranews.com. 2021. "Data Perkembangan COVID-19".

Antons, C. 2017. "Geographical Indications, Heritage, and Decentralization Policies: The Case of Indonesia". In *Geographical Indications at the Crossroads of Trade, Development, and Culture: Focus on Asia-Pacific*, edited by I. Calboli and W.L. Ng-Loy, pp. 485–507. Cambridge: Cambridge University Press.

Arbainsyah, H.H. de Iongh, W. Kustiawan, and G.R. de Snoo. 2014. "Structure, Composition and Diversity of Plant Communities in FSC-Certified, Selectively Logged Forests of Different Ages Compared to Primary Rain Forest". *Biodiversity and Conservation* 23, no. 10: 2445–72. https://doi.org/10.1007/s10531-014-0732-4

Arifanti, V.B., J.B. Kauffman, D. Hadriyanto, D. Murdiyarso, and R. Diana. 2019. "Carbon Dynamics and Land Use Carbon Footprints in Mangrove-Converted Aquaculture: The Case of the Mahakam Delta, Indonesia". *Forest Ecology and Management* 432: 17–29. https://doi.org/10.1016/j.foreco.2018.08.047

Arsanti, I.W., and Hardiyanto. 2020. "Benefiting Communities by Using Plant Genetic Resources in Some Community Biodiversity Management Areas in Indonesia. In *Acta Horticulturae: International Society for Horticultural Science.*

Artati, Y., W. Jaung, K.S. Juniwaty, S. Andini, S.M. Lee, H. Segah, and H. Baral. 2019. "Bioenergy Production on Degraded Land: Landowner Perceptions in Central Kalimantan, Indonesia". *Forests* 10, no. 2. https://doi.org/10.3390/f10020099

Arvola, A., M. Brockhaus, M. Kallio, T.T. Pham, D.T.L. Chi, H.T. Long, A.A. Nawir,

S. Phimmavong, R. Mwamakimbullah, and P. Jacovelli. 2020. "What Drives Smallholder Tree Growing? Enabling Conditions in a Changing Policy Environment". *Forest Policy and Economics* 116: 102173. https://doi.org/10.1016/j.forpol.2020.102173

Asa, R.S. 2019. "An Overview of the Developments of Halal Certification Laws in Malaysia, Singapore, Brunei and Indonesia". *Jurnal Syariah* 27, no. 1: 173–200.

ASEAN GI Database. 2019. "ASEAN GI Database". ASEAN.

Ashworth, K., G. Folberth, C.N. Hewitt, and O. Wild. 2012. "Impacts of Near-Future Cultivation of Biofuel Feedstocks on Atmospheric Composition and Local Air Quality". *Atmospheric Chemistry and Physics* 12, no. 2: 919–39. https://doi.org/10.5194/acp-12-919-2012

Asner, G.P., P.G. Brodrick, C. Philipson, N.R. Vaughn, R.E. Martin, D.E. Knapp, J. Heckler, L.J. Evans, T. Jucker, B. Goossens, D.J. Stark, G. Reynolds, R. Ong, N. Renneboog, F. Kugan, and D.A. Coomes. 2018. "Mapped Aboveground Carbon Stocks to Advance Forest Conservation and Recovery in Malaysian Borneo". *Biological Conservation* 217: 289–310. https://doi.org/10.1016/j.biocon.2017.10.020

Astuti, R., and A. McGregor. 2017. "Indigenous Land Claims or Green Grabs? Inclusions and Exclusions Within Forest Carbon Politics in Indonesia". *Journal of Peasant Studies* 44, no. 2: 445–66. https://doi.org/10.1080/03066150.2016.1197908

Atmadja, S., Y. Indriatmoko, N. Utomo, M. Komalasari, and A. Ekaputri. 2014. "Kalimantan Forests and Climate Partnership, Central Kalimantan, Indonesia". In *REDD+ on the Ground: A Case Book of Subnational Initiatives Across the Globe*, edited by E.O. Sills, S.S. Atmadja, C. de Sassi, A.E. Duchelle, D.L. Kweka, I.A.P. Resosudarmo, and W.D. Sunderlin. Bogor, Indonesia: CIFOR.

Austin, K.G., P.S. Kasibhatla, D.L. Urban, F. Stolle, and J. Vincent. 2015. "Reconciling Oil Palm Expansion and Climate Change Mitigation in Kalimantan, Indonesia". *PLoS ONE* 10, no. 5: e0127963. https://doi.org/10.1371/journal.pone.0127963

———, A. Mosnier, J. Pirker, I. McCallum, S. Fritz, and P.S. Kasibhatla. 2017. "Shifting Patterns of Oil Palm Driven Deforestation in Indonesia and Implications for Zero-Deforestation Commitments". *Land Use Policy* 69: 41–48. https://doi.org/10.1016/j.landusepol.2017.08.036

Avé, J.B., and V.T. King. 1986. *People of the Weeping Forest: Tradition and Change in Borneo*. Leiden, Netherlands: National Museum of Ethnology.

Axelsson, E.P., K.C. Grady, M.L.T. Lardizabal, I.B.S. Nair, D. Rinus, and U. Ilstedt. 2019. "A Pre-adaptive Approach for Tropical Forest Restoration During Climate Change Using Naturally Occurring Genetic Variation in Response to Water Limitation". *Restoration Ecology*. https://doi.org/10.1111/rec.13030

Azhar, B., N. Saadun, C.L. Puan, N. Kamarudin, N. Aziz, S. Nurhidayu, and J. Fischer. 2015. "Promoting Landscape Heterogeneity to Improve the Biodiversity Benefits of Certified Palm Oil Production: Evidence from Peninsular Malaysia". *Global Ecology and Conservation* 3: 553–61.

Azman, I., S.M. Ahmad, A.Z. Ali Nordin, N.N. Kamil, A.S. Shahidan, K. Hashim, M.A. Johari, S. Alid, and N. Balu. 2018. "Labour Requirement in the Oil Palm

Independent Smallholder Sector in Sabah and Sarawak, Malaysia". *Oil Palm Industry Economic Journal* 18: 37–45.

———, A. Zulhusni, A. Norhidayu, S. Mashani, H. Khairuman, S. Ainul, and N. Balu. 2018. "Labour Requirements in the Independent Oil Palm Smallholder Sector in Peninsular Malaysia". *Oil Palm Industry Economic Journal* 18, no. 1: 41–49.

Bakhtyar, B., K. Sopian, A. Zaharim, E. Salleh, and C.H. Lim. 2013. "Potentials and Challenges in Implementing Feed-in Tariff Policy in Indonesia and the Philippines". *Energy Policy* 60: 418–23. https://doi.org/10.1016/j.enpol.2013.05.034

Bakkegaard, R. K., N. J. Hogarth, I. W. Bong, A. S. Bosselmann, and S. Wunder. 2017. "Measuring Forest and Wild Product Contributions to Household Welfare: Testing a Scalable Household Survey Instrument in Indonesia". *Forest Policy and Economics* 84: 20–28. https://doi.org/10.1016/j.forpol.2016.10.005

Bamba, J. 2010. "Indigenous Peoples Self-Determined Development and Lessons from Kalimantan Credit Union Movement". International Expert Group Meeting, United Nations, New York.

BAPPENAS. 2014. "Rencana Pembangunan Jangka Menengah Nasional 2015–2019" (Medium-term Development Plan of 2015–2019), edited by BAPPENAS. Jakarta: BAPPENAS.

———. 2019. "Low Carbon Development Report: A Paradigm Shift Towards a Green Economy in Indonesia". Indonesian Ministry of National Development Planning/ National Development Planning Agency (BAPPENAS), Jakarta.

Barbier, E.B., N. Bockstael, J.C. Burgess, and I. Strand. 1995. "The Linkages Between the Timber Trade and Tropical Deforestation—Indonesia". *World Economy* 18, no. 3: 411–42.

Barker, G., C. Hunt, H. Barton, C. Gosden, S. Jones, L. Lloyd-Smith, L. Farr, B. Nyirí, and S. O'Donnell. 2017. "The 'Cultured Rainforests' of Borneo". *Quaternary International* 448: 44–61. https://doi.org/10.1016/j.quaint.2016.08.018

Barr, C.M., I.A.P. Resosudarmo, A. Dermawan, J. McCarthy, M. Moeliono, and B. Setiono. 2006. *Decentralization of Forest Administration in Indonesia: Implications for Forest Sustainability, Economic Development, and Community Livelihoods*. Bogor, Indonesia: CIFOR. https://www.cifor.org/library/2113/

Barton, H. 2012. "The Reversed Fortunes of Sago and Rice, Oryza Sativa, in the Rainforests of Sarawak, Borneo". *Quaternary International* 249: 96–104. https://doi.org/10.1016/j.quaint.2011.03.037

Basri, M., R. Rahman, and A.B. Salleh. 2013. "Specialty Oleochemicals from Palm Oil Via Enzymatic Syntheses". *J. Oil Palm Res* 25, no. 1: 22.

Basuki, I., J.B. Kauffman, J. Peterson, G. Anshari, and D. Murdiyarso. 2019. "Land Cover Changes Reduce Net Primary Production in Tropical Coastal Peatlands of West Kalimantan, Indonesia". *Mitigation and Adaptation Strategies for Global Change* 24, no. 4: 557–73. https://doi.org/10.1007/s11027-018-9811-2

Bataille, C., C. Guivarch, S. Hallegatte, J. Rogelj, and H. Waisman. 2018. "Carbon Prices Across Countries". *Nature Climate Change* 8, no. 8: 648–50. https://doi.org/10.1038/s41558-018-0239-1

BCCK. 2020. "Borneo Convention Centre Kuching". Kuching, Sarawak http://www.bcck.
    com.my/wp-content/files_mf/1578023439CorporateBrochure_compressed.pdf
Beaudoin, G., S. Rafanoharana, M. Boissière, A. Wijaya, and W. Wardhana. 2016.
    "Completing the Picture: Importance of Considering Participatory Mapping for
    REDD+ Measurement, Reporting and Verification (MRV)". *PLoS ONE* 11, no. 12.
    https://doi.org/10.1371/journal.pone.0166592
BEIS. 2020. "2018 UK Greenhouse Gas Emissions, Final Figures". Department for
    Business, Energy & Industrial Strategy (BEIS), United Kingdom, 4 February
    2020. https://www.gov.uk/environment/energy-and-climate-change-evidence-
    and-analysis
Berkes, F., and H. Ross. 2013. "Community Resilience: Toward an Integrated Approach".
    Society & Natural Resources 26, no. 1: 5–20. https://doi.org/10.1080/08941920.2
    012.736605
Bernama. 2020. "Focus Is on Productivity, Yield Rather Than Expanding Oil Palm
    Planting Area". Bernama, 13 March 2020. https://www.theedgemarkets.com/article/
    focus-productivity-yield-rather-expanding-oil-palm-planting-area
Bernard, S., Y. Roche, and B. Sarrasin. 2016. "Écotourisme, aires protégées et expansion
    agricole : quelle place pour les systèmes socio-écologiques locaux?". *Canadian
    Journal of Development Studies* 37, no. 4: 422–45. https://doi.org/10.1080/02255
    189.2016.1202813
Berninger, A., S. Lohberger, D. Zhang, and F. Siegert. 2019. "Canopy Height and Above-
    Ground Biomass Retrieval in Tropical Forests Using Multi-Pass X-And C-Band
    Pol-Insar Data". *Remote Sensing* 11, no. 18. https://doi.org/10.3390/rs11182105
Besar, N.A., H. Suardi, M.H. Phua, D. James, M.B. Mokhtar, and M.F. Ahmed. 2020.
    "Carbon Stock and Sequestration Potential of an Agroforestry System in Sabah,
    Malaysia". *Forests* 11, no. 2. https://doi.org/10.3390/f11020210
Beschorner, N., M. Bartley Johns, B. Guermazi, J.L. Treadwell, P.W.B. Prakosa, N.A. binte
    A. Karim, D.A. Van Tuijll, L. Bennis, and J. Van Rees. 2019. "The Digital Economy
    in Southeast Asia: Strengthening the Foundations for Future Growth". World Bank
    Working Paper no. 137143.
Bhullar, L. 2013. "REDD+ and the Clean Development Mechanism: A Comparative
    Perspective". *International Journal of Rural Law and Policy*, no. 1: 1.
BIG Indonesia. 2020. "Portal One Map Policy" (Portal Kebijakan Satu Peta). Jakarta,
    Indonesia.
Bioenergy International. 2020. "Pertamina Selects Honeywell OUP for Biorefinery and
    Refinery Revamp". Bioenergy International.
Bissonnette, J.-F. 2011. "Representations as Practices: Producing a Native Space in
    Sarawak, Malaysia". *Journal of Cultural Geography* 28, no. 2: 339–63. https://doi.
    org/10.1080/08873631.2011.583448
⸺. 2013. "Development Through Large-Scale Oil Palm Agribusiness Schemes:
    Representations of Possibilities and the Experience of Limits in West Kalimantan".
    Sojourn 28, no. 3: 485–511. https://doi.org/10.1355/sj28-3d
Blackham, G.V., E.L. Webb, and R.T. Corlett. 2014. "Natural Regeneration in a Degraded

Tropical Peatland, Central Kalimantan, Indonesia: Implications for Forest Restoration". *Forest Ecology and Management* 324: 8–15. https://doi.org/10.1016/j. foreco.2014.03.041

Blackmore, E., J. Keeley, R. Pyburn, E. Mangus, L. Chen, and Q. Yuhui. 2012. "Pro-poor Certification: Assessing the Benefits of Sustainability Certification for Small-Scale Farmers in Asia". International Institute for Environment and Development (UK).

Blanchet-Cohen, N., and M. Urud. 2017. "Tana' Bawang (Homeland): Cultural Safety and the Kelabit Land Struggle in Borneo". *AlterNative* 13, no. 3: 170–78. https://doi.org/10.1177/1177180117714409

BLD Plantation. 2020. "Annual Report 2019". BLD Plantation Berhad, Kuching, Sarawak. https://www.bldpb.com.my/investor-relations/annual-report/

BMF. 2019. "The Mulu Land Grab: Results of a Fact-Finding Mission to Sarawak (Malaysia) on Palm Oil-Related Deforestation and a Land Conflict Near the UNESCO-Protected Gunung Mulu World Heritage Site". Bruno Manser Fonds, CH. https://portals.iucn.org/library/node/48435

Boer, H. 2017. "Welfare Environmentality and REDD+ Incentives in Indonesia". *Journal of Environmental Policy and Planning* 19, no. 6: 795–809. https://doi.org/10.1080/1523908X.2017.1292872

Boer, H.J. 2019. "Deliberative Engagement and REDD+ in Indonesia". *Geoforum* 104: 170–80. https://doi.org/10.1016/j.geoforum.2019.04.025

Boles, K.S., K. Kannan, J. Gill, M. Felderman, H. Gouvis, B. Hubby, K.I. Kamrud, J.C. Venter, and D.G. Gibson. 2017. "Digital-to-Biological Converter for On-Demand Production of Biologics". *Nat Biotechnol* 35, no. 7: 672–75. https://doi.org/10.1038/nbt.3859

Bong, I.W., M.E. Felker, and A. Maryudi. 2016. "How Are Local People Driving and Affected by Forest Cover Change? Opportunities for Local Participation in REDD+ Measurement, Reporting and Verification". *PLoS ONE* 11, no. 11. https://doi.org/10.1371/journal.pone.0145330

Bong, M.W., Norimah A. Karim, and I.M. Noor. 2018. "Nutritional Status and Complimentary Feeding Among Penan Infants and Young Children in Rural Sarawak, Malaysia". *Mal. J. Nutr* 24, no. 4: 539–50.

Boonratana, R. 2013. "Fragmentation and Its Significance on the Conservation of Proboscis Monkey (Nasalis Larvatus) in the Lower Kinabatangan, Sabah (North Borneo)". In *Primates in Fragments: Complexity and Resilience*, pp. 459–75. New York: Springer.

Borchard, N., M. Bulusu, N. Meyer, A. Rodionov, H. Herawati, S. Blagodatsky, G. Cadisch, G. Welp, W. Amelung, and C. Martius. 2019. "Deep Soil Carbon Storage in Tree-Dominated Land Use Systems in Tropical Lowlands of Kalimantan". *Geoderma* 354. https://doi.org/10.1016/j.geoderma.2019.07.022

Borneo Post. 2012. "PKR Sabah Demands Return of 306,000 Acres from Felda". 13 February 2012. https://www.theborneopost.com/2012/02/13/pkr-sabah-demands-return-of-306000-acres-from-felda/

———. 2015. "Sarawak Freezes Issuance of Timber Licenses to Preserve Forest: Adenan".

1 August 2015. http://www.theborneopost.com/2015/08/01/sarawak-freezes-issuance-of-timber-licenses-to-preserve-forest-adenan/

———. 2017a. "Coffee to Be Big Cash Crop for Sabah—Tan". 2 December 2017a. https://www.theborneopost.com/2017/12/02/coffee-to-be-big-cash-crop-for-sabah-tan/

———. 2017b. "Uggah: Digital Application Crucial for Faster Market Penetration". 31 October 2017b. http://www.theborneopost.com/2017/10/31/uggah-digital-application-crucial-for-faster-market-penetration/

———. 2018a. "CM: Sabah Palm Oil 100% RSPO Certified by 2025". 17 November 2018a. https://www.theborneopost.com/2018/11/17/cm-sabah-palm-oil-100-rspo-certified-by-2025/

———. 2018b. "East M'sia's Mobile Internet Usage Highest in the Country". 10 December 2018b. https://www.theborneopost.com/2018/12/10/east-msias-mobile-internet-usage-highest-in-the-country/

———. 2019a. "Bario Rice Industry under Threat". 22 October 2019a. https://www.theborneopost.com/2019/10/22/bario-rice-industry-under-threat/

———. 2019b. "Organic Farming Brings Huge Returns". 9 January 2019b. https://www.theborneopost.com/2019/01/09/organic-farming-brings-huge-returns/.

———. 2019c. "Penan, Berawan Community File Suit to Stop Oil Palm Plantation Near Mulu National Park". 6 August 2019c. http://www.theborneopost.com/2019/08/06/penan-berawan-community-file-suit-to-stop-oil-palm-plantation-near-mulu-national-park/

———. 2020a. "COVID-19's Push on Digital Banking". 5 July 2020a. https://www.theborneopost.com/2020/07/05/covid-19s-push-on-digital-banking/

———. 2020b. "MATTA: Tourism Industry's Recovery Needs Push from Outside". 2 June 2020b. https://www.theborneopost.com/2020/06/02/matta-tourism-industrys-recovery-needs-push-from-outside/

———. 2020c. "Sarawak Pay—A Fintech Platform for All Sarawakians". 8 February 2020c. https://www.theborneopost.com/2020/02/08/sarawak-pay-a-fintech-platform-for-all-sarawakians/

———. 2020d. "Screening for Small Business Licence Application Intensified". 2 June 2020d. https://www.theborneopost.com/2020/06/02/screening-for-small-business-licence-application-intensified/

———. 2020e. "Uggah Wants Salcra to Increase Productivity, Increase Usage of IoT". 5 January 2020e. https://www.theborneopost.com/2020/01/05/uggah-wants-salcra-to-increase-productivity-increase-usage-of-iot/

———. 2020f. "UMS Student's Tree Hut Video Goes Viral". 17 June 2020f. https://www.theborneopost.com/2020/06/17/ums-students-tree-hut-video-goes-viral/

———. 2020g. "Virtual Hearings Should Be Permanent—Sabah Law Society". 1 June 2020g. https://www.theborneopost.com/2020/06/01/virtual-hearings-should-be-permanent-sabah-law-society/

———. 2021a. "State's Economic Recovery Benefits from Sabah Maju Jaya 1.0". 22 September 2021a. https://www.theborneopost.com/2021/09/22/states-economic-recovery-benefits-from-sabah-maju-jaya-1-0-2/

——. 2021b. "Ultra-Luxury Eco-Tourism Resort Planned at Mengalum Island". 3 October 2021b. https://www.theborneopost.com/2021/10/13/ultra-luxury-eco-tourism-resort-planned-at-mengalum-island/

Bosma, R., A.S. Sidik, P. van Zwieten, A. Aditya, and L. Visser. 2012. "Challenges of a Transition to a Sustainably Managed Shrimp Culture Agro-Ecosystem in the Mahakam Delta, East Kalimantan, Indonesia". *Wetlands Ecology and Management* 20, no. 2: 89–99. https://doi.org/10.1007/s11273-011-9244-0

Bou Dib, J., V.V. Krishna, Z. Alamsyah, and M. Qaim. 2018. "Land-Use Change and Livelihoods of Non-Farm Households: The Role of Income from Employment in Oil Palm and Rubber in Rural Indonesia". *Land Use Policy* 76: 828–38. https://doi.org/10.1016/j.landusepol.2018.03.020

BPDPKS. 2019. "Oleochemical Industry Continues to Make Progress". Badan Pengelola Dana Perkebunan Kelapa Sawit (BPDPKS). https://www.bpdp.or.id/en/Oleochemical-Industry-Continues-to-Make-Progress (accessed 4 January 2021).

BPS. 2013. "Sensus Pertanian 2013" (Agricultural census 2013). Badan Pusat Statistik, Jakarta.

——. 2020. BPS – Statistics Indonesia.

BPS Kalbar. 2020. "Statistics of Kalimantan Barat Province".

BPS Kalsel. 2020. "Statistics of Kalimantan Selatan Province".

BPS Kaltara. 2020. "Statistics of Kalimantan Utara Province".

BPS Kalteng. 2020. "Statistics of Kalimantan Tengah Province".

BPS Kaltim. 2020. "Statistics of Kalimantan Timur Province".

Brede, A. 2018. "The Jurisdictional Approach in Indonesia: An Example of Implementation". Programme Sustainable Supply Chains and Standards GIZ, PowerPoint presentation, Bangkok.

Brock, A. 2015. "'Love for Sale': Biodiversity Banking and the Struggle to Commodify Nature in Sabah, Malaysia". *Geoforum* 65: 278–90. https://doi.org/10.1016/j.geoforum.2015.08.009

Brockerhoff, E.G., H. Jactel, J.A. Parrotta, C.P. Quine, and J. Sayer. 2008. "Plantation Forests and Biodiversity: Oxymoron or Opportunity?". *Biodiversity and Conservation* 17, no. 5: 925–51.

Brookfield, H., and Y. Byron. 1990. "Deforestation and Timber Extraction in Borneo and the Malay Peninsula: The Record since 1965". *Global Environmental Change* 1, no. 1: 42–56.

——, L. Potter, and Y. Byron. 1995. *In Place of the Forest: Environmental and Socio-Economic Transformation in Borneo and the Eastern Malay Peninsula.* Tokyo: UNU Press.

Brown, E., N. Dudley, A. Lindhe, D.R. Muhtaman, C. Stewart, and T. Synnott. 2013. "Common Guidance for the Identification of High Conservation Values". 10/2013. Forest Stewardship Council International (FSC). https://fsc.org/en/for-forests/high-conservation-values

Bruno, D.E., D.A. Ruban, G. Tiess, N. Pirrone, P. Perrotta, A.V. Mikhailenko,

V.A. Ermolaev, and N.N. Yashalova. 2020. "Artisanal and Small-Scale Gold Mining, Meandering Tropical Rivers, and Geological Heritage: Evidence from Brazil and Indonesia". *Science of the Total Environment* 715: 136907. https://doi.org/10.1016/j. scitotenv.2020.136907

Bryan, J.E., P.L. Shearman, G.P. Asner, D.E. Knapp, G. Aoro, and B. Lokes. 2013. "Extreme Differences in Forest Degradation in Borneo: Comparing Practices in Sarawak, Sabah, and Brunei". *PLoS ONE* 8, no. 7: e69679. https://doi.org/10.1371/journal. pone.0069679

Budiharta, S., E. Meijaard, P.D. Erskine, C. Rondinini, M. Pacifici, and K.A. Wilson. 2014. "Restoring Degraded Tropical Forests for Carbon and Biodiversity". *Environmental Research Letters* 9, no. 11. https://doi.org/10.1088/1748-9326/9/11/114020

———, E. Meijaard, D.L.A. Gaveau, M.J. Struebig, A. Wilting, S. Kramer-Schadt, J. Niedballa, N. Raes, M. Maron, and K.A. Wilson. 2018. "Restoration to Offset the Impacts of Developments at a Landscape Scale Reveals Opportunities, Challenges and Tough Choices". *Global Environmental Change* 52: 152–61. https://doi. org/10.1016/j.gloenvcha.2018.07.008

———, E. Meijaard, J.A. Wells, N.K. Abram, and K.A. Wilson. 2016. "Enhancing Feasibility: Incorporating a Socio-Ecological Systems Framework into Restoration Planning". *Environmental Science and Policy* 64: 83–92. https://doi.org/10.1016/j. envsci.2016.06.014

Budiman, M.A., M.M. Sadewa, L. Handayani, M.S. Nurzaman, and F.F. Hastiadi. 2019. "Opportunity and Threat of Developing Halal Tourism Destinations: A Case of Banjarmasin, Indonesia". *International Journal of Economic Behavior and Organization* 7, no. 1: 7–13.

Bugge, M.M., T. Hansen, and A. Klitkou. 2016. "What Is the Bioeconomy? A Review of the Literature". *Sustainability* 8, no. 7: 691.

Buhalis, D., and Y. Sinarta. 2019. "Real-Time Co-creation and Nowness Service: Lessons from Tourism and Hospitality". *Journal of Travel & Tourism Marketing* 36, no. 5: 563–82. https://doi.org/10.1080/10548408.2019.1592059

Buongiorno, J., and S. Zhu. 2017. "Potential Effects of a Trans-Pacific Partnership on Forest Industries". *Forest Policy and Economics* 81: 97–104. https://doi.org/10.1016/j. forpol.2016.08.001

Burivalova, Z., E.T. Game, B. Wahyudi, Ruslandi, M. Rifqi, E. MacDonald, S. Cushman, M. Voigt, S. Wich, and D. S. Wilcove. 2020. "Does Biodiversity Benefit When the Logging Stops? An Analysis of Conservation Risks and Opportunities in Active Versus Inactive Logging Concessions in Borneo". *Biological Conservation* 241. https://doi.org/10.1016/j.biocon.2019.108369

Busch, J., J. Engelmann, S.C. Cook-Patton, B.W. Griscom, T. Kroeger, H. Possingham, and P. Shyamsundar. 2019. "Potential for Low-Cost Carbon Dioxide Removal Through Tropical Reforestation". *Nature Climate Change* 9, no. 6: 463–66. https:// doi.org/10.1038/s41558-019-0485-x

Butarbutar, T., S. Soedirman, P.R. Neupane, and M. Köhl. 2019. "Carbon Recovery Following Selective Logging in Tropical Rainforests in Kalimantan, Indonesia". *Forest Ecosystems* 6, no. 1. https://doi.org/10.1186/s40663-019-0195-x

Butler, R. 2012. "A Desperate Effort to Save the Rainforest of Borneo". *Yale Environment 360*.

Carlson, K.M., L.M. Curran, G.P. Asner, A.M. Pittman, S.N. Trigg, and J. Marion Adeney. 2012. "Carbon Emissions from Forest Conversion by Kalimantan Oil Palm Plantations". *Nature Climate Change* 3, no. 3: 283–87. https://doi.org/10.1038/nclimate1702

——, R. Heilmayr, H.K. Gibbs, P. Noojipady, D.N. Burns, D.C. Morton, N.F. Walker, G.D. Paoli, and C. Kremen. 2018. "Effect of Oil Palm Sustainability Certification on Deforestation and Fire in Indonesia". *Proceedings of the National Academy of Sciences* 115, no. 1: 121–26.

Carmenta, R., A. Zabala, W. Daeli, and J. Phelps. 2017. "Perceptions Across Scales of Governance and the Indonesian Peatland Fires". *Global Environmental Change-Human and Policy Dimensions* 46: 50–59. https://doi.org/10.1016/j.gloenvcha.2017.08.001

Caroko, W., H. Komarudin, K. Obidzinski, and P. Gunarso. 2011. *Policy and Institutional Frameworks for the Development of Palm Oil–Based Biodiesel in Indonesia*". Bogor, Indonesia: CIFOR.

Carolan, M. 2020. "Urban Farming Is Going High Tech". *Journal of the American Planning Association* 86, no. 1: 47–59. https://doi.org/10.1080/01944363.2019.1660205

Casson, A. 2001. "Decentralisation of Policies Affecting Forests and Estate Crops in Kotawaringin Timur District, Central Kalimantan". Case Studies on Decentralisation and Forests in Indonesia No. Case Study 5. Bogor, Indonesia, CIFOR.

——, and K. Obidzinski. 2002. "From New Order to Regional Autonomy: Shifting Dynamics of "Illegal" Logging in Kalimantan, Indonesia". *World Development* 30, no. 12: 2133–51. https://doi.org/10.1016/S0305-750X(02)00125-0

Cattau, M.E., M.E. Marlier, and R. DeFries. 2016. "Effectiveness of Roundtable on Sustainable Palm Oil (RSPO) for Reducing Fires on Oil Palm Concessions in Indonesia from 2012 to 2015". *Environmental Research Letters* 11, no. 10. https://doi.org/10.1088/1748-9326/11/10/105007

Chacko, D.P. 2021. *Local Democracy and State Identity of Sabah*. Kota Kinabalu, Sabah: WISDOM Foundation.

Chaddy, A., L. Melling, K. Ishikura, and R. Hatano. 2019. "Soil N2O Emissions under Different N Rates in an Oil Palm Plantation on Tropical Peatland". *Agriculture (Switzerland)* 9, no. 10. https://doi.org/10.3390/agriculture9100213

Chapman, S., J.I. Syktus, R. Trancoso, A. Salazar, M.J. Thatcher, J.E. Watson, E. Meijaard, D. Sheil, P. Dargusch, and C.A. McAlpine. 2020. "Compounding Impact of Deforestation on Borneo's Climate During El Niño Events". *Environmental Research Letters*, 15, no. 8.

Chatham House. 2021. Resourcetrade.earth. Chatham House.

Chellaiah, D., and C.M. Yule. 2018a. "Effect of Riparian Management on Stream Morphometry and Water Quality in Oil Palm Plantations in Borneo". *Limnologica* 69: 72–80. https://doi.org/10.1016/j.limno.2017.11.007

——. 2018b. "Riparian Buffers Mitigate Impacts of Oil Palm Plantations on Aquatic

Macroinvertebrate Community Structure in Tropical Streams of Borneo". *Ecological Indicators* 95: 53–62. https://doi.org/10.1016/j.ecolind.2018.07.025

Chen, B., J. Wan, L. Shu, P. Li, M. Mukherjee, and B. Yin. 2018. "Smart Factory of Industry 4.0: Key Technologies, Application Case, and Challenges". *IEEE Access* 6: 6505–19. https://doi.org/10.1109/ACCESS.2017.2783682

Chen, J. 2020. "The 2018/2019 Simultaneous Elections in West Kalimantan Province and Its Aftermath: Historical Legacies, Identity Politics, and the Politics of Partition". In *The 2018 and 2019 Indonesian Elections*, pp. 145–66. Routledge.

Cheok, K.Y.M., and J. Mohd-Azlan. 2018. "Preliminary Analysis on the Hunting Activities in Selected Areas in Interior Sarawak". *Malaysian Applied Biology* 47, no. 1: 37–44.

Cheuk, S., A. Atang, and M.-C. Lo. 2012. "Community Attitudes Towards the Telecentre in Bario, Borneo Malaysia: 14 Years On". *International Journal of Innovation, Management and Technology* 3, no. 6: 682.

Chew, W.C., and L.W. Vun. 2013. "Preliminary Ecological Input Assessment of EIAs of Selected Quarries and Oil Palm Plantation Projects in Sabah, Malaysia". *Journal of Sustainability Science and Management* 8, no. 1: 22–31.

Chiang, B., and J.C.-y. Cheng. 2017. "Ethnic Chinese Enterprises in Indonesia: A Case Study of West Kalimantan". In *Chinese Capitalism in Southeast Asia: Cultures and Practices*, edited by Y. Santasombat, pp. 131–53. Singapore: Springer Singapore.

Chin, J. 2014. "Exporting the BN/UMNO Model: Politics in Sabah and Sarawak". In *Routledge Handbook of Contemporary Malaysia*, pp. 83–92. London: Routledge.

———. 2019. "The 1963 Malaysia Agreement (MA63): Sabah and Sarawak and the Politics of Historical Grievances". *Minorities Matter: Malaysians Politics and People Volume III*, edited by Sophie Lemière, pp. 75–92. Singapore and Selangor: ISEAS – Yusof Ishak Institute and SIRD.

Chin, M.J., P.E. Poh, B.T. Tey, E.S. Chan, and K.L. Chin. 2013. "Biogas from Palm Oil Mill Effluent (POME): Opportunities and Challenges from Malaysia's Perspective". *Renewable and Sustainable Energy Reviews* 26: 717–26. https://doi.org/10.1016/j.rser.2013.06.008

Ching, J.Y.L., I.C. Yaman, K.L. Khoon, C.K. Hong, and G. Melayong. 2019. "A Case Study into the Sustainability Journey and Biodiversity Conservation Projects in Sarawak by Sarawak Oil Palms Berhad". *Journal of Oil Palm Research* 31, no. 3: 489–95. https://doi.org/10.21894/jopr.2019.0036

Choy, Y.K. 2014. "Land Ethics from the Borneo Tropical Rain Forests in Sarawak, Malaysia: An Empirical and Conceptual Analysis". *Environmental Ethics* 36, no. 4: 421–41. https://doi.org/10.5840/enviroethics201436446

Christin, S., É. Hervet, and N. Lecomte. 2019. "Applications for Deep Learning in Ecology". *Methods in Ecology and Evolution* 10, no. 10: 1632–44. https://doi.org/10.1111/2041-210x.13256

Chua, L. 2016. "Gifting, Dam(n)ing and the Ambiguation of Development in Malaysian Borneo". *Ethnos* 81, no. 4: 735–57. https://doi.org/10.1080/00141844.2014.986152

———, M.E. Harrison, H. Fair, S. Milne, A. Palmer, J. Rubis, P. Thung, S. Wich, B. Büscher, S.M. Cheyne, R.K. Puri, V. Schreer, A. Stępień, and E. Meijaard. 2020.

"Conservation and the Social Sciences: Beyond Critique and Co-Optation. A Case Study from Orangutan Conservation". *People and Nature* 2, no. 1: 42–60. https://doi.org/10.1002/pan3.10072

CIA. 2020. CIA Library. The Central Intelligence Agency (CIA).

CIFOR. 2020. "Atlas of Deforestation and Industrial Plantation". https://atlas.cifor.org/ (accessed on 29 November 2019).

Cleary, M., and P. Eaton. 1992. *Borneo: Change and Development*. Singapore: Oxford University Press.

Clerc, J. 2013. "Oil Palm Plantations and Negotiations for Access to Land in Indonesia: Reflexions Based on a Case Study in Kapuas Hulu (West Kalimantan)". *Cahiers Agricultures* 22, no. 1: 53–60. https://doi.org/10.1684/agr.2012.0603

Clink, D.J., M.C. Crofoot, and A.J. Marshall. 2019. "Application of a Semi-Automated Vocal Fingerprinting Approach to Monitor Bornean Gibbon Females in an Experimentally Fragmented Landscape in Sabah, Malaysia". *Bioacoustics* 28, no. 3: 193–209. https://doi.org/10.1080/09524622.2018.1426042

Clough, Y., V.V. Krishna, M.D. Corre, K. Darras, L.H. Denmead, A. Meijide, S. Moser, O. Musshoff, S. Steinebach, E. Veldkamp, K. Allen, A.D. Barnes, N. Breidenbach, U. Brose, D. Buchori, R. Daniel, R. Finkeldey, I. Harahap, D. Hertel, A.M. Holtkamp, E. Horandl, B. Irawan, I.N.S. Jaya, M. Jochum, B. Klarner, A. Knohl, M.M. Kotowska, V. Krashevska, H. Kreft, S. Kurniawan, C. Leuschner, M. Maraun, D.N. Melati, N. Opfermann, C. Perez-Cruzado, W.E. Prabowo, K. Rembold, A. Rizali, R. Rubiana, D. Schneider, S.S. Tjitrosoedirdjo, A. Tjoa, T. Tscharntke, and S. Scheu. 2016. "Land-Use Choices Follow Profitability at the Expense of Ecological Functions in Indonesian Smallholder Landscapes". *Nat Commun* 7: 13137. https://doi.org/10.1038/ncomms13137

CMO. 2020. "Post COVID-19 Exit Economic Strategy up to 2030 (Formation of Sarawak Economic Action Council)". http://cm.sarawak.gov.my.

CNN Indonesia. 2019. "WALHI Sebut PLTA untuk Ibu Kota Baru Tenggelamkan 2 Desa", 15 November 2019. https://www.cnnindonesia.com/nasional/20191114081129-20-448184/walhi-sebut-plta-untuk-ibu-kota-baru-tenggelamkan-2-desa

———. 2021a. "Desain Proyek Ibu Kota Baru yang Berlanjut Tahun Ini". 26 March 2021a. https://www.cnnindonesia.com/ekonomi/20210326100528-532-622338/desain-proyek-ibu-kota-baru-yang-berlanjut-tahun-ini

———. 2021b. "WALHI: 427.952 Ha Hutan Kalimantan Jadi Konsesi di Era Jokowi". 21 January 2021b. https://www.cnnindonesia.com/nasional/20210121144916-20-596699/walhi-427952-ha-hutan-kalimantan-jadi-konsesi-di-era-jokowi

Coca, N. 2021. "King Coal: How Indonesia Became the Fossil Fuel's Final Frontier". *Mongabay*, 17 March 2021. Mongabay Series: Indonesian Coal. https://news.mongabay.com/2021/03/king-coal-how-indonesia-became-the-fossil-fuels-final-frontier/

Colchester, M. 2020. "Preliminary Findings from a Review of the Jurisdictional Approach

Initiative in Sabah". Forest Peoples Programme. http://www.forestpeoples.org/ sites/default/files/documents/Case%20study%20-%20Sabah%20Preliminary%20 findings%20-%20Jun%202020.pdf

——, N. Jiwan, M.S. Andiko, A.Y. Firdaus, A. Surambo, and H. Pane. 2007. "Promised Land: Palm Oil and Land Acquisition in Indonesia: Implications for Local Communities and Indigenous Peoples". Perkumpulan Sawit Watch Bogor, Indonesia.

Cole, S., and A.N. Fernando. 2012. "The Value of Advice: Evidence from Mobile Phone-Based Agricultural Extension". Harvard Business School Working Paper no. 13-047.

Corley, R.H.V., and P.B. Tinker. 2015. "Vegetative Propagation and Biotechnology". In *The Oil Palm*, pp. 208–24. Blackwell Science Ltd.

Corpuz, R. 2017. "'Wild Borneo': A Study of Visitor Perception and Experience of Nature Tourism in Sandakan, Sabah, Malaysian Borneo". In *Borneo Studies in History, Society and Culture*, pp. 443–461. Springer.

Cramb, R. 2007. *Land and Longhouse: Agrarian Transformation in the Uplands of Sarawak*. Vol. 110. Copenhagen: NIAS Press.

——. 2011a. "Agrarian Transitions in Sarawak: Intensification and Expansion Reconsidered". *Borneo Transformed: Agricultural Expansion on the Southeast Asian Frontier*, pp. 44–93. Singapore: NUS Press.

——. 2011b. "Re-Inventing Dualism: Policy Narratives and Modes of Oil Palm Expansion in Sarawak, Malaysia". *Journal of Development Studies* 47, no. 2: 274–93. https://doi.org/10.1080/00220380903428381

——. 2013. "Palmed Off: Incentive Problems with Joint-Venture Schemes for Oil Palm Development on Customary Land". *World Development* 43: 84–99. https:// doi.org/10.1016/j.worlddev.2012.10.015

——. 2016. "The Political Economy of Large-Scale Oil Palm Development in Sarawak". In *The Oil Palm Complex: Smallholders, Agribusiness and the State in Indonesia and Malaysia*, edited by R. Cramb and J.F. McCarthy, pp. 189–246. Singapore: NUS Press.

——, and D. Ferraro. 2012. "Custom and Capital: A Financial Appraisal of Alternative Arrangements for Large-Scale Oil Palm Development on Customary Land in Sarawak, Malaysia". *Malaysian Journal of Economic Studies* 49, no. 1: 49–69.

——, and J.F. McCarthy, eds. 2016. *The Oil Palm Complex. Smallholders, Agribusiness and the State in Indonesia and Malaysia*. Singapore: NUS Press.

——, and P.S. Sujang. 2016. "Oil Palm Smallholders and State Policies in Sarawak". In *The Oil Palm Complex: Smallholders, Agribusiness and the State in Indonesia and Malaysia*, edited by R. Cramb and J.F. McCarthy, pp. 247–82. Singapore: NUS Press.

——, and P.S. Sujang. 2013. "The Mouse Deer and the Crocodile: Oil Palm Smallholders and Livelihood Strategies in Sarawak, Malaysia". *Journal of Peasant Studies* 40, no. 1: 129–54. https://doi.org/10.1080/03066150.2012.750241

Crouzeilles, R., M.S. Ferreira, R.L. Chazdon, D.B. Lindenmayer, J.B. Sansevero, L. Monteiro, A. Iribarrem, A.E. Latawiec, and B.B. Strassburg. 2017. "Ecological Restoration Success Is Higher for Natural Regeneration Than for Active Restoration in Tropical Forests". *Science Advances* 3, no. 11: e1701345.

Cushman, S.A., E.A. Macdonald, E.L. Landguth, Y. Malhi, and D.W. Macdonald. 2017. "Multiple-Scale Prediction of Forest Loss Risk Across Borneo". *Landscape Ecology* 32, no. 8: 1581–98. https://doi.org/10.1007/s10980-017-0520-0

Cyranoski, D. 2007. "Biodiversity: Logging: The New Conservation". *Nature* 446, no. 7136: 608–10. https://doi.org/10.1038/446608a

Daisuke, T. 2018. "How Accepting Are Swiddeners of Oil Palm Plantation Developments? Based on Evidence from Besiq Village, Indonesia's Province of East Kalimantan". *Japanese Journal of Southeast Asian Studies* 55, no. 2: 320–45. https://doi.org/10.20495/tak.55.2_320

Dalimpos, Y. 2020. "SLDB to Make Payments in April: GM". *Daily Express*, 22 February 2020. https://www.dailyexpress.com.my/news/147617/sldb-to-make-payments-in-april-gm/

Damara, D. 2021. "Ini Isi Lengkap Tuntutan dari Aksi AMPKT yang Menolak Pemekaran Provinsi Kotawaringin". *Borneo News*, 18 January 2021. https://www.borneonews.co.id/berita/201201-ini-isi-lengkap-tuntutan-dari-aksi-ampkt-yang-menolak-pemekaran-provinsi-kotawaringin

Darmawan, M. 2012. "Forest Degradation Detection Using Modis and Landsat Data in Understanding the Implementation of REDD Scenario in East Kalimantan Province, Indonesia".

Das, M., and B. Chatterjee. 2015. "Ecotourism: A Panacea or a Predicament?". *Tourism Management Perspectives* 14: 3–16.

Dauvergne, P. 1998. "The Political Economy of Indonesia's 1997 Forest Fires". *Australian Journal of International Affairs* 52, no. 1: 13–17. https://doi.org/10.1080/10357719808445234

Davies, R. 2015. "The Indonesia-Australia Forest Carbon Partnership: A Murder Mystery". *CGD Policy Paper* 60.

Davis, J.T., K. Mengersen, N.K. Abram, M. Ancrenaz, J.A. Wells, and E. Meijaard. 2013. "It's Not Just Conflict That Motivates Killing of Orangutans". *PLoS ONE* 8, no. 10. https://doi.org/10.1371/journal.pone.0075373

Dayang Norwana, A., R. Kanjappan, M. Chin, G. Schoneveld, L. Potter, and R. Andriani. 2011. *The Local Impacts of Oil Palm Expansion in Malaysia: An Assessment Based on a Case Study in Sabah State*. Bogor, Indonesia: CIFOR.

de Jong, E.B., and K. Kuipers. 2020. "Perceptions of Change: Adopting the Concept of Livelihood Styles for a More Inclusive Approach to 'Building with Nature'". *Sustainability* 12, no. 23: 10011.

De Koninck, R., S. Bernard, and J.-F. o. Bissonnette. 2011. *Borneo Transformed: Agricultural Expansion on the Southeast Asian Frontier*. Singapore: NUS Press.

de Royer, S., L.E. Visser, G. Galudra, U. Pradhan, and M. Van Noordwijk. 2015. "Self-Identification of Indigenous People in Post-Independence Indonesia: A Historical Analysis in the Context of REDD+". *International Forestry Review* 17, no. 3: 282–97. https://doi.org/10.1505/146554815815982648

de Vos, R.E. 2016. "Multi-functional Lands Facing Oil Palm Monocultures: A Case Study of a Land Conflict in West Kalimantan, Indonesia". *Austrian Journal of South-East Asian Studies* 9, no. 1: 11–32. https://doi.org/10.14764/10.ASEAS-2016.1-2

de Vos, R. 2018. "Counter-Mapping Against Oil Palm Plantations: Reclaiming Village Territory in Indonesia with the 2014 Village Law". *Critical Asian Studies* 50, no. 4: 615–33. https://doi.org/10.1080/14672715.2018.1522595

——, and I. Delabre. 2018. "Spaces for Participation and Resistance: Gendered Experiences of Oil Palm Plantation Development". *Geoforum* 96: 217–26. https://doi.org/10.1016/j.geoforum.2018.08.011

——, M. Köhne, and D. Roth. 2018. "'We'll Turn Your Water into Coca-Cola': The Atomizing Practices of Oil Palm Plantation Development in Indonesia". *Journal of Agrarian Change* 18, no. 2: 385–405. https://doi.org/10.1111/joac.12246

Deere, N.J., G. Guillera-Arroita, E.L. Baking, H. Bernard, M. Pfeifer, G. Reynolds, O.R. Wearn, Z.G. Davies, and M.J. Struebig. 2018. "High Carbon Stock Forests Provide Co-benefits for Tropical Biodiversity". *Journal of Applied Ecology* 55, no. 2: 997–1008. https://doi.org/10.1111/1365-2664.13023

Deichmann, U., A. Goyal, and D. Mishra. 2016. "Will Digital Technologies Transform Agriculture in Developing Countries?". *Agricultural Economics* 47 (S1): 21–33. https://doi.org/10.1111/agec.12300

Delphin, S., F.J. Escobedo, A. Abd-Elrahman, and W.P. Cropper. 2016. "Urbanization as a Land Use Change Driver of Forest Ecosystem Services". *Land Use Policy* 54: 188–99. https://doi.org/10.1016/j.landusepol.2016.02.006

den Besten, J.W., B. Arts, and P. Verkooijen. 2014. "The Evolution of REDD+: An Analysis of Discursive-Institutional Dynamics". *Environmental Science & Policy* 35: 40–48. https://doi.org/10.1016/j.envsci.2013.03.009

Dent, C.M., and P. Richter. 2011. "Sub-Regional Cooperation and Developmental Regionalism: The Case of BIMP-EAGA". *Contemporary Southeast Asia* 33, no. 1: 29–55.

DEPS. 2020. "National Statistics. Bandar Seri Begawan, Brunei Darussalam". Department of Economic Planning and Statistics, Ministry of Finance and Economy, Brunei Darussalam.

DG Estate Crop Indonesia, ed. 1996. "Tree Crop Estate Statistics of Indonesia 1995–1997 Palm Oil". Jakarta, Indonesia.

——. 2012. "Komoditas Kelapa Sawit di Indonesia 2011–2013". Jakarta, Indonesia.

——. 2014. "Tree Crop Estate Statistics of Indonesia 2013–2015 Palm Oil". Jakarta, Indonesia.

——. 2016. "Tree Crop Estate Statistics of Indonesia 2015–2017 Palm Oil". Jakarta, Indonesia.

——. 2018. "Tree Crop Estate Statistics of Indonesia 2017–2019 Palm Oil". Jakarta, Indonesia.

——. 2019. "Tree Crop Estate Statistics of Indonesia 2018–2020 Palm Oil". Jakarta, Indonesia.

Dharmawan, A.H., D.I. Mardiyaningsih, H. Komarudin, J. Ghazoul, P. Pacheco, and F. Rahmadian. 2020. "Dynamics of Rural Economy: A Socio-Economic Understanding of Oil Palm Expansion and Landscape Changes in East Kalimantan, Indonesia". *Land* 9, no. 7. https://doi.org/10.3390/land9070213

Dhindsa, H.S., and A.-Z.-A. Md-Hamdilah. 2015. "Societal Perceptions of Agriculture: A Brunei Case Study". *Journal of Agricultural Education and Extension* 21, no. 5: 441–65.

Dileep Kumar, M., N.A. Ismail, and N.S. Govindarajo. 2014. "Way to Measure the Concept Precarious Working Conditions in Oil Palm Plantations". *Asian Social Science* 10, no. 21: 99–108. https://doi.org/10.5539/ass.v10n21p99

DOA. 2020. "Skim Organik Malaysia (SOM)". Malaysia's Department of Agriculture. http://www.doa.gov.my/index.php/pages/view/377 (accessed 26 March 2020).

Döbert, T.F., B.L. Webber, J.B. Sugau, K.J.M. Dickinson, and R.K. Didham. 2018. "Logging, Exotic Plant Invasions, and Native Plant Reassembly in a Lowland Tropical Rain Forest". *Biotropica* 50, no. 2: 254–65. https://doi.org/10.1111/btp.12521

Dohong, A., A.A. Aziz, and P. Dargusch. 2018. "Carbon Emissions from Oil Palm Development on Deep Peat Soil in Central Kalimantan Indonesia". *Anthropocene* 22: 31–39. https://doi.org/10.1016/j.ancene.2018.04.004

Dollah, R., and K. Abdullah. 2018. "The Securitization of Migrant Workers in Sabah, Malaysia". *Journal of International Migration and Integration* 19, no. 3: 717–35. https://doi.org/10.1007/s12134-018-0566-0

Dooley, K., and S. Ozinga. 2011. "Building on Forest Governance Reforms through FLEGT: The Best Way of Controlling Forests' Contribution to Climate Change?". *Review of European Community & International Environmental Law* 20, no. 2: 163–70. https://doi.org/10.1111/j.1467-9388.2011.00717.x

DOSM. 1991. "Siaran Perangkaan Tahunan Sarawak. Annual Statistical Bulletin, Sarawak 1972–1991". Kuching, Sarawak.

———. 2020. Department of Statistics Malaysia.

Dounias, E., and A. Froment. 2011. "From Foraging to Farming Among Present-Day Forest Hunter-Gatherers: Consequences on Diet and Health". *International Forestry Review* 13, no. 3: 294–304. https://doi.org/10.1505/146554811798293818

Dove, M.R. 2019. "Plants, Politics, and the Imagination over the Past 500 Years in the Indo-Malay Region". *Current Anthropology* 60, no. S20: S309–S320. https://doi.org/10.1086/702877

Drabble, J. 2000. *An Economic History of Malaysia, C. 1800–1990: The Transition to Modern Economic Growth.* Springer.

Dragone, G., A.A.J. Kerssemakers, J.L.S.P. Driessen, C.K. Yamakawa, L.P. Brumano, and S.I. Mussatto. 2020. "Innovation and Strategic Orientations for the Development of Advanced Biorefineries". *Bioresource Technology* 302: 122847. https://doi.org/10.1016/j.biortech.2020.122847.

DTE. 2010. "Coal in East Kalimantan: Taking the Toxic Tour". Down to Earth (DTE). https://www.downtoearth-indonesia.org/story/coal-east-kalimantan-taking-toxic-tour (accessed 27 April 2021).

Economic Planning Unit Sarawak, ed. 2021. "Post COVID-19 Development Strategy 2030". Kuching, Sarawak: Economic Planning Unit Sarawak, Chief Minister's Department.

Edge Markets, The. 2020. "Malaysia to File Legal Action with WTO Against EU's Palm

Oil Ban". 1 January 2020. https://www.theedgemarkets.com/article/malaysia-file-wto-legal-action-against-eu-over-palm-oil

Edwards, D.P., J.J. Gilroy, P. Woodcock, F.A. Edwards, T.H. Larsen, D.J.R. Andrews, M.A. Derhé, T.D.S. Docherty, W.W. Hsu, S.L. Mitchell, T. Ota, L.J. Williams, W.F. Laurance, K.C. Hamer, and D.S. Wilcove. 2014. "Land-Sharing Versus Land-Sparing Logging: Reconciling Timber Extraction with Biodiversity Conservation". *Global Change Biology* 20, no. 1: 183–91. https://doi.org/10.1111/gcb.12353

———, T.H. Larsen, T.D.S. Docherty, F.A. Ansell, W.W. Hsu, M.A. Derhé, K.C. Hamer, and D.S. Wilcove. 2011. "Degraded Lands Worth Protecting: The Biological Importance of Southeast Asia's Repeatedly Logged Forests". *Proceedings of the Royal Society B: Biological Sciences* 278, no. 1702: 82–90. https://doi.org/10.1098/rspb.2010.1062

———, P. Woodcock, F.A. Edwards, T.H. Larsen, W.W. Hsu, S. Benedick, and D.S. Wilcove. 2012. "Reduced-Impact Logging and Biodiversity Conservation: A Case Study from Borneo". *Ecological Applications* 22, no. 2: 561–71. https://doi.org/10.1890/11-1362.1

Edwards, F.A., D.P. Edwards, S. Sloan, and K. C. Hamer. 2014. "Sustainable Management in Crop Monocultures: The Impact of Retaining Forest on Oil Palm Yield". *PLoS ONE* 9, no. 3. https://doi.org/10.1371/journal.pone.0091695

Edwards, R.B., R.L. Naylor, M.M. Higgins, and W.P. Falcon. 2020. "Causes of Indonesia's Forest Fires". *World Development* 127. https://doi.org/10.1016/j.worlddev.2019.104717

Eghenter, C. 2008. "Whose Heart of Borneo? Critical Issues in Building Constituencies for Equitable Conservation". *Reflections on the Heart of Borneo*: 131–40.

———. 2018. "Indigenous Effective Area-Based Conservation Measures: Conservation Practices Among the Dayak Kenyah of North Kalimantan". *Parks* 24 (Special issue): 69–78. https://doi.org/10.2305/IUCN.CH.2018.PARKS-24-SICE.en

EIA, and Grassroots. 2015. "Who Watches the Watchmen? Auditors and the Breakdown of Oversight in the RSPO". Environmental Investigation Agency, London. https://eia-international.org/wp-content/uploads/EIA-Who-Watches-the-Watchmen-FINAL.pdf

Eilenberg, M. 2015. "Shades of Green and REDD: Local and Global Contestations over the Value of Forest Versus Plantation Development on the Indonesian Forest Frontier". *Asia Pacific Viewpoint* 56, no. 1: 48–61. https://doi.org/10.1111/apv.12084

———, and R. L. Wadley. 2009. "Borderland Livelihood Strategies: The Socio-Economic Significance of Ethnicity in Cross-Border Labour Migration, West Kalimantan, Indonesia". *Asia Pacific Viewpoint* 50, no. 1: 58–73. https://doi.org/10.1111/j.1467-8373.2009.01381.x

Ekawati, S., K. Budiningsih, G.K. Sari, and M.Z. Muttaqin. 2019. "Policies Affecting the Implementation of REDD+ in Indonesia (Cases in Papua, Riau and Central Kalimantan)". *Forest Policy and Economics* 108.

Eki, A.T. 2002. "International Labour Emigration from Eastern Flores Indonesia to Sabah Malaysia: A Study of Patterns, Causes and Consequences". PhD, University of Adelaide.

Elmhirst, R., M. Siscawati, B.S. Basnett, and D. Ekowati. 2017. "Gender and Generation in Engagements with Oil Palm in East Kalimantan, Indonesia: Insights from Feminist Political Ecology". *Journal of Peasant Studies* 44, no. 6: 1137–59. https://doi.org/10.1080/03066150.2017.1337002

Emang, D., T.H. Lundhede, and B.J. Thorsen. 2016. "Funding Conservation Through Use and Potentials for Price Discrimination Among Scuba Divers at Sipadan, Malaysia". *Journal of Environmental Management* 182: 436–45. https://doi.org/10.1016/j.jenvman.2016.07.033

Ember. 2020. "EUA Price". Ember.

Enrici, A.M., and K. Hubacek. 2018. "Challenges for REDD+ in Indonesia". *Ecology and Society* 23, no. 2.

Ernawati, J. 2017. "Tane'Olen Setulang. Omens of the Isij Bird for the Oma Lung Tribe. A Tradition of Forest Conservation at Setulang Village, Malinau, North Kalimantan". Malinau, Indonesia: Setulang Tourist Village Government, North Kalimantan.

European Commission. 2011. "Commission Regulation (EU) No 550/2011 of 7 June 2011 on Determining, Pursuant to Directive 2003/87/EC of the European Parliament and of the Council, Certain Restrictions Applicable to the Use of International Credits from Projects Involving Industrial Gases". Text with EEA relevance. edited by European Commission.

———. 2019. "Sustainability Criteria for Biofuels Specified". https://ec.europa.eu/commission/presscorner/detail/en/MEMO_19_1656 (accessed 26 August 2021).

Evans, L., B. Goossens, and G.P. Asner. 2017. "Underproductive Agriculture Aids Connectivity in Tropical Forests". *Forest Ecology and Management* 401: 159–65. https://doi.org/10.1016/j.foreco.2017.07.015

Evans, L.J., B. Goossens, A.B. Davies, G. Reynolds, and G.P. Asner. 2020. "Natural and Anthropogenic Drivers of Bornean Elephant Movement Strategies". *Global Ecology and Conservation* 22: e00906. https://doi.org/10.1016/j.gecco.2020.e00906

Faeh, D. 2011. "Development of Global Timber Tycoons in Sarawak, East Malaysia: History and Company Profiles". A report produced for Bruno Manser Fund, Switzerland (February 2011).

Fairhurst, T., M. McLeish, and R. Prasodjo. 2010. "Conditions Required by the Private Sector for Oil Palm Expansion on Degraded Land in Indonesia". Tropical Crop Consultants Limited. http://www.tropcropconsult.com/downloads_files/Fairhurst2010a.pdf

FAOSTAT. 2021. "Food and Agriculture Data". The Food and Agriculture Organization (FAO).

Faridah Aini, M., M. Elias, H. Lamers, U. Shariah, P. Brooke, and H. Mohd Hafizul. 2017. "Evaluating the Usefulness and Ease of Use of Participatory Tools for Forestry and Livelihoods Research in Sarawak, Malaysia". *Forests Trees and Livelihoods* 26, no. 1: 29–46. https://doi.org/10.1080/14728028.2016.1246213

Fatimah, Y.A. 2015. "Fantasy, Values, and Identity in Biofuel Innovation: Examining the Promise of Jatropha for Indonesia". *Energy Research & Social Science* 7: 108–16. https://doi.org/10.1016/j.erss.2015.04.002

Fawcett, D., B. Azlan, T.C. Hill, L.K. Kho, J. Bennie, and K. Anderson. 2019. "Unmanned

Aerial Vehicle (UAV) Derived Structure-from-Motion Photogrammetry Point Clouds For Oil Palm (Elaeis Guineensis) Canopy Segmentation and Height Estimation". *International Journal of Remote Sensing* 40, no. 1: 7538–60. https://doi.org/10.1080/01431161.2019.1591651

Fawzi, N.I., J. Helms, A. Novianto, A. Supianto, A.M. Indrayani, and N. Febriani. 2020. "Reducing Illegal Logging through a Chainsaw Buyback and Entrepreneurship Program at Gunung Palung National Park". *Forest and Society* 4, no. 1: 151–61.

Fay, C., and H.-M.S. Denduangrudee. 2016. "Emerging Options for the Recognition and Protection of Indigenous Community Rights in Indonesia". In *Land and Development in Indonesia: Searching for the People's Sovereignty*, edited by F. McCarthy, and K. Robinson, pp. 91–112. Singapore: ISEAS – Yusof Ishak Institute.

Fazil, M., and M. Firdhous. 2018. "IoT-Enabled Smart Elephant Detection System for Combating Human Elephant Conflict". 3rd International Conference on Information Technology Research (ICITR), 5–7 December 2018.

Feng, X., F. Yan, and X. Liu. 2019. "Study of Wireless Communication Technologies on Internet of Things for Precision Agriculture". *Wireless Personal Communications* 108, no. 3: 1785–802. https://doi.org/10.1007/s11277-019-06496-7

Fernandes, K., L. Verchot, W. Baethgen, V. Gutierrez-Velez, M. Pinedo-Vasquez, and C. Martius. 2017. "Heightened Fire Probability in Indonesia in Non-Drought Conditions: The Effect of Increasing Temperatures". *Environmental Research Letters* 12, no. 5: 054002. https://doi.org/10.1088/1748-9326/aa6884

Ferraz, A., S. Saatchi, L. Xu, S. Hagen, J. Chave, Y. Yu, V. Meyer, M. Garcia, C. Silva, O. Roswintiart, A. Samboko, P. Sist, S. Walker, T.R.H. Pearson, A. Wijaya, F.B. Sullivan, E. Rutishauser, D. Hoekman, and S. Ganguly. 2018. "Carbon Storage Potential in Degraded Forests of Kalimantan, Indonesia". *Environmental Research Letters* 13, no. 9. https://doi.org/10.1088/1748-9326/aad782

FGV Holdings. 2020. "Annual Integrated Report 2019". https://www.fgvholdings.com/investor-relations/annual-reports-presentations/

Fidiashtry, A., C. Aryudiawan, L. Awaluddin, and M.A. Marfai. 2017. "Food Insecurity as a Basis for Drafting a Strategic Food Sovereignty Plan: A Case Study of the Kutai Kartanegara District, Indonesia". *Quaestiones Geographicae* 36, no. 4: 141–58.

Field, R.D., G.R. Van Der Werf, T. Fanin, E.J. Fetzer, R. Fuller, H. Jethva, R. Levy, N.J. Livesey, M. Luo, O. Torres, and H.M. Worden. 2016. "Indonesian Fire Activity and Smoke Pollution in 2015 Show Persistent Nonlinear Sensitivity to El Niño-Induced Drought". *Proceedings of the National Academy of Sciences of the United States of America* 113, no. 33: 9204–9. https://doi.org/10.1073/pnas.1524888113

Filer, C., S. Mahanty, and L. Potter. 2020. "The FPIC Principle Meets Land Struggles in Cambodia, Indonesia and Papua New Guinea". *Land* 9, no. 3: 67.

Firdaus, R., P.M. Wibowo, and Y. Rochmayanto. 2017. "Developing Strategies for Landscape Sustainability: An Indonesian National Strategic Plan of Action in the Heart of Borneo". In *Landscape Ecology for Sustainable Society*, pp. 67–84. Springer.

Fisher, B., D.P. Edwards, X. Giam, and D.S. Wilcove. 2011. "The High Costs of Conserving Southeast Asia's Lowland Rainforests". *Frontiers in Ecology and the Environment* 9, no. 6: 329–34. https://doi.org/10.1890/100079

———, D.P. Edwards, T.H. Larsen, F.A. Ansell, W.W. Hsu, C.S. Roberts, and D.S. Wilcove. 2011. "Cost-Effective Conservation: Calculating Biodiversity and Logging Trade-offs in Southeast Asia". *Conservation Letters* 4, no. 6: 443–50. https://doi.org/10.1111/j.1755-263X.2011.00198.x

———, D.P. Edwards, and D.S. Wilcove. 2014. "Logging and Conservation: Economic Impacts of the Stocking Rates and Prices of Commercial Timber Species". *Forest Policy and Economics* 38: 65–71. https://doi.org/10.1016/j.forpol.2013.05.006

Flach, B., S. Lieberz, and S. Bolla. 2020. "EU Biofuels Annual 2019". USDA. https://www.fas.usda.gov/data/european-union-biofuels-annual-0

Fleiss, S., E.H. Waddell, B. Bala Ola, L.F. Banin, S. Benedick, A. Bin Sailim, D.S. Chapman, A. Jelling, H. King, C. J. McClean, K.L. Yeong, and J.K. Hill. 2020. "Conservation Set-Asides Improve Carbon Storage and Support Associated Plant Diversity in Certified Sustainable Oil Palm Plantations". *Biological Conservation* 248: 108631. https://doi.org/10.1016/j.biocon.2020.108631

FORCLIME. 2016. "Setulang Becomes the First Village in North Kalimantan with Full Forest Management Rights". https://www.forclime.org/index.php/en/more-news/30-2016/676-setulang-becomes-the-first-village-in-north-kalimantan-with-full-forest-management-rights (accessed 18 May 2021).

Fornace, K.M., N. Alexander, T.R. Abidin, P.M. Brock, T.H. Chua, I. Vythilingam, H.M. Ferguson, B.O. Manin, M.L. Wong, S.H. Ng, J. Cox, and C. Drakeley. 2019. "Local Human Movement Patterns and Land Use Impact Exposure to Zoonotic Malaria in Malaysian Borneo". *eLife* 8. https://doi.org/10.7554/eLife.47602

Forsyth, T. 2014. "Public Concerns About Transboundary Haze: A Comparison of Indonesia, Singapore, and Malaysia". *Global Environmental Change* 25: 76–86. https://doi.org/10.1016/j.gloenvcha.2014.01.013

Fox, J., Y. Fujita, D. Ngidang, N. Peluso, L. Potter, N. Sakuntaladewi, J. Sturgeon, and D. Thomas. 2009. "Policies, Political-Economy, and Swidden in Southeast Asia". *Human Ecology* 37, no. 3: 305–22.

Fraser, E.D.G., and M. Campbell. 2019. "Agriculture 5.0: Reconciling Production with Planetary Health". *One Earth* 1, no. 3: 278–80. https://doi.org/10.1016/j.oneear.2019.10.022

Fritsche, U., G. Brunori, D. Chiaramonti, C. Galanakis, S. Hellweg, R. Matthews, and C. Panoutsou. 2020. "Future Transitions for the Bioeconomy Towards Sustainable Development and a Climate-Neutral Economy—Knowledge Synthesis: Final Report". Luxembourg: Publications Office of the EU. https://op.europa.eu/en/publication-detail/-/publication/54a1e679-f634-11ea-991b-01aa75ed71a1

FSC. 2019. "FSC Annual Report 2018 – English". Forest Stewardship Council. https://annual-reports.fsc.org/en

———. 2020. "Public Certificate Search". Forest Stewardship Council. https://info.fsc.org/certificate.php (accessed 3 June 2020).

Fujiwara, E. 2017. "First Come, First Served? The Partial Devolution of Forest Management Promotes Rights Competition—From the Application Process for Hutan Desa, East Kalimantan, Indonesia". *International Forestry Review* 19, no. 4: 423–36. https://doi.org/10.1505/146554817822272312

Funakawa, S. 2017. "Comparison of Nutrient Utilization Strategies of Traditional Shifting Agriculture under Different Climatic and Soil Conditions in Zambia, Thailand, Indonesia, and Cameroon: Examples of Temporal Redistribution of Ecosystem Resources". In *Soils, Ecosystem Processes, and Agricultural Development: Tropical Asia and Sub-Saharan Africa*, pp. 275–92. Springer Japan.

Furchtgott-Roth, D. 2012. "The Elusive and Expensive Green Job". *Energy Economics* 34: S43–S52. https://doi.org/10.1016/j.eneco.2012.08.034

Galante, M.V., M. Dutschke, G. Patenaude, and B. Vickers. 2012. "Climate Change Mitigation Through Reduced-Impact Logging and the Hierarchy of Production Forest Management". *Forests* 3, no. 1: 59–74. https://doi.org/10.3390/f3010059

Gallagher, J.B., and C.H. Chuan. 2018. "Chlorophyll *a* and Turbidity Distributions: Applicability of Using a Smartphone 'App' Across Two Contrasting Bays". *Journal of Coastal Research* 34, no. 5: 1236–43. https://doi.org/10.2112/JCOASTRES-D-16-00221.1

Gallemore, C. 2017. "Transaction Costs in the Evolution of Transnational Polycentric Governance". *International Environmental Agreements: Politics, Law and Economics* 17, no. 5: 639–54. https://doi.org/10.1007/s10784-016-9335-8

Gallemore, C.T., H. Rut Dini Prasti, and M. Moeliono. 2014. "Discursive Barriers and Cross-Scale Forest Governance in Central Kalimantan, Indonesia". *Ecology and Society* 19, no. 2. https://doi.org/10.5751/ES-06418-190218

Galudra, G., M. Van Noordwijk, S. Suyanto, I. Sardi, U. Pradhan, and D. Catacutan. 2011. "Hot Spots of Confusion: Contested Policies and Competing Carbon Claims in the Peatlands of Central Kalimantan, Indonesia". *International Forestry Review* 13, no. 4: 431–41. https://doi.org/10.1505/146554811798811380

GAR. 2020. *Annual Report 2019*. Singapore: Golden Agri-Resources Ltd.

Garcia-Nunez, J.A., N.E. Ramirez-Contreras, D.T. Rodriguez, E. Silva-Lora, C.S. Frear, C. Stockle, and M. Garcia-Perez. 2016. "Evolution of Palm Oil Mills into Bio-Refineries: Literature Review on Current and Potential Uses of Residual Biomass and Effluents". *Resources, Conservation and Recycling* 110: 99–114. https://doi.org/10.1016/j.resconrec.2016.03.022

Garnett, T., M.C. Appleby, A. Balmford, I.J. Bateman, T.G. Benton, P. Bloomer, B. Burlingame, M. Dawkins, L. Dolan, and D. Fraser. 2013. "Sustainable Intensification in Agriculture: Premises and Policies". *Science* 341, no. 6141: 33–34.

Gaveau, D., A. Salim, Husnayaen, and R.A. Alam. 2021. "Nusantara Atlas". https://nusantara-atlas.org/#en (accessed 7 May 2021).

Gaveau, D.L.A., M. Kshatriya, D. Sheil, S. Sloan, E. Molidena, A. Wijaya, S. Wich, M. Ancrenaz, M. Hansen, M. Broich, M.R. Guariguata, P. Pacheco, P. Potapov, S. Turubanova, and E. Meijaard. 2013. "Reconciling Forest Conservation and Logging in Indonesian Borneo". *PLoS ONE* 8, no. 8. https://doi.org/10.1371/journal.pone.0069887

———, B. Locatelli, M.A. Salim, H. Yaen, P. Pacheco, and D. Sheil. 2018. "Rise and Fall of Forest Loss and Industrial Plantations in Borneo (2000–2017)". *Conservation Letters*. https://doi.org/10.1111/conl.12622

Gaworecki, M. 2015a. "Opponents of Malaysian Dam Project Cautiously Optimistic about Moratorium". *Mongabay*, 23 September 2015a. https://news.mongabay.com/2015/09/opponents-of-malaysian-dam-project-cautiously-optimistic-about-moratorium/

———. 2015b. "Sarawak Can Meet Energy Needs Without Mega-Dams: Report". *Mongabay*, 8 July 2015b. https://news.mongabay.com/2015/07/sarawak-can-meet-energy-needs-without-mega-dams-report/

GEM. 2021. "Global Coal Mine Tracker (GCMT)". Global Energy Monitor (GEM).

GFED. 2020. "Global Fire Emissions Database". https://globalfiredata.org/ (accessed 7 December 2020).

Gibbs, H.K., and J.M. Salmon. 2015. "Mapping the World's Degraded Lands". *Applied Geography* 57: 12–21. https://doi.org/10.1016/j.apgeog.2014.11.024

Giesen, W., and E. Nirmala. 2018. "Tropical Peatland Restoration Report: The Indonesian Case". Berbak Green Prosperity Partnership, MCA-Indonesia, Jakarta.

Gillespie, P. 2011. "How Does Legislation Affect Oil Palm Smallholders in the Sanggau District of Kalimantan, Indonesia?". *Australasian Journal of Natural Resources Law and Policy* 14, no. 1: 1–35.

———. 2016. "People, Participation, Power: The Upstream Complexity of Indonesian Oil Palm Plantations". In *The Oil Palm Complex: Smallholders, Agribusiness and the State in Indonesia and Malaysia*, edited by R. Cramb and J.F. McCarthy, pp. 301–26. Singapore: NUS Press.

Gingold, B., A. Rosenbarger, Y. Muliastra, F. Stolle, I.M. Sudana, M. Manessa, A. Murdimanto, S. Tiangga, C. Madusari, and P. Douard. 2012. "How to Identify Degraded Land for Sustainable Palm Oil in Indonesia". World Resources Institute and Sekala, USA, pp. 1–24.

GIZ. 2020. "Sustainable Use of Peatland and Haze Mitigation in ASEAN (SUPA)". *Deutsche Gesellschaft fürInternationaleZusammenarbeit* (GIZ) GmbH. https://www.giz.de/en/worldwide/81673.html

Glasbergen, P. 2018. "Smallholders Do Not Eat Certificates". *Ecological Economics* 147: 243–52. https://doi.org/10.1016/j.ecolecon.2018.01.023

Glauber, A., S. Moyer, M. Adriani, and I. Gunawan. 2016. "The Cost of Fire: An Economic Analysis of Indonesia's 2015 Fire Crisis". World Bank, Washington, DC. http://documents.worldbank.org/curated/en/776101467990969768/The-cost-of-fire-an-economic-analysis-of-Indonesia-s-2015-fire-crisis

Glenday, S., and G. Paoli. 2015. "Overview of Indonesian Oil Palm Smallholder Farmers: A Typology of Organizational Models, Needs, and Investment Opportunities". Daemeter Consulting, Bogor, Indonesia.

Gnaniah, J., A.W. Yeo, H. Zen, P. Songan, and K.A. Hamid. 2005. "e-Bario and e-Bedian Project Implementation in Malaysia". In *Encyclopedia of Developing Regional Communities with Information and Communication Technology*, pp. 214–19. Hershey, PA: IGI Global.

Gnych, S.M., G. Limberg, and G. Paoli. 2015. *Risky Business: Uptake and Implementation of Sustainability Standards and Certification Schemes in the Indonesian Palm Oil Sector*. Bogor, Indonesia: CIFOR. https://www.cifor.org/library/5748/

Goh, C.S. 2016. "Can We Get Rid of Palm Oil?". *Trends in Biotechnology* 34, no. 12: 948–50. https://doi.org/10.1016/j.tibtech.2016.08.007

———, A. Ahl, and W.T. Woo. 2020. "Sustainable Transformation of Land-Based Economic Development in the Era of Digital Revolution". *Trends in Biotechnology.* https://doi.org/10.1016/j.tibtech.2020.05.010

———, T. Aikawa, A. Ahl, K. Ito, C. Kayo, Y. Kikuchi, Y. Takahashi, T. Furubayashi, T. Nakata, Y. Kanematsu, O. Saito, and Y. Yamagata. 2020. "Rethinking Sustainable Bioenergy Development in Japan: Decentralised System Supported by Local Forestry Biomass". *Sustainability Science* 15: 1461–71. https://doi.org/10.1007/s11625-019-00734-4

———, M. Junginger, and A. Faaij. 2014. "Monitoring Sustainable Biomass Flows: General Methodology Development". *Biofuels, Bioproducts and Biorefining* 8, no. 1: 83–102. https://doi.org/10.1002/bbb.1445

———, M. Junginger, L. Potter, A. Faaij, and B. Wicke. 2018. "Identifying Key Factors for Mobilising Under-Utilised Low Carbon Land Resources: A Case Study on Kalimantan". *Land Use Policy* 70: 198–211. https://doi.org/10.1016/j.landusepol.2017.10.016

———, and K.T. Lee. 2010. "Will Biofuel Projects in Southeast Asia Become White Elephants?". *Energy Policy* 38, no. 8: 3847–48. https://doi.org/10.1016/j.enpol.2010.04.009

———, K.T. Tan, K.T. Lee, and S. Bhatia. 2010. "Bio-ethanol from Lignocellulose: Status, Perspectives and Challenges in Malaysia". *Bioresource Technology* 101, no. 13: 4834–41. https://doi.org/10.1016/j.biortech.2009.08.080

———, B. Wicke, A. Faaij, D. N. Bird, H. Schwaiger, and M. Junginger. 2016. "Linking Carbon Stock Change from Land-Use Change to Consumption of Agricultural Products: Alternative Perspectives". *J Environ Manage* 182: 542–56. https://doi.org/10.1016/j.jenvman.2016.08.004

———, B. Wicke, L. Potter, A. Faaij, A. Zoomers, and M. Junginger. 2017. "Exploring Under-Utilised Low Carbon Land Resources from Multiple Perspectives: Case Studies on Regencies in Kalimantan". *Land Use Policy* 60: 150–68. https://doi.org/10.1016/j.landusepol.2016.10.033

———, B. Wicke, J. Verstegen, A. Faaij, and M. Junginger. 2016. "Linking Carbon Stock Change from Land-Use Change to Consumption of Agricultural Products: A Review with Indonesian Palm Oil as a Case Study". *J Environ Manage* 184 (Pt 2): 340–52. https://doi.org/10.1016/j.jenvman.2016.08.055

Goh, H. C. 2021. "Strategies for Post-COVID-19 Prospects of Sabah's Tourist Market: Reactions to Shocks Caused by Pandemic or Reflection for Sustainable Tourism?". *Research in Globalization* 3: 100056. https://doi.org/10.1016/j.resglo.2021.100056

———, and Z. Rosilawati. 2014. "Conservation Education in Kinabalu Park, Malaysia: Analysis of Visitors' Satisfaction". *Journal of Tropical Forest Science* 26, no. 2: 208–17.

Gokkon, B. 2019. "In Borneo, Dwindling Forests Face Further Fragmentation, as Roads Spread". *Mongabay*, 22 January 2019. https://news.mongabay.com/2019/01/in-borneo-dwindling-forests-face-further-fragmentation-as-roads-spread/

Gómez-Baggethun, E., R. De Groot, P.L. Lomas, and C. Montes. 2010. "The History of Ecosystem Services in Economic Theory and Practice: From Early Notions to Markets and Payment Schemes". *Ecological Economics* 69, no. 6: 1209–18.

Gomez, L., and C.R. Shepherd. 2019. "Bearly on the Radar: An Analysis of Seizures of Bears in Indonesia". *European Journal of Wildlife Research* 65, no. 6. https://doi.org/10.1007/s10344-019-1323-1

Gönner, C. 2011. "Surfing on Waves of Opportunities: Resource Use Dynamics in a Dayak Benuaq Community in East Kalimantan, Indonesia". *Society and Natural Resources* 24, no. 2: 165–73. https://doi.org/10.1080/08941920902724990

Govindarajo, N.S., M. Dileep Kumar, and S.S. Ramulu. 2014. "Why Workers Disengage? Factors from 'Head' or 'Heart' to Be Tagged on?". *Asian Social Science* 10, no. 17: 108–19. https://doi.org/10.5539/ass.v10n17p108

Gray, C.L., and O.T. Lewis. 2014. "Do Riparian Forest Fragments Provide Ecosystem Services or Disservices in Surrounding Oil Palm Plantations?". *Basic and Applied Ecology* 15, no. 8: 693–700. https://doi.org/10.1016/j.baae.2014.09.009

——, E.M. Slade, D.J. Mann, and O.T. Lewis. 2014. "Do Riparian Reserves Support Dung Beetle Biodiversity and Ecosystem Services in Oil Palm-Dominated Tropical Landscapes?". *Ecology and Evolution* 4, no. 7: 1049–60. https://doi.org/10.1002/ece3.1003

Greenpeace. 2019. "Documentation of Forest Fires Investigation in PT GAL Concession (Genting), Central Kalimantan 2019 – Photos & Video (GP0STTW0X)". Greenpeace.

——. 2020. "Burning Issues: Five Years of Fires". Greenpeace Southeast Asia-Indonesia. https://www.greenpeace.org/southeastasia/publication/44140/burning-issues-five-years-of-fire/

——. 2021. "Restoration Up in Smoke: Losing the Battle to Protect Peatlands". https://www.greenpeace.org/southeastasia/publication/44387/restoration-up-in-smoke-losing-the-battle-to-protect-peatlands (accessed 28 October 2021).

Grignard, L., S. Shah, T.H. Chua, T. William, C.J. Drakeley, and K.M. Fornace. 2019. "Natural Human Infections With Plasmodium cynomolgi and Other Malaria Species in an Elimination Setting in Sabah, Malaysia". *Journal of Infectious Diseases* 220, no. 12: 1946–49. https://doi.org/10.1093/infdis/jiz397

Griscom, B.W., P.W. Ellis, Z. Burivalova, J. Halperin, D. Marthinus, R.K. Runting, Ruslandi, D. Shoch, and F.E. Putz. 2019. "Reduced-Impact Logging in Borneo to Minimize Carbon Emissions and Impacts on Sensitive Habitats While Maintaining Timber Yields". *Forest Ecology and Management* 438: 176–85. https://doi.org/10.1016/j.foreco.2019.02.025

Grobelak, A., P. Kokot, D. Hutchison, A. Grosser, and M. Kacprzak. 2018. "Plant Growth-Promoting Rhizobacteria as an Alternative to Mineral Fertilizers in Assisted Bioremediation: Sustainable Land and Waste Management". *Journal of Environmental Management* 227: 1–9. https://doi.org/10.1016/j.jenvman.2018.08.075

Großmann, K. 2018. "Conflicting Ecologies in a 'Failed' Gaharu Nursery Programme in Central Kalimantan". *Sojourn* 33, no. 2: 319–40. https://doi.org/10.1355/sj33-2d

——. 2019. "'Dayak, Wake Up': Land, Indigeneity, and Conflicting Ecologies in Central Kalimantan, Indonesia". *Bijdragen tot de Taal-, Land- en Volkenkunde* 175, no. 1: 1–28. https://doi.org/10.1163/22134379-17501021

Guerry, A.D., S. Polasky, J. Lubchenco, R. Chaplin-Kramer, G.C. Daily, R. Griffin, M. Ruckelshaus, I.J. Bateman, A. Duraiappah, T. Elmqvist, M.W. Feldman, C. Folke, J. Hoekstra, P.M. Kareiva, B.L. Keeler, S. Li, E. McKenzie, Z. Ouyang, B. Reyers, T.H. Ricketts, J. Rockstrom, H. Tallis, and B. Vira. 2015. "Natural Capital and Ecosystem Services Informing Decisions: From Promise to Practice". *Proc Natl Acad Sci U S A* 112, no. 24: 7348–55. https://doi.org/10.1073/pnas.1503751112

Guèze, M., and L. Napitupulu. 2016. "Trailing Forest Uses Among the Punan Tubu of North Kalimantan, Indonesia". In *Hunter-Gatherers in a Changing World*, pp. 41–58. Springer International Publishing.

Gunarso, P., M.E. Hartoyo, F. Agus, and T.J. Killeen. 2013. "Oil Palm and Land Use Change in Indonesia, Malaysia and Papua New Guinea". Reports from the Technical Panels of the 2nd Greenhouse Gas Working Group of the Roundtable on Sustainable Palm Oil (RSPO).

Gunton, R.M., E.N. van Asperen, A. Basden, D. Bookless, Y. Araya, D.R. Hanson, M.A. Goddard, G. Otieno, and G.O. Jones. 2017. "Beyond Ecosystem Services: Valuing the Invaluable". *Trends in Ecology & Evolution* 32, no. 4: 249–57.

Guo, Z., E. Ngai, C. Yang, and X. Liang. 2015. "An RFID-Based Intelligent Decision Support System Architecture for Production Monitoring and Scheduling in a Distributed Manufacturing Environment". *International Journal of Production Economics* 159: 16–28.

Haddock-Fraser, J., and M.P. Hampton. 2012. "Multistakeholder Values on the Sustainability of Dive Tourism: Case Studies of Sipadan and Perhentian Islands, Malaysia". *Tourism Analysis* 17, no. 1: 27–41.

Hadian, O., I. Wedastra, T. Barano, A. Dixon, I. Peterson, and M. Lange. 2014. "Promoting Sustainable Land Use Planning in Sumatra and Kalimantan, Indonesia". WWF Indonesia. https://globallandusechange.org/en/projects/sulu/results-reports/

Hadin, A.F., and E.N. Oemar. 2020. "Problematika Tata Kelola Sumber Daya Alam dan Tantangan Penegakan Hukum Sektor Sumber Daya Alam di Kalimantan Selatan. Auriga Nusantara (Jakarta)". https://auriga.or.id/resource/reference/ahmad-fikri-2020-problematika-tata-kelola-sumber-daya-alam-dan-tantangan-penegakan-hukum-sektor-sumber-daya-alam-di-kalimantan-selatan.pdf

Haeruddin, H. Johan, U. Hairah, and E. Budiman. 2017. "Ethnobotany Database: Exploring Diversity Medicinal Plants of Dayak Tribe Borneo". *Proceeding of the Electrical Engineering Computer Science and Informatics* 4, no. 1.

Haigh, M. 2020. "Cultural Tourism Policy in Developing Regions: The Case of Sarawak, Malaysia". *Tourism Management* 81: 104166. https://doi.org/10.1016/j.tourman.2020.104166

Hairiah, K., M. van Noordwijk, R.R. Sari, D.D. Saputra, Widianto, D. Suprayogo, S. Kurniawan, C. Prayogo, and S. Gusli. 2020. "Soil Carbon Stocks in Indonesian (Agro) Forest Transitions: Compaction Conceals Lower Carbon Concentrations in Standard Accounting". *Agriculture, Ecosystems and Environment* 294. https:// doi.org/10.1016/j.agee.2020.106879

Halik, M., and P. Webley. 2011. "Adolescents' Understanding of Poverty and the Poor in Rural Malaysia". *Journal of Economic Psychology* 32, no. 2: 231–39. https://doi. org/10.1016/j.joep.2009.02.006

Halim, M.A., N.M. Saraf, N.I. Hashim, A.R.A. Rasam, A.N. Idris, and N.M. Saad. 2019. "Discovering New Tourist Attractions Through Social Media Data: A Case Study in Sabah Malaysia". IEEE 8th International Conference on System Engineering and Technology.

Hamdi, E., and P. Adhiguna. 2021. "Putting PLN's Net Zero Ambition into Context: The Numbers Will Need to Add Up". Institute for Energy Economics and Financial Analysis (IEEFA).

Hamzah, A., and N.H. Mohamad. 2012. "Critical Success Factors of Community Based Ecotourism: Case Study of Miso Walaihomestay, Kinabatangan, Sabah". *Malaysian Forester* 75, no. 1: 29–42.

Hamzah, N.W.H., S.A.H. Jalil, and W.S.H. Suhaili. 2018. "Towards Developing a Peatland Fire Prevention System for Brunei Darussalam". International Conference on Computational Intelligence in Information System.

Han, X., M.J. Gill, H. Hamilton, S.G. Vergara, and B.E. Young. 2020. "Progress on National Biodiversity Indicator Reporting and Prospects for Filling Indicator Gaps in Southeast Asia". *Environmental and Sustainability Indicators* 5: 100017. https:// doi.org/10.1016/j.indic.2019.100017

Hanafi, M., and A. Raj. 2011. "Socio-economic and Feasibility Study of Utilising Palm Oil Derived Biofuel in Malaysia". *Oil Palm Industry Economic Journal* 11, no. 1: 23–27.

Hance, J. 2020. "Conservationists Replant Legal Palm Oil Plantation with Forest in Borneo". *Mongabay*, 9 November 2020. Mongabay Series: Saving Life on Earth: Words on the Wild. https://news.mongabay.com/2020/11/conservationists-replant-legal-palm-oil-plantation-with-forest-in-borneo/?utm_source=Mongabay+Newsletter&utm_campaign=95035e3ba8-Newsletter_2020_04_30_COPY_01&utm_medium=email&utm_term=0_940652e1f4-95035e3ba8-77238222&mc_cid=95035e3ba8&mc_eid=0f84ac1bd4

Handayani, R. 2019. "The Potential Herbs of Medicinal Forests from Central Kalimantan as a Inhibitor of Staphylococcus aureus". *Pharmacognosy Journal* 11, no. 4: 740–44. https://doi.org/10.5530/pj.2019.11.117

Hao, Y., C. Tian, and C. Wu. 2020. "Modelling of Carbon Price in Two Real Carbon Trading Markets". *Journal of Cleaner Production* 244: 118556. https://doi. org/10.1016/j.jclepro.2019.118556

Harahap, F., S. Leduc, S. Mesfun, D. Khatiwada, F. Kraxner, and S. Silveira. 2020. "Meeting the Bioenergy Targets from Palm Oil Based Biorefineries: An Optimal Configuration in Indonesia". *Applied Energy* 278: 115749. https://doi.org/10.1016/j. apenergy.2020.115749

Hardi, W., N. Herbasuki, and R.K. Thalita. 2018. "Social Movement at Indonesia–Malaysia

Border (A Case Study of Indonesian Migrant Workers' Education in Sebatik Island, a Land Border of Indonesia–Malaysia)". *E3S Web of Conferences* 73: 11013.

Harding, A. 2018. "'A Measure of Autonomy': Federalism as Protection for Malaysia's Indigenous Peoples". *Federal Law Review* 46, no. 4: 557–74. https://doi. org/10.1177/0067205x1804600405

Haridison, A., A. Sandi, and J. Retei. 2019. "The Patterns of Collaborative Governance in Dayak Land, Central Borneo, Indonesia". 28 August 2019.

Harrington, M. 2015. "'Hanging by Rubber': How Cash Threatens the Agricultural Systems of the Siang Dayak". *Asia Pacific Journal of Anthropology* 16, no. 5: 481–95.

Harris, R., N.A.N.K. Ramaiyer, and J. Tarawe. 2018. "The eBario Story: ICTs for Rural Development". 2018 International Conference on ICT for Rural Development (IC-ICTRuDev), 17–18 October 2018.

Harris, R.W. 2009. "Tourism in Bario, Sarawak, Malaysia: A Case Study of Pro-Poor Community-Based Tourism Integrated into Community Development". *Asia Pacific Journal of Tourism Research* 14, no. 2: 125–35.

Harrison, M.E., and G.D. Paoli. 2012. "Managing the Risk of Biodiversity Leakage from Prioritising REDD+ in the Most Carbon-Rich Forests: The Case Study of Peat-Swamp Forests in Kalimantan, Indonesia". *Tropical Conservation Science* 5, no. 4: 426–33. https://doi.org/10.1177/194008291200500402

Harsono, N. 2020. "Coal Miner Bukit Asam Eyes Tuhup Mine Amid Corruption Scandal". *Jakarta Post*, 17 July 2020. https://www.thejakartapost.com/news/2020/07/17/coal-miner-bukit-asam-eyes-tuhup-mine-amid-corruption-scandal.html

———. 2021. "ADB, PLN Consider Plan to Retire Indonesian Coal Plants Early". *Jakarta Post,* 24 August 2021. https://www.thejakartapost.com/news/2021/08/24/adb-pln-consider-plan-to-retire-indonesian-coal-plants-early.html

Harsono, S.S., A. Prochnow, P. Grundmann, A. Hansen, and C. Hallmann. 2012. "Energy Balances and Greenhouse Gas Emissions of Palm Oil Biodiesel in Indonesia". *GCB Bioenergy* 4, no. 2: 213–28. https://doi.org/10.1111/j.1757-1707.2011.01118.x

Harun, S., A. Baker, C. Bradley, and G. Pinay. 2016. "Spatial and Seasonal Variations in the Composition of Dissolved Organic Matter in a Tropical Catchment: The Lower Kinabatangan River, Sabah, Malaysia". *Environmental Sciences: Processes and Impacts* 18, no. 1: 137–50. https://doi.org/10.1039/c5em00462d

Hashim, A.H., A.K. Khairuddin, and J.B. Ibrahim. 2015. "Integration of Renewable Energy into Grid System: The Sabah Green Grid". 2015 IEEE Eindhoven PowerTech, 29 June – 2 July 2015.

Hashim, S.M. 1998. *Income Inequality and Poverty in Malaysia*. Lanham, MD: Rowman & Littlefield.

Hassan, Z.H., S. Lesmayati, R. Qomariah, and A. Hasbianto. 2013. "Effective Postharvest Management of Tangerine Citrus (Citrus Reticulata 'Siam Banjar') to Reduce Losses, Maintain Quality, and Protect Safety". *Acta Horticulturae: International Society for Horticultural Science.*

Hata, S., and M.H. Wahab. 2018. "Malaysia: Longhouse of Sarawak". In *Sustainable Houses and Living in the Hot-Humid Climates of Asia*, pp. 37–45. Singapore: Springer.

Hattori, D., T. Kenzo, T. Shirahama, Y. Harada, J.J. Kendawang, I. Ninomiya, and K. Sakurai. 2019. "Degradation of soil nutrients and slow recovery of biomass following shifting cultivation in the heath forests of Sarawak, Malaysia". Forest Ecology and Management 432: 467–77. https://doi.org/10.1016/j.foreco.2018. 09.051.

Haug, M. 2014. "Resistance, Ritual Purification and Mediation: Tracing a Dayak Community's Sixteen-Year Search for Justice in East Kalimantan". Asia Pacific Journal of Anthropology 15, no. 4: 357–75. https://doi.org/10.1080/14442213.20 14.927522

———. 2018a. "Claiming Rights to the Forest in East Kalimantan: Challenging Power and Presenting Culture". Sojourn 33, no. 2: 341–61. https://doi.org/10.1355/ sj33-2e

———. 2018b. "A Future Without Forests? Indigenous Perspectives on Environmental Change, Deforestation and Development in Kalimantan, Indonesia". Geographische Rundschau 70, no. 4: 32–38.

Hazard, L., P. Steyaert, G. Martin, N. Couix, M.-L. Navas, M. Duru, A. Lauvie, and J. Labatut. 2018. "Mutual Learning Between Researchers and Farmers During Implementation of Scientific Principles for Sustainable Development: The Case of Biodiversity-Based Agriculture". Sustainability Science 13, no. 2: 517–30. https:// doi.org/10.1007/s11625-017-0440-6

Heidhues, M.F.S. 2003. Golddiggers, Farmers, and Traders in the "Chinese Districts" of West Kalimantan, Indonesia. Ithaca: Southeast Asia Program Publications, Cornell University.

Hein, L., and P.J. van der Meer. 2012. "REDD+ in the Context of Ecosystem Management". Current Opinion in Environmental Sustainability 4, no. 6: 604–11. https://doi. org/10.1016/j.cosust.2012.09.016.

Herawati, H., and H. Santoso. 2011. "Tropical Forest Susceptibility to and Risk of Fire Under Changing Climate: A Review of Fire Nature, Policy and Institutions in Indonesia". Forest Policy and Economics 13, no. 4: 227–33. https://doi.org/10.1016/j. forpol.2011.02.006

———, S. Suripin, S. Suharyanto, and T. Hetwisari. 2018. "Analysis of River Flow Regime Changes Related to Water Availability on the Kapuas River, Indonesia". Irrigation and Drainage 67: 66–71. https://doi.org/10.1002/ird.2103

Heredia, I. 2017. "Large-Scale Plant Classification with Deep Neural Networks". Proceedings of the Computing Frontiers Conference.

Hew, C.S. 2011. "Coping with Change: Rural Transformation and Women in Contemporary Sarawak, Malaysia". Critical Asian Studies 43, no. 4: 595–616. https:// doi.org/10.1080/14672715.2011.623524

Hidayat, N.K., A. Offermans, and P. Glasbergen. 2018. "Sustainable Palm Oil as a Public Responsibility? On the Governance Capacity of Indonesian Standard for Sustainable Palm Oil (ISPO)". Agriculture and Human Values 35, no. 1: 223–42.

Hideki, H. 2018. "The Replanting Problems of Plasma Estates in the Indonesian State-Owned Oil Palm Estate: A Case in Sanggau Regency, West Kalimantan

Province". *Japanese Journal of Southeast Asian Studies* 55, no. 2: 292–319. https://doi.org/10.20495/tak.55.2_292

Hiratsuka, M., E. Nakama, T. Satriadi, H. Fauzi, M. Aryadi, and Y. Morikawa. 2019. "An Approach to Achieve Sustainable Development Goals Through Participatory Land and Forest Conservation: A Case Study in South Kalimantan Province, Indonesia". *Journal of Sustainable Forestry* 38, no. 6: 558–71. https://doi.org/10.1080/10549811.2019.1598440

Hirbli, T. 2018. "Palm Oil Traceability: Blockchain Meets Supply Chain". Master of Engineering in Supply Chain Management, Massachusetts Institute of Technology.

Hisano, S., M. Akitsu, and S.R. McGreevy. 2018. "Revitalising Rurality under the Neoliberal Transformation of Agriculture: Experiences of Re-agrarianisation in Japan". *Journal of Rural Studies* 61: 290–301.

Hitchner, S.L., F.L. Apu, L. Tarawe, S. Galih@Sinah Nabun Aran, and E. Yesaya. 2009. "Community-Based Transboundary Ecotourism in the Heart of Borneo: A Case Study of the Kelabit Highlands of Malaysia and the Kerayan Highlands of Indonesia". *Journal of Ecotourism* 8, no. 2: 193–213. https://doi.org/10.1080/14724040802696064

Ho, S.Y., M.E.B. Wasli, and M. Perumal. 2019. "Evaluation of Physicochemical Properties of Sandy-Textured Soils under Smallholder Agricultural Land Use Practices in Sarawak, East Malaysia". *Applied and Environmental Soil Science* 2019: 1–14. https://doi.org/10.1155/2019/7685451

Hoffmann, M.P., C.R. Donough, S.E. Cook, M.J. Fisher, C.H. Lim, Y.L. Lim, J. Cock, S.P. Kam, S.N. Mohanaraj, K. Indrasuara, P. Tittinutchanon, and T. Oberthür. 2017. "Yield Gap Analysis in Oil Palm: Framework Development and Application in Commercial Operations in Southeast Asia". *Agricultural Systems* 151: 12–19. https://doi.org/10.1016/j.agsy.2016.11.005

Hooijer, A., R. Vernimmen, M. Visser, and N. Mawdsley. 2015. "Flooding Projections from Elevation and Subsidence Models for Oil Palm Plantations in the Rajang Delta peatlands, Sarawak, Malaysia". *Deltares Report* 1207384: 76.

Horn, C., P. Philip, and C.L. Sabang. 2018. "Getting Connected: Indigeneity, Information, and Communications Technology Use and Emerging Media Practices in Sarawak". *Verge: Studies in Global Asias* 4, no. 2: 163–93.

———, E. Rennie, S. Gifford, R.M. Riman, and G.L.H. Wee. 2018. "Digital Inclusion and Mobile Media in Remote Sarawak". Swinburne University of Technology, Melbourne, Australia.

Horton, A.J., E.D. Lazarus, T.C. Hales, J.A. Constantine, M.W. Bruford, and B. Goossens. 2018. "Can Riparian Forest Buffers Increase Yields from Oil Palm Plantations?". *Earth's Future* 6, no. 8: 1082–96. https://doi.org/10.1029/2018EF000874

Hovani, L., T. Varns, H. Hartanto, S. Rahman, N. Makinuddin, and R. Cortez. 2018. "Jurisdictional Approaches to Sustainable Landscapes: Berau and East Kalimantan, Indonesia". *The Nature Conservancy* (Arlington, VA).

How, V., and K. Othman. 2017. "A Snapshot of Environmental Health Conditions Among Indigenous Baram Communities at Borneo, Sarawak". *Annals of Tropical Medicine and Public Health* 10, no. 1. https://doi.org/10.4103/atmph.Atmph_80_17

Howe, B.M., and N. Kamaruddin. 2016. "Good Governance and Human Security in Malaysia: Sarawak's Hydroelectric Conundrum". *Contemporary Southeast Asia* 38, no. 1: 81–105. https://doi.org/10.1355/cs38-1d

Howson, P. 2018a. "Can Cryptocurrencies Save Indonesia's Carbon Forests? (Commentary)". *Mongabay*, 4 June 2018a. https://news.mongabay.com/2018/06/can-cryptocurrencies-save-indonesias-carbon-forests-commentary/

———. 2018b. "Slippery Violence in the REDD+ Forests of Central Kalimantan, Indonesia". *Conservation and Society* 16, no. 2: 136–46. https://doi.org/10.4103/cs.cs_16_150

———. 2020. "Climate Crises and Crypto-Colonialism: Conjuring Value on the Blockchain Frontiers of the Global South". *Frontiers in Blockchain* 3. https://doi.org/10.3389/fbloc.2020.00022

———, and S. Kindon. 2015. "Analysing Access to the Local REDD+ Benefits of Sungai Lamandau, Central Kalimantan, Indonesia". *Asia Pacific Viewpoint* 56, no. 1: 96–110. https://doi.org/10.1111/apv.12089

Hughes, A.C. 2018. "Have Indo-Malaysian Forests Reached the End of the Road?". *Biological Conservation* 223: 129–37. https://doi.org/10.1016/j.biocon.2018.04.029

Human Rights Watch. 2020. "Indonesia: New Law Hurts Workers, Indigenous Groups". https://www.hrw.org/news/2020/10/15/indonesia-new-law-hurts-workers-indigenous-groups (accessed 16 November 2021).

Hunt, C.O., D.D. Gilbertson, and G. Rushworth. 2012. "A 50,000-Year Record of Late Pleistocene Tropical Vegetation and Human Impact in Lowland Borneo". *Quaternary Science Reviews* 37: 61–80. https://doi.org/10.1016/j.quascirev.2012.01.014

Husnina, Z., A.C.A. Clements, and K. Wangdi. 2019. "Forest Cover and Climate as Potential Drivers for Dengue Fever in Sumatra and Kalimantan 2006–2016: A Spatiotemporal Analysis". *Tropical Medicine and International Health* 24, no. 7: 888–98. https://doi.org/10.1111/tmi.13248

Ibnu, M., A. Offermans, and P. Glasbergen. 2018. "Certification and Farmer Organisation: Indonesian Smallholder Perceptions of Benefits". *Bulletin of Indonesian Economic Studies* 54, no. 3: 387–415.

Idris, A., and S. Mohamad. 2014. "The continuing Dominance of Barisan Nasional in Sabah in the 13th General Elections". *Kajian Malaysia* 32: 171–206.

Idris, M. 2021. "Daftar 5 Perusahaan Besar Tambang Batu Bara di Kalsel". *Kompas.com*, 19 January 2021. https://money.kompas.com/read/2021/01/19/082241026/daftar-5-perusahaan-besar-tambang-batu-bara-di-kalsel?page=all

Idris, R., K. Mansur, and R.Z. Idris. 2019. *Studies on The Economy of Sabah and Kalimantan Towards Greater Economic Interaction in Borneo*. Bogor, Indonesia: IPB Press.

Imai, N., T. Seino, S. Aiba, M. Takyu, J. Titin, and K. Kitayama. 2012. "Effects of Selective Logging on Tree Species Diversity and Composition of Bornean Tropical Rain Forests at Different Spatial Scales". *Plant Ecology* 213, no. 9: 1413–24. https://doi.org/10.1007/s11258-012-0100-y

Iman Sapari. 2018. "Response from Iman Sapari, Yayorin, to 'Slippery Violence' Paper

about Sungai Lamandau REDD+ Project, Indonesia". *REDD-monitor.org*. https://
redd-monitor.org/2018/06/05/response-from-iman-sapari-yayorin-to-slippery-
violence-paper-about-sungai-lamandau-redd-project-indonesia/ (accessed 6 April
2020).

IndexMundi. 2021. "Commodity Prices".

Indra, S. Nazara, D. Hartono, and S. Sumarto. 2019. "Roles of Income Polarization,
Income Inequality and Ethnic Fractionalization in Social Conflicts: An Empirical
Study of Indonesian Provinces, 2002–2012". *Asian Economic Journal* 33, no. 2:
165–90. https://doi.org/10.1111/asej.12179

Indrajaya, Y., E. van der Werf, H.-P. Weikard, F. Mohren, and E.C. van Ierland. 2016.
"The Potential of REDD+ for Carbon Sequestration in Tropical Forests: Supply
Curves for Carbon Storage for Kalimantan, Indonesia". *Forest Policy and Economics*
71: 1–10. https://doi.org/10.1016/j.forpol.2016.06.032

Indriatmoko, Y., S. Atmadja, A. Ekaputri, and M. Komalasari. 2014. "Rimba Raya
Biodiversity Reserve Project, Central Kalimantan, Indonesia". In *REDD+ on
the Ground: A Case Book of Subnational Initiatives Across the Globe*, edited by
E.O. Sills, S.S. Atmadja, C. de Sassi, A.E. Duchelle, D.L. Kweka, I.A.P. Resosudarmo,
and W.D. Sunderlin. Bogor, Indonesia: CIFOR.

Indriatmoko, Y., S. Atmadja, N. A. Utomo, A.D. Ekaputri, and M. Komalasari. 2014.
"Katingan Peatland Restoration and Conservation Project, Central Kalimantan,
Indonesia". In *REDD+ on the Ground: A Case Book of Subnational Initiatives Across
the Globe*, edited by E.O. Sills, S.S. Atmadja, C. de Sassi, A.E. Duchelle, D.L. Kweka,
I.A.P. Resosudarmo, and W.D. Sunderlin. Bogor, Indonesia: CIFOR.

Inoue, M., M. Kawai, N. Imang, D. Terauchi, F. Pambudhi, and M.A. Sardjono. 2013.
"Implications of Local Peoples' Preferences in Terms of Income Source and Land
Use for Indonesia's National REDD-Plus Policy: Evidence in East Kalimantan,
Indonesia". *International Journal of Environment and Sustainable Development* 12,
no. 3: 244–63. https://doi.org/10.1504/IJESD.2013.054951.

Intarini, D., I. Resosudarmo, M. Komalasari, A. Ekaputri, and M. Agustavia. 2014.
"Ketapang Community Carbon Pools, West Kalimantan, Indonesia". In *REDD+
on the Ground: A Case Book of Subnational Initiatives Across the Globe*, edited by
E.O. Sills, S.S. Atmadja, C. de Sassi, A.E. Duchelle, D.L. Kweka, I.A.P. Resosudarmo,
and W.D. Sunderlin. Bogor, Indonesia: CIFOR.

IOI Group. 2019. "IOI Group Annual Report 2019". https://www.ioigroup.com/Content/
IR/PDF/AR/2019_AR.pdf

Ioki, K., N.M. Din, R. Ludwig, D. James, S.W. Hue, S.A. Johari, R.A. Awang, R. Anthony,
and M.H. Phua. 2019. "Supporting Forest Conservation Through Community-Based
Land Use Planning and Participatory GIS: Lessons from Crocker Range Park,
Malaysian Borneo". *Journal for Nature Conservation* 52. https://doi.org/10.1016/j.
jnc.2019.125740

IPCC. 2019. "2019 Refinement to the 2006 IPCC Guidelines for National Greenhouse
Gas Inventories". https://www.ipcc.ch/report/2019-refinement-to-the-2006-ipcc-
guidelines-for-national-greenhouse-gas-inventories/

Irawan, A.W., A. Yusufianto, D. Agustina, and R. Dean. 2019. "Laporan Survei Internet APJII 2019-2020 (Q2)". Indonesia Survey Center.

Irawan, S., T. Widiastomo, L. Tacconi, J.D. Watts, and B. Steni. 2019. "Exploring the Design of Jurisdictional REDD+: The Case of Central Kalimantan, Indonesia". *Forest Policy and Economics* 108. https://doi.org/10.1016/j.forpol.2018.12.009

IRENA. 2020. "IRENA Statistics". IRENA.

———, and ACE. 2016. "Renewable Energy Outlook for ASEAN. International Renewable Energy Agency (IRENA) & ASEAN Centre for Energy (ACE)". https://www.irena.org/publications/2016/Oct/Renewable-Energy-Outlook-for-ASEAN

Ishak, A., R.D. Rusmadi, and B. Yusuf. 2013. "Visi Kaltim 2030: Pertumbuhan Kaltim Hijau yang Berkeadilan dan Berkelanjutan: Sebuah Pemikiran Kebijakan Transformasi Ekonomi Pasca Migas dan Batubara". Edited by Pemerintah Provinsi Kalimantan Timur.

Ishikawa, N., and R. Soda. 2019. *Anthropogenic Tropical Forests: Human–Nature Interfaces on the Plantation Frontier.* Springer Nature.

Islam, S. N., S.M.B.H. Mohamad, and A.K. Azad. 2019. "Acacia spp.: Invasive Trees along the Brunei Coast, Borneo". In *Coastal Research Library.* Springer.

Ismail, A., and C.J. Nazirah. 2015. "The Effects of Establishing Sustainable Oil Palm Growers' Cooperatives on the Incomes of Oil Palm Smallholders". *Oil Palm Industry Economic Journal* 15: 1–7.

Izadyar, N., H.C. Ong, W.T. Chong, J.C. Mojumder, and K.Y. Leong. 2016. "Investigation of Potential Hybrid Renewable Energy at Various Rural Areas in Malaysia". *Journal of Cleaner Production* 139: 61–73. https://doi.org/10.1016/j.jclepro.2016.07.167

Jaafar, M., S.M. Rasoolimanesh, and K.A.T. Lonik. 2015. "Tourism Growth and Entrepreneurship: Empirical Analysis of Development of Rural Highlands". *Tourism Management Perspectives* 14: 17–24. https://doi.org/10.1016/j.tmp.2015.02.001

Jagger, P., and P. Rana. 2017. "Using Publicly Available Social and Spatial Data to Evaluate Progress on REDD+ Social Safeguards in Indonesia". *Environmental Science and Policy* 76: 59–69. https://doi.org/10.1016/j.envsci.2017.06.006

Jakarta Globe. 2020. "Indonesia Accelerates Digital Transformation to Meet Pandemic Demand". 6 May 2020. https://jakartaglobe.id/news/indonesia-accelerates-digital-transformation-to-meet-pandemic-demand/

Jakarta Post. 2018. "PLN Operates First Biomass Power Plant". 25 April 2018. http://www.thejakartapost.com/news/2018/04/25/pln-operates-first-biomass-power-plant.html

Janssen, M., and U. Hamm. 2012. "Product Labelling in the Market for Organic Food: Consumer Preferences and Willingness-to-Pay for Different Organic Certification Logos". *Food Quality and Preference* 25, no. 1: 9–22.

Jarias, S. 2020. "Community Groups of Dayak Misik Struggle for Justice, Well-Being and Sustainable Forestry in Central Kalimantan". *International Journal of Management* 11, no. 3.

Jati, A.S., H. Samejima, S. Fujiki, Y. Kurniawan, R. Aoyagi, and K. Kitayama. 2018. "Effects of Logging on Wildlife Communities in Certified Tropical Rainforests in East Kalimantan, Indonesia". *Forest Ecology and Management* 427: 124–34. https://doi.org/10.1016/j.foreco.2018.05.054

Jaung, W., E. Wiraguna, B. Okarda, Y. Artati, C. Goh, R. Syahru, B. Leksono, L. Prasetyo, S. Lee, and H. Baral. 2018. "Spatial Assessment of Degraded Lands for Biofuel Production in Indonesia". *Sustainability* 10, no. 12. https://doi.org/10.3390/su10124595

Javed Muhammad, A., M.Z. Abdullah, N. Muhammad, and W. Ratnam. 2017. "Detecting Mislabelling and Identifying Unique Progeny in Acacia Mapping Population Using SNP Markers". *Journal of Forestry Research* 28, no. 6: 1119–27. https://doi.org/10.1007/s11676-017-0405-8

Jeffree, S.M., K. Ahmed, N. Safian, R. Hassan, O. Mihat, K.A. Lukman, S.B. Shamsudin, and F. Kamaludin. 2018. "Falciparum Malaria Outbreak in Sabah Linked to an Immigrant Rubber Tapper". *American Journal of Tropical Medicine and Hygiene* 98, no. 1: 45–50.

Jelsma, I., G.C. Schoneveld, A. Zoomers, and A.C.M. van Westen. 2017. "Unpacking Indonesia's Independent Oil Palm Smallholders: An Actor-Disaggregated Approach to Identifying Environmental and Social Performance Challenges". *Land Use Policy* 69: 281–97. https://doi.org/10.1016/j.landusepol.2017.08.012

———, L.S. Woittiez, J. Ollivier, and A.H. Dharmawan. 2019. "Do Wealthy Farmers Implement Better Agricultural Practices? An Assessment of Implementation of Good Agricultural Practices among Different Types of Independent Oil Palm Smallholders in Riau, Indonesia". *Agricultural Systems* 170: 63–76. https://doi.org/10.1016/j.agsy.2018.11.004

Jenkins, D. 1978. "The Dyaks: Goodbye to All That". *Far Eastern Economic Review*, 30 June 1978.

Jespersen, K., and C. Gallemore. 2018. "The Institutional Work of Payments for Ecosystem Services: Why the Mundane Should Matter". *Ecological Economics* 146: 507–19. https://doi.org/10.1016/j.ecolecon.2017.12.013

Jewitt, S.L., D. Nasir, S.E. Page, J.O. Rieley, and K. Khanal. 2014. "Indonesia's Contested Domains. Deforestation, Rehabilitation and Conservation-with-Development in Central Kalimantan's Tropical Peatlands". *International Forestry Review* 16, no. 4: 405–20. https://doi.org/10.1505/146554814813484086.

Jiménez, D., S. Delerce, H. Dorado, J. Cock, L.A. Muñoz, A. Agamez, and A. Jarvis. 2019. "A Scalable Scheme to Implement Data-Driven Agriculture for Small-Scale Farmers". *Global Food Security* 23: 256–66.

Jo, R.S., V. Raman, M. Lu, Y. Sebastian, S.J. Cameron, J.Y.H. Ten, T.K.S. Chong, F.L. Yap, V. Chiew, and D. Yeo. 2019. "Design of IoT Monitoring Architecture for Smart Organic Farming in Sarawak State of Malaysian Borneo". 24th International Conference of Society for Design and Process Science Transformative Research Through Transdisciplinary Means.

Johansah, M., P. Rupang, T. Apriando, Zamzami, H. Meutia, A. Saini, Z. Suhadi, A.A. Birry, M. Nasution, Y. Indradi, and A.P. Prayoga. 2019. "Ibu Kota Baru Buat

Siapa? Report for 'Bersihkan Indonesia'". WALHI. https://www.walhi.or.id/ibu-kota-negara-baru-untuk-siapa

Johari, A., S.I. Ahmed, H. Hashim, H. Alkali, and M. Ramli. 2012. "Economic and Environmental Benefits of Landfill Gas from Municipal Solid Waste in Malaysia". *Renewable and Sustainable Energy Reviews* 16, no. 5: 2907–12. https://doi.org/10.1016/j.rser.2012.02.005

———, B.B. Nyakuma, S.H. Mohd Nor, R. Mat, H. Hashim, A. Ahmad, Z. Yamani Zakaria, and T.A. Tuan Abdullah. 2015. "The Challenges and Prospects of Palm Oil Based Biodiesel in Malaysia". *Energy* 81: 255–61. https://doi.org/10.1016/j.energy.2014.12.037

Johnson, F.X., H. Pacini, and E. Smeets. 2013. *Transformations in EU Biofuels Markets under the Renewable Energy Directive and the Implications for Land Use, Trade and Forests*. Bogor, Indonesia: CIFOR. https://www.cifor.org/library/3775/.

Johnson, T.G., and I. Altman. 2014. "Rural Development Opportunities in the Bioeconomy". *Biomass and Bioenergy* 63: 341–44.

Jomo, K.S., Y.T. Chang, and K.J. Khoo. 2004. *Deforesting Malaysia: The Political Economy and Social Ecology of Agricultural Expansion and Commercial Logging*. London: Zed Books.

———, and M. Rock. 1998. "Economic Diversification and Primary Commodity Processing in the Second-Tier South-East Asian Newly Industrializing Countries". UNCTAD Discussion Papers 136, United Nations Conference on Trade and Development.

———, and C.H. Wee. 2003. "The Political Economy of Malaysian Federalism: Economic Development, Public Policy and Conflict Containment". *Journal of International Development* 15, no. 4: 441–56. https://doi.org/10.1002/jid.995

Jong, H.N. 2018. "Report Finds APP and APRIL Violating Zero-Deforestation Policies with Wood Purchases from Djarum Group Concessions in East Kalimantan". *Mongabay*, 21 August 2018. https://news.mongabay.com/2018/08/report-finds-app-and-april-violating-zero-deforestation-policies-with-wood-purchases-from-djarum-group-concessions-in-east-kalimantan/

———. 2019a. "Customary Land Map, A First for Indonesia, Launches to Mixed Reception". *Mongabay*, 26 June 2019a. https://news.mongabay.com/2019/06/customary-land-map-a-first-for-indonesia-launches-to-mixed-reception/

———. 2019b. "'Dangerous' New Regulation Puts Indonesia's Carbon-Rich Peatlands at Risk". *Mongabay*, 12 July 2019b.

———. 2019c. "Indonesia to Get First Payment from Norway under $1b REDD+ Scheme". *Mongabay*, 20 February 2019c. https://news.mongabay.com/2019/02/indonesia-to-get-first-payment-from-norway-under-1b-redd-scheme/

———. 2019d. "Indonesian Court Fines Palm Oil Firm $18.5m over Forest Fires in 201". *Mongabay*, 28 October 2019d. https://news.mongabay.com/2019/10/palm-oil-indonesia-arjuna-utama-sawit-musim-mas-forest-fires/

———. 2019e. "Indonesia Fires Cost Nation $5 billion This Year: World Bank". *Mongabay*, 20 December 2019e. https://news.mongabay.com/2019/12/indonesia-fires-cost-nation-5-billion-this-year-world-bank/

———. 2020a. "Indonesia's 'Militarized Agriculture' Raises Social, Environmental Red Flags". *Mongabay*, 27 October 2020a. https://news.mongabay.com/2020/10/indonesia-militarized-agriculture-food-estate-kalimantan-sumatra/

———. 2020b. "Indonesia Aims for Sustainability Certification for Oil Palm Smallholders". *Mongabay*, 29 April 2020b. https://news.mongabay.com/2020/04/indonesia-aims-for-sustainability-certification-for-oil-palm-smallholders/

———. 2020c. "Indonesia Bill Weakening Environmental Safeguards to Pass in October". *Mongabay*, 24 August 2020c. https://news.mongabay.com/2020/08/indonesia-omnibus-deregulation-bill-pass-october/

———. 2020d. "Indonesia Moves to End Smallholder Guarantee Meant to Empower Palm Oil Farmers". *Mongabay*, 12 May 2020d. https://news.mongabay.com/2020/05/indonesia-palm-oil-plasma-plantation-farmers-smallholders/

———. 2020e. "Indonesia Pushes Rice Estate Project Despite Environmental Red Flags". *Mongabay* (Mongabay Series: Indonesian Forests), 17 August 2020e, https://news.mongabay.com/2020/08/indonesia-mega-rice-estate-project-kalimantan-borneo-peat-wetland/

———. 2020f. "Indonesia to Receive $56m Payment from Norway for Reducing Deforestation". *Mongabay*, 29 May 2020f. https://news.mongabay.com/2020/05/indonesia-norway-redd-payment-deforestation-carbon-emission-climate-change/

———. 2020g. "Report Identifies Tycoons Controlling Site of New Indonesian Capital". *Mongabay*, 6 January 2020g. https://news.mongabay.com/2020/01/indonesia-capital-relocation-borneo-kalimantan-tycoons-coal-mining-pulpwood/

———. 2020h. "Upgrade of Indonesian Palm Oil Certification Falls Short, Observers Say". *Mongabay*, 22 January 2020h. https://news.mongabay.com/2020/07/ispo-indonesia-update-palm-oil-sustainable-certification-review/

———. 2021a. "Indonesia Says No New Coal Plants from 2023 (After the Next 100 or So)". *Mongabay*, 12 May 2021a. https://news.mongabay.com/2021/05/indonesia-says-no-new-coal-plants-from-2023-after-the-next-100-or-so/

———. 2021b. "Plantations, Mines Didn't Worsen Flood, Indonesia Says. The Data Begs to Differ". *Mongabay*, 22 January 2021b. https://news.mongabay.com/2021/01/plantations-mines-south-kalimantan-indonesia-borneo-flood-environment-minister-denies/

Jordan, N., G. Boody, W. Broussard, J. Glover, D. Keeney, B. McCown, G. McIsaac, M. Muller, H. Murray, and J. Neal. 2007. "Sustainable Development of the Agricultural Bio-Economy". *Science* 316, no. 5831: 1570–71.

Joshi, L., v. N.M. Janudianto, U. Pradhan, and M. van Noordwijk. 2010. "Investment in Carbon Stocks in the Eastern Buffer Zone of Lamandau River Wildlife Reserve, Central Kalimantan Province, Indonesia: A REDD+ Feasibility Study". Project Report. World Agroforestry Centre (ICRAF) Southeast Asia Regional Office, Bogor.

Jucker, T., G.P. Asner, M. Dalponte, P.G. Brodrick, C.D. Philipson, N.R. Vaughn, Y. Arn Teh, C. Brelsford, D.F.R. P. Burslem, N.J. Deere, R.M. Ewers, J. Kvasnica, S.L. Lewis, Y. Malhi, S. Milne, R. Nilus, M. Pfeifer, O.L. Phillips, L. Qie, N. Renneboog, G. Reynolds, T. Riutta, M.J. Struebig, M. Svátek, E.C. Turner, and D.A. Coomes.

2018. "Estimating Aboveground Carbon Density and Its Uncertainty in Borneo's Structurally Complex Tropical Forests Using Airborne Laser Scanning". *Biogeosciences* 15, no. 12: 3811–30. https://doi.org/10.5194/bg-15-3811-2018

Julia, and B. White. 2012. "Gendered Experiences of Dispossession: Oil Palm Expansion in a Dayak Hibun Community in West Kalimantan". *Journal of Peasant Studies* 39, no. 3–4: 995–1016. https://doi.org/10.1080/03066150.2012.676544

Jupesta, J., A.A. Supriyanto, G. Martin, J. Piliang, S. Yang, A. Purnomo, A. Neville, and J.-P. Caliman. 2020. "Establishing Multi-Partnerships Environmental Governance in Indonesia: Case of Desa Makmur Perduli Api (Prosperous and Fire Free Village) Program". In *Food Security and Land Use Change under Conditions of Climatic Variability: A Multidimensional Perspective*, edited by V.R. Squires and M.K. Gaur, pp. 181–96. Cham: Springer International Publishing.

Jurriëns, E., and R. Tapsell. 2017. *Digital Indonesia: Connectivity and Divergence.* Singapore: ISEAS – Yusof Ishak Institute.

Jusoh, A., L. Kamarulzaman, and Z. Zakaria. 2017. "The Implementation of Halal Cosmetic Standard in Malaysia: A Brief Overview". *Contemporary Issues and Development in the Global Halal Industry.* Singapore.

Kabir, S., S. Shams, and R. Lawrey. 2019. "Halal Market Emergence and Export Opportunity: The Comparative Advantage Perspective". *Proceedings of the Twelfth International Conference on Management Science and* Engineering Management, edited by J. Xu, F. L. Cooke, M. Gen and S. E. Ahmed. Cham: Springer.

Kadir, E.A., H. Irie, and S.L. Rosa. 2019. "Modeling of Wireless Sensor Networks for Detection Land and Forest Fire Hotspot". In *2019 International Conference on Electronics, Information, and Communication*, pp. 185–89.

Kadir, N.A.A., A. Hussin, and H. Hashim. 2019. "Minimum Wages: Helping or Hurting Producers?". In *Proceedings of the Regional Conference on Science, Technology and Social Sciences*, edited by M.Y.M. Noor, B.E. Ahmad, M.R. Ismail, H. Hashim, and M.A.A. Baharum. Singapore: Springer Nature Singapore.

Kallio, M.H., M. Kanninen, and D. Rohadi. 2011. "Farmers' Tree Planting Activity in Indonesia—Case Studies in the Provinces of Central Java, Riau, and South Kalimantan". *Forests Trees and Livelihoods* 20, no. 2–3: 191–209. https://doi.org/10.1080/14728028.2011.9756706

———, H. Krisnawati, D. Rohadi, and M. Kanninen. 2011. "Mahogany and Kadam Planting Farmers in South Kalimantan: The Link Between Silvicultural Activity and Stand Quality". *Small-scale Forestry* 10, no. 1: 115–32. https://doi.org/10.1007/s11842-010-9137-8

———, M. Moeliono, C. Maharani, M. Brockhaus, N. J. Hogarth, W. Daeli, W. Tauhid, and G. Wong. 2016. "Information Exchange in Swidden Communities of West Kalimantan: Lessons for Designing REDD+". *International Forestry Review* 18, no. 2: 203–17. https://doi.org/10.1505/146554816818966336

Kallis, G., C. Kerschner, and J. Martinez-Alier. 2012. "The Economics of Degrowth". *Ecological Economics* 84: 172–80. https://doi.org/10.1016/j.ecolecon.2012.08.017

Kamri, T., and A. Radam. 2013. "Visitors' Visiting Motivation: Bako National Park,

Sarawak". *Procedia – Social and Behavioral Sciences* 101: 495–505. https://doi. org/10.1016/j.sbspro.2013.07.223

Kannan, P., N.H. Mansor, N.K. Rahman, T. Peng, and S.M. Mazlan. 2021. "A Review on the Malaysian Sustainable Palm Oil Certification Process Among Independent Oil Palm Smallholders". *Journal of Oil Palm Research* 33, no. 1: 171–80.

Karim, M.F. 2019. "State Transformation and Cross-Border Regionalism in Indonesia's Periphery: Contesting the Centre". *Third World Quarterly* 40, no. 8: 1554–70. https:// doi.org/10.1080/01436597.2019.1620598

Karsenty, A., A. Vogel, and F. Castell. 2014. "'Carbon Rights', REDD+ and Payments for Environmental Services". *Environmental Science & Policy* 35: 20–29.

Kartika, P., Hariyadi, and Cerdikwan. 2020. "The Programme for the Endorsement of Forest Certification (PEFC) and Its Contribution to Sustainable Forest Management in Indonesia". In *Sustainability Standards and Global Governance: Experiences of Emerging Economies*, edited by A. Negi, J.A. Pérez-Pineda and J. Blankenbach, pp. 145–61. Singapore: Springer Singapore.

Kasa, M., J. Kho, D. Yong, K. Hussain, and P. Lau. 2020. "Competently Skilled Human Capital Through Education for the Hospitality and Tourism Industry". *Worldwide Hospitality and Tourism Themes* 12, no. 2: 175–84. https://doi.org/10.1108/ WHATT-12-2019-0081

Kassim, M.R.M., A.N. Harun, I.M. Yusoff, I. Mat, C.P. Kuen, and N. Rahmad. 2017. "Applications of Wireless Sensor Networks in Shiitake Mushroom Cultivation". 2017 Eleventh International Conference on Sensing Technology (ICST).

Kato, Y. 2014. "Changes in Resource Use and Subsistence Activities Under the Plantation Expansion in Sarawak, Malaysia". In *Social-Ecological Systems in Transition*, pp. 179–94. Springer.

———, and H. Samejima. 2020. "The Effects of Landscape and Livelihood Transitions on Hunting in Sarawak". In *Advances in Asian Human-Environmental Research*. Springer International Publishing.

———, and R. Soda. 2020. "The Impact of RSPO Certification on Oil Palm Smallholdings in Sarawak". In *Advances in Asian Human-Environmental Research*. Springer International Publishing.

Kaur, A. 1998. "Economic Change in East Malaysia: Sabah and Sarawak since 1850". *Studies in the Economies of East and South-East Asia*. London: Palgrave Macmillan.

Kaur, D. 2020. "Up to 96% of Oil Palm Estates in Malaysia MSPO-Certified". *The Malaysian Reserve*, 7 July 2020. https://themalaysianreserve.com/2020/07/07/up-to-96-of-oil-palm-estates-in-malaysia-mspo-certified/

Kawai, M., and M. Inoue. 2016. "Alternative Development Strategies for Large Scale Oil Palm Plantations in East Kalimantan, Indonesia". In *Monoculture Farming: Global Practices, Ecological Impact and Benefits/Drawbacks*, pp. 129–60. Nova Science Publishers, Inc.

Keeton-Olsen, D. 2021. "In Malaysian Borneo's Rainforests, Powerful State Governments Set Their Own Rules". *Mongabay*, 18 February 2021. https://news.mongabay. com/2021/02/in-malaysian-borneos-rainforests-powerful-state-government-set-their-own-rules/

Kelley, L.C., N.L. Peluso, K.M. Carlson, and S. Afiff. 2020. "Circular Labor Migration and Land-Livelihood Dynamics in Southeast Asia's Concession Landscapes". *Journal of Rural Studies* 73: 21–33. https://doi.org/10.1016/j.jrurstud.2019.11.019

Khan, T. 2014. "Kalimantan's Biodiversity: Developing Accounting Models to Prevent Its Economic Destruction". *Accounting, Auditing and Accountability Journal* 27, no. 1: 150–82. https://doi.org/10.1108/AAAJ-07-2013-1392

Khasanah, N., M. van Noordwijk, M. Slingerland, M. Sofiyudin, D. Stomph, A.F. Migeon, and K. Hairiah. 2020. "Oil Palm Agroforestry Can Achieve Economic and Environmental Gains as Indicated by Multifunctional Land Equivalent Ratios". *Frontiers in Sustainable Food Systems* 3, no. 122. https://doi.org/10.3389/fsufs.2019.00122

Khasanah, N.m., M. van Noordwijk, A. Ekadinata, S. Dewi, S. Rahayu, H. Ningsih, A. Setiawan, E. Dwiyanti, and R. Octaviani. 2012. "The Carbon Footprint of Indonesian Palm Oil Production". World Agroforestry Centre – ICRAF, Bogor, Indonesia. http://outputs.worldagroforestry.org/record/6548/files/ICRAF-2014-392.PDF

Khatiwada, D., C. Palmén, and S. Silveira. 2018. "Evaluating the Palm Oil Demand in Indonesia: Production Trends, Yields, and Emerging Issues". *Biofuels*: 1–13. https://doi.org/10.1080/17597269.2018.1461520

Khoiriati, S.D., I. Krisnajaya, and D. Dinarto. 2018. "Debating Halal Tourism Between Values and Branding: A Case Study of Lombok, Indonesia". *KnE Social Sciences*: 494–515.

Khoon, K.L., E. Rumpang, N. Kamarudin, and M.H. Harun. 2019. "Quantifying Total Carbon Stock of Mature Oil Palm". *Journal of Oil Palm Research* 31, no. 3: 521–27. https://doi.org/10.21894/jopr.2019.0044

Khor, Y., J. Saravanamuttu, and D. Augustin. 2015. *Consulting Study 12: The Felda Case Study—The High Carbon Stock* http://www.simedarbyplantation.com/sites/default/files/sustainability/high-carbon-stock/consulting-reports/socio-economic/hcs-consulting-report-12-the-felda-case-study.pdf

Kiat, P.E., M.A. Malek, and S.M. Shamsuddin. 2020. "Net Carbon Stocks Change in Biomass from Wood Removal of Tropical Forests in Sarawak, Malaysia". *Journal of King Saud University—Science* 32, no. 1: 1096–99. https://doi.org/10.1016/j.jksus.2019.09.012

Kibanov, M., G. Stumme, I. Amin, and J.G. Lee. 2017. "Mining Social Media to Inform Peatland Fire and Haze Disaster Management". *Social Network Analysis and Mining* 7, no. 1. https://doi.org/10.1007/s13278-017-0446-1

Kieft, J., T. Smith, S. Someshwar, and R. Boer. 2016. "Towards Anticipatory Management of Peat Fires to Enhance Local Resilience and Reduce Natural Capital Depletion". In *Advances in Natural and Technological Hazards Research*. Springer Netherlands.

Killeen, T.J., G. Schroth, W. Turner, C.A. Harvey, M.K. Steininger, C. Dragisic, and R.A. Mittermeier. 2011. "Stabilizing the Agricultural Frontier: Leveraging REDD with Biofuels for Sustainable Development". *Biomass and Bioenergy* 35, no. 12: 4815–23. https://doi.org/10.1016/j.biombioe.2011.06.027

King, V.T. 1993. *The Peoples of Borneo: 1460–1610*. Oxford, UK: Blackwell.

———. 2016. "Convergence and Divergence: Issues of State and Region in Tourism Development in Malaysian Borneo, Brunei Darussalam and Indonesian Kalimantan". Working Paper no. 24, Institute of Asian Studies, Universiti Brunei Darussalam, Gadong.

———. 2017. "Identities in Borneo: Constructions and Transformations". In *Borneo Studies in History, Society and Culture*, pp. 177–207. Springer.

Kirchherr, J., D. Reike, and M. Hekkert. 2017. "Conceptualizing the Circular Economy: An Analysis of 114 Definitions". *Resources, Conservation and Recycling* 127: 221–32. https://doi.org/10.1016/j.resconrec.2017.09.005

Kitayama, K., S. Fujiki, R. Aoyagi, N. Imai, J. Sugau, J. Titin, R. Nilus, P. Lagan, Y. Sawada, R. Ong, F. Kugan, and S. Mannan. 2018. "Biodiversity Observation for Land and Ecosystem Health (BOLEH): A Robust Method to Evaluate the Management Impacts on the Bundle of Carbon and Biodiversity Ecosystem Services in Tropical Production Forests". *Sustainability* (Switzerland) 10, no. 11. https://doi.org/10.3390/su10114224

Kitayama, K., R.C. Ong, and Y.F. Lee. 2013. "Synthesis: Co-benefits of Sustainable Production Forestry". In *Co-benefits of Sustainable Forestry: Ecological Studies of a Certified Bornean Rain Forest*, edited by K. Kitayama, pp. 149–57. Tokyo: Springer Japan.

Kitchen, L., and T. Marsden. 2009. "Creating Sustainable Rural Development through Stimulating the Eco-economy: Beyond the Eco-economic Paradox?". *Sociologia Ruralis* 49, no. 3: 273–94. https://doi.org/10.1111/j.1467-9523.2009.00489.x

KLK. 2019. "Kuala Lumpur Kepong Berhad. Annual Report 2019". Kuala Lumpur Kepong Berhad. https://www.klk.com.my/wp-content/uploads/2019/12/1-KLK-Annual-Report-2019.pdf

Koalisi Anti Mafia Hutan, 2019. "Asia Pulp and Paper and APRIL Groups Continued in 2018 to Source Wood from Controversial Supplier Owned by Djarum Group". October 2019. https://environmentalpaper.org/wp-content/uploads/2019/10/Borneo-Deforestation-Update-October-2019.pdf

Koh, L.P., H.K. Gibbs, P.V. Potapov, and M.C. Hansen. 2012. "REDD Calculator. com: A Web-Based Decision-Support Tool for Implementing Indonesia's Forest Moratorium". *Methods in Ecology and Evolution* 3, no. 2: 310–16. https://doi.org/10.1111/j.2041-210X.2011.00147.x

Koizumi, M., D. Mamung, and P. Levang. 2012. "Hunter-Gatherers' Culture, a Major Hindrance to a Settled Agricultural Life: The Case of the Penan Benalui of East Kalimantan". *Forests Trees and Livelihoods* 21, nos. 1–2: 1–15. https://doi.org/10.1080/14728028.2012.662626

Komalasari, M., S. Peteru, and S. Atmadja. 2018. "North Kalimantan, Indonesia: Low-Emission Rural Development (LED-R) at a Glance". Earth Innovation Institute (EII).

———, S. Peteru, S. Atmadja, and C. Chan. 2018. "East Kalimantan, Indonesia: Low-emission Rural Development (LED-R) at a Glance". Earth Innovation Institute (EII). https://www.cifor.org/knowledge/publication/7047/

Konecny, K., U. Ballhorn, P. Navratil, J. Jubanski, S.E. Page, K. Tansey, A. Hooijer,

R. Vernimmen, and F. Siegert. 2016. "Variable Carbon Losses from Recurrent Fires in Drained Tropical Peatlands". *Global Change Biology* 22, no. 4: 1469–80. https://doi.org/10.1111/gcb.13186

Krisnawati, H. 2015. "National Inventory of Greenhouse Gas Emissions and Removals on Indonesia's Forests and Peatlands: Indonesian National Carbon Accounting System (INCAS)". Ministry of Environment and Forestry, Research, Development and Innovation.

Kubo, H., A. Wibawanto, and D. Rossanda. 2019. "Toward a Policy Mix in Conservation Governance: A Case of Gunung Palung National Park, West Kalimantan, Indonesia". *Land Use Policy* 88. https://doi.org/10.1016/j.landusepol.2019.104108

Kugan, F. 2018. "Jurisdictional Approaches: Delivering Sustainable and Deforestation-Free Palm Oil". RT 16, Kota Kinabalu, Sabah.

Kumagai, T., and A. Porporato. 2012. "Drought-Induced Mortality of a Bornean Tropical Rain Forest Amplified by Climate Change". *Journal of Geophysical Research: Biogeosciences* 117, no. 2. https://doi.org/10.1029/2011JG001835

Kunjuraman, V. 2020. "Community-Based Ecotourism Managing to Fuel Community Empowerment? An Evidence from Malaysian Borneo". *Tourism Recreation Research*: 1–16. https://doi.org/10.1080/02508281.2020.1841378

———, and R. Hussin. 2017. "Challenges of Community-Based Homestay Programme in Sabah, Malaysia: Hopeful or Hopeless?". *Tourism Management Perspectives* 21: 1–9. https://doi.org/10.1016/j.tmp.2016.10.007

Kurlantzick, J. 2020. "A Controversial Omnibus Law Could Spell Trouble for Indonesia's Democracy". *World Politics Review*. https://www.worldpoliticsreview.com/articles/29281/a-controversial-omnibus-law-could-spell-trouble-for-indonesian-democracy (accessed 16 November 2021).

Kurniawan, N.I., and D. Rahmawati. 2018. "Framing Needs, Politicising Cooperatives: Credit Unions In West Kalimantan in a Context of Market Economy". In *The Politics of Welfare: Contested Welfare Regimes in Indonesia*, edited by W. Mas'udi and C. Lay. Jakarta: Yayasan Pustaka Obor Indonesia.

Kushairi, A., R. Singh, and M. Ong-Abdullah. 2017. "The Oil Palm Industry in Malaysia: Thriving with Transformative Technologies". *Journal of Oil Palm Research* 29, no. 4: 431–39. https://doi.org/10.21894/jopr.2017.00017

Kusumawati, R., and S.R. Bush. 2015. "Co-producing Better Management Practice Standards for Shrimp Aquaculture in Indonesia". *Maritime Studies* 14, no. 1: 1–18. https://doi.org/10.1186/s40152-015-0039-4

———, S.R. Bush, and L.E. Visser. 2013. "Can Patrons Be Bypassed? Frictions Between Local and Global Regulatory Networks over Shrimp Aquaculture in East Kalimantan". *Society & Natural Resources* 26, no. 8: 898–911.

Kwan, M.S., F.T. Tangang, and L. Juneng. 2014. "Present-Day Regional Climate Simulation over Malaysia and Western Maritime Continent Region Using PRECIS Forced with ERA40 Reanalysis". *Theoretical and Applied Climatology* 115, nos. 1–2: 1–14. https://doi.org/10.1007/s00704-013-0873-5

Labrière, N., Y. Laumonier, B. Locatelli, G. Vieilledent, and M. Comptour. 2015.

"Ecosystem Services and Biodiversity in a Rapidly Transforming Landscape in Northern Borneo". *PLoS ONE* 10, no. 10. https://doi.org/10.1371/journal. pone.0140423

Lahjie, A.M., B. Nouval, A.A. Lahjie, Y. Ruslim, and R. Kristiningrum. 2019. "Economic Valuation from Direct Use of Mangrove Forest Restoration in Balikpapan Bay, East Kalimantan, Indonesia". *F1000Research* 8: 9. https://doi.org/10.12688/f1000research.17012.1

Lam, M.K., and K.T. Lee. 2011. "Renewable and Sustainable Bioenergies Production from Palm Oil Mill Effluent (POME): Win-Win Strategies Toward Better Environmental Protection". *Biotechnology Advances* 29, no. 1: 124–41. https://doi.org/10.1016/j. biotechadv.2010.10.001

Langner, A., H. Samejima, R.C. Ong, J. Titin, and K. Kitayama. 2012. "Integration of Carbon Conservation into Sustainable Forest Management Using High Resolution Satellite Imagery: A Case Study in Sabah, Malaysian Borneo". *International Journal of Applied Earth Observation and Geoinformation* 18, no. 1: 305–12. https://doi. org/10.1016/j.jag.2012.02.006

Langston, J.D., R.A. Riggs, Y. Sururi, T. Sunderland, and M. Munawir. 2017. "Estate Crops More Attractive Than Community Forests in West Kalimantan, Indonesia". *Land* 6, no. 1. https://doi.org/10.3390/land6010012

Lanzafame, P., S. Perathoner, and G. Centi. 2016. "A Vision for Future Biorefineries". In *Chemicals and Fuels from Bio-Based Building Blocks*, pp. 497–518. Wiley Online Library.

Larsen, R.K., N. Jiwan, A. Rompas, J. Jenito, M. Osbeck, and A. Tarigan. 2014. "Towards 'Hybrid Accountability' in EU Biofuels Policy? Community Grievances and Competing Water Claims in the Central Kalimantan Oil Palm Sector". *Geoforum* 54: 295–305. https://doi.org/10.1016/j.geoforum.2013.09.010

———, M. Osbeck, E. Dawkins, H. Tuhkanen, H. Nguyen, A. Nugroho, T.A. Gardner, Zulfahm, and P. Wolvekamp. 2018. "Hybrid Governance in Agricultural Commodity Chains: Insights from Implementation of 'No Deforestation, No Peat, No Exploitation' (NDPE) Policies in the Oil Palm Industry". *Journal of Cleaner Production* 183: 544–54. https://doi.org/10.1016/j.jclepro.2018.02.125

Latip, N.A., N. Badarulzaman, A. Marzuki, and M.U. Umar. 2013. "Sustainable Forest Management in Lower Kinabatangan, Sabah: Issues and Current Practices". *Planning Malaysia* 11: 59–84.

———, M. Jaafar, A. Marzuki, K.M. Roufechaei, M.U. Umar, and R. Karim. 2020. "The Impact of Tourism Activities on the Environment of Mount Kinabalu, UNESCO World Heritage Site". *Planning Malaysia* 18, no. 14.

Laurance, W.F. 2016. "Lessons from Research for Sustainable Development and Conservation in Borneo". *Forests* 7, no. 12. https://doi.org/10.3390/f7120314

Law, E.A., B.A. Bryan, E. Meijaard, T. Mallawaarachchi, M. Struebig, and K.A. Wilson. 2015. "Ecosystem Services from a Degraded Peatland of Central Kalimantan: Implications for Policy, Planning, and Management". *Ecological Applications* 25, no. 1: 70–87. https://doi.org/10.1890/13-2014.1

———, B.A. Bryan, E. Meijaard, T. Mallawaarachchi, M.J. Struebig, M.E. Watts, and K.A. Wilson. 2017. "Mixed Policies Give More Options in Multifunctional Tropical Forest Landscapes". *Journal of Applied Ecology* 54, no. 1: 51–60. https://doi.org/10.1111/1365-2664.12666

———, B.A. Bryan, N. Torabi, S.A. Bekessy, C.A. McAlpine, and K.A. Wilson. 2015. "Measurement Matters in Managing Landscape Carbon". *Ecosystem Services* 13: 6–15.

———, E. Meijaard, B.A. Bryan, T. Mallawaarachchi, L.P. Koh, and K.A. Wilson. 2015. "Better Land-Use Allocation Outperforms Land Sparing and Land Sharing Approaches to Conservation in Central Kalimantan, Indonesia". *Biological Conservation* 186: 276–86. https://doi.org/10.1016/j.biocon.2015.03.004

Lawson, S., and L. MacFaul. 2010. *Illegal Logging and Related Trade: Indicators of the Global Response*. London: Chatham House.

Le, Q.V., K.U. Tennakoon, F. Metali, and R.S. Sukri. 2019. "Photosynthesis in Co-occurring Invasive Acacia spp. and Native Bornean Heath Forest Trees at the Post-Establishment Invasion Stage". *Journal of Sustainable Forestry* 38, no. 3: 230–43. https://doi.org/10.1080/10549811.2018.1530602

Leasor, H.C., and O.J. Macgregor. 2014. "Proboscis Monkey Tourism: Can We Make It 'Ecotourism'?". In *Primate Tourism: A Tool for Conservation*, pp. 56–75. Cambridge: Cambridge University Press.

Lee, P.O. 2018a. "Property Rights, Food Security, and Gender: The Impact of the Expansion of Palm Oil Plantations on Native Communities in Sarawak, Malaysia". In *Ensuring a Square Meal: Women and Food Security in Southeast Asia*, pp. 147–70. Singapore: World Scientific Publishing.

Lee, S.S. 2018b. "Observations on the Successes and Failures of Acacia Plantations in Sabah and Sarawak and the Way Forward". *Journal of Tropical Forest Science* 30, no. 5: 468–75. https://doi.org/10.26525/jtfs2018.30.5.468475

Lee, T., and J. van der Heijden. 2019. "Does the Knowledge Economy Advance the Green Economy? An Evaluation of Green Jobs in the 100 Largest Metropolitan Regions in the United States". *Energy & Environment* 30, no. 1: 141–55.

Lee, W.C., K.K. Viswanathan, and J. Ali. 2015. "Compensation Policy in a Large Development Project: The Case of the Bakun Hydroelectric Dam". *International Journal of Water Resources Development* 31, no. 1: 64–72. https://doi.org/10.1080/07900627.2014.914429

Leonald, L., and D. Rowland. 2016. *Drivers and Effects of Agrarian Change in Kapuas Hulu Regency, West Kalimantan, Indonesia*. Bogor, Indonesia: CIFOR. https://www.cifor.org/library/6365.

Lesniewska, F., and C.L. McDermott. 2014. "FLEGT VPAs: Laying a Pathway to Sustainability Via Legality Lessons from Ghana and Indonesia". *Forest Policy and Economics* 48: 16–23. https://doi.org/10.1016/j.forpol.2014.01.005

Lestari, O., and S. Purwayantie. 2018. "The Glycemic Index and Organoleptic Test of Pekawai (Durio kutejensis) Chips". *Pro Food* 3, no. 2: 235–39.

Levang, P., W. F. Riva, and M.G. Orth. 2016. "Oil Palm Plantations and Conflict in

Indonesia: Evidence from West Kalimantan". In *The Oil Palm Complex: Smallholders, Agribusiness and the State in Indonesia and Malaysia*, edited by R. Cramb and J.F. McCarthy, pp. 283–300. Singapore: NUS Press.

Li, T.M. 2017a. "Intergenerational Displacement in Indonesia's Oil Palm Plantation Zone". *Journal of Peasant Studies* 44, no. 6: 1160–78. https://doi.org/10.1080/030 66150.2017.1308353

———. 2017b. "The Price of Un/Freedom: Indonesia's Colonial and Contemporary Plantation Labor Regimes". *Comparative Studies in Society and History* 59, no. 2: 245–76. https://doi.org/10.1017/S0010417517000044

———. 2018. "After the Land Grab: Infrastructural Violence and the 'Mafia System' in Indonesia's Oil Palm Plantation Zones". *Geoforum* 96: 328–37. https://doi. org/10.1016/j.geoforum.2017.10.012

Lilleskov, E., K. McCullough, K. Hergoualc'h, D. del Castillo Torres, R. Chimner, D. Murdiyarso, R. Kolka, L. Bourgeau-Chavez, J. Hribljan, J. del Aguila Pasquel, and C. Wayson. 2019. "Is Indonesian Peatland Loss a Cautionary Tale for Peru? A Two-Country Comparison of the Magnitude and Causes of Tropical Peatland Degradation". *Mitigation and Adaptation Strategies for Global Change* 24, no. 4: 591–623. https://doi.org/10.1007/s11027-018-9790-3

Lim, C.I., and W. Biswas. 2019. "Sustainability Assessment for Crude Palm Oil Production in Malaysia Using the Palm Oil Sustainability Assessment Framework". *Sustainable Development* 27, no. 3: 253–69. https://doi.org/10.1002/sd.1872

Lim, H.Y., P.C. Gardner, N.K. Abram, K.M. Yusah, and B. Goossens. 2019. "Identifying Habitat and Understanding Movement Resistance for the Endangered Bornean Banteng *Bos javanicus lowi* in Sabah, Malaysia". *Oryx*. https://doi.org/10.1017/ S0030605318001126

Lim, T.W., and A.A. Noorainie. 2010. *Wood for the Trees: A Review of the Agarwood (Gaharu) Trade in Malaysia*. Petaling Jaya, Selangor: TRAFFIC Southeast Asia.

Lindsay, E., I. Convery, A. Ramsey, and E. Simmons. 2012. "Changing Place: Palm Oil and Sense of Place in Borneo". *Human Geographies* 6, no. 2: 45–53. https://doi. org/10.5719/hgeo.2012.62.45

Liswanti, N., D. Sheil, I. Basuki, M. Padmanaba, and G. Mulcahy. 2011. "Falling Back on Forests: How Forest-Dwelling People Cope with Catastrophe in a Changing Landscape". *International Forestry Review* 13, no. 4: 442–55. https://doi. org/10.1505/146554811798811326

Liu, J., Z. Feng, A. Mannan, and L. Yang. 2019. "Positioning of Coordinates and Precision Analysis of Sample Trees Using the Intelligent Forest Survey Calculator". *Computers and Electronics in Agriculture* 159: 157–64.

Loh, S.K., A.B. Nasrin, S. Mohamad Azri, B. Nurul Adela, N. Muzzammil, T. Daryl Jay, R.A. Stasha Eleanor, W.S. Lim, Y.M. Choo, and M. Kaltschmitt. 2017. "First Report on Malaysia's Experiences and Development in Biogas Capture and Utilization from Palm Oil Mill Effluent under the Economic Transformation Programme: Current and Future Perspectives". *Renewable and Sustainable Energy Reviews* 74: 1257–74. https://doi.org/10.1016/j.rser.2017.02.066

Long, S.P., A. Marshall-Colon, and X.G. Zhu. 2015. "Meeting the Global Food Demand of the Future by Engineering Crop Photosynthesis and Yield Potential". *Cell* 161, no. 1: 56–66. https://doi.org/10.1016/j.cell.2015.03.019

Lord, M., and S. Chang. 2018. "Pre-Feasibility Study of Sabah-North Kalimantan Cross-Border Value Chains". Asian Development Bank (ADB). https://bimp-eaga. asia/documents-and-publications/pre-feasibility-study-sabah-north-kalimantan-cross-border-value-chains

Lounela, A. 2015. "Climate Change Disputes and Justice in Central Kalimantan, Indonesia". *Asia Pacific Viewpoint* 56, no. 1: 62–78. https://doi.org/10.1111/apv.12088

———. 2019. "Morality, Sharing and Change Among the Ngaju People in Central Kalimantan". *Hunter Gatherer Research* 3, no. 3: 515–36. https://doi.org/10.3828/hgr.2017.25

———. 2020. "Contested Values and Climate Change Mitigation in Central Kalimantan, Indonesia". *Social Anthropology* 28, no. 4: 862–80. https://doi.org/10.1111/1469-8676.12790

Low, K.O., and J. Pugh-Kitingan. 2015. "The Impact of Christianity on Traditional Agricultural Practices and Beliefs Among the Kimaragang of Sabah: A Preliminary Study". *Asian Ethnology* 74, no. 2: 401.

Lu, C., Z. Meng, X. Wang, G. Wu, N. Gao, and J. Dong. 2016. "Application Feasibility Analysis of Precision Agriculture in Equipment for Controlled Traffic Farming System: A Review". In *Computer and Computing Technologies in Agriculture IX. CCTA 2015. IFIP Advances in Information and Communication Technology*, vol 478, edited by D. Li and Z. Li. Cham: Springer. https://doi.org/10.1007/978-3-319-48357-3_34

Lu, H., and G. Liu. 2012. "A Case Study of REDD+ Challenges in the Post-2012 Climate Regime: The Scenarios Approach". *Natural Resources Forum* 36, no. 3: 192–201. https://doi.org/10.1111/j.1477-8947.2012.01452.x.

———, and G. Liu. 2013. "Distributed Land Use Modeling And Sensitivity Analysis for REDD+". *Land Use Policy* 33: 54–60. https://doi.org/10.1016/j.landusepol.2012.12.008.

Lucarelli, B. 2010. "The History and Future of Indonesia's Coal Industry: Impact of Politics and Regulatory Framework on Industry Structure and Performance". Working Paper 93, Program on Energy and Sustainable Development, Stanford University, USA. https://pesd.fsi.stanford.edu/sites/default/files/WP_93_Lucarelli_revised_Oct_2010.pdf (accessed 10 May 2011).

Lucey, J.M., N. Tawatao, M.J.M. Senior, V.K. Chey, S. Benedick, K.C. Hamer, P. Woodcock, R.J. Newton, S.H. Bottrell, and J.K. Hill. 2014. "Tropical Forest Fragments Contribute to Species Richness in Adjacent Oil Palm Plantations". *Biological Conservation* 169: 268–76. https://doi.org/10.1016/j.biocon.2013.11.014

Lukman, K.M., Y. Uchiyama, J.M.D. Quevedo, and R. Kohsaka. 2020. "Local Awareness as an Instrument for Management and Conservation of Seagrass Ecosystem: Case of Berau Regency, Indonesia". *Ocean & Coastal Management* 203: 105451. https://doi.org/10.1016/j.ocecoaman.2020.105451

Lunkapis, G.J. 2013. "Confusion Over Land Rights and Development Opportunities Through Communal Titles in Sabah, Malaysia". *Asia Pacific Viewpoint* 54, no. 2: 198–205. https://doi.org/10.1111/apv.12019

———. 2015. "Secure Land Tenure as Prerequisite Towards Sustainable Living: A Case Study of Native Communities in Mantob Village, Sabah, Malaysia". *SpringerPlus* 4, no. 1. https://doi.org/10.1186/s40064-015-1329-4

Luo, X., and C. Niu. 2019. "E-Commerce Participation and Household Income Growth in Taobao Villages". Policy Research Working Paper, No. 8811. Washington, DC: World Bank.

Lussetti, D., K. Kuljus, B. Ranneby, U. Ilstedt, J. Falck, and A. Karlsson. 2019. "Using Linear Mixed Models to Evaluate Stand Level Growth Rates for Dipterocarps and Macaranga Species Following Two Selective Logging Methods in Sabah, Borneo". *Forest Ecology and Management* 437: 372–79. https://doi.org/10.1016/j.foreco.2019.01.044

Lynch, J., A. Perdiguero, and J. Rush. 2017. "The Role of ADB in ASEAN Integration: Harnessing Connectivity for Regional Cooperation and Integration". In *Economic Integration and Regional Development*, pp. 34–44. Routledge.

Macfie, E.J., and E.A. Williamson. 2010. *Best Practice Guidelines for Great Ape Tourism*. Gland, Switzerland: IUCN/SSC Primate Specialist Group (PSG).

MacInnes, A. 2020. "Breaking the Heart of Borneo: A Plan to Plunder Borneo's Final Frontier". Forest Peoples Programme (FPP), UK.

MacKinnon, Kathy, Gusti Hatta, Hakimah Halim, and Arthur Mangalik. 1996. *The Ecology of Kalimantan*. Volume III in The Ecology of Indonesia series. Dalhousie University, Periplus Editions [H.K.] Ltd).

Mafira, T., S. Muluk, and S. Conway. 2019. "From Digging to Planting: A Sustainable Economic Transition for Berau, East Kalimantan". Climate Policy Initiative (CPI) Report. https://climatepolicyinitiative.org/wp-content/uploads/2019/08/From-Digging-to-Planting.pdf

———, R. Rakhmadi, and C. Novianti. 2018. "Towards a More Sustainable and Efficient Palm Oil Supply Chain in Berau, East Kalimantan". Climate Policy Initiative (CPI) Report. https://climatepolicyinitiative.org/wp-content/uploads/2018/07/Towards-a-more-sustainable-and-efficient-palm-oil-supply-chain-in-Berau-East-Kalimantan-Full-publication.pdf.

Mahadi, S.A.R.S., H. Hussin, and A. Khoso. 2018. "Migrant Workers: Recruitment and Travelling from Indonesia to Tawau (Sabah) Malaysia". *Borneo Research Journal* 12: 20–35.

Maharani, C.D., M. Moeliono, G.Y. Wong, M. Brockhaus, R. Carmenta, and M. Kallio. 2019. "Development and Equity: A Gendered Inquiry in a Swidden Landscape". *Forest Policy and Economics* 101: 120–28. https://doi.org/10.1016/j.forpol.2018.11.002

Mahayani, N.P.D., F.J.W. Slik, T. Savini, E.L. Webb, and G.A. Gale. 2020. "Rapid Recovery of Phylogenetic Diversity, Community Structure and Composition of Bornean Tropical Forest a Decade After Logging and Post-Logging Silvicultural Interventions". *Forest Ecology and Management* 476: 118467. https://doi.org/10.1016/j.foreco.2020.118467

Mai-Moulin, T., S. Armstrong, J. van Dam, and M. Junginger. 2019. "Toward a Harmonization of National Sustainability Requirements and Criteria for Solid Biomass". *Biofuels, Bioproducts and Biorefining* 13, no. 2: 405–21.

Mai-Moulin, T., L. Visser, K.R. Fingerman, W. Elbersen, B. Elbersen, G.J. Nabuurs, U.R. Fritsche, I. Del Campo Colmenar, D. Rutz, and R.A. Diaz-Chavez. 2019. "Sourcing Overseas Biomass for EU Ambitions: Assessing Net Sustainable Export Potential from Various Sourcing Countries". *Biofuels, Bioproducts and Biorefining* 13, no. 2: 293–324.

Majid Cooke, F. 2002. "Vulnerability, Control and Oil Palm in Sarawak: Globalization and a New Era?". *Development and Change* 33, no. 2: 189–211. https://doi.org/10.1111/1467-7660.00247

———. 2012. "In the Name of Poverty Alleviation: Experiments with Oil Palm Smallholders and Customary Land in Sabah, Malaysia". *Asia Pacific Viewpoint* 53, no. 3: 240–53. https://doi.org/10.1111/j.1467-8373.2012.01490.x

———, 2013. "Constructing Rights: Indigenous Peoples at the Public Hearings of the National Inquiry into Customary Rights to Land in Sabah, Malaysia". *Sojourn* 28, no. 3: 512–37. https://doi.org/10.1355/sj28-3e

———, and D.S. Mulia. 2012. "Migration and Moral Panic: The Case of Oil Palm in Sabah, East Malaysia". In *The Palm Oil Controversy in Southeast Asia: A Transnational Perspective*, pp. 140–63. Singapore: ISEAS – Yusof Ishak Institute.

———, S. Toh, and J. Vaz. 2011. *Community-Investor Business Models: Lessons Oil Palm Sector in East Malaysia*. London; Rome; Kota Kinabalu: IIED; IFAD; FAO; Universiti Malaysia Sabah https://pubs.iied.org/sites/default/files/pdfs/migrate/12570IIED.pdf.

Malaysia's Energy Commission. 2020. "Malaysia Energy Information Hub". Edited by Energy Commission, Putrajaya, Malaysia.

Malaysia Tourism Promotion Board. 2018. "Key Performance Indicators 2018". Edited by Malaysia Tourism Promotion Board, Ministry of Tourism, Arts and Culture Malaysia.

Managi, S., and P. Kumar. 2018. *Inclusive Wealth Report 2018: Measuring Progress Towards Sustainability*. Routledge.

Marius, P., and F. Pinont. 2013. "Indonesia Internet Usage for Business Sector 2013". Asosiasi Penyelenggara Jasa Internet Indonesia (APJII), Jakarta, Indonesia. https://apjii.or.id/downfile/file/SurveiPenggunaanInternetSektorBisnis2013versienglish.pdf

Marsden, T., and F. Farioli. 2015. "Natural Powers: From the Bio-Economy to the Eco-economy and Sustainable Place-Making". *Sustainability Science* 10, no. 2: 331–44.

Marshall, G.R. 2009. "Polycentricity, Reciprocity, and Farmer Adoption of Conservation Practices Under Community-Based Governance". *Ecological Economics* 68, no. 5: 1507–20.

Martin, P., N. Cherukuru, A.S.Y. Tan, N. Sanwlani, A. Mujahid, and M. Müller. 2018. "Distribution and Cycling of Terrigenous Dissolved Organic Carbon in Peatland-Draining Rivers and Coastal Waters of Sarawak, Borneo". *Biogeosciences* 15, no. 22: 6847–65. https://doi.org/10.5194/bg-15-6847-2018

Martin, S., A. Rieple, J. Chang, B. Boniface, and A. Ahmed. 2015. "Small Farmers and Sustainability: Institutional Barriers to Investment and Innovation in the Malaysian Palm Oil Industry in Sabah". *Journal of Rural Studies* 40: 46–58. https://doi. org/10.1016/j.jrurstud.2015.06.002

Martindale, L. 2021. "From Land Consolidation and Food Safety to Taobao Villages and Alternative Food Networks: Four Components of China's Dynamic Agri-Rural Innovation System". *Journal of Rural Studies* 82: 404–16. https://doi.org/10.1016/j. jrurstud.2021.01.012

Marvin, D.C., L.P. Koh, A.J. Lynam, S. Wich, A.B. Davies, R. Krishnamurthy, E. Stokes, R. Starkey, and G.P. Asner. 2016. "Integrating Technologies for Scalable Ecology and Conservation". *Global Ecology and Conservation* 7: 262–75. https://doi. org/10.1016/j.gecco.2016.07.002

Maryudi, A., H. Kurniawan, B.D. Siswoko, W. Andayani, and B. Murdawa. 2017. "What Do Forest Audits Say? The Indonesian Mandatory Forest Certification". *International Forestry Review* 19, no. 2: 170–79.

Maseyk, F.J., A.D. Mackay, H.P. Possingham, E.J. Dominati, and Y.M. Buckley. 2017. "Managing Natural Capital Stocks for the Provision of Ecosystem Services". *Conservation Letters* 10, no. 2: 211–20.

Masni, Z., and M.E. Wasli. 2019. "Yield Performance and Nutrient Uptake of Red Rice Variety (MRM 16) at Different NPK Fertilizer Rates". *International Journal of Agronomy* 2019: 1–6. https://doi.org/10.1155/2019/5134358

Masuda, Y.J., B. Castro, I. Aggraeni, N.H. Wolff, K. Ebi, T. Garg, E.T. Game, J. Krenz, and J. Spector. 2019. "How Are Healthy, Working Populations Affected by Increasing Temperatures in the Tropics? Implications for Climate Change Adaptation Policies". *Global Environmental Change* 56: 29–40. https://doi.org/10.1016/j. gloenvcha.2019.03.005

Matsumoto, K., W.A. Noerdjito, and K. Fukuyama. 2015. "Restoration of Butterflies in Acacia Mangium Plantations Established on Degraded Grasslands in East Kalimantan". *Journal of Tropical Forest Science* 27, no. 1: 47–59.

Mauerhofer, V., K. Hubacek, and A. Coleby. 2013. "From Polluter Pays to Provider Gets: Distribution of Rights and Costs under Payments for Ecosystem Services". *Ecology and Society* 18, no. 4. https://doi.org/10.5751/ES-06025-180441

Maulia, E. 2019. "Jokowi Announces Indonesia's New Capital in East Kalimantan". *Nikkei Asian Review*, 2019. https://asia.nikkei.com/Politics/Jokowi-announces-Indonesia-s-new-capital-in-East-Kalimantan.

Mayrowani, H. 2012. "Pengembangan Pertanian Organik di Indonesia". *Forum Penelitian Agro Ekonomi* 30, no. 2: 91–108.

Mba, O.I., M.-J. Dumont, and M. Ngadi. 2015. "Palm Oil: Processing, Characterization and Utilization in the Food Industry—A Review". *Food Bioscience* 10: 26–41. https://doi.org/10.1016/j.fbio.2015.01.003

McAlpine, C.A., A. Johnson, A. Salazar, J. Syktus, K. Wilson, E. Meijaard, L. Seabrook, P. Dargusch, H. Nordin, and D. Sheil. 2018. "Forest Loss and Borneo's Climate". *Environmental Research Letters* 13, no. 4. https://doi.org/10.1088/1748-9326/aaa4ff

McArthur, J.W., and G.C. McCord. 2017. "Fertilizing Growth: Agricultural Inputs and Their Effects in Economic Development". *Journal of Development Economics* 127: 133–52. https://doi.org/10.1016/j.jdeveco.2017.02.007

McBeth, J. 1995. "Swamp for Sale: Indonesia Woos Private Sector for Huge Rice Scheme". *Far Eastern Economic Review* 158: 58–59.

McCarthy, J.F. 2012. "Certifying in Contested Spaces: Private Regulation in Indonesian Forestry and Palm Oil". *Third World Quarterly* 33, no. 10: 1871–88. https://doi.org/10.1080/01436597.2012.729721

———. 2013. "Tenure and Transformation in Central Kalimantan After the 'Million Hectare' Project". In *Land for the People: The State and Agrarian Conflict in Indonesia*, pp. 183–214. Athens, US: Ohio University Press.

———, and K. Obidzinski. 2017. "Framing the Food Poverty Question: Policy Choices and Livelihood Consequences in Indonesia". *Journal of Rural Studies* 54: 344–54. https://doi.org/10.1016/j.jrurstud.2017.06.004

———, and K. Robinson. 2016. *Land and Development in Indonesia: Searching for the People's Sovereignty*. Singapore: ISEAS – Yusof Ishak Institute.

McClure, M., C. Machalaba, C. Zambrana-Torrelio, Y. Feferholtz, K.D. Lee, P. Daszak, W.B. Karesh, and Future Earth oneHEALTH Global Research Project. 2019. "Incorporating Health Outcomes into Land-Use Planning". *EcoHealth* 16, no. 4: 627–37. https://doi.org/10.1007/s10393-019-01439-x

MCMC. 2020. "Facts & Figures 1Q 2020". Malaysian Communications and Multimedia Commission (MCMC) Cyberjaya, Malaysia: MCMC. https://www.mcmc.gov.my/skmmgovmy/media/General/pdf/Q1-2019.pdf

Medrilzam, M., P. Dargusch, J. Herbohn, and C. Smith. 2014. "The Socio-Ecological Drivers of Forest Degradation in Part of the Tropical Peatlands of Central Kalimantan, Indonesia". *Forestry* 87, no. 2: 335–45. https://doi.org/10.1093/forestry/cpt033

Meijaard, E., N.K. Abram, J.A. Wells, A.S. Pellier, M. Ancrenaz, D.L. Gaveau, R.K. Runting, and K. Mengersen. 2013. "People's Perceptions About the Importance of Forests on Borneo". *PLoS ONE* 8, no. 9: e73008. https://doi.org/10.1371/journal.pone.0073008

———, T.M. Brooks, K.M. Carlson, E.M. Slade, J. Garcia-Ulloa, D.L.A. Gaveau, J.S.H. Lee, T. Santika, D. Juffe-Bignoli, M.J. Struebig, S.A. Wich, M. Ancrenaz, L.P. Koh, N. Zamira, J.F. Abrams, H.H.T. Prins, C.N. Sendashonga, D. Murdiyarso, P.R. Furumo, N. Macfarlane, R. Hoffmann, M. Persio, A. Descals, Z. Szantoi, and D. Sheil. 2020. "The Environmental Impacts of Palm Oil in Context". *Nature Plants* 6, no. 12: 1418–26. https://doi.org/10.1038/s41477-020-00813-w

———, C. Morgans, N. Abram, and M. Ancrenaz. 2017. "An Impact Analysis of RSPO Certification on Borneo Forest Cover And Orangutan Populations".

———, and D. Sheil. 2019. "The Moral Minefield of Ethical Oil Palm and Sustainable Development". *Frontiers in Forests and Global Change* 2. https://doi.org/10.3389/ffgc.2019.00022

Meilani, M.M., R. Thwaites, D. Race, W. Andayani, L.R.W. Faida, and A. Maryudi. 2019.

"Finding Alternatives of Livelihood Sources for Forest Dependent Communities in Protected Areas: A Case Study of Sebangau National Park, Central Kalimantan Province, Indonesia". *IOP Conf. Ser.: Earth Environ. Sci.* 285: 012005

Meilasari-Sugiana, A. 2018. "Oil Palm Companies, Privatization and Social Dissonance: Towards a Socially Viable and Ecologically Sustainable Land Reform in Tanah Laut Regency, South Kalimantan, Indonesia". *Journal of Political Ecology* 25, no. 1: 548–68. https://doi.org/10.2458/v25i1.22045

Melendy, L., S.C. Hagen, F.B. Sullivan, T.R.H. Pearson, S.M. Walker, P. Ellis, Kustiyo, A.K. Sambodo, O. Roswintiarti, M.A. Hanson, A.W. Klassen, M.W. Palace, B.H. Braswell, and G.M. Delgado. 2018. "Automated Method for Measuring the Extent of Selective Logging Damage with Airborne LiDAR Data". *ISPRS Journal of Photogrammetry and Remote Sensing* 139: 228–40. https://doi.org/10.1016/j.isprsjprs.2018.02.022

Melling, L. 2016. "Peatland in Malaysia". In *Tropical Peatland Ecosystems*, pp. 59–73. Springer Japan.

Méndez, V.E., C.M. Bacon, M. Olson, S. Petchers, D. Herrador, C. Carranza, L. Trujillo, C. Guadarrama-Zugasti, A. Cordon, and A. Mendoza. 2010. "Effects of Fair Trade and Organic Certifications on Small-Scale Coffee Farmer Households in Central America and Mexico". *Renewable Agriculture and Food Systems* 25, no. 3: 236–51.

Menon, S.J. 2018. "Highland Tales in the Heart of Borneo: Postcolonial Capitalism, Multiculturalism, and Survivance". *Ariel* 49, no. 4: 163–88. https://doi.org/10.1353/ari.2018.0033

Mersat, N.I. 2018. "The Sarawak Dayaks' Shift in Malaysia's 2018 Election". *The Round Table* 107, no. 6: 729–37. https://doi.org/10.1080/00358533.2018.1545940

Mertz, O., K. Egay, T.B. Bruun, and T.S. Colding. 2013. "The Last Swiddens of Sarawak, Malaysia". *Human Ecology* 41, no. 1: 109–18. https://doi.org/10.1007/s10745-012-9559-3

MESTECC Malaysia. 2018. "Malaysia: Third National Communication and Second Biennial Update Report to the UNFCCC". Edited by Ministry of Energy, S., Technology, Environment and Climate Change. Putrajaya, Malaysia: Ministry of Energy, Science, Technology, Environment and Climate Change.

Mewah Group. 2021. "Our Manufacturing Facilities". https://www.mewahgroup.com/OurBusiness.html (accessed 26 October 2021).

Miard, P., K.A.I. Nekaris, and H. Ramlee. 2017. "Hiding in the Dark: Local Ecological Knowledge About Slow Loris in Sarawak Sheds Light on Relationships Between Human Populations and Wild Animals". *Hum Ecol Interdiscip J* 45, no. 6: 823–31. https://doi.org/10.1007/s10745-017-9954-x

MIDA. 2018. "Malaysia Investment Performance Report 2018". Malaysia Investment Development Authority (MIDA), Kuala Lumpur. https://www.mida.gov.my/home/malaysia:-investment-performance/posts/

Milano, S., R. Ponzio, and P. Sardo. 2018. "The Ark of Taste. How to Build the World's Largest Catalog of Flavors: A Heritage to Discover and To Save". Slow Food Foundation. www.slowfoodfoundation.com

Milner, A. 2009. *The Malays*. John Wiley & Sons.

Ming, R.Y.C., Y. Sobeng, F. Zaini, and N. Busri. 2018. "Suitability of Peat Swamp Areas for Commercial Production of Sago Palms: The Sarawak Experience". In *Sago Palm: Multiple Contributions to Food Security and Sustainable Livelihoods*, pp. 91–108. Singapore: Springer Singapore.

Mintz-Habib, N. 2013. "Malaysian Biofuels Industry Experience: A Socio-Political Analysis of the Commercial Environment". *Energy Policy* 56: 88–100. https://doi.org/10.1016/j.enpol.2012.08.069

———. 2016. *Biofuels, Food Security, and Developing Economies*. Taylor and Francis Inc.

Missemer, A. 2018. "Natural Capital as an Economic Concept, History and Contemporary Issues". *Ecological Economics* 143: 90–96. https://doi.org/10.1016/j.ecolecon.2017.07.011

Miteva, D.A., C.J. Loucks, and S.K. Pattanayak. 2015. "Social and Environmental Impacts of Forest Management Certification in Indonesia". *PLoS ONE* 10, no. 7. https://doi.org/10.1371/journal.pone.0129675

Miwil, O. 2021. "WWF-Malaysia Calls for Inclusion of SDGs in Sabah Maju Jaya Development". *New Straits Times*, 24 January 2021. https://www.nst.com.my/news/nation/2021/01/660099/wwf-malaysia-calls-inclusion-sdgs-sabah-maju-jaya-development

MoA Indonesia. 2018. "Food Security and Vulnerability Atlas". Food Security Dvision (Badan Ketahanan Pangan), Ministry of Agriculture Indonesia.

MoEF. 2020a. "Sistem Informasi Legalitas Kayu (SILK)". http://liu.dephut.go.id/index.php (accessed 30 March 2020).

———. 2020b. *The State of Indonesia's Forests 2020*. Edited by Ministry of Environment and Forest.

MoEF Indonesia. 2018. *Indonesia: Second Biennial Update Report Under the United Nations Framework Convention on Climate Change*. Edited by Directorate General of Climate Change, MOEF, Jakarta.

———. 2019. "Statistik Lingkungan Hidup dan Kehutanan Tahun 2018" [Statistics Environment and Forest Year 2018]. Ministry of Environment and Forest Indonesia, Jakarta.

Moeliono, M., E. Wollenberg, and G. Limberg. 2009. *The Decentralization of Forest Governance: Politics, Economics and the Fight for Control of Forests in Indonesian Borneo*. London: Earthscan Publications.

MoH. 2021. "COVID-19 Cases in Malaysia". Ministry of Health (MoH) Malaysia.

Moh, Y., and L. Abd Manaf. 2017. "Solid Waste Management Transformation and Future Challenges of Source Separation and Recycling Practice in Malaysia". *Resources, Conservation and Recycling* 116: 1–14. https://doi.org/10.1016/j.resconrec.2016.09.012

Mohamad Naim, H., A.N. Yaakub, and D.A. Awang Hamdan. 2016. "Commercialization of Sago through Estate Plantation Scheme in Sarawak: The Way Forward". *International Journal of Agronomy* 2016: 1–6. https://doi.org/10.1155/2016/8319542

Mohammad, H.S., and I. Bujang. 2019. "Does Intellectual Capital Influence Firms'

Financial Performance? A Comparative Analysis into Three Malaysian Industries". *International Journal of Business and Society* 20, no. 1: 260–76.

Montefrio, M.J.F., Y.Y. Ortiga, and M.R.C.B. Josol. 2014. "Inducing Development: Social Remittances and the Expansion of Oil Palm". *International Migration Review* 48, no. 1: 216–42. https://doi.org/10.1111/imre.12075

Morgans, C.L., E. Meijaard, T. Santika, E. Law, S. Budiharta, M. Ancrenaz, and K.A. Wilson. 2018. "Evaluating the Effectiveness of Palm Oil Certification in Delivering Multiple Sustainability Objectives". *Environmental Research Letters* 13, no. 6. https://doi.org/10.1088/1748-9326/aac6f4

Morishita, A. 2016. "Political Dynamics of Foreign-Invested Development Projects in Decentralized Indonesia: The Case of Coal Railway Projects in Kalimantan". *Southeast Asian Studies* 5, no. 3: 413–42. https://doi.org/10.20495/seas.5.3_413

MOTAC. 2015. "National Ecotourism Plan 2016–2025: Executive Summary". Edited by Ministry of Tourism.

MPOB. 2021. "Economic and Industry Development Division". Malaysian Palm Oil Board. http://bepi.mpob.gov.my/index.php/en/ (accessed 4 January 2021).

MTCC. 2020. "Certified Forests". Malaysian Timber Certification Council (MTCC). http://mtcc.com.my/certified-forests/ (accessed 11 November 2020).

Muazir, S., and H.-C. Hsieh. 2012. "Borderlands and Tourism Development in Kalimantan Island: Kalimantan Barat, Indonesia-Sarawak, Malaysia 'Head to Head'". *Journal of Design and Built Environment* 13, no. 1.

———, and H.C. Hsieh. 2014. "Lagging Yet Strategic: Tourism and Regional Development Planning in a Lagging-Outermost-Forefront Area (Borderland) in Indonesia". *Tourism* 62, no. 4: 361–76.

Muhdar, M., M. Tavip, and R. Al Hidayah. 2019. "State Failure in Recognition and Protection of Indigenous Peoples Over Natural Resource Access in East Kalimantan". *Asia Pacific Law Review* 27, no. 1: 127–43. https://doi.org/10.1080/10192557.2019.1665921

Mulyana, R.N. 2021. "Jatam: Banjir Kalsel Karena Banyaknya Izin Tambang Batubara dan Sawit". *Kontan.co.id*, 20 January 2021. https://nasional.kontan.co.id/news/jatam-banjir-kalsel-karena-banyaknya-izin-tambang-batubara-dan-sawit.

Mulyani, A., and M. Syarwani. 2013. "Karakteristik dan Potensi Lahan Sub-Optimal untuk Pengembangan Pertanian di Indonesia". Prosiding Seminar Nasional Lahan Sub-optimal "Intensifikasi Pengelolaan Lahan Sub-optimal dalam Rangka Mendukung Kemandirian Pangan Nasional", Palembang, 20–21 September 2013.

Mulyani, M., and P. Jepson. 2015. "Social Learning Through a REDD+ 'Village Agreement': Insights from the KFCP in Indonesia". *Asia Pacific Viewpoint* 56, no. 1: 79–95. https://doi.org/10.1111/apv.12083

———, and P. Jepson. 2016. "Does the 'One Map Initiative' Represent a New Path for Forest Mapping in Indonesia? Assessing the Contribution of the REDD+ Initiative in Effecting Forest Governance Reform". *Forests* 8, no. 1. https://doi.org/10.3390/f8010014

Murdiyarso, D., S. Dewi, D. Lawrence, and F. Seymour. 2011. "Indonesia's Forest

Moratorium: A Stepping Stone to Better Forest Governance?". Bogor, Indonesia: CIFOR. https://www.cifor.org/library/3561/

——, M.F. Saragi-Sasmito, and A. Rustini. 2019. "Greenhouse Gas Emissions in Restored Secondary Tropical Peat Swamp Forests". *Mitigation and Adaptation Strategies for Global Change* 24, no. 4: 507–20. https://doi.org/10.1007/s11027-017-9776-6

Murni, S., J. Whale, T. Urmee, J.K. Davis, and D. Harries. 2013. "Learning from Experience: A Survey of Existing Micro-Hydropower Projects in Ba'Kelalan, Malaysia". *Renewable Energy* 60: 88–97. https://doi.org/10.1016/j.renene.2013.04.009

Murphy, D.J. 2014. "The Future of Oil Palm as a Major Global Crop: Opportunities and Challenges". *J Oil Palm Res* 26, no. 1: 1–24.

Musim Mas. 2020. "Sustainability Report 2020". https://www.musimmas.com/wp-content/uploads/2020/11/Musim-Mas-SR-2019.pdf

Mustafa, F.H., A. Bagul, S. Senoo, and R. Shapawi. 2016. "A Review of Smart Fish Farming Systems". *J Aqua Eng Fish Res* 2, no. 4: 193–200.

Muttaqin, M.Z., I. Alviya, M. Lugina, F.A.U. Hamdani, and Indartik. 2019. "Developing Community-Based Forest Ecosystem Service Management to Reduce Emissions from Deforestation and Forest Degradation". *Forest Policy and Economics* 108. https://doi.org/10.1016/j.forpol.2019.05.024

Naito, D., and N. Ishikawa. 2020. "Certifying Borneo's Forest Landscape: Implementation Processes of Forest Certification in Sarawak". In *Advances in Asian Human-Environmental Research*. Springer International Publishing.

Nambiar, E.K.S., C.E. Harwood, and D.S. Mendham. 2018. "Paths to Sustainable Wood Supply to the Pulp and Paper Industry in Indonesia after Diseases Have Forced a Change of Species from Acacia to Eucalypts". *Australian Forestry* 81, no. 3: 148–61. https://doi.org/10.1080/00049158.2018.1482798

Nasution, M.A., A. Wulandari, T. Ahamed, and R. Noguchi. 2020. "Alternative POME Treatment Technology in the Implementation of Roundtable on Sustainable Palm Oil, Indonesian Sustainable Palm Oil (ISPO), and Malaysian Sustainable Palm Oil (MSPO) Standards Using LCA and AHP Methods". *Sustainability* 12, no. 10: 4101.

Naylor, R.L., M.M. Higgins, R.B. Edwards, and W.P. Falcon. 2019. "Decentralization and the Environment: Assessing Smallholder Oil Palm Development in Indonesia". *Ambio*: 1–14.

Nectoux, F., and Y. Kuroda. 1989. *Timber from the South Seas: An Analysis of Japan's Tropical Timber Trade and Its Environmental Impact*. WWF International.

Nelson, J., N. Muhammed, and R.A. Rashid. 2016. "An Empirical Study on Compatibility of Sarawak Forest Ordinance and Bidayuh Native Customary Laws in Forest Management". *Small-Scale Forestry* 15, no. 2: 135–48. https://doi.org/10.1007/s11842-015-9313-y

——, H. Yahya, M.S.H. Chowdhury, and N. Muhammed. 2014. "Indigenous Community Awareness and Rights to Forest in Kawang Forest Reserve, Sabah, Malaysia". *International Journal of Sustainable Development and World Ecology* 21, no. 2: 127–37. https://doi.org/10.1080/13504509.2014.880959

NEPCon. 2013. "Evaluation and Revision of the Sabah TLAS Standard and Audit Checklists". NEPCon. https://preferredbynature.org/library/report/sabah-tlas-review

Ng, K.K.S., S.L. Lee, L.H. Tnah, Z. Nurul-Farhanah, C.H. Ng, C.T. Lee, N. Tani, B. Diway, P.S. Lai, and E. Khoo. 2016. "Forensic Timber Identification: A Case Study of a CITES Listed Species, Gonystylus bancanus (Thymelaeaceae)". *Forensic Sci Int Genet* 23: 197–209. https://doi.org/10.1016/j.fsigen.2016.05.002

Nga, J.L., W.K. Ramlan, and S. Naim. 2021. "COVID-19 Pandemic and Unemployment in Malaysia: A Case Study from Sabah". *Cosmopolitan Civil Societies: An Interdisciplinary Journal* 13, no. 2: 73–90.

Ngan, S.L., B.S. How, S.Y. Teng, M.A.B. Promentilla, P. Yatim, A.C. Er, and H.L. Lam. 2019. "Prioritization of Sustainability Indicators for Promoting the Circular Economy: The Case of Developing Countries". *Renewable and Sustainable Energy Reviews* 111: 314–31. https://doi.org/10.1016/j.rser.2019.05.001

Nguitragool, P. 2010. *Environmental Cooperation in Southeast Asia: ASEAN's Regime for Transboundary Haze Pollution*. Routledge Contemporary Southeast Asia Series, Vol. 21. London: Routledge.

Nkrumah, P.N., R. Tisserand, R.L. Chaney, A.J.M. Baker, J.L. Morel, R. Goudon, P.D. Erskine, G. Echevarria, and A. van der Ent. 2019. "The First Tropical 'Metal Farm': Some Perspectives from Field and Pot Experiments". *Journal of Geochemical Exploration* 198: 114–22. https://doi.org/10.1016/j.gexplo.2018.12.003

Nobre, C.A., G. Sampaio, L.S. Borma, J.C. Castilla-Rubio, J.S. Silva, and M. Cardoso. 2016. "Land-Use and Climate Change Risks in the Amazon and the Need of a Novel Sustainable Development Paradigm". *Proc Natl Acad Sci U S A* 113, no. 39: 10759–68. https://doi.org/10.1073/pnas.1605516113

Nofyanza, S., K. Barney, S. Peteru, R. Paembonan, and R. Kristanti. 2021. *The Politics of the Green Economy in Provincial Indonesia: Insights from Coal and Oil Palm Sector Reforms in East Kalimantan*. Bogor, Indonesia: CIFOR.

Noojipady, P., D.C. Morton, W. Schroeder, K.M. Carlson, C. Huang, H.K. Gibbs, D. Burns, N.F. Walker, and S.D. Prince. 2017. "Managing Fire Risk During Drought: The Influence of Certification and El Niño on Fire-Driven Forest Conversion for Oil Palm in Southeast Asia". *Earth Syst. Dynam.* 8, no. 3: 749–71. https://doi.org/10.5194/esd-8-749-2017

Normelani, E. 2016. "The Floating Market of Lok Baitan, South Kalimantan". *Journal of Indonesian Tourism and Development Studies* 4, no. 1: 1–4.

Novindra, N., B.M. Sinaga, S. Hartoyo, and E. Erwidodo. 2019. "Impact of Increasing in Production Capacity of CPO Downstream Industries on Competitiveness and Welfare of Oil Palm Farmers in Indonesia". *International Journal of Oil Palm* 2, no. 2: 88–100.

Nugraha, B., L.P. Putri, and J. Suprihanto. 2018. "Krayan Heart of Borneo: Indonesian Potential Tourism Destination Enjoyed by Malaysia". *KnE Social Sciences*: 118–29.

Nugroho, B., A. Dermawan, and L. Putzel. 2013. "Financing Smallholder Timber Planting in Indonesia: Mismatches Between Loan Scheme Attributes and Smallholder

Borrowing Characteristics". *International Forestry Review* 15, no. 4: 499–508. https://doi.org/10.1505/146554813809025702

Nugroho, H.Y.S.H., A. Skidmore, and Y.A. Hussin. 2020. "Verifying Indigenous Based-Claims to Forest Rights Using Image Interpretation and Spatial Analysis: A Case Study in Gunung Lumut Protection Forest, East Kalimantan, Indonesia". *GeoJournal.* https://doi.org/10.1007/s10708-020-10260-x

———, A. van der Veen, A.K. Skidmore, and Y.A. Hussin. 2018. "Expansion of Traditional Land-Use and Deforestation: A Case Study of an Adat Forest in the Kandilo Subwatershed, East Kalimantan, Indonesia". *Journal of Forestry Research* 29, no. 2: 495–513. https://doi.org/10.1007/s11676-017-0449-9

Nurrochmat, D.R., R. Boer, M. Ardiansyah, G. Immanuel, and H. Purwawangsa. 2020. "Policy Forum: Reconciling Palm Oil Targets and Reduced Deforestation: Landswap and Agrarian Reform in Indonesia". *Forest Policy and Economics* 119: 102291. https://doi.org/10.1016/j.forpol.2020.102291

Obeth, E. 2013. "Trust and Commitment in Horticultural Supply Chains of Small Scale Business: A Case Study in East Kalimantan, Indonesia". In *Acta Horticulturae,* edited by P.J. Batt.

Obidzinski, K., and A. Dermawan. 2010. "Smallholder Timber Plantation Development in Indonesia: What Is Preventing Progress?". *International Forestry Review* 12, no. 4: 339–48.

Octania, G. 2021. "The Government's Role in the Indonesian Rice Supply Chain". Center for Indonesian Policy Studies (CIPS). https://repository.cips-indonesia.org/publications/338075/the-governments-role-in-the-indonesian-rice-supply-chain

OECD. 2020. "Digitalisation in the Bioeconomy: Convergence for the Bio-Based Industries". In *The Digitalisation of Science, Technology and Innovation.*

Oettli, P., S.K. Behera, and T. Yamagata. 2018. "Climate Based Predictability of Oil Palm Tree Yield in Malaysia". *Sci Rep* 8, no. 1: 2271. https://doi.org/10.1038/s41598-018-20298-0

Ogg, C. 2020. "Transforming Farm-Program Incentives to Preserve Tropical Forests". *Conservation Biology* 34, no. 3: 762–65. https://doi.org/10.1111/cobi.13393

Okuno, K., and T. Ichikawa. 2020. "Oil Palm Plantations and Bezoar Stones: An Ethnographic Sketch of Human-Nature Interactions in Sarawak". In *Advances in Asian Human-Environmental Research*. Springer International Publishing.

Olbrei, E., and S. Howes. 2012. "A Very Real and Practical Contribution? Lessons from the Kalimantan Forests and Climate Partnership". *Climate Law* 3, no. 2: 103–37. https://doi.org/10.3233/CL-2012-059

Ong, C., and K. Wilson. 2020. "Rice Revitalization and Food Sovereignty in Sabah". *Agriculture and Human Values* 37, no. 3: 555–56. https://doi.org/10.1007/s10460-020-10082-0

Ong, C.E., M. Ormond, and D. Sulianti. 2017. "Performing 'Chinese-ness' in Singkawang: Diasporic Moorings, Festivals and Tourism". *Asia Pacific Viewpoint* 58, no. 1: 41–56. https://doi.org/10.1111/apv.12149

Onitsuka, K., A.R.T. Hidayat, and W. Huang. 2018. "Challenges for the Next Level of

Digital Divide in Rural Indonesian Communities". *Electronic Journal of Information Systems in Developing Countries* 84, no. 2: e12021. https://doi.org/10.1002/isd2.12021

Oosterveer, P. 2015. "Promoting Sustainable Palm Oil: Viewed from a Global Networks and Flows Perspective". *Journal of Cleaner Production* 107: 146–53. https://doi.org/10.1016/j.jclepro.2014.01.019

Orsato, R.J., S.R. Clegg, and H. Falcão. 2013. "The Political Ecology of Palm Oil Production". *Journal of Change Management* 13, no. 4: 444–59. https://doi.org/10.1080/14697017.2013.851916

Osaki, M., B. Setiadi, H. Takahashi, and M. Evri. 2016. "Peatland in Kalimantan". In *Tropical Peatland Ecosystems*, pp. 91–112. Springer Japan.

Ota, T., K. Kusin, F.M. Kilonzi, A. Usup, K. Moji, and S. Kobayashi. 2020. "Sustainable Financing for Payment for Ecosystem Services (PES) to Conserve Peat Swamp Forest Through Enterprises Based on Swiftlets' Nests: An Awareness Survey in Central Kalimantan, Indonesia". *Small-scale Forestry*. https://doi.org/10.1007/s11842-020-09452-7

Pacheco, P., G.C. Schoneveld, A. Dermawan, H. Komarudin, and M. Djama. 2017. *The Public and Private Regime Complex for Governing Palm Oil Supply: What Scope for Building Connections and Enhancing Complementarities?* Bogor, Indonesia: CIFOR.

Padmanabhan, E., and H. Eswaran. 2011. "Impact of Shifting Agriculture on the Sustainability of Anthroscapes in Sarawak, Malaysia". In *Sustainable Land Management: Learning from the Past for the Future*, pp. 285–92. Springer Berlin Heidelberg.

Padoch, C., and N.L. Peluso. 1996. *Borneo in Transition*. Oxford University Press.

Page, S., and A. Hoscilo. 2018. "Fire in Borneo Peatlands". In *The Wetland Book I: Structure and Function, Management, and Methods*, pp. 65–71. Springer Netherlands.

Page, S.E., F. Siegert, J.O. Rieley, H.D.V. Boehm, A. Jaya, and S. Limin. 2002. "The Amount of Carbon Released from Peat and Forest Fires in Indonesia during 1997". *Nature* 420, no. 6911: 61–65. https://doi.org/10.1038/nature01131

Palmer, C., and S. Engel. 2007. "For Better or for Worse? Local Impacts of the Decentralization of Indonesia's Forest Sector". *World Development* 35, no. 12: 2131–49. https://doi.org/10.1016/j.worlddev.2007.02.004

Pandong, J., M. Gumal, Z.M. Aton, M.S. Sabki, and L.P. Koh. 2019. "Threats and Lessons Learned from Past Orangutan Conservation Strategies in Sarawak, Malaysia". *Biological Conservation* 234: 56–63. https://doi.org/10.1016/j.biocon.2019.03.016

Pang, T.W., and M.T. Lee. 2013. "Investment Opportunities at Palm Oil Industrial Cluster (POIC) Lahad Datu with Special Reference to Biofuels". In *Advances in Biofuels*, edited by R. Pogaku and R.H. Sarbatly, pp. 15–26. Boston, MA: Springer US.

Paoli, G.D., D.R. Peart, M. Leighton, and I. Samsoedin. 2001. "An Ecological and Economic Assessment of the Nontimber Forest Product Gaharu Wood in Gunung Palung National Park, West Kalimantan, Indonesia". *Conservation Biology* 15, no. 6: 1721–32. https://doi.org/10.1046/j.1523-1739.2001.98586.x

Pariatamby, A. 2014. "MSW Management in Malaysia-Changes for Sustainability". In

Municipal Solid Waste Management in Asia and the Pacific Islands: Challenges and Strategic Solutions, edited by A. Pariatamby and M. Tanaka, pp. 195–232. Singapore: Springer Singapore.

Pascual, U., P. Balvanera, S. Díaz, G. Pataki, E. Roth, M. Stenseke, R.T. Watson, E.B. Dessane, M. Islar, and E. Kelemen. 2017. "Valuing Nature's Contributions to People: The IPBES Approach". *Current Opinion in Environmental Sustainability* 26: 7–16.

Paterson, R.R.M., L. Kumar, S. Taylor, and N. Lima. 2015. "Future Climatic Effects on Suitability for Growth of Oil Palms in Malaysia and Indonesia". *Sci Rep* 5, no. 14457. https://doi.org/10.1038/srep14457

Paturusi, S. 2019. "Ibu Kota Negara di Kaltim, Harga Tanah di Sepaku, Penajam Naik Dua Kali Lipat". *Tribunnews.com*, 28 August 2019. https://kaltim.tribunnews.com/2019/08/28/ibu-kota-negara-di-kaltim-harga-tanah-di-sepaku-penajam-naik-dua-kali-lipat?page=2

Pauli, N., C. Donough, T. Oberthür, J. Cock, R. Verdooren, Rahmadsyah, G. Abdurrohim, K. Indrasuara, A. Lubis, T. Dolong, and J.M. Pasuquin. 2014. "Changes in Soil Quality Indicators under Oil Palm Plantations Following Application of 'Best Management Practices' in a Four-Year Field Trial". *Agriculture, Ecosystems and Environment* 195: 98–111. https://doi.org/10.1016/j.agee.2014.05.005

PEFC. 2020, "Double Certification FSC and PEFC – 2019 Estimation". https://www.pefc.org/discover-pefc/facts-and-figures

Pellier, A.S., J.A. Wells, N.K. Abram, D. Gaveau, and E. Meijaard. 2014. "Through the Eyes of Children: Perceptions of Environmental Change in Tropical Forests". *PLoS ONE* 9, no. 8: e103005. https://doi.org/10.1371/journal.pone.0103005

Peluso, N.L. 2017. "Plantations and Mines: Resource Frontiers and the Politics of the Smallholder Slot". *Journal of Peasant Studies* 44, no. 4: 954–89. https://doi.org/10.1080/03066150.2017.1339692

———. 2018. "Entangled Territories in Small-Scale Gold Mining Frontiers: Labor Practices, Property, and Secrets in Indonesian Gold Country". *World Development* 101: 400–16. https://doi.org/10.1016/j.worlddev.2016.11.003

PEMANDU. 2010. "Economic Transformation Programme (ETP): A Roadmap for Malaysia". Edited by Performance Management and Delivery Unit, Prime Minister's Department, Malaysia.

Pengiran Bagul, A. 2009. "Success of Ecotourism Sites and Local Community Participation in Sabah". PhD, School of Management, Victoria University of Wellington.

Permadi, D.B., M. Burton, R. Pandit, D. Race, C. Ma, D. Mendham, and E.B. Hardiyanto. 2018. "Socio-economic Factors Affecting the Rate of Adoption of Acacia Plantations by Smallholders in Indonesia". *Land Use Policy* 76: 215–23. https://doi.org/10.1016/j.landusepol.2018.04.054

———, M. Burton, R. Pandit, I. Walker, and D. Race. 2017. "Which Smallholders Are Willing to Adopt Acacia Mangium under Long-Term Contracts? Evidence from a Choice Experiment Study in Indonesia". *Land Use Policy* 65: 211–23. https://doi.org/10.1016/j.landusepol.2017.04.015

Persoon, G.A., and M. Osseweijer. 2008. *Reflections on the Heart of Borneo*. Series 24. Wageningen: Tropenbos International.

——, and R. Simarmata. 2014. "Undoing 'Marginality': The Islands of the Mahakam Delta, East Kalimantan (Indonesia)". *Journal of Marine and Island Cultures* 3, no. 2: 43–53. https://doi.org/10.1016/j.imic.2014.11.002

Peter, B.G., J.P. Messina, Z. Lin, and S.S. Snapp. 2020. "Crop Climate Suitability Mapping on the Cloud: A Geovisualization Application for Sustainable Agriculture". *Scientific Reports* 10, no. 1: 15487. https://doi.org/10.1038/s41598-020-72384-x

Pfeifer, M., L. Kor, R. Nilus, E. Turner, J. Cusack, I. Lysenko, M. Khoo, V.K. Chey, A.C. Chung, and R.M. Ewers. 2016. "Mapping the Structure of Borneo's Tropical Forests Across a Degradation Gradient". *Remote Sensing of Environment* 176: 84–97. https://doi.org/10.1016/j.rse.2016.01.014

Phua, M.H., W. Wong, M.H. Goh, K.U. Kamlun, J. Kodoh, S. Teo, F.M. Cooke, and S. Tsuyuki. 2014. "Deforestation, Forest Degradation and Readiness of Local People of Lubuk Antu, Sarawak for REDD". *Sains Malaysiana* 43, no. 10: 1461–70.

Pierce Colfer, C., and I. Resosudarmo. 2002. *Which Way Forward: People, Forests, and Policymaking in Indonesia*. Taylor and Francis.

Pirard, R., N. Schulz, J. Benedict, R. Heilmayr, B. Ayre, and H. Bellfield. 2020. "Corporate Ownership and Dominance of Indonesia's Palm Oil Supply Chains". *Trase Infobrief* 9. http://resources.trase.earth/documents/infobriefs/infobrief09EN.pdf

Pohnan, E., H. Ompusunggu, and C. Webb. 2015. "Does Tree Planting Change Minds? Assessing the Use of Community Participation in Reforestation to Address Illegal Logging in West Kalimantan". *Tropical Conservation Science* 8, no. 1: 45–57. https://doi.org/10.1177/194008291500800107

Polasky, S., B. Bryant, P. Hawthorne, J. Johnson, B. Keeler, and D. Pennington. 2015. "Inclusive Wealth as a Metric of Sustainable Development". *Annual Review of Environment and Resources* 40, no. 1: 445–66. https://doi.org/10.1146/annurev-environ-101813-013253

Pontianak Post. 2020. "Teh Borneo Lahir di Sintang". 28 January 2020. https://pontianakpost.co.id/teh-borneo-lahir-di-sintang/

Possingham, H.P., M. Bode, and C.J. Klein. 2015. "Optimal Conservation Outcomes Require Both Restoration and Protection". *PLoS Biology* 13, no. 1. https://doi.org/10.1371/journal.pbio.1002052

Potter, L. 1988. "Eating the Forests in Gulps and Nibbles: Concessionaires, Transmigrants and Free Loggers in South Kalimantan". *Inside Indonesia* (October): 19–21.

——. 1993. "Banjarese in and beyond the Hulu Sungai. A Study in Cultural Independence, Economic Opportunity and Mobility". In *New Challenges in the Modern Economic History of Indonesia*, edited by J.T. Lindblad, pp. 264–98. Proceedings of the First Conference in Indonesia's Modern Economic History, Jakarta, 1–4 October 1991, Bureau of Indonesian Studies, University of Leiden (also in Indonesian).

——. 1996. "Forestry in Contemporary Indonesia". In *Historical Foundations of a National Economy in Indonesia, 1890s–1990s*, edited by J.Th. Lindblad. Proceedings of the Colloquium, 20–22 September 1994, Amsterdam. Koninklijke Nederlandse

Akademie van Wetenschappen Verhandelingen, Afd. Letterkunde. Nieuwe Reeks, deel 167 (also in Indonesian).

———. 1997a. "The Dynamics of Imperata: Historical Overview and Current Farmer Perspectives, with Special Reference to South Kalimantan, Indonesia". *Agroforestry Systems* 36, no. 1: 31–51.

———. 1997b. "A Forest Product Out of Control. Gutta Percha in Indonesia and the Wider Malay World 1845–1915". In *Paper Landscapes: Explorations in the Environmental History of Indonesia*, edited by P. Boomgaard, F. Colombijn, and D. Henley, pp. 281–308. Leiden: KITLV Press.

———. 2005. "Commodifying, Consuming and Converting Kalimantan's Forests, 1950–2002". In *Muddied Waters: Historical and Contemporary Perspectives on Management of Forests and Fisheries in Island Southeast Asia*, pp. 373–400. Leiden: KITLV Press.

———. 2008. "The Oil Palm Question in Borneo". In *Reflections on the Heart of Borneo*, edited by G.A. Persoon and Manon Osseweijer, Series 24, pp. 69–90. Wageningen: Tropenbos International.

———. 2009a. "Oil Palm and Resistance in West Kalimantan, Indonesia". In *Agrarian Angst and Rural Resistance in Contemporary Southeast Asia*, edited by Dominique Caouette and Sarah Turner, pp. 125–54. Routledge.

———. 2009b. "Resource Periphery, Corridor, Heartland: Contesting Land Use in the Kalimantan/Malaysia Borderlands". *Asia Pacific Viewpoint* 50, no. 1: 88–106. https://doi.org/10.1111/j.1467-8373.2009.01383.x

———. 2010. "Kalimantan in the Firing Line: A Note on the Effects of the Global Financial Crisis". *Bulletin of Indonesian Economic Studies* 46, no. 1: 99–109. https://doi.org/10.1080/00074911003642260

———. 2012. "New Transmigration 'Paradigm' in Indonesia: Examples from Kalimantan". *Asia Pacific Viewpoint* 53, no. 3: 272–87. https://doi.org/10.1111/j.1467-8373.2012.01492.x.

———. 2015a. *Managing Oil Palm Landscapes. A Seven-Country Survey of the Modern Palm Oil Industry in Southeast Asia, Latin America and West Africa*. Bogor, Indonesia: CIFOR.

———. 2015b. "Where Are the Swidden Fallows Now? An Overview of Oil Palm and Dayak Agriculture across Kalimantan, with Case Studies from Sanggau, in West Kalimantan". In *Shifting Cultivation and Environmental Change: Indigenous People, Agriculture and Forest Conservation*, edited by M. Cairns, pp. 742–69. Routledge.

———. 2016a. "Alternative Pathways for Smallholder Oil Palm in Indonesia. International Comparisons". In *The Oil Palm Complex: Smallholders, Agribusiness and the State in Indonesia and Malaysia*, edited by R. Cramb and J.F. McCarthy, pp. 155–88. Singapore: NUS Press.

———. 2016b. "How Can the People's Sovereignty Be Achieved in the Oil Palm Sector? Is the Plantation Model Shifting in Favour of Smallholders". In *Land and Development in Indonesia: Searching for the People's Sovereignty*, edited by J. McCarthy and K. Robinson, pp. 315–42. Singapore: ISEAS – Yusof Ishak Institute.

———, and S. Badcock. 2001. *The Effect of Indonesia's Decentralisation on Forests and*

Estate Crops: Case Study of Riau Province, the Original Districts of Kampar and Indragiri Hulu. Bogor, Indonesia: CIFOR.

———, and S. Badcock 2006. "Can Indonesia's Complex Agroforests Survive Globalisation and Decentralisation? Sanggau District, West Kalimantan". In *Environment, Development and Change in Rural Asia-Pacific*, pp. 181–99. Routledge.

———, and J. Lee. 1998. *Tree Planting in Indonesia: Trends, Impacts and Directions.* Bogor, Indonesia: CIFOR.

Potts, J., M. Lynch, A. Wilkings, G. Huppé, M. Cunningham, and V. Voora. 2014. "The State of Sustainability Initiatives Review: Standards and the Green Economy". International Institute for Sustainable Development. https://www.iisd.org/pdf/2014/ssi_2014.pdf

Poynton, S. 2015. *Beyond Certification.* London: Routledge.

Prabowo, D., A. Maryudi, Senawi, and M.A. Imron. 2017. "Conversion of Forests into Oil Palm Plantations in West Kalimantan, Indonesia: Insights from Actors' Power and Its Dynamics". *Forest Policy and Economics* 78: 32–39. https://doi.org/10.1016/j.forpol.2017.01.004

Pramova, E., B. Locatelli, A. Mench, E. Marbyanto, K. Kartika, and H. Prihatmaja. 2013. *Integrating Adaptation into REDD+: Potential Impacts and Social Return on Investment in Setulang, Malinau District, Indonesia".* Vol. 112. Bogor, Indonesia: CIFOR.

Prasad, K. 2015. *Identity Politics and Elections in Malaysia and Indonesia: Ethnic Engineering in Borneo.* Routledge.

Prasetyo, L.B., and M.S. Zulkifli. 2010. "Orchids as a Catalyst for Conservation by the Local Communities of Danau Sentarum". *Borneo Research Bulletin* 41: 162+.

Proctor, S., C.J. McClean, and J. K. Hill. 2011. "Protected Areas of Borneo Fail to Protect Forest Landscapes with High Habitat Connectivity". *Biodiversity and Conservation* 20, no. 12: 2693–704. https://doi.org/10.1007/s10531-011-0099-8

PT Jasa Marga. 2021. "Balikpapan-Samarinda Toll Road Will Be Fully Operational Soon and Sections 1 and 5 are Ready for Operating". https://www.jasamarga.com/public/en/activity/detailactivity.aspx?title=Balikpapan-Samarinda%20Toll%20Road%20Will%20be%20Fully%20Operational%20Soon%20and%20Sections%201%20and%205%20are%20Ready%20for%20Operating (accessed 9 November 2021).

Puder, J. 2019. "Excluding Migrant Labor from the Malaysian Bioeconomy: Working and Living Conditions of Migrant Workers in the Palm Oil Sector in Sabah". *Austrian Journal of South-East Asian Studies* 12, no. 1: 31–48. https://doi.org/10.14764/10.ASEAS-0012

Purnomo, H., B. Okarda, A. Dermawan, Q.P. Ilham, P. Pacheco, F. Nurfatriani, and E. Suhendang. 2020. "Reconciling Oil Palm Economic Development and Environmental Conservation in Indonesia: A Value Chain Dynamic Approach". *Forest Policy and Economics* 111: 102089. https://doi.org/10.1016/j.forpol.2020.102089

———, B. Okarda, B. Shantiko, R. Achdiawan, A. Dermawan, H. Kartodihardjo, and A.A. Dewayani. 2019. "Forest and Land Fires, Toxic Haze and Local Politics

in Indonesia". *International Forestry Review* 21, no. 4: 486–500. https://doi.
org/10.1505/146554819827906799

——, Shantiko, S. Sitorus, H. Gunawan, R. Achdiawan, H. Kartodihardjo, and
A.A. Dewayani. 2017. "Fire Economy and Actor Network of Forest and Land Fires
in Indonesia". *Forest Policy and Economics* 78: 21–31. https://doi.org/10.1016/j.
forpol.2017.01.001

Purwanto, E., ed. 2019. *HCV Mainstreaming in Indonesia: Tropenbos Indonesia's
Experience (2004–2017)*. Bogor, Indonesia: Tropenbos Indonesia.

Purwanto, S.A. 2018. "Back to the River. Changing Livelihood Strategies in Kapuas
Hulu, West Kalimantan, Indonesia". *Forests Trees and Livelihoods* 27, no. 3: 141–57.
https://doi.org/10.1080/14728028.2018.1446849

Pusat Pengembangan Kawasan Perkotaan. 2015. "Metropolitan Banjarmasin, Banjarbaru,
Banjar, Barito Kuala, Tanah Laut". http://perkotaan.bpiw.pu.go.id/n/metropolitan/9
(accessed 20 May 2021).

Puspitaloka, D., Y.-S. Kim, H. Purnomo, and P.Z. Fulé. 2020. "Defining Ecological
Restoration of Peatlands in Central Kalimantan, Indonesia". *Restoration Ecology*
28, no. 2: 435–46. https://doi.org/10.1111/rec.13097

Pye, O. 2016. "Deconstructing the Roundtable on Sustainable Palm Oil". In *The Oil Palm
Complex: Smallholders, Agribusiness and the State in Indonesia and Malaysia*, edited
by R. Cramb and J.F. McCarthy, pp. 409–41. Singapore: NUS Press.

——. 2019. "Commodifying Sustainability: Development, Nature and Politics in the
Palm Oil Industry". *World Development* 121: 218–28. https://doi.org/10.1016/j.
worlddev.2018.02.014

——, R. Daud, Y. Harmono, and Tatat. 2012. "Precarious Lives: Transnational
Biographies of Migrant Oil Palm Workers". *Asia Pacific Viewpoint* 53, no. 3: 330–42.
https://doi.org/10.1111/j.1467-8373.2012.01496.x

Qamariah, N., D.S. Mulia, and D. Fakhrizal. 2020. "Indigenous Knowledge of Medicinal
Plants by Dayak Community in Mandomai Village, Central Kalimantan, Indonesia".
Pharmacognosy Journal 12, no. 2.

Qie, L., S.L. Lewis, M.J.P. Sullivan, G. Lopez-Gonzalez, G.C. Pickavance, T. Sunderland,
P. Ashton, W. Hubau, K. Abu Salim, S.I. Aiba, L.F. Banin, N. Berry, F.Q. Brearley,
D.F.R.P. Burslem, M. Dančák, S.J. Davies, G. Fredriksson, K.C. Hamer, R. Hédl,
L.K. Kho, K. Kitayama, H. Krisnawati, S. Lhota, Y. Malhi, C. Maycock, F. Metali,
E. Mirmanto, L. Nagy, R. Nilus, R. Ong, C.A. Pendry, A.D. Poulsen, R.B. Primack,
E. Rutishauser, I. Samsoedin, B. Saragih, P. Sist, J.W.F. Slik, R.S. Sukri, M. Svátek,
S. Tan, A. Tjoa, M. Van Nieuwstadt, R.R.E. Vernimmen, I. Yassir, P.S. Kidd,
M. Fitriadi, N.K.H. Ideris, R.M. Serudin, L.S. Abdullah Lim, M.S. Saparudin,
and O.L. Phillips. 2017. "Long-Term Carbon Sink in Borneo's Forests Halted by
Drought and Vulnerable to Edge Effects". *Nature Communications* 8, no. 1. https://
doi.org/10.1038/s41467-017-01997-0

Qie, L., E.M. Telford, M.R. Massam, H. Tangki, R. Nilus, A. Hector, and R.M. Ewers.
2019. "Drought Cuts Back Regeneration in Logged Tropical Forests". *Environmental
Research Letters* 14, no. 4. https://doi.org/10.1088/1748-9326/ab0783

Radel, C., B D. Jokisch, B. Schmook, L. Carte, M. Aguilar-Støen, K. Hermans, K. Zimmerer, and S. Aldrich. 2019. "Migration as a Feature of Land System Transitions". *Current Opinion in Environmental Sustainability* 38: 103–10. https://doi.org/10.1016/j. cosust.2019.05.007

Radius, D.B. 2012. "Pemprov Kalteng Lakukan Moratorium Transmigrasi" [The Provincial Government of Central Kalimantan executes a Moratorium on Trans-migration], *Kompas*, 26 April 2012. https://regional.kompas.com/read/2012/04/26/21374178/~Regional~Kalimantan

Radjawali, I., and O. Pye. 2017. "Drones for Justice: Inclusive Technology and River-Related Action Research Along the Kapuas". *Geographica Helvetica* 72, no. 1: 17–27. https://doi.org/10.5194/gh-72-17-2017

Rahajoe, J.S., L. Alhamd, E.B. Walujo, H.S. Limin, M.S. Suneetha, A.K. Braimoh, and T. Kohyama. 2014. "Impacts of Agricultural Land Change on Biodiversity and Ecosystem Services in Kahayan Watershed, Central Kalimantan". In *Vulnerability of Land Systems in Asia*, pp. 195–214. Wiley Blackwell.

Rahman, A.F., D. Dragoni, K. Didan, A. Barreto-Munoz, and J.A. Hutabarat. 2013. "Detecting Large Scale Conversion of Mangroves to Aquaculture with Change Point and Mixed-Pixel Analyses of High-Fidelity MODIS Data". *Remote Sensing of Environment* 130: 96–107. https://doi.org/10.1016/j.rse.2012.11.014

Rahman, D.F. 2020. "Explainer: All You Need to Know About the Govt's Food Estates". *Jakarta Post*, 30 September 2020. https://www.thejakartapost.com/news/2020/09/30/explainer-all-you-need-to-know-about-the-govts-food-estates.html

Rahman, N., A. de Neergaard, J. Magid, G.W.J. van de Ven, K.E. Giller, and T.B. Bruun. 2018. "Changes in Soil Organic Carbon Stocks after Conversion from Forest to Oil Palm Plantations in Malaysian Borneo". *Environmental Research Letters* 13, no. 10. https://doi.org/10.1088/1748-9326/aade0f

Rahman, S.A., J.B. Jacobsen, J.R. Healey, J.M. Roshetko, and T. Sunderland. 2016. "Finding Alternatives to Swidden Agriculture: Does Agroforestry Improve Livelihood Options and Reduce Pressure on Existing Forest?". *Agroforestry Systems* 91, no. 1: 185–99. https://doi.org/10.1007/s10457-016-9912-4

Rahmanulloh, A. 2020. "Indonesia Biofuels Annual Report 2020". USDA. https://www.fas.usda.gov/data

Rahyla, R.S., R.B. Radin Firdaus, and F. Purwaningrum. 2017. "Upgrading of Malaysian Palm Oil Biofuel Industry: Lessons Learned from the USA and Germany's Policies". *Cogent Food & Agriculture* 3, no. 1: 1279760. https://doi.org/10.1080/23311932.2017.1279760

Rakatama, A., and R. Pandit. 2020. "Reviewing Social Forestry Schemes in Indonesia: Opportunities and Challenges". *Forest Policy and Economics* 111. https://doi.org/10.1016/j.forpol.2019.102052

Rakib, M.R.M., C.F.J. Bong, A. Khairulmazmi, A.S. Idris, M.B. Jalloh, and O.H. Ahmed. 2017. "Association of Copper and Zinc Levels in Oil Palm (Elaeis guineensis) to the Spatial Distribution of Ganoderma Species in the Plantations on Peat". *Journal of Phytopathology* 165, no. 4: 276–82. https://doi.org/10.1111/jph.12559

Rambli, J., W.A. W.A.K. Ghani, M.A.M. Salleh, and R. Khezri. 2019. "Evaluation of Biochar from Sago (Metroxylon Spp.) as a Potential Solid Fuel". *BioResources* 14, no. 1: 1928–40. https://doi.org/10.15376/biores.14.1.1928-1940

Rana, P., and E.O. Sills. 2018. "Does Certification Change the Trajectory of Tree Cover in Working Forests in the Tropics? An Application of the Synthetic Control Method of Impact Evaluation". *Forests* 9, no. 3. https://doi.org/10.3390/f9030098

Rana, R., and F.S. Oliveira. 2015. "Dynamic Pricing Policies for Interdependent Perishable Products or Services Using Reinforcement Learning". *Expert Systems with Applications* 42, no. 1: 426–36. https://doi.org/10.1016/j.eswa.2014.07.007

Rana, S., L. Singh, Z. Wahid, and H. Liu. 2017. "A Recent Overview of Palm Oil Mill Effluent Management via Bioreactor Configurations". *Current Pollution Reports* 3, no. 4: 254–67. https://doi.org/10.1007/s40726-017-0068-2

Rasat, M.S.M., R. Wahab, O. Sulaiman, J. Moktar, A. Mohamed, T.A. Tabet, and I. Khalid. 2011. "Properties of Composite Boards from Oil Palm Frond Agricultural Waste". *BioResources* 6, no. 4: 4389–403.

Rasmussen, L.V., B. Coolsaet, A. Martin, O. Mertz, U. Pascual, E. Corbera, N. Dawson, J.A. Fisher, P. Franks, and C.M. Ryan. 2018. "Social-Ecological Outcomes of Agricultural Intensification". *Nature Sustainability* 1, no. 6: 275–82.

Rasoolimanesh, S.M., M. Jaafar, and T.M. Tangit. 2018. "Community Involvement in Rural Tourism: A Case of Kinabalu National Park, Malaysia". *Anatolia* 29, no. 3: 337–50.

———, C. Khoo-Lattimore, S. Md Noor, M. Jaafar, and R. Konar. 2020. "Tourist Engagement and Loyalty: Gender Matters?". *Current Issues in Tourism*: 1–15. https://doi.org/10.1080/13683500.2020.1765321

———, S. Md Noor, F. Schuberth, and M. Jaafar. 2019. "Investigating the Effects of Tourist Engagement on Satisfaction and Loyalty". *Service Industries Journal* 39, no. 7–8: 559–74. https://doi.org/10.1080/02642069.2019.1570152

RECODA. 2016. "RECODA Annual Report 2016". Edited by Regional Corridor Development Authority, Kuching, Sarawak.

Resosudarmo, I.A.P. 2002. "Timber Management and Related Policies: A Review". In *Which Way Forward?: People, Forests, and Policymaking in Indonesia*, pp. 161–90. Resources for the Future, Center for International Forestry Research (CIFOR).

———, L. Tacconi, S. Sloan, F.A.U. Hamdani, Subarudi, I. Alviya, and M.Z. Muttaqin. 2019. "Indonesia's Land Reform: Implications for Local Livelihoods and Climate Change". *Forest Policy and Economics* 108. https://doi.org/10.1016/j.forpol.2019.04.007

Reyes-García, V., Á. Fernández-Llamazares, M. Guèze, and S. Gallois. 2018. "Does Weather Forecasting Relate to Foraging Productivity? An Empirical Test Among Three Hunter-Gatherer Societies". *Weather, Climate, and Society* 10, no. 1: 163–77.

———, and S. Gallois. 2016. "How Does Social Status Relate to Traditional Ecological Knowledge?" In *Introduction to Ethnobiology*, pp. 257–60. Springer.

———, S. Gallois, I. Diáz-Reviriego, Á. Fernández-Llamazares, and L. Napitupulu. 2018. "Dietary Patterns of Children on Three Indigenous Societies". *Journal of Ethnobiology* 38, no. 2: 244–60. https://doi.org/10.2993/0278-0771-38.2.244

Reynolds, G., J. Payne, W. Sinun, G. Mosigil, and R.P.D. Walsh. 2011. "Changes in Forest Land Use and Management in Sabah, Malaysian Borneo, 1990–2010, with a Focus on the Danum Valley Region". *Philosophical Transactions of the Royal Society B: Biological Sciences* 366, no. 1582: 3168–76. https://doi.org/10.1098/rstb.2011.0154

Reza, M.S., A. Ahmed, W. Caesarendra, M.S. Abu Bakar, S. Shams, R. Saidur, N. Aslfattahi, and A.K. Azad. 2019. "*Acacia holosericea:* An Invasive Species for Bio-Char, Bio-Oil, and Biogas Production". *Bioengineering* 6, no. 2. https://doi.org/10.3390/bioengineering6020033

Rezaul Islam, M., H. A. Wahab, and L. a. Anggum. 2020. "The Influence of Leadership Quality Towards Community Cohesion in Iban Community in Malaysia". *Heliyon* 6, no. 2: e03370. https://doi.org/10.1016/j.heliyon.2020.e03370.

Rhama, B. 2019. "The Analysis of the Central Kalimantan Tourism Development Plan Based on Ecotourism Policy Perspective". *Policy & Governance Review* 3: 204-016%V 2. https://doi.org/10.30589/pgr.v2i3.110

Rietberg, P.I., and O. Hospes. 2018. "Unpacking Land Acquisition at the Oil Palm Frontier: Obscuring Customary Rights and Local Authority in West Kalimantan, Indonesia". *Asia Pacific Viewpoint* 59, no. 3: 338–48. https://doi.org/10.1111/apv.12206

Rimbunan Hijau. 2020. "Annual Report 2019". Rimbunan Hijau. http://www.rsb.com.my/investor_relations.html

Robinson, D., I. Fraser, E. Dominati, B. Davíðsdóttir, J. Jónsson, L. Jones, S. Jones, M. Tuller, I. Lebron, and K. Bristow. 2014. "On the Value of Soil Resources in the Context of Natural Capital and Ecosystem Service Delivery". *Soil Science Society of America Journal* 78, no. 3: 685–700.

Robinson, R.N.S., A. Martins, D. Solnet, and T. Baum. 2019. "Sustaining Precarity: Critically Examining Tourism and Employment". *Journal of Sustainable Tourism* 27, no. 7: 1008–25. https://doi.org/10.1080/09669582.2018.1538230

Rochmyaningsih, D. 2016. "Massive Hydroelectricity Project Planned for Indonesian Borneo". *Mongabay*, 7 November 2016. https://news.mongabay.com/2016/11/massive-hydroelectricity-project-planned-for-indonesian-borneo/

Rockstrom, J., J. Williams, G. Daily, A. Noble, N. Matthews, L. Gordon, H. Wetterstrand, F. DeClerck, M. Shah, P. Steduto, C. de Fraiture, N. Hatibu, O. Unver, J. Bird, L. Sibanda, and J. Smith. 2017. "Sustainable Intensification of Agriculture for Human Prosperity and Global Sustainability". *Ambio* 46, no. 1: 4–17. https://doi.org/10.1007/s13280-016-0793-6

Rofiqi, D.M., M.S. Maarif, and A. Hermawan. 2016. "Strategi Percepatan Pengembangan Industri Turunan Minyak Sawit Mentah (MSM) di Indonesia". *Journal of Agroindustrial Technology* 26, no. 3.

Roopsind, A., B. Sohngen, and J. Brandt. 2019. "Evidence That a National REDD+ Program Reduces Tree Cover Loss and Carbon Emissions in a High Forest Cover, Low Deforestation Country". *Proceedings of the National Academy of Sciences* 116, no. 49: 24492–99. https://doi.org/10.1073/pnas.1904027116

Rosenbarger, A., B. Gingold, R. Prasodjo, A. Alisjahbana, A. Putraditama, and D. Tresya.

2013. "How to Change Legal Land Use Classifications to Support More Sustainable Palm Oil Production in Indonesia". World Resources Institute, Washington, DC, USA.

Rosoman, G., S.S. Sheun, C. Opal, P. Anderson, and R. Trapshah, eds. 2017. *The HCS Approach Toolkit*. Singapore: High Carbon Stock (HCS) Approach Steering Group.

Rothenberg, A.D., and D. Temenggung. 2019. *Place-Based Policies in Indonesia: A Critical Review*. Washington, DC: World Bank Group. https://elibrary.worldbank.org/doi/abs/10.1596/32593

Rozlaily, Z., W.E. Wan Rozita, M.N. Farah Zaidat, and M.S. Nor Hazlina. 2015. "Orchid Breeding Programme in MARDI". In *Acta Horticulturae* (International Society for Horticultural Science) 1078: 35–40.

RSPO. 2018. "One Year On, Smallholder Farmer Programme Delivers Results". Roundtable on Sustainable Palm Oil. https://rspo.org/news-and-events/news/one-year-on-smallholder-farmer-programme-delivers-results (accessed 11 May 2021).

———. 2020a. "GeoRSPO: RSPO Mapbuilder App". Roundtable on Sustainable Palm Oil. https://www.rspo.org/members/georspo (accessed 7 February 2020).

———. 2020b. "Official Website". Roundtable on Sustainable Palm Oil. https://www.rspo.org/impact (accessed 7 December 2020).

Rubis, J.M. 2020. "The Orang Utan Is Not an Indigenous Name: Knowing and Naming the Maias as a Decolonizing Epistemology". *Cultural Studies* 34, no. 5: 811–30. https://doi.org/10.1080/09502386.2020.1780281

———, and N. Theriault. 2019. "Concealing Protocols: Conservation, Indigenous Survivance, and the Dilemmas of Visibility". *Social & Cultural Geography*: 1–23. https://doi.org/10.1080/14649365.2019.1574882

Runting, R.K., E. Meijaard, N.K. Abram, J.A. Wells, D.L. Gaveau, M. Ancrenaz, H.P. Possingham, S.A. Wich, F. Ardiansyah, M.T. Gumal, L.N. Ambu, and K.A. Wilson. 2015. "Alternative Futures for Borneo Show the Value of Integrating Economic and Conservation Targets Across Borders". *Nat Commun* 6: 6819. https://doi.org/10.1038/ncomms7819

———, Ruslandi, B.W. Griscom, M.J. Struebig, M. Satar, E. Meijaard, Z. Burivalova, S.M. Cheyne, N.J. Deere, E.T. Game, F.E. Putz, J.A. Wells, A. Wilting, M. Ancrenaz, P. Ellis, F.A.A. Khan, S.M. Leavitt, A.J. Marshall, H.P. Possingham, J.E.M. Watson, and O. Venter. 2019. "Larger Gains from Improved Management over Sparing-Sharing for Tropical Forests". *Nature Sustainability* 2, no. 1: 53–61. https://doi.org/10.1038/s41893-018-0203-0

Ruslandi, W.P. Cropper, Jr., and F.E. Putz. 2017. "Effects of Silvicultural Intensification on Timber Yields, Carbon Dynamics, and Tree Species Composition in a Dipterocarp Forest in Kalimantan, Indonesia: An Individual-Tree-Based Model Simulation". *Forest Ecology and Management* 390: 104–18. https://doi.org/10.1016/j.foreco.2017.01.019

Russon, A.E., and A. Susilo. 2014. "Orangutan Tourism and Conservation: 35 Years' Experience". In *Primate Tourism: A Tool for Conservation*, pp. 76–97. Cambridge University Press.

Ruysschaert, D., and D. Salles. 2014. "Towards Global Voluntary Standards: Questioning the Effectiveness in Attaining Conservation Goals". *Ecological Economics* 107: 438–46. https://doi.org/10.1016/j.ecolecon.2014.09.016

Rye, S.A., and N.I. Kurniawan. 2017. "Claiming Indigenous Rights Through Participatory Mapping and the Making of Citizenship". *Political Geography* 61: 148–59. https://doi.org/10.1016/j.polgeo.2017.08.008

Sa'adi, Z., S. Shahid, T. Ismail, E.-S. Chung, and X.-J. Wang. 2017. "Trends Analysis of Rainfall and Rainfall Extremes in Sarawak, Malaysia Using Modified Mann–Kendall Test". *Meteorology and Atmospheric Physics* 131, no. 3: 263–77. https://doi.org/10.1007/s00703-017-0564-3

———, M.S. Shiru, S. Shahid, and T. Ismail. 2019. "Selection of General Circulation Models for the Projections of Spatio-Temporal Changes in Temperature of Borneo Island Based on CMIP5". *Theoretical and Applied Climatology*. https://doi.org/10.1007/s00704-019-02948-z

Saadun, N., E.A.L. Lim, S.M. Esa, F. Ngu, F. Awang, A. Gimin, I.H. Johari, M.A. Firdaus, N.I. Wagimin, and B. Azhar. 2018. "Socio-ecological Perspectives of Engaging Smallholders in Environmental-Friendly Palm Oil Certification Schemes". *Land Use Policy* 72: 333–40.

Sabah Forestry Department. 2013. "Strategic Plan of Action (Sabah)". *The Heart of Borneo Initiative (2014–2020)*. Sabah, Malaysia: WWF-Malaysia.

———. 2018. "Demonstration Initiative for Community-Based Forest & Management & REDD+ in Sabah". Kota Kinabalu, Sabah.

———. 2020. "Annual Report 2020". Kota Kinabalu, Sabah: http://www.forest.sabah.gov.my/publications/annual-reports.html

Sachs, J.D., G. Schmidt-Traub, M. Mazzucato, D. Messner, N. Nakicenovic, and J. Rockström. 2019. "Six Transformations to Achieve the Sustainable Development Goals". *Nature Sustainability* 2, no. 9: 805–14. https://doi.org/10.1038/s41893-019-0352-9

Sada, C., Y. Alas, and M. Anshari. 2019. "Indigenous People of Borneo (Dayak): Development, Social Cultural Perspective and Its Challenges". *Cogent Arts and Humanities* 6, no. 1. https://doi.org/10.1080/23311983.2019.1665936

Sadhukhan, J., E. Martinez-Hernandez, R.J. Murphy, D.K.S. Ng, M.H. Hassim, K. Siew Ng, W. Yoke Kin, I.F.M. Jaye, M.Y. Leung Pah Hang, and V. Andiappan. 2018. "Role of Bioenergy, Biorefinery and Bioeconomy in Sustainable Development: Strategic Pathways for Malaysia". *Renewable and Sustainable Energy Reviews* 81: 1966–87. https://doi.org/10.1016/j.rser.2017.06.007

Safitri, L., H. Hermantoro, S. Purboseno, V. Kautsar, S.K. Saptomo, and A. Kurniawan. 2018. "Water Footprint and Crop Water Usage of Oil Palm (*Eleasis guineensis*) in Central Kalimantan: Environmental Sustainability Indicators for Different Crop Age and Soil Conditions". *Water* (Switzerland) 11, no. 1. https://doi.org/10.3390/w11010035

Saharjo, B.H. 2014. "Community-Based Peatland Management for Greenhouse Gas Reduction Based on Fire-Free Land Preparation". In *Vulnerability of Land Systems in Asia*, pp. 285–96. Wiley Blackwell.

Sahide, M.A.K., and L. Giessen. 2015. "The Fragmented Land Use Administration in Indonesia: Analysing Bureaucratic Responsibilities Influencing Tropical Rainforest Transformation Systems". *Land Use Policy* 43: 96–110. https://doi.org/10.1016/j.landusepol.2014.11.005

Said, B. 2015. "Optimization of River Transport to Strengthen Multimodal Passenger Transport System in Inland Region". *Procedia Engineering* 125: 498–503.

Saikim, F.H., and B. Prideaux. 2014. "Rainforest Wildlife a Key Element in Sabah's Destination Appeal". In *Rainforest Tourism, Conservation and Management: Challenges for Sustainable Development*, edited by B. Prideaux. London: Routledge.

Saikim, F.H., B. Prideaux, M. Mohamed, and Z. Hamzah. 2016. "Using Tourism as a Mechanism to Reduce Poaching and Hunting: A Case Study of the Tidong Community, Sabah". In *Advances in Hospitality and Leisure*, pp. 119–44. Bingley, UK: Emerald Group Publishing Limited.

Saito-Jensen, M., T. Sikor, Y. Kurniawan, M. Eilenberg, E.P. Setyawan, and S.J. Kustini. 2015. "Policy Options for Effective REDD+ Implementation in Indonesia: The Significance of Forest Tenure Reform". *International Forestry Review* 17, no. 1: 86–97. https://doi.org/10.1505/146554815814725040

Sakuma, K. 2017. "The Longhouse as Trade Hub in Inland Borneo: Sarawak's Riverine Trade in the Late Nineteenth Century". *Japanese Journal of Southeast Asian Studies* 54, no. 2: 153–81. https://doi.org/10.20495/tak.54.2_153

Salam, A., M.C. Vuran, and S. Irmak. 2019. "Di-Sense: In Situ Real-Time Permittivity Estimation and Soil Moisture Sensing Using Wireless Underground Communications". *Computer Networks* 151: 31–41.

SALCRA. 2020. "Sarawak Land Consolidation and Rehabilitation Authority (SALCRA)". http://www.salcra.gov.my/en/ (accessed 10 December 2020).

Salimon, J., N. Salih, and E. Yousif. 2012. "Industrial Development and Applications of Plant Oils and Their Biobased Oleochemicals". *Arabian Journal of Chemistry* 5, no. 2: 135–45.

Salzman, J., G. Bennett, N. Carroll, A. Goldstein, and M. Jenkins. 2018. "The Global Status and Trends of Payments for Ecosystem Services". *Nature Sustainability* 1, no. 3: 136–44. https://doi.org/10.1038/s41893-018-0033-0

Samejima, H. 2020. "Tropical Timber Trading from Southeast Asia to Japan". In *Advances in Asian Human-Environmental Research*. Springer International Publishing.

———, M. Demies, M. Koizumi, and S. Fujiki. 2020. "Above-Ground Biomass and Tree Species Diversity in the Anap Sustainable Development Unit, Sarawak". In *Advances in Asian Human-Environmental Research*: Springer International Publishing.

Samsudin, Y.B. 2016. "Policies, Drivers and Land-Use Trends in Industrial Forest Plantation Development in Indonesia". MSc thesis, Michigan State University.

Sanders, A.J.P., R.M. Ford, R.J. Keenan, and A.M. Larson. 2020. "Learning Through Practice? Learning from the REDD+ Demonstration Project, Kalimantan Forests and Climate Partnership (KFCP) in Indonesia". *Land Use Policy* 91. https://doi.org/10.1016/j.landusepol.2019.104285

———, R.M. Ford, L. Mulyani, R.D. Prasti H, A.M. Larson, Y. Jagau, and R.J. Keenan. 2019. "Unrelenting Games: Multiple Negotiations and Landscape Transformations in the Tropical Peatlands of Central Kalimantan, Indonesia". *World Development* 117: 196–210. https://doi.org/10.1016/j.worlddev.2019.01.008

———, H.d.S. Hyldmo, R.D. Prasti H, R.M. Ford, A.M. Larson, and R.J. Keenan. 2017. "Guinea Pig or Pioneer? Translating Global Environmental Objectives Through to Local Actions in Central Kalimantan, Indonesia's REDD+ Pilot Province". *Global Environmental Change* 42: 68–81. https://doi.org/10.1016/j.gloenvcha.2016.12.003

Sanderson, S. 2016. "Malaysian Oil Palm and Indonesian Labour Migration: A Perspective from Sarawak". In *The Oil Palm Complex: Smallholders, Agribusiness and the State in Indonesia and Malaysia*, edited by R. Cramb and J.F. McCarthy, pp. 378–408. Singapore: NUS Press.

———. 2017. "Processes of Large-Scale Oil Palm Development on Native Customary Land in Sarawak: A Rural Livelihoods Approach". PhD, School of Agriculture and Food Sciences, University of Queensland.

Sang, A.J., K.M. Tay, C.P. Lim, and S. Nahavandi. 2018. "Application of a Genetic-Fuzzy FMEA to Rainfed Lowland Rice Production in Sarawak: Environmental, Health, and Safety Perspectives". *IEEE Access* 6: 74628–47. https://doi.org/10.1109/access.2018.2883115

Santika, T., E. Meijaard, and K.A. Wilson. 2015. "Designing Multifunctional Landscapes for Forest Conservation". *Environmental Research Letters* 10, no. 11. https://doi.org/10.1088/1748-9326/10/11/114012

———, E. Meijaard, S. Budiharta, E.A. Law, A. Kusworo, J.A. Hutabarat, T.P. Indrawan, M. Struebig, S. Raharjo, I. Huda, Sulhani, A.D. Ekaputri, S. Trison, M. Stigner, and K.A. Wilson. 2017. "Community Forest Management in Indonesia: Avoided Deforestation in the Context of Anthropogenic and Climate Complexities". *Global Environmental Change* 46: 60–71. https://doi.org/10.1016/j.gloenvcha.2017.08.002

———, K.A. Wilson, S. Budiharta, A. Kusworo, E. Meijaard, E.A. Law, R. Friedman, J.A. Hutabarat, T.P. Indrawan, F.A.V. St. John, and M.J. Struebig. 2019. "Heterogeneous Impacts of Community Forestry on Forest Conservation and Poverty Alleviation: Evidence from Indonesia". *People and Nature* 1, no. 2: 204–19. https://doi.org/10.1002/pan3.25

———, K.A. Wilson, S. Budiharta, E.A. Law, T.M. Poh, M. Ancrenaz, M.J. Struebig, and E. Meijaard. 2019. "Does Oil Palm Agriculture Help Alleviate Poverty? A Multidimensional Counterfactual Assessment of Oil Palm Development in Indonesia". *World Development* 120: 105–17. https://doi.org/10.1016/j.worlddev.2019.04.012

———, S. Budiharta, E.A. Law, R.A. Dennis, A. Dohong, M.J. Struebig, Medrilzam, H. Gunawan, E. Meijaard, and K.A. Wilson. 2020. "Interannual Climate Variation, Land Type and Village Livelihood Effects on Fires in Kalimantan, Indonesia". *Global Environmental Change* 64: 102129. https://doi.org/10.1016/j.gloenvcha.2020.102129

———, K.A. Wilson, E.A. Law, F.A.V. St John, K.M. Carlson, H. Gibbs, C.L. Morgans, M. Ancrenaz, E. Meijaard, and M.J. Struebig. 2020. "Impact of Palm Oil Sustainability Certification on Village Well-Being and Poverty in Indonesia". *Nature Sustainability*. https://doi.org/10.1038/s41893-020-00630-1

——, K.A. Wilson, E. Meijaard, S. Budiharta, E.E. Law, M. Sabri, M. Struebig, M. Ancrenaz, and T.M. Poh. 2019. "Changing Landscapes, Livelihoods and Village Welfare in the Context of Oil Palm Development". *Land Use Policy* 87. https://doi.org/10.1016/j.landusepol.2019.104073

Saragi-Sasmito, M.F., D. Murdiyarso, T. June, and S.D. Sasmito. 2019. "Carbon Stocks, Emissions, and Aboveground Productivity in Restored Secondary Tropical Peat Swamp Forests". *Mitigation and Adaptation Strategies for Global Change* 24, no. 4: 521–33. https://doi.org/10.1007/s11027-018-9793-0

Saragih, I. N. 2019. "Jurisdictional Approach in Indonesia: Current Development and Way Forward". *Tropical Forest Alliance.* https://www.tropicalforestalliance.org/assets/Uploads/JAupdate-April-2019.pdf

Saravanamuttu, J. 2016. *Power Sharing in a Divided Nation: Mediated Communalism and New Politics in Six Decades of Malaysia's Elections.* Singapore: ISEAS – Yusof Ishak Institute.

Sarawak Report. 2013. "Resettlement Chaos: Outrage Grows Over Murum Natives". https://www.sarawakreport.org/2013/10/resettlement-chaos-outrage-grows-over-murum-natives/ (accessed 6 October 2021).

——. 2014. "SEB's 'Generous' School Bus for Murum!". https://www.sarawakreport.org/2014/07/sebs-generous-school-bus-for-murum/ (accessed 6 October 2021).

Sayer, J., J. Ghazoul, P. Nelson, and A.K. Boedhihartono. 2012. "Oil Palm Expansion Transforms Tropical Landscapes and Livelihoods". *Global Food Security-Agriculture Policy Economics and Environment* 1, no. 2: 114–19. https://doi.org/10.1016/j.gfs.2012.10.003

——, T. Sunderland, J. Ghazoul, J.L. Pfund, D. Sheil, E. Meijaard, M. Venter, A.K. Boedhihartono, M. Day, C. Garcia, C. van Oosten, and L.E. Buck. 2013. "Ten Principles for a Landscape Approach to Reconciling Agriculture, Conservation, and Other Competing Land Uses". *Proc Natl Acad Sci U S A* 110, no. 21: 8349–56. https://doi.org/10.1073/pnas.1210595110

——, C. Margules, A. K. Boedhihartono, T. Sunderland, J.D. Langston, J. Reed, R. Riggs, L.E. Buck, B.M. Campbell, K. Kusters, C. Elliott, P.A. Minang, A. Dale, H. Purnomo, J.R. Stevenson, P. Gunarso, and A. Purnomo. 2016. "Measuring the Effectiveness of Landscape Approaches to Conservation and Development". *Sustainability Science* 12, no. 3: 465–76. https://doi.org/10.1007/s11625-016-0415-z

Schaafsma, M., P.J.H. van Beukering, and I. Oskolokaite. 2017. "Combining Focus Group Discussions and Choice Experiments for Economic Valuation of Peatland Restoration: A Case Study in Central Kalimantan, Indonesia". *Ecosystem Services* 27: 150–60. https://doi.org/10.1016/j.ecoser.2017.08.012

Scheitz, C.J.F., L.J. Peck, and E.S. Groban. 2018. "Biotechnology Software in the Digital Age: Are You Winning?". *Journal of Industrial Microbiology & Biotechnology* 45, no. 7: 529–34.

Schleifer, P. 2013. "Orchestrating Sustainability: The Case of European Union Biofuel Governance". *Regulation & Governance* 7, no. 4: 533–46. https://doi.org/10.1111/rego.12037

Schneider, M.N., A. Iaconi, and S. Larocca. 2016. "Oleochemical Biorefinery". *Chemicals and Fuels from Bio-Based Building Blocks*. Weinheim: Wiley. https://doi.org/10.1002/9783527698202.ch19

Schoneveld, G.C., D. Ekowati, A. Andrianto, and S. Van Der Haar. 2019. "Modeling Peat- and Forestland Conversion by Oil Palm Smallholders in Indonesian Borneo". *Environmental Research Letters* 14, no. 1. https://doi.org/10.1088/1748-9326/aaf044

———, S. van der Haar, D. Ekowati, A. Andrianto, H. Komarudin, B. Okarda, I. Jelsma, and P. Pacheco. 2019. "Certification, Good Agricultural Practice and Smallholder Heterogeneity: Differentiated Pathways for Resolving Compliance Gaps in the Indonesian Oil Palm Sector". *Global Environmental Change* 57. https://doi.org/10.1016/j.gloenvcha.2019.101933

Schreer, V. 2016. "Learning Knowledge about Rattan (Calamoideae arecaceae) and Its Uses Amongst Ngaju Dayak in Indonesian Borneo". *Journal of Ethnobiology* 36, no. 1: 125–46. https://doi.org/10.2993/0278-0771-36.1.125

———. 2020. "'Only Gold Can Become Hope': Resource Rushes and Risky Conviviality in Indonesian Borneo". *Ethnos*: 1–23. https://doi.org/10.1080/00141844.2020.1743337

Sconfienza, U.M. 2019. "The Post-Sustainability Trilemma". *Journal of Environmental Policy & Planning* 21, no. 6: 769–84. https://doi.org/10.1080/1523908X.2019.1673156

Scriven, S.A., K.M. Carlson, J.A. Hodgson, C.J. McClean, R. Heilmayr, J.M. Lucey, and J.K. Hill. 2019. "Testing the Benefits of Conservation Set-Asides for Improved Habitat Connectivity in Tropical Agricultural Landscapes". *Journal of Applied Ecology* 56, no. 10: 2274–85. https://doi.org/10.1111/1365-2664.13472

Searle, S., and K. Bitnere. 2018. "Compatibility of Mid-Level Biodiesel Blends in Vehicles in Indonesia". International Council on Clean Transportation, Working Paper (2018-08).

Sears, R., S. Phuntsho, T. Dorji, K. Choden, N. Norbu, and H. Baral. 2017. *Forest Ecosystem Services and the Pillars of Bhutan's Gross National Happiness*. Bogor, Indonesia: CIFOR.

SEDIA. 2016. "SEDIA Annual Report 2016". Kota Kinabalu, Sabah.

Selvadurai, S., A.C. Er, N. Lyndon, S.M. Sum, S. Saad, A.A. Manaf, and Z. Ramli. 2013. "Penan Natives' Discourse for and Against Development". *Asian Social Science* 9, no. 8. https://doi.org/10.5539/ass.v9n8p72

Semedi, P. 2014. "Palm Oil Wealth and Rumour Panics in West Kalimantan". *Forum for Development Studies* 41, no. 2: 233–52. https://doi.org/10.1080/08039410.2014.901240

———, and L. Bakker. 2014. "Between Land Grabbing and Farmers' Benefits: Land Transfers in West Kalimantan, Indonesia". *Asia Pacific Journal of Anthropology* 15, no. 4: 376–90. https://doi.org/10.1080/14442213.2014.928741

Senawi, R., N.K. Rahman, N. Mansor, and A. Kuntom. 2019. "Transformation of Oil Palm Independent Smallholders Through Malaysian Sustainable Palm Oil". *Journal of Oil Palm Research* 31: 496–507.

Sephton, P.S. 2011. "Spatial Arbitrage in Sarawak Pepper Prices". *Canadian Journal of Agricultural Economics/Revue canadienne d'agroeconomie* 59, no. 3: 405–16. https://doi.org/10.1111/j.1744-7976.2010.01207.x

Sercombe, P., and B. Sellato. 2007. *Beyond the Green Myth: Borneo's Hunter-Gatherers in the Twenty-First Century*. Copenhagen: NIAS Press.

Setiawan, E.N., A. Maryudi, R.H. Purwanto, and G. Lele. 2016. "Opposing Interests in the Legalization of Non-Procedural Forest Conversion to Oil Palm in Central Kalimantan, Indonesia". *Land Use Policy* 58: 472–81. https://doi.org/10.1016/j. landusepol.2016.08.003

SETKAB. 2020. "Remarks of President of the Republic of Indonesia at the Opening of Indonesia's SDGs Annual Conference 2020, 17 December 2020, from the Bogor Presidential Palace, West Java province". Office of Assistant to Deputy Cabinet Secretary for State Documents & Translation.

Seymour, F.J., L. Aurora, and J. Arif. 2020. "The Jurisdictional Approach in Indonesia: Incentives, Actions, and Facilitating Connections". *Frontiers in Forests and Global Change* 3, no. 124. https://doi.org/10.3389/ffgc.2020.503326

Shafie, F.A., and D. Rennie. 2012. "Consumer Perceptions Towards Organic Food". *Procedia: Social and Behavioral Sciences* 49: 360–367. https://doi.org/10.1016/j. sbspro.2012.07.034

Shah, K., A.H. Mustafa Kamal, Z. Rosli, K.R. Hakeem, and M.M. Hoque. 2016. "Composition and Diversity of Plants in Sibuti Mangrove Forest, Sarawak, Malaysia". *Forest Science and Technology* 12, no. 2: 70–76. https://doi.org/10.1080/2158010 3.2015.1057619

Shanmuganathan, S., A. Narayanan, M. Mohamed, R. Ibrahim, and H. Khalid. 2014. "A Hybrid Approach to Modelling the Climate Change Effects on Malaysia's Oil Palm Yield at the Regional Scale". In *Recent Advances on Soft Computing and Data Mining. Advances in Intelligent Systems and Computing*, vol. 287. Cham: Springer.

Sharma, S.K., H. Baral, Y. Laumonier, B. Okarda, H. Purnomo, and P. Pacheco. 2019. "Ecosystem Services Under Future Oil Palm Expansion Scenarios in West Kalimantan, Indonesia". *Ecosystem Services* 39. https://doi.org/10.1016/j. ecoser.2019.100978

Shayea, I., M. Ergen, M.H. Azmi, D. Nandi, A.A. El-Salah, and A. Zahedi. 2020. "Performance Analysis of Mobile Broadband Networks With 5G Trends and Beyond: Rural Areas Scope in Malaysia". *IEEE Access* 8: 65211–29. https://doi. org/10.1109/ACCESS.2020.2978048

Sheena, B., M. Mariapan, and A. Aziz. 2015. "Characteristics of Malaysian Ecotourist Segments in Kinabalu Park, Sabah". *Tourism Geographies* 17, no. 1: 1–18. https:// doi.org/10.1080/14616688.2013.865069

Sheil, D., A. Casson, E. Meijaard, M. Van Noordwijk, J. Gaskell, J. Sunderland-Groves, K. Wertz, and M. Kanninen. 2009. *The Impacts and Opportunities of Oil Palm in Southeast Asia: What Do We Know and What Do We Need to Know?* Bogor, Indonesia: Center for International Forestry Research.

———, and A. Salim. 2011. "Diversity of Locally Useful Tropical Forest Wild-Plants as a Function of Species Richness and Informant Culture". *Biodiversity and Conservation* 21, no. 3: 687–99. https://doi.org/10.1007/s10531-011-0208-8

Sheldon, R.A. 2014. "Green and Sustainable Manufacture of Chemicals from Biomass: State of the Art". *Green Chemistry* 16, no. 3: 950–63.

Shen, L., E. Worrell, and M. Patel. 2010. "Present and Future Development in Plastics from Biomass". *Biofuels, Bioproducts and Biorefining: Innovation for a Sustainable Economy* 4, no. 1: 25–40.

Sherman, J., M. Ancrenaz, and E. Meijaard. 2020. "Shifting Apes: Conservation and Welfare Outcomes of Bornean Orangutan Rescue and Release in Kalimantan, Indonesia". *Journal for Nature Conservation* 55: 125807. https://doi.org/10.1016/j.jnc.2020.125807

Shirley, R., and D. Kammen. 2015. "Energy Planning and Development in Malaysian Borneo: Assessing the Benefits of Distributed Technologies Versus Large Scale Energy Mega-Projects". *Energy Strategy Reviews* 8: 15–29. https://doi.org/10.1016/j.esr.2015.07.001

Shuib, A., L.S. Yee, and S. Edman. 2012. "Attitudes of Local Communities Towards Conservation of the Mangrove Ecosystem in Kuching, Sarawak". *Malaysian Forester* 75, no. 1: 15–28.

Shukri, M., and N.Y. Sam Shor. 2015. "Forest Certification in Malaysia: Current Status and Challenges". *Malaysian Forester* 78, nos. 1–2: 1–10.

Shukri, S. 2020. "Shared Prosperity: Inclusivity Drives Digital Growth". The 5th ASEAN Rice Bowl Startup Awards, Kuala Lumpur, Malaysia, 15 January 2020.

Siahaya, M.E., T.R. Hutauruk, H.S.E.S. Aponno, J.W. Hatulesila, and A.B. Mardhanie. 2016. "Traditional Ecological Knowledge on Shifting Cultivation and Forest Management in East Borneo, Indonesia". *International Journal of Biodiversity Science, Ecosystem Services and Management* 12, nos. 1–2: 14–23. https://doi.org/10.1080/21513732.2016.1169559

Siebel, T.M. 2019. *Digital Transformation: Survive and Thrive in an Era of Mass Extinction.* New York: Rosetta Books.

Sills, E.O., S.S. Atmadja, C. de Sassi, A.E. Duchelle, D.L. Kweka, I.A.P. Resosudarmo, and W.D. Sunderlin. 2014. *REDD+ on the Ground: A Case Book of Subnational Initiatives Across the Globe.* Bogor, Indonesia: CIFOR.

Silveira, S., and F.X. Johnson. 2016. "Navigating the Transition to Sustainable Bioenergy in Sweden and Brazil: Lessons Learned in a European and International Context". *Energy Research & Social Science* 13: 180–93. https://doi.org/10.1016/j.erss.2015.12.021

Silvianingsih, Y.A., K. Hairiah, D. Suprayogo, and M. van Noordwijk. 2020. "Agroforests, Swiddening and Livelihoods Between Restored Peat Domes and River: Effects of the 2015 Fire Ban in Central Kalimantan (Indonesia)". *International Forestry Review* 22, no. 3: 382–96. https://doi.org/10.1505/146554820830405645

Simangunsong, B.C.H., V.J. Sitanggang, E.G.T. Manurung, A. Rahmadi, G.A. Moore, L. Aye, and A.H. Tambunan. 2017. "Potential Forest Biomass Resource as Feedstock for Bioenergy and Its Economic Value in Indonesia". *Forest Policy and Economics* 81: 10–17. https://doi.org/10.1016/j.forpol.2017.03.022

Sime Darby. 2020. "Annual Report 2019". https://www.simedarbyplantation.com/investor-relations/annual-reports

SIMTARU. 2021. "Sistem Informasi Tata Ruang Provinsi Kalimantan Utara".

Sinar Mas. 2020. "Annual Report 2020". https://www.smart-tbk.com/wp-content/uploads/2021/05/AR-2020-SMART-Final.pdf

Siswoyo Jo, R., M. Lu, V. Raman, and P. Hanghui Then. 2019. "Design and Implementation of IoT-Enabled Compost Monitoring System". *9th IEEE Symposium on Computer Applications & Industrial Electronics 2019*, pp. 23–28. IEEE.

Siti Maimunah, and S. Agustiorini. 2020. "The Story of Mahakam River in Indonesia: From the Commons to Extractivism and Back". *Global Water Forum* (blog), 23 October 2020 https://globalwaterforum.org/2020/10/23/the-story-of-mahakam-river-in-indonesia-from-the-commons-to-extractivism-and-back/

———, S.A. Rahman, Y.B. Samsudin, Y. Artati, T.I. Simamora, S. Andini, S.M. Lee, and H. Baral. 2018. "Assessment of Suitability of Tree Species for Bioenergy Production on Burned and Degraded Peatlands in Central Kalimantan, Indonesia". *Land* 7, no. 4. https://doi.org/10.3390/land7040115

Slamet, A.S., A. Nakayasu, and M. Ichikawa. 2017. "Small-Scale Vegetable Farmers' Participation in Modern Retail Market Channels in Indonesia: The Determinants of and Effects on Their Income". *Agriculture* 7, no. 2: 11.

SLDB. 2020. "About Us". Sabah Land Development Board (SLDB). http://www.sldb.com.my/about/ (accessed 1 December 2020).

Sloan, S., M.J. Campbell, M. Alamgir, A.M. Lechner, J. Engert, and W.F. Laurance. 2019. "Trans-national Conservation and Infrastructure Development in the Heart of Borneo". *PLoS ONE* 14, no. 9. https://doi.org/10.1371/journal.pone.0221947

Smajgl, A., and E. Bohensky. 2012. "When Households Stop Logging: Evidence for Household Adaptation from East Kalimantan". *Forest Policy and Economics* 20: 58–65. https://doi.org/10.1016/j.forpol.2012.01.013

———. 2013. "Behaviour and Space in Agent-Based Modelling: Poverty Patterns in East Kalimantan, Indonesia". *Environmental Modelling and Software* 45: 8–14. https://doi.org/10.1016/j.envsoft.2011.10.014

Smit, H.H., E. Meijaard, C. van der Laan, S. Mantel, A. Budiman, and P. Verweij. 2013. "Breaking the Link between Environmental Degradation and Oil Palm Expansion: A Method for Enabling Sustainable Oil Palm Expansion". *PLoS ONE* 8, no. 9. https://doi.org/10.1371/journal.pone.0068610

Smith, B.G. 2008. "Developing Sustainable Food Supply Chains". *Philosophical Transactions of the Royal Society B: Biological Sciences* 363, no. 1492: 849–61.

Smith, J., K. Obidzinski, Subarudi, and I. Suramenggala. 2003. "Illegal Logging, Collusive Corruption and Fragmented Governments in Kalimantan, Indonesia". *International Forestry Review* 5, no. 3: 293–302. https://doi.org/10.1505/IFOR.5.3.293.19138

Smith, W.R., A.J. Atala, R.P. Terlecki, E.E. Kelly, and C.A. Matthews. 2020. "Implementation Guide for Rapid Integration of an Outpatient Telemedicine Program During the COVID-19 Pandemic". *Journal of the American College of Surgeons* 231, no. 2: 216–22e2. https://doi.org/10.1016/j.jamcollsurg.2020.04.030

Soda, R., and Y. Kato. 2020. "The Autonomy and Sustainability of Small-Scale Oil Palm Farming in Sarawak". In *Advances in Asian Human-Environmental Research*. Springer International Publishing.

————, N. Ishikawa, and Y. Kato. 2020. "From River to Road? Changing Living Patterns and Land Use of Inland Indigenous Peoples in Sarawak". In *Advances in Asian Human-Environmental Research*. Springer International Publishing.

————, Y. Kato, and J. Hon. 2016. "The Diversity of Small-Scale Oil Palm Cultivation in Sarawak, Malaysia". *The Geographical Journal* 182, no. 4: 353–63. https://doi.org/10.1111/geoj.12152

Solidaridad. 2020. "Solidaridad in West Kalimantan". https://solidaridadsseablog.wordpress.com/2018/05/22/solidaridad-in-west-kalimantan/ (accessed 6 May 2020).

Somasundram, C., Z. Razali, and V. Santhirasegaram. 2016. "A Review on Organic Food Production in Malaysia". *Horticulturae* 2, no. 3: 12.

Soon, C., and W.-H. Lam. 2013. "The Growth of Seaports in Peninsular Malaysia and East Malaysia for 2007–2011". *Ocean & Coastal Management* 78: 70–76. https://doi.org/10.1016/j.ocecoaman.2013.03.007

SOP. 2020. "Annual Report 2019". Sarawak Oil Palms Berhad. http://www.sop.com.my/wp-content/uploads/2020/05/annual-report-2019.pdf.

Sopian, A., S. Hardwinarto, M.I. Aipassa, and Sumaryono. 2019. "Gap Analysis of Land Availability and Land Needs to Identify Potential Development of Agricultural Lands in Santan Watersheds, East Kalimantan, Indonesia". *Biodiversitas* 20, no. 4: 1097–105. https://doi.org/10.13057/biodiv/d200422

Sovacool, B.K., and L.C. Bulan. 2011. "Behind an Ambitious Megaproject in Asia: The History and Implications of the Bakun Hydroelectric Dam in Borneo". *Energy Policy* 39, no. 9: 4842–59. https://doi.org/10.1016/j.enpol.2011.06.035

————, and L.C. Bulan. 2012. "Energy Security and Hydropower Development in Malaysia: The Drivers and Challenges Facing the Sarawak Corridor of Renewable Energy (SCORE)". *Renewable Energy* 40, no. 1: 113–29. https://doi.org/10.1016/j.renene.2011.09.032

Spiegel, S.J. 2019. "Visual Storytelling and Socioenvironmental Change: Images, Photographic Encounters, and Knowledge Construction in Resource Frontiers". *Annals of the American Association of Geographers*. https://doi.org/10.1080/24694452.2019.1613953

SPU. 2016. "Sarawak Facts and Figure 2015". State Planning Unit (SPU), Chief Minister's Department of Sarawak, Kuching, Sarawak.

————. 2019. "Sarawak Facts and Figure 2017/2018". State Planning Unit (SPU), Chief Minister's Department of Sarawak, Kuching, Sarawak.

Star, The. 2020. "S'wak to Set Aside RM1.6mil for Mobile Banking Services in Rural Areas". 8 May 2020.

————. 2021. "Sarawak State Assembly Automatically Dissolved with Emergency Lifted, Say Experts". 3 November 2021. https://www.thestar.com.my/news/nation/2021/11/03/sarawak-state-assembly-automatically-dissolved-with-emergency-lifted-say-experts

Stark, D.J., K.M. Fornace, P.M. Brock, T.R. Abidin, L. Gilhooly, C. Jalius, B. Goossens, C.J. Drakeley, and M. Salgado-Lynn. 2019. "Long-Tailed Macaque Response to

Deforestation in a Plasmodium knowlesi-Endemic Area". *EcoHealth*. https://doi.org/10.1007/s10393-019-01403-9

———, I.P. Vaughan, L.J. Evans, H. Kler, and B. Goossens. 2018. "Combining Drones and Satellite Tracking as an Effective Tool for Informing Policy Change in Riparian Habitats: A Proboscis Monkey Case Study". *Remote Sensing in Ecology and Conservation* 4, no. 1: 44–52. https://doi.org/10.1002/rse2.51

STB. 2020. "Official Tourism Website of Sabah, Malaysian Borneo". Sabah Tourism Board. https://www.sabahtourism.com/ (accessed 5 May 2020).

Stickler, C., A. Duchelle, J. Ardila, D. Nepstad, O. David, C. Chan, J. Rojas, R. Vargas, T. Bezerra, and L. Pritchard. 2018. *The State of Jurisdictional Sustainability*. San Francisco: Earth Innovation Institute.

Stolle, F., R.A. Dennis, I. Kurniwan, and E.F. Lambin. 2010. "Evaluation of Remote Sensing-Based Active Fire Datasets in Indonesia". *International Journal of Remote Sensing* 25, no. 2: 471–79. https://doi.org/10.1080/01431160310001618022

Struebig, M.J., A. Turner, E. Giles, F. Lasmana, S. Tollington, H. Bernard, and D. Bell. 2013. "Quantifying the Biodiversity Value of Repeatedly Logged Rainforests. Gradient and Comparative Approaches from Borneo". In *Advances in Ecological Research*. Academic Press Inc.

———, A. Wilting, D.L.A. Gaveau, E. Meijaard, R.J. Smith, M. Fischer, K. Metcalfe, S. Kramer-Schadt, T. Abdullah, N.K. Abram, R. Alfred, M. Ancrenaz, D.M. Augeri, J.L. Belant, H. Bernard, M. Bezuijen, A. Boonman, R. Boonratana, T. Boorsma, C. Breitenmoser-Würsten, J. Brodie, S.M. Cheyne, C. Devens, J.W. Duckworth, N. Duplaix, J. Eaton, C. Francis, G. Fredriksson, A.J. Giordano, C. Gonner, J. Hall, M.E. Harrison, A.J. Hearn, I. Heckmann, M. Heydon, H. Hofer, J. Hon, S. Husson, F.A.A. Khan, T. Kingston, D. Kreb, M. Lammertink, D. Lane, F. Lasmana, L.B. Liat, N.T.L. Lim, J. Lindenborn, B. Loken, D.W. Macdonald, A.J. Marshall, I. Maryanto, J. Mathai, W.J. McShea, A. Mohamed, M. Nakabayashi, Y. Nakashima, J. Niedballa, S. Noerfahmy, S. Persey, A. Peter, S. Pieterse, J.D. Pilgrim, E. Pollard, S. Purnama, A. Rafiastanto, V. Reinfelder, C. Reusch, C. Robson, J. Ross, R. Rustam, L. Sadikin, H. Samejima, E. Santosa, I. Sapari, H. Sasaki, A.K. Scharf, G. Semiadi, C.R. Shepherd, R. Sykes, T. Van Berkel, K. Wells, B. Wielstra, A. Wong, and C. The Borneo Mammal Distribution. 2015. "Targeted Conservation to Safeguard a Biodiversity Hotspot from Climate and Land-Cover Change". *Current Biology* 25, no. 3: 372–78. https://doi.org/10.1016/j.cub.2014.11.067

Suba, R.B., J. van der Ploeg, M. van't Zelfde, Y.W. Lau, T.F. Wissingh, W. Kustiawan, G.R. de Snoo, and H.H. de Iongh. 2017. "Rapid Expansion of Oil Palm Is Leading to Human–Elephant Conflicts in North Kalimantan Province of Indonesia". *Tropical Conservation Science* 10. https://doi.org/10.1177/1940082917703508

Sukri, W., B. Oktavianus, Anastasia, F. Parwadi, Y. Prawiyanto, A. Isnandar, E. Subariyanti, Hermanto, Firdaus, P. Epi, Perdana, S. Susanti, H. Setiawan, S. Putri, S. Wihastuti, P. Pasaribu, R. Istant, and S. Peteru. 2020. *Profil Keberlanjutan Yurisdiksional. Sintang District, West Kalimantan, Indonesia*. Bogor: Indonesia: CIFOR. https://www.cifor.org/knowledge/publication/7797/

Sulok, T. 2017. "Fourth Hydroelectric Dam Approved in Sarawak". *Malay Mail*, 21 July 2017. https://www.malaymail.com/news/malaysia/2017/07/21/sarawak-to-go-ahead-with-the-construction-of-trusan-dam/1426059

Sumarga, E. 2017. "Spatial Indicators for Human Activities May Explain the 2015 Fire Hotspot Distribution in Central Kalimantan Indonesia". *Tropical Conservation Science* 10. https://doi.org/10.1177/1940082917706168

———, and L. Hein. 2014. "Mapping Ecosystem Services for Land Use Planning, the Case of Central Kalimantan". *Environmental Management* 54, no. 1: 84–97. https://doi.org/10.1007/s00267-014-0282-2

———, and L. Hein. 2016. "Benefits and Costs of Oil Palm Expansion in Central Kalimantan, Indonesia, under Different Policy Scenarios". *Reg Environ Change* 16: 1011–21. https://doi.org/10.1007/s10113-015-0815-0

———, L. Hein, B. Edens, and A. Suwarno. 2015. "Mapping Monetary Values of Ecosystem Services in Support of Developing Ecosystem Accounts". *Ecosystem Services* 12: 71–83. https://doi.org/10.1016/j.ecoser.2015.02.009

Surahman, A., G.P. Shivakoti, and P. Soni. 2019. "Climate Change Mitigation Through Sustainable Degraded Peatlands Management in Central Kalimantan, Indonesia". *International Journal of the Commons* 13, no. 2: 859–66. https://doi.org/10.5334/ijc.893

———, P. Soni, and G.P. Shivakoti. 2018a. "Are Peatland Farming Systems Sustainable? Case Study on Assessing Existing Farming Systems in the Peatland of Central Kalimantan, Indonesia". *Journal of Integrative Environmental Sciences* 15, no. 1: 1–19. https://doi.org/10.1080/1943815X.2017.1412326

———, P. Soni, and G.P. Shivakoti. 2018b. "Reducing CO2 Emissions and Supporting Food Security in Central Kalimantan, Indonesia, with Improved Peatland Management". *Land Use Policy* 72: 325–32. https://doi.org/10.1016/j.landusepol.2017.12.050

Suruhanjaya Tenaga (ST). 2014. *Sabah Electricity Supply Industry Outlook 2014*. Putrajaya: Suruhanjaya Tenaga.

Susanto, D. 2019. "Kalsel Batasi Produksi Batu Bara". *Media Indonesia*, 30 August 2019. https://mediaindonesia.com/nusantara/256425/kalsel-batasi-produksi-batu-bara

———, 2021. "4.662 Hektar Kebun Jeruk di Kalsel Rusak Karena Banjir". *Media Indonesia*, 24 February 2021. https://mediaindonesia.com/nusantara/386677/4662-hektar-kebun-jeruk-di-kalsel-rusak-karena-banjir

Suter, M.K., K.A. Miller, I. Anggraeni, K.L. Ebi, E.T. Game, J. Krenz, Y.J. Masuda, L. Sheppard, N.H. Wolff, and J.T. Spector. 2019. "Association between Work in Deforested, Compared to Forested, Areas and Human Heat Strain: An Experimental Study in a Rural Tropical Environment". *Environmental Research Letters* 14, no. 8. https://doi.org/10.1088/1748-9326/ab2b53

Sutrisno, E. 2021. "Perkembangan Food Estate Kalteng Menggembirakan". *Portal Informasi Indonesia*, 21 April 2021. https://www.indonesia.go.id/kategori/editorial/2749/perkembangan-food-estate-kalteng-menggembirakan

Suwarno, A., R.E. de Vos, M.A. Slingerland, P.J. v. d. Meer, and J. Lucey. 2019. "A Study on Outcomes of Rspo Certification for Independent Smallholders in Central Kalimantan: Technical Report by the SEnSOR Programme".

——, L. Hein, and E. Sumarga. 2015. "Governance, Decentralisation and Deforestation: The Case of Central Kalimantan Province, Indonesia". *Quarterly Journal of International Agriculture* 54, no. 1: 77–100.

——, L. Hein, H.-P. Weikard, M. van Noordwijk, and B. Nugroho. 2018. "Land-Use Trade-Offs in the Kapuas Peat Forest, Central Kalimantan, Indonesia". *Land Use Policy* 75: 340–51. https://doi.org/10.1016/j.landusepol.2018.03.015

——, M. van Noordwijk, H.P. Weikard, and D. Suyamto. 2018. "Indonesia's Forest Conversion Moratorium Assessed with an Agent-Based Model of Land-Use Change and Ecosystem Services (LUCES)". *Mitig Adapt Strateg Glob Chang* 23, no. 2: 211–29. https://doi.org/10.1007/s11027-016-9721-0

Suwastoyo, B. 2019. "The Jurisdictional Approach in Palm Oil Production: The Case of Central Kalimantan". *Environment and Sustainability*. https://thepalmscribe.id/the-jurisdictional-approach-in-palm-oil-production-the-case-of-central-kalimantan/ (accessed 11 May 2021).

Suzuki, K., N. Tsuji, Y. Shirai, M.A. Hassan, and M. Osaki. 2017. "Evaluation of Biomass Energy Potential Towards Achieving Sustainability in Biomass Energy Utilization in Sabah, Malaysia". *Biomass and Bioenergy* 97: 149–54. https://doi.org/10.1016/j.biombioe.2016.12.023

Sweet, J., and M. Kelly. 2014. "Dynamics of Cultural Heritage Development in Sarawak". *IIAS 2014: Proceedings of the Conference on State Policy and the Cultural Politics of Heritage-Making in East and Southeast Asia.*

Syahrinudin, M. Denich, M. Becker, W. Hartati, and P.L.G. Vlek. 2020. "Biomass and Carbon Distribution on Imperata Cylindrica Grasslands". *Biodiversitas* 21, no. 1: 74–79. https://doi.org/10.13057/biodiv/d210111

Syaufina, L. 2018. "Forest and Land Fires in Indonesia: Assessment and Mitigation". In *Integrating Disaster Science and Management: Global Case Studies in Mitigation and Recovery*, pp. 109–21. Elsevier Inc.

——, and I.S. Sitanggang. 2018. "Peatland Fire Detection Using Spatio-Temporal Data Mining Analysis in Kalimantan, Indonesia". *Journal of Tropical Forest Science* 30, no. 2: 154–62. https://doi.org/10.26525/jtfs2018.30.2.154162

Tabassum, M., M.K. Haldar, and D.F.S. Khan. 2020. "Implementation and Performance Evaluation of Advance Metering Infrastructure for Borneo-Wide Power Grid". *Frontiers in Energy* 14, no. 1: 192–211. https://doi.org/10.1007/s11708-016-0438-2

Tacconi, L., and M.Z. Muttaqin. 2019. "Reducing Emissions from Land Use Change in Indonesia: An Overview". *Forest Policy and Economics* 108: 101979. https://doi.org/10.1016/j.forpol.2019.101979

Tagliacozzo, E. 2001. "Border Permeability and the State in Southeast Asia: Contraband and Regional Security". *Contemporary Southeast Asia* 23, no. 2: 254–74.

Tai, B. 2018. "The WWF Spatial Planning Experiences in Borneo". WWF.

Takahashi, H., A. Jaya, and S.H. Limin. 2015. "Compact Firefighting System for Villages and Water Resources for Firefighting in Peatland Area of Central Kalimantan". In *Tropical Peatland Ecosystems*, pp. 407–17. Springer Japan.

Takeuchi, Y., M. Nakagawa, B. Diway, and T. Nakashizuka. 2013. "Reproductive Success of a Tropical Tree, *Shorea laxa*, in a Pulau (Forest Reserve) Managed by a Local

Community in Borneo". *Forest Ecology and Management* 289: 416–24. https://doi.org/10.1016/j.foreco.2012.10.027

———, R. Soda, B. Diway, T.A. Kuda, M. Nakagawa, H. Nagamasu, and T. Nakashizuka. 2017. "Biodiversity Conservation Values of Fragmented Communally Reserved Forests, Managed by Indigenous People, in a Human-Modified Landscape in Borneo". *PLoS ONE* 12, no. 11: e0187273. https://doi.org/10.1371/journal.pone.0187273

Tan-Soo, J.S., and S.K. Pattanayak. 2019. "Seeking Natural Capital Projects: Forest Fires, Haze, and Early-Life Exposure in Indonesia". *Proc Natl Acad Sci U S A* 116, no. 12: 5239–45. https://doi.org/10.1073/pnas.1802876116

Tan, K.-L. 1965. "The Oil Palm Industry in Malaya". MA thesis, Faculty of Arts and Social Sciences, University of Malaya.

Tang, K.H.D. 2020. "Hydroelectric Dams and Power Demand in Malaysia: A Planning Perspective". *Journal of Cleaner Production* 252: 119795. https://doi.org/10.1016/j.jclepro.2019.119795

Tanilink.com. 2020. "Tempat Jual Beli Produk-Produk Pertanian dan Peternakan". Tani Link. https://tanilink.com/ (accessed 15 May 2020).

Tao, H.H., C. Donough, J. Gerendas, M.P. Hoffmann, A. Cahyo, H. Sugianto, R. Wandri, G.A. Rahim, M. Fisher, R.P. Rötter, K. Dittert, L. Pardon, and T. Oberthür. 2018. "Fertilizer Management Effects on Oil Palm Yield and Nutrient Use Efficiency on Sandy Soils with Limited Water Supply in Central Kalimantan". *Nutrient Cycling in Agroecosystems* 112, no. 3: 317–33. https://doi.org/10.1007/s10705-018-9948-0

———, C. Donough, M.P. Hoffmann, Y.L. Lim, S. Hendra, Rahmadsyah, G. Abdurrohim, K. Indrasuara, A. Lubis, T. Dolong, and T. Oberthür. 2017. "Effects of Best Management Practices on Dry Matter Production and Fruit Production Efficiency of Oil Palm". *European Journal of Agronomy* 90: 209–15. https://doi.org/10.1016/j.eja.2017.07.008

Taswell, R. 1986. "Dam in Sarawak Forces 3,000 Iban to Resettle". *Cultural Survival Quarterly Magazine.*

Tata, H.L. 2019. "Mixed Farming Systems on Peatlands in Jambi and Central Kalimantan Provinces, Indonesia: Should They Be Described as Paludiculture?". *Mires and Peat* 25. https://doi.org/10.19189/MaP.2018.KHR.360

Tay, K.X., and J.K.L. Chan. 2016. "Tour Operator Perspectives on Responsible Tourism Practices: A Case of Kinabalu National Park, Sabah". *International Journal of Culture, Tourism, and Hospitality Research* 10, no. 2: 121–37. https://doi.org/10.1108/IJCTHR-07-2014-0057

———, J.K.L. Chan, C.A. Vogt, and B. Mohamed. 2016. "Comprehending the Responsible Tourism Practices Through Principles of Sustainability: A Case of Kinabalu Park". *Tourism Management Perspectives* 18: 34–41. https://doi.org/10.1016/j.tmp.2015.12.018

TDD. 2018. "Tourism Statistics for the Year 2018". Tourism Development Department, M.o.P.R.a.T., Brunei Darussalam.

ten Kate, A., B. Kuepper, and M. Piotrowski. 2020. "NDPE Policies Cover 83% of Palm Oil Refining Market". *Chain Reaction Research*. https://chainreactionresearch. com/report/ndpe-policies-cover-83-of-palm-oil-refineries-implementation-at-75/

Teo, H.C., A.M. Lechner, S. Sagala, and A. Campos-Arceiz. 2020. "Environmental Impacts of Planned Capitals and Lessons for Indonesia's New Capital". *Land* 9, no. 11: 438.

Terauchi, D. 2020. "Reorganization of a Swidden Society with the Development of Coal Mining in East Kalimantan: Focusing on Land-Use Practices and Social Relationships over Labor and Land. In Japanese". *Southeast Asian Studies* 58, no. 1: 33–76. https://doi.org/10.20495/tak.58.1_33

———, N. Imang, M. Nanang, M. Kawai, M.A. Sardjono, F. Pambudhi, and M. Inoue. 2014. "Implication for Designing a REDD+ Program in a Frontier of Oil Palm Plantation Development: Evidence in East Kalimantan, Indonesia". *Open Journal of Forestry* 2014.

———, and M. Inoue. 2016. "Swiddeners' Perception on Monoculture Oil Palm in East Kalimantan, Indonesia". In *Monoculture Farming: Global Practices, Ecological Impact and Benefits/Drawbacks*, pp. 99–128. Nova Science Publishers, Inc.

Thaler, G.M., and C.A.M. Anandi. 2017. "Shifting Cultivation, Contentious Land Change and Forest Governance: The Politics of Swidden in East Kalimantan". *Journal of Peasant Studies* 44, no. 5: 1066–87. https://doi.org/10.1080/03066150.2016.1243531

Thompson, B.S. 2018. "Institutional Challenges for Corporate Participation in Payments for Ecosystem Services (PES): Insights from Southeast Asia". *Sustainability Science* 13, no. 4: 919–35. https://doi.org/10.1007/s11625-018-0569-y

Thung, P.H. 2018. "A Case Study on the Persistence of Swidden Agriculture in the Context of Post-2015 Anti-Haze Regulation in West-Kalimantan". *Human Ecology* 46, no. 2: 197–205.

TIES. 2019. "What Is Ecotourism?". The International Ecotourism Society. https:// ecotourism.org/what-is-ecotourism/ (accessed 30 March 2020).

Tilman, D., C. Balzer, J. Hill, and B.L. Befort. 2011. "Global Food Demand and the Sustainable Intensification of Agriculture". *Proceedings of the National Academy of Sciences* 108, no. 50: 20260–64. https://doi.org/10.1073/pnas.1116437108

Timotius, T. 2021. "Kapuas Hulu Gelar Festival Danau Sentarum Desember 2021". *Antara Kalbar*, 29 March 2021. https://kalbar.antaranews.com/berita/465894/ kapuas-hulu-gelar-festival-danau-sentarum-desember-2021

Tiraieyari, N., A. Hamzah, and B.A. Samah. 2017. "Organic Farming and Sustainable Agriculture in Malaysia: Organic Farmers' Challenges Towards Adoption". *Sustainable Development of Organic Agriculture: Historical Perspectives*: 135.

Tisen, O.B., S.L. Kheng, and F. Gombek. 2015. "Sarawak Hornbill Conservation Initiatives: Engaging the Society". *Malayan Nature Journal* 67, no. 2: 216–23.

Tokuchi, N., H. Samejima, J. Hon, and K. Fukushima. 2020. "Influence of Herbicide Use in Oil Palm Plantations on Stream Water Chemistry in Sarawak". In *Advances in Asian Human-Environmental Research*. Springer International Publishing.

Tong, Y.-S. 2017. "Vertical Specialisation or Linkage Development for Agro-Commodity

Value Chain Upgrading? The Case of Malaysian Palm Oil". *Land Use Policy* 68: 585–96. https://doi.org/10.1016/j.landusepol.2017.08.020

Topalovic, M. 2016. "Palm Oil: A New Ethics of Visibility for the Production Landscape". *Architectural Design* 86, no. 4: 42–47. https://doi.org/10.1002/ad.2066

Toulec, T., S. Lhota, H. Soumarová, A.K.S. Putera, and W. Kustiawan. 2020. "Shrimp Farms, Fire or Palm Oil? Changing Causes of Proboscis Monkey Habitat Loss". *Global Ecology and Conservation* 21. https://doi.org/10.1016/j.gecco.2019.e00863

Toumbourou, T.D., and W.H. Dressler. 2020. "Sustaining Livelihoods in a Palm Oil Enclave: Differentiated Gendered Responses in East Kalimantan, Indonesia". *Asia Pacific Viewpoint*. https://doi.org/10.1111/apv.12265

Trase. 2022. Trase. Intelligence for Sustainable Trade.

Ubukata, F., and Y. Sadamichi. 2020. "Estate and Smallholding Oil Palm Production in Sarawak: A Comparison of Profitability and Greenhouse Gas Emissions". In *Advances in Asian Human-Environmental Research*. Springer International Publishing.

Uda, S.K., L. Hein, and A. Adventa. 2020. "Towards Better Use of Indonesian Peatlands with Paludiculture and Low-Drainage Food Crops". *Wetlands Ecology and Management* 28, no. 3: 509–26. https://doi.org/10.1007/s11273-020-09728-x

———, G. Schouten, and L. Hein. 2018. "The Institutional Fit of Peatland Governance in Indonesia". *Land Use Policy*. https://doi.org/10.1016/j.landusepol.2018.03.031

Ueda, A., D. Dwibadra, W.A. Noerdjito, Sugiarto, M. Kon, T. Ochi, M. Takahashi, and K. Fukuyama. 2015. "Effect of Habitat Transformation from Grassland to Acacia Mangium Plantation on Dung Beetle Assemblage in East Kalimantan, Indonesia". *Journal of Insect Conservation* 19, no. 4: 765–80. https://doi.org/10.1007/s10841-015-9798-x

Umahuk, D. 2017. "Republik Jagoi". *Kompas*, 31 July 2017. https://nasional.kompas.com/read/2017/07/31/12141781/republik-jagoi?page=all

Umar, M.S., P. Jennings, and T. Urmee. 2014. "Generating Renewable Energy from Oil Palm Biomass in Malaysia: The Feed-in Tariff Policy Framework". *Biomass and Bioenergy* 62: 37–46. https://doi.org/10.1016/j.biombioe.2014.01.020

———, T. Urmee, and P. Jennings. 2018. "A Policy Framework and Industry Roadmap Model for Sustainable Oil Palm Biomass Electricity Generation in Malaysia". *Renewable Energy* 128: 275–84. https://doi.org/10.1016/j.renene.2017.12.060

UN COMTRADE. 2021. "UN COMTRADE Database". UN Department of Economic and Social Affair, New York.

UNCTAD. 2003. "Energy and Environmental Services: Negotiating Objectives and Development Priorities". United Nations, New York and Geneva. https://unctad.org/system/files/official-document/ditctncd20033_en.pdf

UNDP Malaysia. 2018. "Project Document: SDG Localization in Sabah and Sarawak". ATLAS Project Number: 00110460. UNDP.

UNFCCC. 2016a. "First Nationally Determined Contribution Republic of Indonesia". https://www4.unfccc.int/sites/NDCStaging/pages/Party.aspx?party=IDN

———. 2016b. "Intended Nationally Determined Contribution of The Government of Malaysia". https://www4.unfccc.int/sites/NDCStaging/pages/Party.aspx?party=MYS

Urano, M. 2014. "Impacts of Newly Liberalised Policies on Customary Land Rights of Forest-Dwelling Populations: A Case Study from East Kalimantan, Indonesia". *Asia Pacific Viewpoint* 55, no. 1: 6–23. https://doi.org/10.1111/apv.12042

———. 2020. "Why the Principle of Informed Self-Determination Does Not Help Local Farmers Facing Land Loss: A Case Study from Oil Palm Development in East Kalimantan, Indonesia". *Globalizations* 17, no. 4: 593–607. https://doi.org/10.108 0/14747731.2019.1654703

USDA. 2019. "Organic Market Overview". United States Department of Agriculture. https://www.ers.usda.gov/topics/natural-resources-environment/organic-agriculture/organic-market-overview/ (accessed 26 March 2020).

Ushio, M., Y. Osada, T. Kumagai, T. Kume, R.A.S. Pungga, T. Nakashizuka, T. Itioka, and S. Sakai. 2019. "Dynamic and Synergistic Influences of Air Temperature and Rainfall on General Flowering in a Bornean Lowland Tropical Forest". *Ecological Research*. https://doi.org/10.1111/1440-1703.12057

van der Ent, A., A.J.M. Baker, R.D. Reeves, R.L. Chaney, C.W.N. Anderson, J.A. Meech, P.D. Erskine, M.-O. Simonnot, J. Vaughan, J.L. Morel, G. Echevarria, B. Fogliani, Q. Rongliang, and D.R. Mulligan. 2015. "Agromining: Farming for Metals in the Future?". *Environmental Science & Technology* 49, no. 8: 4773–80. https://doi. org/10.1021/es506031u

Van der Laan, C., B. Wicke, P.A. Verweij, and A.P.C. Faaij. 2017. "Mitigation of Unwanted Direct and Indirect Land-Use Change: An Integrated Approach Illustrated for Palm Oil, Pulpwood, Rubber and Rice Production in North and East Kalimantan, Indonesia". *GCB Bioenergy* 9, no. 2: 429–44. https://doi.org/10.1111/gcbb.12353

van Gevelt, T., H. Abok, M.M. Bennett, S.D. Fam, F. George, N. Kulathuramaiyer, C.T. Low, and T. Zaman. 2019. "Indigenous Perceptions of Climate Anomalies in Malaysian Borneo". *Global Environmental Change* 58. https://doi.org/10.1016/j. gloenvcha.2019.101974

van Oosten, C., M. Moeliono, and F. Wiersum. 2018. "From Product to Place: Spatializing Governance in a Commodified Landscape". *Environmental Management* 62, no. 1: 157–69. https://doi.org/10.1007/s00267-017-0883-7

Varkkey, H. 2012. "Patronage Politics as a Driver of Economic Regionalisation: The Indonesian Oil Palm Sector and Transboundary Haze". *Asia Pacific Viewpoint* 53, no. 3: 314–29. https://doi.org/10.1111/j.1467-8373.2012.01493.x

———. 2018. "Transboundary Haze, ASEAN, and the SDGs: Normative and Structural Considerations". In *Sustainable Development Goals in Southeast Asia and ASEAN*, pp. 235–257. Leiden: Brill.

———. A. Tyson, and S.A.B. Choiruzzad. 2018. "Palm Oil Intensification and Expansion in Indonesia and Malaysia: Environmental and Socio-Political Factors Influencing Policy". *Forest Policy and Economics* 92: 148–59. https://doi.org/10.1016/j. forpol.2018.05.002

Vaz, J., and A.L. Agama. 2013. "Seeking Synergy Between Community and State-Based Governance for Biodiversity Conservation: The Role of Indigenous and Community-Conserved Areas in Sabah, Malaysian Borneo". *Asia Pacific Viewpoint* 54, no. 2: 141–57. https://doi.org/10.1111/apv.12015

Veloo, R., S. Paramananthan, and E. Van Ranst. 2014. "Classification of Tropical Lowland Peats Revisited: The Case of Sarawak". *Catena* 118: 179–85. https://doi.org/10.1016/j.catena.2014.01.004

Venter, O., H.P. Possingham, L. Hovani, S. Dewi, B. Griscom, G. Paoli, P. Wells, and K.A. Wilson. 2013. "Using Systematic Conservation Planning to Minimize REDD+ Conflict with Agriculture and Logging in the Tropics". *Conservation Letters* 6, no. 2: 116–24. https://doi.org/10.1111/j.1755-263X.2012.00287.x

Verstegen, J.A., F. van der Hilst, G. Woltjer, D. Karssenberg, S.M. de Jong, and A. Faaij. 2016. "What Can and Can't We Say About Indirect Land-Use Change in Brazil Using an Integrated Economic - Land-Use Change Model?". *Global Change Biology Bioenergy* 8, no. 3: 561–78. https://doi.org/10.1111/gcbb.12270

———, C. van der Laan, S.C. Dekker, A. Faaij, and M.J. Santos. 2019. "Recent and Projected Impacts of Land Use and Land Cover Changes on Carbon Stocks and Biodiversity in East Kalimantan, Indonesia". *Ecological Indicators* 103: 563–75. https://doi.org/10.1016/j.ecolind.2019.04.053

Vicol, M., J. Neilson, D.F.S. Hartatri, and P. Cooper. 2018. "Upgrading for Whom? Relationship Coffee, Value Chain Interventions and Rural Development in Indonesia". *World Development* 110: 26–37. https://doi.org/10.1016/j.worlddev.2018.05.020

Vijge, M.J., M. Brockhaus, M. Di Gregorio, and E. Muharrom. 2016. "Framing National REDD+ Benefits, Monitoring, Governance and Finance: A Comparative Analysis of Seven Countries". *Global Environmental Change* 39: 57–68. https://doi.org/10.1016/j.gloenvcha.2016.04.002

Vijith, H., and D. Dodge-Wan. 2020. "Applicability of MODIS Land Cover and Enhanced Vegetation Index (EVI) for the Assessment of Spatial and Temporal Changes in Strength of Vegetation in Tropical Rainforest Region of Borneo". *Remote Sensing Applications: Society and Environment* 18: 100311. https://doi.org/10.1016/j.rsase.2020.100311

Vincent, J.R., and R.M. Ali. 1997. "Environment and Development in a Resource-Rich Economy: Malaysia under the New Economic Policy". Harvard Institute for International Development, Harvard University.

Visser, L., R. Hoefnagels, and M. Junginger. 2020. "Wood Pellet Supply Chain Costs: A Review and Cost Optimization Analysis". *Renewable and Sustainable Energy Reviews* 118: 109506. https://doi.org/10.1016/j.rser.2019.109506

Vlam, M., G.A. de Groot, A. Boom, P. Copini, I. Laros, K. Veldhuijzen, D. Zakamdi, and P.A. Zuidema. 2018. "Developing Forensic Tools for an African Timber: Regional Origin Is Revealed by Genetic Characteristics, but Not by Isotopic Signature". *Biological Conservation* 220: 262–71. https://doi.org/10.1016/j.biocon.2018.01.031

Vong, J., P. Mandal, and I. Song. 2016. "Digital Banking for Alleviating Rural Poverty in Indonesia: Some Evidences". In *Smart Technologies for Smart Nations: Perspectives from the Asia-Pacific Region*, edited by P. Mandal and J. Vong, pp. 3–18. Singapore: Springer Singapore.

Vos, R., and A. Cattaneo. 2020. "Smallholders and Rural People - Making Food System Value Chains Inclusive". In *2020 Global Food Policy Report: Building Inclusive Food*

System, edited by P. Stedman-Edwards, pp. 14–27. Washington, DC: International Food Policy Research Institute (IFPRI).

Wadley, R.L., and M. Eilenberg. 2005. "Autonomy, Identity, and 'Illegal' Logging in the Borderland of West Kalimantan, Indonesia". *Asia Pacific Journal of Anthropology* 6, no. 1: 19–34. https://doi.org/10.1080/14442210500074853

——, and O. Mertz. 2005. "Pepper in a Time of Crisis: Smallholder Buffering Strategies in Sarawak, Malaysia and West Kalimantan, Indonesia". *Agricultural Systems* 85, no. 3: 289–305. https://doi.org/10.1016/j.agsy.2005.06.012

Wahab, A.G. 2020. "Malaysia Biofuels Annual Report 2020". USDA. https://www.fas.usda.gov/data

Wahi, R., E.R. Bidin, N.M.M. Asif, N.A.N. Hamizat, Z. Ngaini, R. Omar, and J. Jamel. 2019. "Nutrient Availability in Sago Bark and Empty Fruit Bunch Composts for the Growth of Water Spinach and Green Mustard". *Environmental Science and Pollution Research*: 1–8.

Walker, B., J. Sayer, N.L. Andrew, and B. Campbell. 2010. "Should Enhanced Resilience Be an Objective of Natural Resource Management Research for Developing Countries?". *Crop Science* 50 (Supplement 1). https://doi.org/10.2135/cropsci2009.10.0565

Walker, O. 2018. "A Pilot Investigation of a Wildlife Tourism Experience Using Photographs Shared to Social Media: Case Study on the Endangered Borneo Pygmy Elephant". Murdoch University.

Wan Mohd Jaafar, W.S., N.F.S. Said, K.N. Abdul Maulud, R. Uning, M.T. Latif, A.M. Muhmad Kamarulzaman, M. Mohan, B. Pradhan, S.N.M. Saad, and E.N. Broadbent. 2020. "Carbon Emissions from Oil Palm Induced Forest and Peatland Conversion in Sabah and Sarawak, Malaysia". *Forests* 11, no. 12: 1285.

Wang, S.Y., J.F. Wan, D. Li, and C.H. Zhang. 2016. "Implementing Smart Factory of Industry 4.0: An Outlook". *International Journal of Distributed Sensor Networks*. https://doi.org/10.1155/2016/3159805

Watanabe, C., N. Naveed, and P. Neittaanmäki. 2019. "Digitalized Bioeconomy: Planned Obsolescence-Driven Circular Economy Enabled by Co-Evolutionary Coupling". *Technology in Society* 56: 8–30. https://doi.org/10.1016/j.techsoc.2018.09.002

Watts, J., D. Nepstad, and S. Irawan. 2019. "Can Jurisdictional Certification Curb Palm Oil Deforestation in Indonesia? (Commentary)". *Mongabay*, 10 July 2019 (Mongabay Series on Indonesian Palm Oil). https://news.mongabay.com/2019/07/can-jurisdictional-certification-curb-palm-oil-deforestation-in-indonesia/

Watts, J.D., L. Tacconi, N. Hapsari, S. Irawan, S. Sloan, and T. Widiastomo. 2019. "Incentivizing Compliance: Evaluating the Effectiveness of Targeted Village Incentives for Reducing Burning in Indonesia". *Forest Policy and Economics* 108. https://doi.org/10.1016/j.forpol.2019.101956

Wells, J.A., K.A. Wilson, N.K. Abram, M. Nunn, D.L.A. Gaveau, R.K. Runting, N. Tarniati, K.L. Mengersen, and E. Meijaard. 2016. "Rising Floodwaters: Mapping Impacts and Perceptions of Flooding in Indonesian Borneo". *Environmental Research Letters* 11, no. 6. https://doi.org/10.1088/1748-9326/11/6/064016

Wetland International and Tropenbos International. 2016. "Can Peatland Landscapes in Indonesia be Drained Sustainably? An Assessment of the 'eko-hidro' Water Management Approach". Wetlands International, Tropenbos International.

Wibowo, A., and L. Giessen. 2015. "Absolute and Relative Power Gains Among State Agencies in Forest-Related Land Use Politics: The Ministry of Forestry and Its Competitors in the REDD+ Programme and the One Map Policy in Indonesia". *Land Use Policy* 49: 131–41. https://doi.org/10.1016/j.landusepol.2015.07.018

———, and L. Giessen. 2018. "From Voluntary Private to Mandatory State Governance in Indonesian Forest Certification: Reclaiming Authority by Bureaucracies". *Forest and Society* 2, no. 1: 28–46.

Wicke, B., R. Sikkema, V. Dornburg, and A. Faaij. 2011. "Exploring Land Use Changes and the Role of Palm Oil Production in Indonesia and Malaysia". *Land Use Policy* 28, no. 1: 193–206. https://doi.org/10.1016/j.landusepol.2010.06.001

Widodo, J., A. Sulaiman, A. Awaluddin, A. Riyadi, M. Nasucha, D. Perissin, and J.T.S. Sumantyo. 2019. "Application of SAR Interferometry Using ALOS-2 PALSAR-2 Data as Precise Method to Identify Degraded Peatland Areas Related to Forest Fire". *Geosciences* (Switzerland) 9, no. 11. https://doi.org/10.3390/geosciences 9110484

Wijedasa, L.S., J. Jauhiainen, M. Könönen, M. Lampela, H. Vasander, M.-C. Leblanc, S. Evers, T.E.L. Smith, C.M. Yule, H. Varkkey, M. Lupascu, F. Parish, I. Singleton, G.R. Clements, S.A. Aziz, M.E. Harrison, S. Cheyne, G.Z. Anshari, E. Meijaard, J.E. Goldstein, S. Waldron, K. Hergoualc'h, R. Dommain, S. Frolking, C.D. Evans, M.R.C. Posa, P.H. Glaser, N. Suryadiputra, R. Lubis, T. Santika, R. Padfield, S. Kurnianto, P. Hadisiswoyo, T.W. Lim, S.E. Page, V. Gauci, P.J. Van Der Meer, H. Buckland, F. Garnier, M.K. Samuel, L.N.L.K. Choo, P. O'Reilly, M. Warren, S. Suksuwan, E. Sumarga, A. Jain, W.F. Laurance, J. Couwenberg, H. Joosten, R. Vernimmen, A. Hooijer, C. Malins, M.A. Cochrane, B. Perumal, F. Siegert, K.S.-H. Peh, L.-P. Comeau, L. Verchot, C.F. Harvey, A. Cobb, Z. Jaafar, H. Wösten, S. Manuri, M. Müller, W. Giesen, J. Phelps, D.L. Yong, M. Silvius, B.M.M. Wedeux, A. Hoyt, M. Osaki, T. Hirano, H. Takahashi, T.S. Kohyama, A. Haraguchi, N.P. Nugroho, D.A. Coomes, L.P. Quoi, A. Dohong, H. Gunawan, D.L.A. Gaveau, A. Langner, F.K.S. Lim, D.P. Edwards, X. Giam, G. Van Der Werf, R. Carmenta, C.C. Verwer, L. Gibson, L. Gandois, L.L.B. Graham, J. Regalino, S.A. Wich, J. Rieley, N. Kettridge, C. Brown, R. Pirard, S. Moore, B.R. Capilla, U. Ballhorn, H.C. Ho, A. Hoscilo, S. Lohberger, T.A. Evans, N. Yulianti, G. Blackham, Onrizal, S. Husson, D. Murdiyarso, S. Pangala, L.E.S. Cole, L. Tacconi, H. Segah, P. Tonoto, J.S.H. Lee, G. Schmilewski, S. Wulffraat, E.I. Putra, M.E. Cattau, R.S. Clymo, R. Morrison, A. Mujahid, J. Miettinen, S.C. Liew, S. Valpola, D. Wilson, L. D'Arcy, M. Gerding, S. Sundari, S.A. Thornton, B. Kalisz, S.J. Chapman, A.S.M. Su, I. Basuki, M. Itoh, C. Traeholt, S. Sloan, A.K. Sayok, and R. Andersen. 2017. "Denial of Long-Term Issues with Agriculture on Tropical Peatlands Will Have Devastating Consequences". *Global Change Biology* 23, no. 3: 977–82. https://doi.org/10.1111/gcb.13516

Wijedasa, L.S., S. Sloan, S.E. Page, G.R. Clements, M. Lupascu, and T.A. Evans. 2018. "Carbon Emissions from South-East Asian Peatlands Will Increase Despite

Emission-Reduction Schemes". *Global Change Biology* 24, no. 10: 4598–613. https://doi.org/10.1111/gcb.14340

Wilkinson, C.L., D.C.J. Yeo, H.H. Tan, A.H. Fikri, and R.M. Ewers. 2018. "Land-Use Change Is Associated with a Significant Loss of Freshwater Fish Species and Functional Richness in Sabah, Malaysia". *Biological Conservation* 222: 164–71. https://doi.org/10.1016/j.biocon.2018.04.004

Willer, H., G. Sampson, V. Voora, D. Dang, and J. Lernoud. 2019. "The State of Sustainable Markets 2019". International Trade Centre (ITC). Geneva, Switzerland: ITC.

Williams, A., G. Whiteman, and S. Kennedy. 2019. "Cross-Scale Systemic Resilience: Implications for Organization Studies". *Business & Society*: 0007650319825870.

Williams, S.H., S.A. Scriven, D.F.R.P. Burslem, J.K. Hill, G. Reynolds, A.L. Agama, F. Kugan, C.R. Maycock, E. Khoo, A.Y.L. Hastie, J.B. Sugau, R. Nilus, J.T. Pereira, S.L.T. Tsen, L.Y. Lee, S. Juiling, J.A. Hodgson, L.E. S. Cole, G.P. Asner, L.J. Evans, and J.F. Brodie. 2020. "Incorporating Connectivity into Conservation Planning for the Optimal Representation of Multiple Species and Ecosystem Services". *Conservation Biology* 34, no. 4: 934–42. https://doi.org/10.1111/cobi.13450

Wilman, E.A. 2019. "Market Redirection Leakage in the Palm Oil Market". *Ecological Economics* 159: 226–34. https://doi.org/10.1016/j.ecolecon.2019.01.014

Wilmar International. 2020. "Traceability: Supply Chain Map". https://www.wilmar-international.com/sustainability/traceability/supply-chain-map (accessed 3 November 2020).

Wilson, K., N.K.K. Abram, P. Chin, C. Ong, E. Latik, H.H. Jitilon, M. Ramlan, N.B. Amat Nor, C.I. Kinsui, M.D.B. Rosli, J. Wasai, and M. Kumar. 2018. "Smallholder Readiness for Roundtable on Sustainable Palm Oil (RSPO) Jurisdictional Certification of Palm Oil by 2025: Results from Field Studies in Sabah's Telupid, Tongod, Beluran & Kinabatangan Districts". Forever Sabah. Kota Kinabalu, Sabah.

Winosa, Y. 2020. "Indonesia Mulling Special Economic Status for Halal Industrial Zones". Salaam Gateway. https://www.salaamgateway.com/story/indonesia-mulling-special-economic-status-for-halal-industrial-zones (accessed 20 May 2021).

Woittiez, L.S., M. Slingerland, R. Rafik, and K.E. Giller. 2018. "Nutritional Imbalance in Smallholder Oil Palm Plantations in Indonesia". *Nutrient Cycling in Agroecosystems* 111, no. 1: 73–86. https://doi.org/10.1007/s10705-018-9919-5

———, M.T. van Wijk, M. Slingerland, M. van Noordwijk, and K.E. Giller. 2017. "Yield Gaps in Oil Palm: A Quantitative Review of Contributing Factors". *European Journal of Agronomy* 83: 57–77. https://doi.org/10.1016/j.eja.2016.11.002

Wolff, N.H., Y.J. Masuda, E. Meijaard, J.A. Wells, and E.T. Game. 2018. "Impacts of Tropical Deforestation on Local Temperature and Human Well-Being Perceptions". *Global Environmental Change* 52: 181—89. https://doi.org/10.1016/j.gloenvcha.2018.07.004

Wong, G.X., R. Hirata, T. Hirano, F. Kiew, E.B. Aeries, K.K. Musin, J.W. Waili, K.S. Lo, and L. Melling. 2020. "How Do Land Use Practices Affect Methane Emissions from Tropical Peat Ecosystems?". *Agricultural and Forest Meteorology*, pp. 282–83: 107869. https://doi.org/10.1016/j.agrformet.2019.107869

Wong, W.V.C., and S. Tsuyuki. 2017. "High Resolution of Three-Dimensional Dataset for

Aboveground Biomass Estimation in Tropical Rainforests". In *Redefining Diversity and Dynamics of Natural Resources Management in Asia*, pp. 115–30. Elsevier Inc.

Woodcock, P., D.P. Edwards, T.M. Fayle, R.J. Newton, C.V. Khen, S.H. Bottrell, and K.C. Hamer. 2011. "The Conservation Value of South East Asia's Highly Degraded Forests: Evidence from Leaf-Litter Ants". *Philosophical Transactions of the Royal Society B: Biological Sciences* 366, no. 1582: 3256–64. https://doi.org/10.1098/rstb.2011.0031

World Bank. 2020a. "State and Trends of Carbon Pricing 2020". World Bank, Washington, DC. https://openknowledge.worldbank.org/bitstream/handle/10986/33809/9781464815867.pdf?sequence=4

——. 2020b. "World Development Indicators (WDI)". http://datatopics.worldbank.org/world-development-indicators/ (accessed 1 February 2020).

——. 2021. *State and Trends of Carbon Pricing 2021*. Washington, DC: World Bank.

Wulan, Y.C., S. Budidarsono, and L. Joshi. 2008. "Economic Analysis of Improved Smallholder Rubber Agroforestry Systems in West Kalimantan, Indonesia-Implications for Rubber Development". Sustainable Sloping Lands and Watershed Management Conference, Luang Prabang, Lao PDR.

Wulffraat, S., and J. Morrison. 2013. "Measuring Biological Indicators dor Status Assessment of the Heart of Borneo". *Environmental Conservation* 40, no. 3: 277–86. https://doi.org/10.1017/S0376892913000064

Wunder, S., B. Campbell, P.G.H. Frost, J.A. Sayer, R. Iwan, and L. Wollenberg. 2008. "When Donors Get Cold Feet: The Community Conservation Concession in Setulang (Kalimantan, Indonesia) That Never Happened". *Ecology and Society* 13, no. 1.

WWF. 2005. "Heart of Borneo: Three Countries, One Conservation Vision". Heart of Borneo Workshop by WWF, Brunei Darussalam, 5–6 April 2005.

——. 2015. "Highland Tales in the Heart of Borneo Unveiled". 6 August 2015. https://www.wwf.org.my/?20105/Highland-Tales-in-the-Heart-of-Borneo-Unveiled

——. 2019. "Visit the Heart of Borneo: An Ecotourism Promotion in the Heart of Borneo". WWF. https://wwf.panda.org/wwf_news/?347695/Visit-the-Heart-of-Borneo-An-Ecotourism-Promotion-in-the-Heart-of-Borneo (accessed 18 October 2021).

——. 2021. "Sabah: A Global Leader in Sustainable Palm Oil". https://www.wwf.org.my/?28486/Sabah-A-Global-Leader-in-Sustainable-Palm-Oil (accessed 7 November 2021).

Yamamoto, Y., and K. Takeuchi. 2012. "Estimating the Break-Even Price for Forest Protection in Central Kalimantan". *Environmental Economics and Policy Studies* 14, no. 3: 289–301. https://doi.org/10.1007/s10018-012-0030-x

——, and K. Takeuchi. 2015. "The Potential for REDD+ in Peatland of Central Kalimantan, Indonesia". In *Tropical Peatland Ecosystems*, pp. 599–612. Springer Japan.

——, and K. Takeuchi. 2016. "Mitigating Climate Change by Preventing Peatland Fire: Conditions for Successful REDD+ in Indonesia". In *Climate Change Policies and Challenges in Indonesia*, pp. 145–58. Springer Japan.

Yan, J., and F. Su. 2018. "An Analysis of the Developmental Differences in Borneo's Southeastern and Northwestern Coastal Zones". *Journal of Coastal Conservation* 22, no. 6: 1045–55. https://doi.org/10.1007/s11852-018-0622-0

——, M. Wang, F. Su, X. Zhang, S. Gao, and M. Xu. 2020. "Changes in Land Cover and Ecological Stress in Borneo Based on Remote Sensing and an Ecological Footprint Method". *Landscape and Ecological Engineering.* https://doi.org/10.1007/s11355-020-00425-8

Yanindraputri, P. 2016. "Balancing Sustainable Growth and Forest Conservation through Spatial Planning for a Green Economy in the Heart of Borneo". ASEAN-Canada Research Partnership, Working Paper Series, Working Paper No. 3. October 2016.

Yau, K.A., S.L. Lau, A.F.L. Chua, M.H. Ling, V. Iranmanesh, and S.C.C. Kwan. 2016. "Greater Kuala Lumpur as a Smart City: A Case Study on Technology Opportunities". 2016 8th International Conference on Knowledge and Smart Technology (KST), 3–6 February 2016.

Yeo, T.C., M. Naming, and R. Manurung. 2014. "Building a Discovery Partnership with Sarawak Biodiversity Centre: A Gateway to Access Natural Products from the Rainforests". *Combinatorial Chemistry & High Throughput Screening* 17, no. 3: 192–200.

Yoon, I., D.K. Noh, D. Lee, R. Teguh, T. Honma, and H. Shin. 2012. "Reliable Wildfire Monitoring with Sparsely Deployed Wireless Sensor Networks". 2012 IEEE 26th International Conference on Advanced Information Networking and Applications.

Yoshikura, T., M. Amano, and G.Z. Anshari. 2018. "Exploring Potential of REDD+ Readiness with Social Safeguard through Diverse Forest Use Practices in Gunung Palung National Park in West Kalimantan, Indonesia". *Open Journal of Forestry* 8, no. 2: 141.

——, M. Amano, H. Chikaraishi, B. Supriyanto, and D. Wardhana. 2016. "Evaluation of Appropriate Identification of Deforestation Agents and Drivers for Designing Redd+ Readiness Activities Through an Examination of the Area Around Gunung Palung National Park, Indonesia". *Open Journal of Forestry* 6, no. 2: 106–22.

——, M. Amano, B. Supriyanto, and D. Wardhana. 2016. "Identifying the Agents and Drivers of Deforestation: An Examination Around Gunung Palung National Park, West Kalimantan, Indonesia". *International Journal of Agricultural Resources, Governance and Ecology* 12, no. 4: 327–43. https://doi.org/10.1504/IJARGE.2016.080884

Yovanda. 2019. "Plans for a New Indonesian Capital Put Borneo's Abandoned Mines in the Spotlight". *Mongabay*, 20 December 2019. https://news.mongabay.com/2019/12/plans-for-a-new-indonesian-capital-put-borneos-abandoned-mines-in-the-spotlight/

Yuliani, E.L., H. Adnan, R. Achdiawan, D. Bakara, V. Heri, J. Sammy, M.A. Salim, and T. Sunderland. 2018. "The Roles of Traditional Knowledge Systems in Orang-Utan Pongo Spp. and Forest Conservation: A Case Study of Danau Sentarum, West Kalimantan, Indonesia". *Oryx* 52, no. 1: 156–65. https://doi.org/10.1017/S0030605316000636

———, W.T. de Groot, L. Knippenberg, and D.O. Bakara. 2020. "Forest or Oil Palm Plantation? Interpretation of Local Responses to the Oil Palm Promises in Kalimantan, Indonesia". *Land Use Policy* 96: 104616. https://doi.org/10.1016/j.landusepol.2020.104616

———. E.B.P. de Jong, L. Knippenberg, D.O. Bakara, M.A. Salim, and T. Sunderland. 2018. "Keeping the Land: Indigenous Communities' Struggle Over Land Use and Sustainable Forest Management in Kalimantan, Indonesia". *Ecology and Society* 23, no. 4. https://doi.org/10.5751/ES-10640-230449

Yuliyanto. 2017. "The Role of the Dayak Customary Law in Resolving Conflict to Realize Justice and Peace". *Jurnal RechtsVinding* 6, no. 1: 55–70.

Yusuf, A.A., E.L. Roos, and J.M. Horridge. 2018. "Indonesia's Moratorium on Palm Oil Expansion from Natural Forests: Economy-Wide Impacts and the Role of International Transfers". *Asian Development Review* 35, no. 2: 85–112. https://doi.org/10.1162/adev_a_00115

Yuyun, M., Kaarieni, and N.T. Sunaryo. 2020. "Analysis of Ecotourism Development Strategy in Tanjung Puting Province National Park, Central Kalimantan". *KnE Social Sciences* 4, no. 6. https://doi.org/10.18502/kss.v4i6.6655

Zahari, M.A.K.M., H. Ariffin, M.N. Mokhtar, J. Salihon, Y. Shirai, and M.A. Hassan. 2015. "Case Study for a Palm Biomass Biorefinery Utilizing Renewable Non-Food Sugars from Oil Palm Frond for the Production of Poly(3-Hydroxybutyrate) Bioplastic". *Journal of Cleaner Production* 87: 284–90. https://doi.org/10.1016/j.jclepro.2014.10.010

Zaremohzzabieh, Z., B.A. Samah, M. Muhammad, S.Z. Omar, J. Bolong, S.B.H. Hassan, and H.A. Mohamed Shaffril. 2016. "Information and Communications Technology Acceptance by Youth Entrepreneurs in Rural Malaysian Communities: The Mediating Effects of Attitude and Entrepreneurial Intention". *Information Technology for Development* 22, no. 4: 606–29. https://doi.org/10.1080/02681102.2015.1128384

Zeppel, H.D. 1998. "Entertainers or Entrepreneurs". *Tourism Recreation Research* 23, no. 1: 39–45. https://doi.org/10.1080/02508281.1998.11014818

Zhang, J.J., and V.R. Savage. 2019. "Southeast Asia's Transboundary Haze Pollution: Unravelling the Inconvenient Truth". *Asia Pacific Viewpoint* 60, no. 3: 355–69. https://doi.org/10.1111/apv.12245

Zhou, A., and E. Thomson. 2009. "The Development of Biofuels in Asia". *Applied Energy* 86: S11–S20. https://doi.org/10.1016/j.apenergy.2009.04.028

Zhou, Q., X. Chen, and S. Li. 2018. "Innovative Financial Approach for Agricultural Sustainability: A Case Study of Alibaba". *Sustainability* 10, no. 3: 891.

Zhou, Z., Z. Li, S. Waldron, and A. Tanaka. 2019. "InSAR Time Series Analysis of L-Band Data for Understanding Tropical Peatland Degradation and Restoration". *Remote Sensing* 11, no. 21. https://doi.org/10.3390/rs11212592

Index

www.ingramcontent.com/pod-product-compliance
Lightning Source LLC
Chambersburg PA
CBHW041254040426
42334CB00028BA/3014